CHANGE OVER TIME
IN CHILDREN'S LITERACY DEVELOPMENT

CHANGE OVER TIME
IN CHILDREN'S LITERACY DEVELOPMENT

Marie M. Clay

Heinemann

Published by Heinemann Education, a division of Reed Publishing (NZ) Ltd,
39 Rawene Road, Birkenhead, Auckland, New Zealand. Associated companies,
branches and representatives throughout the world.

In the United States: Heinemann, a division of Reed Elsevier (USA) Inc.,
361 Hanover Street, Portsmouth, NH 03801-3912.

ISBN 0-86863-300-3 (NZ)

Library of Congress Cataloging-in-Publication Data
CIP data is on file with the Library of Congress
ISBN 0-325-00383-1 (USA)

© 2001 Marie M. Clay
First published 2001

Printed in Singapore by Imago Production

Cover: Brenda Cantell

Acknowledgements:
The following have generously given permission to use quotations from copyrighted
works.

Chapter 2, selections from *Five Kids* by Susan O'Leary, published by The Wright
Group/McGraw-Hill, 19201 120th Avenue NE, Bothell, WA 98011, phone
800-648-2970.

Chapter 3, excerpts from pages 120–129 in *GNYS AT WRK* by Glenda Bissex,
Cambridge, MA: Harvard University Press, Copyright © 1980 by the President and
Fellows of Harvard College.

Chapter 8, Figure 4 from 'The epigenetic landscape revisited: A dynamic
interpretation' by M. Muchisky, L. Gershkoffe-Stowe, E. Cole and E. Thelen in *Advances
in Infancy Research*, Volume 10, 1996, page 38, Carolyn Rovee-Collier and Lewis Lipsitt
(eds), Ablex Publishing, Greenwood, Westport CT 06881.

Chapter 8, Figure 5 derived from 'Time scale dynamics and the development of an
embodied cognition' by E. Thelen in *Mind in Motion*, R. Port and T. van Gelder (eds),
MIT Press, Cambridge, 1995.

Contents

List of figures

List of tables

Introduction and dedication

Reading is a message-getting, problem-solving activity, which increases in power and flexibility the more it is practised. It is complex because:

- Within the directional constraints of written language

- verbal and

- perceptual behaviours

- are purposefully directed

- in some integrated way

- to the problems of extracting sequences of information from texts

- to yield meaningful and specific communications (Clay 1966).

One view of children's progress in reading and writing is to observe on a daily basis the changes taking place as young children engage with language in print as that definition suggests. Teachers then adjust their interactions with learners in ways that are sensitive to individual differences. That is one reading of the title of this book, *Change Over Time in Children's Literacy Development*.

Theoretical arguments can be made for many working systems in the brain which search for and pick up verbal and perceptual information governed by directional rules; other systems which work on that information and make decisions; other systems which monitor and verify those decisions; and systems which produce responses. Working in complex networks these systems make literacy processing possible.

Young children put fragments of these processes together before they come to school. When societies expect children to learn to read and write, and open the doors to formal education, the children begin to construct and integrate the complex network of working systems that will enable them to lift their literacy performance on increasingly difficult texts, until they become silent readers with self-extending systems for reading and writing.

Constructive children use the scaffolds which teachers provide to lift their progress. It is not the parent, or the teacher, or the politician, or the administrator, or the publisher who builds the neurological power pack: that can only be done by the child. For low-achieving children this 'construction' is not going well and something extra must be provided by teachers who are expert at fostering constructiveness.

How do people make decisions about how to read or write something? When do I slow down, or skim, or reread, or stop and think? in either reading or writing? Do I know when I have lost the message? and is it me or the print that is wrong? My attention is always on the messages, and not on how I am getting them, so what explains that?

How do children work on texts? How do young children make decisions about what to do next as they read? Are they working on getting a message? and calling off words? and sounding out words? and looking at the spelling of words? Does this happen all at once? or in some instructional sequence? or in some developmental sequence? or could it be both more personal and more chaotic than that, as chance would have it, for example? When we observe closely whether the child knows *how to generate and carry out some literacy process* this immediately informs daily teaching in important ways. Perhaps 'What bits will I teach?' and ' Which items do they know?' are not the most important questions.

After the first day at school, children can be disappointed because they didn't learn to read! The myriad of *'how to do'* learnings stretch out before them for the next few years. My assumption is that classroom teachers will find most children put literacy learning together as easily as they sort out the complexities of speaking their dominant language; we need to remember that learning to talk took several years! Issues about beginning literacy learning become critical for a small minority of children who need supplementary help for a period to establish order within chaos. They find the tasks difficult for diverse reasons.

Narrowing the book's scope

A range of readers read my rough drafts; conference audiences and discussion groups tossed the arguments in, out, and round about. *My questions were about the perceptual/ cognitive changes in processing in reading and writing of young low-achieving students anywhere.* Here are some expectations my readers had which I have not tried to address in this book. I do not explore a range of theoretical paradigms and pronounce my perspective on each. I do not answer all early intervention critics. I had to leave out many interesting things: theories on language development and socio-cultural issues, comments on classroom programmes, and everyone's choice of famous or recognised authorities in different countries. When I wrote this book I had in mind early intervention researchers, change agents in education systems, graduate students and academics, and tutors or teacher leaders preparing early intervention teachers for their work with children.

I live in a perpetual state of enquiry, finding new questions to ask, then moving on. I do not have 'a position' or a safe haven where what is 'right' exists. Pragmatism precludes idealism. I search for questions which need answers. What exists in the real world? and how well do our theories explain what exists? Opposing arguments in debates seem to block my search for new solutions, although I have great enthusiasm for brain-clearing discussions. I want to find evidence to convince me of the need for changes in understanding. The frequent reference to Reading Recovery (RR) arises from 25 years of working with this early intervention in many countries, in both English and Spanish. What we have learned can be shared with other early interventions, for our task is a huge one. This is not so much an advocacy of RR as it is for early intervention in literacy learning in general.

Some of my rough-draft readers explained what they thought I was doing in this book, and they did that very well.

- This writing is a shift from 'These are the things we know how to do' to 'Why these things we do make us consider a set of questions for further understanding.'

- This is an elaboration of current understandings from which new questions are derived.

- This writing is seeking a better understanding of internal processing so that teachers can help children to construct it (literacy processing power) more flexibly.

- This writing advances a stronger cognitive view; acts of processing will be clearer than vague strategies; and the hierarchical view is abandoned for a stronger, more flexible view consistent with the brain's learning to deal with more complex stimuli. Because other authorities give detailed attention to the language subsystems of structure and meaning, this text addresses the frequently neglected areas of visual, self-correction and writing systems.

- The sequential parsing of sentences that we do as we speak, listen, write and read, emerges freshly in this account. Somehow implicit in RR lesson activities (like oral reading, writing and rereading, remaking the cut-up story, and reading texts with more complex language structures) it should be easier to talk about during training.

- A strong metaphor emerges describing reading as a symphony being played, rather than a solo performance on a single instrument.

- A clean-cut, stripped-down definition of the book's content was a framework for considering revisions needed in new editions of workhorse publications used in RR training courses.

I can agree with most of those statements.

Provocative alternatives

This book says very little about a) implementing effective interventions or b) teaching teachers, or c) teaching practices, all of which are essential for the success of any early intervention. The book's focus is on children's learning (which of course can never really be separated from those other aspects).

Early intervention professionals need to ask more questions and get to even better theory in order to be more effective in their work. This book begins that process by posing an alternative way of viewing literacy progress as changes over time in literacy processing. Each of the following chapters might stand alone, and raise its own set of research questions. There is a need for new descriptive accounts recording sequences of children's learning in detail. We need research which makes well-designed tests of hypotheses, and we need *explanations of why children succeed*. The research base for my writing lies partly in developmental psychology, and in the psychology of literacy behaviours in older successful readers. The ideas in this book edge us a little closer to a cognitive or neurological account of what occurs during the successful acquisition of reading and writing but we will not benefit from new insights from neuropsychology unless we first articulate clearly what we already know and what we need to find out.

The challenge of writing

Most theorists in the field of reading acquisition ignore the fact that children are learning and practising writing *at the same time*. The two literacy activities are kept far apart. Experience with teaching reading and writing together has enabled early intervention teachers to support their most difficult students in important ways.

The challenge of describing processing information

How do *acts of processing* change over time during literacy acquisition? Would a description of changes in processing improve teachers' judgements about what and when to teach, and when or whether to discontinue children from an early intervention?

The challenges of reading and writing continuous text

What is it about continuous texts that challenges a reader or writer? What does a child have to do when reading or writing continuous text? What is the child likely to miss out on when the instruction places a heavy emphasis on letters, sounds, and words in reading or spelling, which steals all the child's attention?

The challenge of explaining self-correction

Self-correction, so easily observed, is challenging to explain even in a complex theory. Early intervention teachers make use of it daily as they interpret the Running Records of their children. Some theorists, on the other hand, have claimed it to be unimportant. Is it an executive control mechanism in the making, or merely the result of correcting for a poor memory search?

The creation of constructiveness

The idea of giving 'lessons in becoming constructive' challenges early intervention professionals to think about the perceptual/cognitive learning required in each lesson activity. It calls for more attention to what makes an early intervention preventive of subsequent difficulties, in contrast to one which only adds more items to knowledge sources.

The challenges of research

New theory calls for ingenuity in designing research to test that theory but critics of early interventions urge us to use well-established research logic and methodologies which do not always fit with the logic of early intervention. Sound research will be necessary to sustain support for early interventions like RR. So how do we design our research in the future to get quality information?

The explanations given in the critical literature for why RR is successful with children are unconvincing. This can only be because RR academics have not yet managed to characterise the programme's complexity in articulate ways. The chapters in this book will begin to clarify some of the issues. RR does not fit with many common assumptions. Yet because it was designed to be adopted by an education system and aims to reduce the number of children identified as learning disabled in that system, it is a contemporary answer to an old problem and it fits easily into several current thrusts to reduce literacy learning difficulties in different countries.

Future research about children's learning in RR should explore the implications of its complex theories. My challenge to RR's theory (from within) invites much discussion, of what special demands reading and writing continuous text place on learners (as distinct from decoding words or knowing them in isolation), and how self-correction is to be explained in a complex theory, and in what ways are lesson activities adjusted to suit individual strengths, and why is this helpful?

Selecting a way forward

A common focus for RR's international efforts is maintaining an effective early intervention in many different education systems with the perpetual efficiency of a hardly-noticeable pendulum. RR's theory could stay theoretically where it is and continue to replicate its current success. But we draw talented people into the programme from different backgrounds and that will keep the 'internal questioning' rich and varied.

Literacy learning has usually been measured by performance scores — like a golf card — rather than by a performer's response to coaching which changed his or her stance, approach, selection of the appropriate club, integration and co-ordination of skill and judgement. Coaching the learners in how to do things changes the score on the score card *and* provides the insurance of long-term effects. This is especially true when an intervention begins *early* in the learning process.

I would attribute a large measure of the success of RR to its links to developmental psychology. It has a view of constructive children guided by observant, flexible and tentative teachers, taking children along different paths to common outcomes, and shaped by local cultural contexts. These contexts change continually, driven by the history of how societies deliver education services to children.

Dedication

Early literacy interventions like RR could be delivered on current theoretical explanations, unaltered, but some of its professionals will want to explore alternative explanations for the work they do. It will be healthy to debate productively how best to introduce change into a successful enterprise. The ideas in this book provide an integration of what I now understand about early literacy intervention and it has been exciting to find out that we are in line with some frontier shifts in a broader field of psychology and developmental psychology.

Literacy processing theory can inform daily instruction and with RR bring a rigour to the teaching of those children who need more help than most. In writing this book I have tried to find words that might help teachers to help more children climb higher mountains … but words that help teaching are hard to find.

This book is dedicated to those who intend to deliver labour-intensive early intervention in ways that could prevent subsequent literacy difficulties, and in particular to countless teaching professionals and administrators who have helped me to stay with this challenge.

My sincere thanks go to a group of early intervention leaders around the world who took time to read rough drafts of some chapters. My readers' comments clearly signalled that we need further elaboration of our theories, clearer conceptualisation of our tasks, and answers to more research questions. I hope these readings contribute to future discussions. I, alone, must take responsibility for the selection and final form of the messages in this book.

1   Extra power from writing in early literacy interventions

1 Extra power from writing in early literacy interventions

Introduction

Beginning reading and writing share common ground irrespective of the teaching approach used in schools. This chapter strongly encourages parents and teachers to think about the common ground between these two literacy activities when young children are exploring literacy. It also calls for valuing the reciprocal contribution of writing to reading when children enter early literacy interventions, and complements the discussion of how writing strengthens early literacy learning in classrooms (Clay 1998). When children are clearly getting left behind by their faster-learning classmates it is very important to work with reading and writing together.

Theory, practice, and reciprocity

Between three and seven years children begin to build a foundation for literacy learning which underpins what follows in formal education. In the past thirty years the term 'emergent literacy' generated proposals, critiques and publications which have raised or lowered the interest in early writing but none of which has made significant changes to how we understand the *reciprocity* of learning to read and write. A better understanding about *reciprocity* could lead to more effective teaching interactions in both activities, and the idea has the pleasant ring of a small 'two for one' bargain allowing the busy teacher some economy in teaching time.

A broad-band theory of literacy learning views it as complex rather than simple and acknowledges that writers have to know how to do certain things with language which overlap with things that readers have to know or do. Teaching practices today often engage the child in tasks described as 'authentic reading and writing tasks' of wide variety, presented with some sort of management of a gradient of difficulty. As children work at these tasks they themselves create some opportunities to discover new things about print which they have not attended to before. Instruction should provide learners with opportunities that are open-ended, allowing the learner to surprise the teacher and expand any aspect of his or her existing knowledge. The challenge for teachers is to understand what is going on before their eyes, as reading and writing come together and influence each other. That is immeasurably more complex than teaching children to spell set lists of words or to specialise narrowly in sounding out new words in reading.

Writing can contribute to building almost every kind of inner control of literacy learning that is needed by the successful reader (see pp. 19–25) and yet there may be no predictable sequence in which the shifts in control occur! Rumelhart (1994) listed relevant knowledge sources available in print, and Chapter 3 examines other knowledge that must be learned in early literacy.

Should writing be taught before, after, or side-by-side with reading? It is important to think about what happens when any one of these three positions is accepted. Mostly the two activities occur in parallel alongside each other, but are treated separately by parents and teachers. Occasionally, even today in some education systems, writing is delayed a year and a half until reading is established; before that children are expected only to copy. And some literacy programmes have begun with writing. *The Writing Road to Reading* (Spalding and Spalding 1962) taught letter-sound relationships as a lead-in to writing which then led to phonics, which then led to reading. One computer program designed for teaching writing prescriptively sequenced the learning to suit a computer delivery system. (My work was quoted as a major source, yet I had already published a 'no set sequence' warning!) Carol Chomsky stressed what writing might do for reading in the early stages of literacy acquisition in both academic (1972, 1975b, 1979) and popular articles (1971, 1975a), urging kindergarten and Grade 1 teachers in the United States to help children explore word and text construction with magnetic letters as a lead-in to reading.

The advocacy of 'writing first and reading later' is as limited as the 'reading first and writing later' approach but the assumption that reading and writing are concurrent sources of learning about print is a relatively recent theme (Shanahan 1990).

Preschool writing

Published accounts of children learning about writing as preschoolers should be compulsory reading for teachers of early writing in schools or in intervention programmes. Preschool children often explore writing without connecting it to reading, as if it were quite a different code. Some preschoolers do not explore it at all, and yet become good writers in school.

A quick read of *GNYS AT WRK* (Bissex 1980), *Literacy Before Schooling* (Ferreiro and Teberosky 1982), *Writing Begins At Home* (Clay 1987), *How Children Construct Literacy* (Goodman 1990) and *Early Spelling: Between Convention and Creativity* (Kress 2000) would take the reader for a journey through preschool writing which highlights *conceptual shifts* made by quite young children. *What Did I Write?* (Clay 1975) and *Writing Superheroes* (Dyson 1997) provide examples from the early years of school. A guiding question to direct to a sample of children's work is, 'Which features of this extremely complex activity is this child attending to?'

The value of reading to preschool children has captured the public imagination and the idea of story-time in the family group has provided a model for the kindergarten story group and sometimes for school instruction, but there is no comparable popular image of the preschool writer. Most parents and teachers believe that preschool *reading* experiences are very important but know almost nothing about the value of preschool *writing* experiences. Then last year I heard a wonderful recommendation: write a letter to a preschooler today! Children love to get mail and a few engaging words are all they need (Booth 1999).

An unavoidable outcome of preschool experiences is that individual differences prevail in the awareness of literacy. Children come to school with different prior experience, from different homes and different communities, and each has experience with different parts of the complex whole that makes up literacy knowledge. (This is captured by the Sheffield jigsaw, explained below.)

They are grappling with a strange thing called a code. One four-year-old boy presented his 'writing' to his father to read. That father made a serious attempt to sound out the jumbled symbols but the son was obviously disappointed and said, 'I didn't write that! I wrote English!' He thought he had used the code that adults seem to use when putting a message on paper, and had not doubted that his father would be able to read it. He protested that he had intended to signify in English. At moments 'when children express the clear desire to signify something for some reason … we learn most about the evolution of their search for equivalences' (Dyson 1994, p. 302).

A blank jigsaw was used by Weinberger, Hannon and Nutbrown (1990) of the University of Sheffield to make parents aware of their children's interest in various aspects of literacy activity. Each different focus of attention was a separate entry on the jigsaw. Different children entering a school programme will have learned to attend to quite different parts of the complex task. The jigsaw helps us to understand the diversity that exists in young children's understanding — in competencies, in prior opportunities to learn, and in the items they have already learned about. *Jigsaws filled-in for several children will show that children have taken hold of different aspects of a complex task before they get to school — a few letters, one or two words, and images from environmental print.*

Writing in the first year of school

Teachers of new entrants to school give a little weight to the reciprocity of reading and writing when they get children to attend to their own names, reading and writing them. A child's own name is a word of high interest and may provide the first insights that print conveys a message. A child who can write his or her name (or some other first word) has learnt about some important features of a code.

1)   It is made up of only special marks,

2)   placed in a certain order,

3)   making a recognisable pattern.

PETER   JIMMY   HөTɛT   Roberta ROPɛtɑ

ᴸᴼᴿᴮ   Kay   Heather   MIO

Pupils' attempts to write their own names differ greatly. The few who have not mastered their names after a full year at school (when there are no handicapping conditions) are long overdue for some close encounters with a good teacher.

These examples emphasise the obvious: *each child brings his or her own repertoire of literacy learning into the first classroom programme.* Each has a little knowledge, an awareness of some small part of the complex whole. Teachers' assumptions about what happens in general can get in the way of individual learning. The historic position that one has *to learn to read* words before one will be able *to learn to write or spell* them is still an assumption made by some teachers, and regrettably it turns out to be true when teachers assume that it is so.

When teachers do not expect children to be able to write, they do not give them opportunities to write, and therefore they will observe that the children do not write. Naturally teachers' experiences with children shape and confirm their practices but then they look for and find what they expect to see. It is not easy for teachers to observe the things that children already know which lie outside the teachers' expectation. Sally-Ann (Clay 1987) showed that before she was four years of age she used three different ways of attempting to write down simple messages: 1) she could take spelling dictation from members of her family; 2) she could 'pretend' to write a story by stringing letters together, and 3) she could use the few words she knew to record a message — she already had three ways of writing text and her teacher could have worked with these. And yet, when Sally-Ann first went to school, her teacher complained that she did not write in the expected way; she did not make up what teachers call 'invented spelling'. By this teachers mean that children 'hear the sounds in words that they speak and try to find letters which will represent those sounds'. Read's (1975) research showed that some children do this. Sally-Ann's teacher missed all the things Sally-Ann could do, and wanted her to do 'invented spelling', which was a new concept teachers were exploring. Sally-Ann was flexible enough to add a fourth option: she could hear the sounds in the words and try to record those sounds. After six weeks of school Sally-Ann had met her teacher's assumptions and was making up her own words from invented spelling. Another child's knowledge on entry to school would be organised quite differently from Sally-Ann's, but both could move forward from his or her personal knowledge base. *As each child learns more about writing it is as if he or she were putting the same jigsaw together but solving it in different ways.*

Cazden (1974) described the ability to attend to our own speaking as a special kind of language performance which we rarely engage in. Yet when children learn to write and read concurrently these activities help them to attend quite analytically to the oral language they already use. We can observe young children making links between speaking, reading and writing as they try to write their earliest messages.

The constructive writer

Many teachers find it difficult to accept the argument that there is no fixed sequence in which the shifts in early writing will occur (Clay 1993b, p. 31). My research and observations led me to conclude that as children explore writing they will:

- attend closely to the features of letters and to learning letters

- construct 'their own words', letter by letter

- direct attention to spatial features like serial order and spaces between words

- work within the order and sequence rules of print, revealing these to themselves while constructing messages

- break down the task to its smallest segments while at the same time synthesising them into words and sentences

- engage in their own form of segmenting sounds in words in order to write them.

A theory of children as constructive thinkers can be applied to preschoolers exploring writing as easily as it can be used to describe seven-year-olds actively organising and learning from self-initiated experiences. We do not need to emphasise memorising. The child needs to learn how to compile or construct new words out of what he or she already knows about words. Constructing a particular word on several occasions creates familiarity, and ultimately leads to knowing it in every respect. The learner who does not readily recall a word can go into 'constructive mode' and generate it from other things he or she knows. Fast recognition, or slower recall, or thoughtful construction from a small repertoire of knowledge can each facilitate the expansion of writing vocabulary.

Words to be solved are of two kinds: those best described as 'words still coming under control', and those which are the 'never-tried-before words'. The goal is to have independent writers able to get to new words in many different ways, sometimes alone, sometimes with easy access to a correct example, and sometimes with an expert's assistance. Writing a word is always sequential, letter by letter. Words constructed come to need less and less attention to produce a correct version. *Many people describe the word as memorised but the learning is good for more than just prompt recall; some kind of programme for producing the word has been learned, and also it is easily taken apart for use in new ways.*

In the early intervention called Reading Recovery (RR) children are specifically taught to hear the sound sequences in words and to construct words in writing from the sounds or sound patterns they can hear. This is one important way to get to a word they have never written before. Teachers give children credit for their attempts, and prompt them to articulate the word slowly to hear the sounds, but teacher and child share the writing of the hard or new parts. This provides two kinds of model for the child: one model of how a writer solves a difficulty and a correct model of the word being written.

The teaching interactions need to encourage other things, however. Children need opportunities to initiate attempts at words (usually on a working page), and teaching interactions should maximise children's opportunities to initiate word-solving and to take control of the task when they can. To work effectively the teacher must at all times know what it is that the child already controls in these writing tasks.

A teacher will deliberately direct children's attention to print features in both reading and writing but children also direct their own attention to parts of the task, switching from one source of information in print to another when necessary. The switching may sometimes be observable but usually it will be hidden. *Teacher demonstrations* are of greater value than *teacher talk* for directing or redirecting attention at this early stage.

When the eye and ear and hand are jointly involved in the management of a task they send three different messages to the brain, messages picked up by different senses. Together they lead to recognising a particular object, say, a familiar toy or a 'known' word. The different messages may be regarded as providing a way of checking one message against the other. Russian developmental psychologists demonstrated how much children at an earlier stage of development need such joint involvement as a precursor to being able to use their eyes alone to do the searching at a later stage (Clay 1991, pp. 284–285).

Writing helps to build:

- the sources of knowledge upon which the reader must draw
- the processes needed to search for information in print
- the strategies used to combine or check information
- an awareness of how to construct messages.

David Pearson claimed in 1990 that:

> it does not (now) sound heretical to assert that reading and writing are driven by the same underlying cognitive and socio-cultural processes, or that the learning of one supports the other, or that reading is an act of composing, or that learning ought to occur within an interpretive community of readers and writers. (p. v)

Before school, reading and writing have rather independent lives but they are most interactive at the point where instruction begins in school. *For about two years they appear to share a great deal of common ground.*

A second chance to learn about early writing

Early literacy interventions are designed to give children a second chance to catch up with their classmates. The challenge for their teachers is to find a place to begin using something the child can do and moving out from there in whatever directions that the learner can go in both reading and writing. Progress must occur immediately and the goal is for the learner to catch up to his or her average peers. One child may have managed to avoid writing and print; another may not have had any opportunities to explore with a pencil and make letter shapes as a preschooler; another child may have inventively explored print without adapting to the rigorous constraints of the printed code. There are many explanations of failure to learn. Given individually designed and individually delivered attention many children can make up the difference quickly, learning to read and write at accelerated rates during effective daily instruction. Occasionally the problem involves a deeper problem related to motor behaviours, or to unexpected difficulty in combining or integrating two or more kinds of activities.

I began thinking about this when a carefully designed master's thesis (Robinson 1973; see Chapter 2) reported that writing vocabulary (the number of words a child could generate and write correctly given a maximum time of ten minutes) was *the main predictor of early reading progress* across the range of achievement between 5:6 and 6:0 and again between 6:0 and 6:5. (Her children were receiving literacy instruction in school.) Robinson demonstrated with a rigorous statistical analysis that writing in the first eighteen months of learning to read was of major importance in the 1970s in New Zealand. Her research influenced the design of the RR early literacy intervention which is now backed by more than twenty years of working in most English-speaking countries (and with speakers of Spanish in the United States). Annually thousands of children complete that intervention and many reach average band for age in both reading and writing with only twelve to twenty weeks of instruction. Why might early writing be a critical part of a successful intervention in early reading and what would the activities look like?

Writing is of critical importance for learning to read in an early literacy intervention because writing prevents learners from neglecting or overlooking many things they must know about print, and reveals things about the learners' ways of working that their teachers need to know about. The following account reports what occurs during ten minutes of a 30-minute RR lesson but my argument is that writing would be very important in *any early literacy intervention*. When teachers do not include writing daily in early intervention lessons they are severely limiting the child's opportunities to learn and they are contributing to slower progress overall, at a time when it is most important to learn quickly.

In a series of one-to-one early intervention lessons writing must be highly valued alongside reading because:

- it is important in its own right, and

- it helps children who are finding it hard to learn about print to begin to attend to print in a detailed way.

Beginning in the first two weeks of the lesson series, a child is invited to use whatever he or she already knows about writing in many different ways. The early intervention teacher needs to know from the beginning the writing repertoire of each child in order to determine that child's starting point for writing. The teacher asks, 'What knowledge does this particular child have about any of the aspects of literacy that we can attend to?' Beginning repertoires are usually meagre. The teacher must work with the child to anchor experience in something memorable; any first words will do. Most children begin a slow but steady expansion of their entry repertoire. There could conceivably be a rare child for whom writing is extraordinarily difficult, for example, a child with mild cerebral palsy affecting eye or hand control, or a child who suffered a physical injury. Such a case would call for innovative teaching, manipulation of magnetic letters, and assistance of many kinds, but *the constructive side to literacy learning which puts messages into print should not be avoided*.

RR teachers must reject common assumptions when they are beginning to work with a new hard-to-teach child. Their judgements about how reading and writing are interacting must be tentative. They are decision-makers: they make decisions about the learning sequence to follow with a particular child. Obviously it is very important for the teacher to be 'reading the signs' as the child works at a writing task, and not missing important signs because of personal assumptions. The one necessary assumption is that reading and writing can help one another.

Children can be made aware that reading and writing *contribute reciprocally* to early progress when teachers prompt for such reciprocity. 'Yes, you can read that word. Think of how you wrote it in your story yesterday', or 'Yes, you can write that word. Do you remember we read it in [name of the book]?' Research tracing children's progress longitudinally has shown that strength in both literacy activities yields a better prognosis. So RR children are expected to reach satisfactory levels in both aspects of literacy acquisition before their lesson series ends.

Teachers assume rightly that they have to make the challenges easy for particular children and they try to simplify the tasks in some way. Certainly the tasks must be made accessible to children but *teacher assumptions about what is simple can actually threaten success!* First, work out what the child already can do. Then do not avoid the hard parts for that avoidance is a weak move. *The challenge is to make those hard things easier to learn.*

- Create context from what the child knows and introduce the 'new' into this.

- Don't alter the task in a way which makes the desired outcome more difficult to attain or which takes longer.

- Don't simplify the complexity if it is that complexity that is the target of the learning. You can share the task and demonstrate the solving process.

- Avoid long detours (long verbal explanations and oblique analogies) which delay attainment of the goal.

- Be aware that what worked for another child could be inappropriate for this child.

The teaching has to provide a gradient of difficulty in the tasks such that learners have many opportunities to try to work at higher levels of complexity. Teachers watch for new things that the child is paying attention to, finding evidence in what the learner initiates, draws, writes, dictates, copies, talks about, points to in text, *and reads.*

How does early writing influence early reading?

Directing attention to print

The vital question is, 'What is the young child attending to as he or she attends to print?' It may be the shape or form of the letters, or some feature which distinguishes two similar letters, or perhaps the order or sequence of the letters, or words. *Often the child's attention is not where the teacher expects it to be.* In reading children must begin by picking up some visual information but in writing children must find visual forms to represent the sounds in the messages they have composed. When they check visually by reading what they wrote they find out whether it says what they intended to write (Clay 1991, 1993b, 1998).

Adults who try to learn some of the symbols in an unfamiliar script (such as Hebrew, Arabic, Burmese or the Cyrillic alphabet) should notice where they begin to 'read', how their eyes scan across the print, how they search for individual symbols, and when they look for patterns or 'words'. Especially when they try to copy the text, writing some letters or 'words', they find out how much attention must be given to features which distinguish the symbols one from the other. If those adults returned to this new script daily for about five days they would be able to observe ways in which their perception of the print had changed because they were learning more things about the unfamiliar print (see Chapter 4, p. 160ff).

Directing attention to particular parts of a print display in an appropriate scanning order is action initiated and carried out by both readers and writers.

Attending closely to the features of letters

As in beginning reading, the young writer has to attend to the particular features that help all of us to distinguish letters, one from another (Smith 1978).

> S is distinct,
> E and F catch the attention,
> a is confused with e, m with n, n with u,
> and I, l, L, and numeral 1 are easily confused.

The young writer must attend to familiar letter features, until each letter can be rapidly distinguished from similar letters. Every letter takes two journeys. The first journey is:

- from being new,

- to only just known,

- to working to get a solution,

- to easily produced but easily thrown,

- to a well-known old response in most contexts,

- and later, known in any variant form.

The second journey is:

- moving from very slow,

- to very fast production or very fast recognition measured in thousandths of a second (or milliseconds).

(Journeys like these can also be traced in the learning of letter clusters, parts of words and words.) Being able to access knowledge about a letter in different ways — by sight, sound, name, key word, and the feel of how you write it — helps to distinguish it from similar forms, and speeds recognition. Rapid access to letter identity speeds up literacy processing.

Individual differences persist at the end of the first year of school even when all children have been taught well in a sound curriculum by the same teacher. Early intervention teachers can discover the individual child's total repertoire of known letters and words in an initial assessment but nothing will tell them how quickly a particular child will take new learning aboard. A low score on writing tasks initially does not necessarily mean the child will be slow to write but may merely indicate writing was something the learner has not wanted to attend to, or did not have the opportunity to learn. And knowing quite a lot about print initially does not necessarily mean writing will come easily.

Each newly learned letter has to find an identity among a rapidly growing set of letters, some 54 symbols for English. Ferreiro and Teberosky (1982) proposed that the little each child knows at any one time is a highly organised set — a temporary universe of letter knowledge. A child coming into an early intervention programme may know only five letters, and as he or she comes to know the sixth and seventh letters that child will be distinguishing those two new letters from the five already known. Letter knowledge may extend rapidly in the early lessons, slow up between 20 and 40 letters, and speed up again when the last letters of 'the set' are being added to what is known. This is partly because of the amount of checking against known letters that must be done.

Constructing words from single phonemes or clusters

Young readers and writers have to become aware of phonemes (the sounds which are the smallest units of information transmitted in language). Phonemes are only sounds. So a question about phonemes or phonemic awareness is a question about whether children can break up the words they *say* into parts. Children learn to hear the sounds that make up the words they speak. They manage syllables very well, but the smallest units of sound that make a difference between two words are harder to attend to.

When learners are writing they need to separate the sounds within the words they are trying to write in order to be able to find some letter forms to represent those sounds. The preschool children studied by the linguist Charles Read (1975) invented ways of writing down what they wanted to record without first learning traditional English spelling. (They knew many letter names and forms already, and would use 'C' for 'see' and other interesting short cuts, like 'NE' for 'any'.) Read demonstrated that some children had made a rather clever analysis of the sounds of English a year before they started school. His children used the sounds they could hear as they said the names of letters in the alphabet with the sounds they could hear in their own speech. He did not claim that children would learn the capricious orthography of English by themselves, and reported (Read 1986) how some spelling errors were related to how hard it is to hear some parts of English words, like the 'n' in 'bent'. Treiman (1993) published further definitive research in this area.

In *The Literacy Dictionary* (Harris and Hodges 1995) Joanna Williams defined phonemic awareness as the awareness of the sounds that make up spoken words. She recalled Elkonin's (1973) recommendation for children in the USSR which was never widely adopted. He thought they should be trained to hear the sounds in words before they were 'exposed to print' in either reading or writing. An adaptation of his approach is used in RR to help children to learn to hear sounds, and sound sequences, in the words they want to write. For hard-to-teach children teachers at first accept *any sounds in any order*, and the teacher indicates the sound's position in the word in a set of boxes he or she has quickly drawn. When the child shows some control over the task the teacher begins to call for the sounds from first to last, that is, in the order in which they occur. That is a harder task. Before long children are able to hear *the sound sequences* in words. Phonemic awareness in the RR early intervention is developed in the writing segment of the lessons, under the title of 'Hearing and recording the sounds in words'. The teaching is systematic and the emphasis shifts in response to the increase of the child's control. New Zealand teachers readily adapted this approach from its individual tutoring format for use in a classroom. Their children wrote and teachers encouraged them to attempt selected words by themselves by saying, 'What can you hear? What else can you hear?' as they moved around the classroom, interacting with children over writing.

Why deal with phonemic awareness during writing? It is mandatory in writing to write letter by letter, so this is a naturally-occurring training situation. In 1977 during the development phase of RR it was recorded how teachers worked with hard-to-teach children having difficulty hearing sounds in words. It was particularly difficult for some children to hear sounds when they were embedded in a sequence of sounds. The children were helped by hearing the teacher articulate the sound sequence slowly, by doing this for themselves, and even by watching themselves do this using a small mirror if necessary. A slowed-up articulation which did not break the sound sequence into discrete single units worked well for most children.

Which words will the early intervention teacher choose for developing phonemic awareness?

- Simple words with sounds that are easy to hear

- and words with uncomplicated sound-to-letter relationships.

- Early in a lesson series children learn how to do this analysis, and practise it daily.

- Later there may be other reasons for using the Elkonin boxes such as to consolidate the learning of a word often needed in this child's writing (that is, another way of knowing the word),

- or to discriminate the order of hard-to-hear sounds in a word,

- or to establish sound sequence in a word the child mispronounces,

- or to work with a letter cluster or spelling pattern,

- or …

Teachers avoid asking children to analyse words for which the relationship of sound to spelling is complex. The child has to learn that phonemic analysis will often work, before being shown all the quirks and exceptions of sound-to-letter relationships in English.

Children in early interventions can be supported by an attentive teacher and by trials and demonstrations on a work-page on which teacher–child interactions occur. What is written in the story today is material for the child to read again at any time in his or her lesson series, so the text appears only in a correct form when the 'story for the day' is completed.

Knowing many different words: a writing vocabulary

The child learns to write a number of words correctly, uses these often, builds up speeded production, and can then give more attention to new challenges.

In the one-to-one interactions of an early intervention lesson a child can try, on a work-page, to write a new word for his or her self-composed story without using the Elkonin boxes, but using instead what he or she already knows about how words work. The new word is analogous to some other words the child knows. The teacher interacts with the child's attempts, prompting, helping, teaching and providing models. The emphasis of the interactions is on finding out something new and interesting about print. From such teaching interactions a new word emerges and can be taken back into the story by the child. What goes into the text is the correct version, the final product of all the child-and-teacher interactions. The special condition of correctness is required for children who are finding it hard to learn because more exposure to correct models is essential. The message construction is a literacy task completed jointly with quality teaching interactions. The child's approximations are saved on the work-page, providing a record which can be referred to by the teacher. When the child rereads what he or she wrote there is a further opportunity for the new learning to be consolidated.

When children compose their messages for the day they venture to write a wide range of words which give the learner a sense of the regularities and exceptions of English spellings. This learning about how words work in writing makes a great contribution to reading similar words in texts.

Words gather information around them. Like tiny drops of mercury coming together to form larger drops, or raindrops running down the windowpane, words gather up information. A particular word accumulates

- oral language knowledge

- writing knowledge

- reading knowledge

- quantitative knowledge about approximate frequency
- personal and cultural knowledge
- spelling knowledge about likenesses and differences, and so on.

A network of knowledge gathers around each word that the child knows, and probably when the learner attends to a particular word, this neural network can potentially be tapped.

The power to construct or generate unknown words comes from having a personal writing vocabulary. A child's writing vocabulary consists of the words he or she knows in every detail and produces easily without help plus any new word he or she can construct correctly using existing strategies and knowledge (Clay 1993a). Knowing many words makes it easier to write stories because much of the text is written quickly, which frees the attention to go to new words that the child does have to work on. Knowing many different words *enlarges one's chances of getting to new words*; knowing only short words, and regular spelling patterns provided by teachers who are 'hooked on word families' of the 'cut, but, nut and shut' type, *restricts options when constructing new words.*

The far too popular practice of teaching word families can be limiting for writing development. I see children who think they have to remember a word and who do not attempt to construct it. I see children who only dare to write short words: they have not memorised the long ones so they do not dare to try them. I see children being taught word families, and being tested on word families because teachers want to show children 'how words are generated'. But teaching word families can create misconceptions such as 'all words belong to word families', or 'this is a memory game', as distinct from a constructing game; or 'English words are regular', when English spelling rules are complex. Children can too easily be drilled into expecting regularity.

Generating words is not about building word families. It is producing a word you need to write *by any means at your disposal* and getting as close as you can to the way it is probably written in English. For that kind of problem-solving a rich collection of known words will be invaluable.

A concept of 'learning words' can be limiting

Building a repertoire of known words is *a valuable by-product of the writing component of early intervention lessons,* but it is not the main reason for including the writing task. The purpose of the writing component of the RR lesson is to learn how to write messages and stories, to be ready after a rather brief series of special lessons to blossom out and write bigger and better stories. In the ideal case we teach children 'how to do things' so that they will forever extend their own competencies. Writing the new words needed for writing interesting texts must become generative far beyond the limitations of word families.

Knowing many different words enlarges writers' chances of getting to the new words they want. The child who knows a lot of words which are different one from another can generate more words than the child who knows a few spelling patterns well. The latter child is being held back by only knowing simple and regular words, usually three- and four-letter words. An early intervention teacher needs to make a distinction between teaching word families and teaching children how to get from something they know to something new by themselves, and having done this, how to check on it.

In a writing vocabulary assessment teachers should *not* prompt for word families. When high writing vocabulary scores come only because a teacher has prompted for word families the children probably do not know enough different words to be independent generators of new words from old words. Writing vocabulary is made up of known vocabulary plus the words that the child knows how to construct, and together those two groups of words are good indicators of future progress. When teachers are testing for writing vocabulary their prompts should keep the child active and thinking about more words, and not merely about the regularity of word families.

Learning how to construct a wide range of different words allows a child to begin to sense something about the regularities in English spelling, the rules of English orthography and something about irregular spellings.

Any word a child can write is taking the two journeys discussed earlier in relation to letters. And that new word has also to find its place in all other literacy knowledge about similar words which this child has accumulated so far. It must be accessible when needed.

Teachers should ask themselves: 'Is my teaching facilitating these changes?' 'Do I make it easy for my students to learn more for themselves about how words work?' 'Do I give my students many opportunities to initiate writing a word?' 'Do I hold back and encourage initiation or do I butt in, protectively?' 'What encourages the student to speed up the writing of the word?' 'Is this child's repertoire of words expanding, giving the learner more tools to work with?' 'How can I tell which words have settled into the child's repertoire?' 'Do my lessons facilitate or obstruct any of that learning?'

Becoming aware of the construction of sentences

Here is a young speaker, struggling, as he tries to find a syntactic structure that will carry his message. He wants to convey a message in which one thing had an influence on something else. The speaker, about three and a half years old, had been playing outside with his brother Mark and came into the house to get a ball.

Adult: You're covered in mud. What happened?
Child: Falled me. Markie me. Markie me pushed.
　　　　Markie pushed me … falled me.

Spoken utterances have to be composed and in sentences ideas are subject to sequence rules. It is not just the stories that have to be composed: sentences have to be composed and the rules of order are essential if we are to transmit the message. Composing a sentence means constructing a sequence of meanings within an acceptable sequence of grammatical rules.

Writing activities force children to bring many things together:

- the ideas
- the composing of their own messages, constrained both by meaning and structure
- the search for ways to record them
- the monitoring of that recording
- and the reading of the record made.

In writing down a simple message like, 'My brother hit the ball and broke the window', a child faces a challenge to manipulate the order of words within the rules of syntax. When four-year-old Penny tried to reply to a birthday party invitation the word 'come' dominated her composing (see Note 1, p. 35) and she did not seem to understand that in writing she had to do just what she always did in speaking, which was to formulate an utterance according to the syntax of the language. Young children learn that if you fail to do this you are not understood when speaking, and the same is true of writing.

In the early weeks of their supplementary lessons children in an early intervention need time to think about constructing sentences in order to write them. Their interactions with teachers must support their early attempts to initiate slightly more complex writing at each encounter. By the time children complete their early intervention lessons they need to have fluent control of writing sentences and be well-prepared to produce stories of greater length and quality back in their classrooms. Early intervention teachers should get some samples of average to above-average writing from the child's classroom so that as teachers they understand what the goal 'average for class' really is.

Elkonin recognised this as an important time when children begin to examine the language they speak more closely, at all levels — at the level of sounds, of words, and of composed utterances. He also understood the challenges for children in the hearing of sound sequences in words.

> While actively utilizing grammatical knowledge and while defining with words the corresponding objects and actions the child cannot make a word ... the object of his awareness. During this period the word may be used but not noticed by the child, and frequently it presents things seemingly like a glass through which the child looks at the surrounding world, not making the word itself the object of awareness and not suspecting that it has its own existence, its own aspects of construction. (Elkonin 1971)

Which of the many things in written language should the child who is having difficulty with literacy learning attend to? A big challenge in the writing of a simple sentence is how to direct one's attention to detail while holding the whole message in mind. It is a task to learn about in just those terms, and cannot be avoided by concentrating only on single words and trying to string them together. Many teachers assume that they make the learning task easy by attending to words in isolation. The more difficult challenge is to be able to construct and write a sentence, cycling back and forth between the constraints of the phonemic, grammatical and meaning levels.

Children who are learning more about the language of instruction at the same time as they are learning to read and write it may already have a rich and complex knowledge of how to work with their home language. But many of the language rules they implicitly use for their home language or dialect will be different from the language of school instruction. They have to learn how to construct utterances or written sentences in new ways in order to read and write. In classrooms children who have a limited control of the language of instruction need more *oral language learning* opportunities as well as literacy instruction, and more interactions over meanings are needed when reading stories to them. In a one-to-one lesson for 30 minutes each day a child has a teacher who knows about his or her language and literacy progress in detail, and a little more time must be borrowed from each lesson activity to allow for more conversation.

Getting children to compose stories

In an early intervention lesson the reluctant child is expected to learn to compose and write his or her own stories. This is not done by copying words and it is *not* about mimicking the texts in storybooks. Teachers help children to compose oral messages and recount simple events in their lives. To write these down children are:

- going from ideas
- to spoken words
- to printed messages.

It is about constructing sentences from ideas, and about constructing words from their parts, all in the context of getting down a message.

The invitation is open-ended. The teacher talks with the child engaging the child in conversation. When a turn in the conversation produces a likely utterance the teacher can select one of many eliciting comments, like, 'What can we write about that?', a question which invites composing. No matter how limited a child's language, teachers can almost always get a spoken utterance which can become the written message for that lesson.

A teacher's goal is to increase the initiation by the child and to avoid participating in ways which make the child pull back. For example, questions that sound like interrogation to the insecure child, and even a 'helpful' expansion of his or her limited utterance, could be utterly intimidating. When the child offers something to be written down it should sound just like another move in the conversation. Even in the first lessons when the teacher acts as a scribe writing all the message at the child's dictation, in this or the next lesson, there should be a call for the child to participate in the 'writing' in some small way. When a teacher has to give a great deal of help during the first lessons it is useful because he or she can be an action model of what a writer does. (Hopefully the teacher will not distract the child from watching what the teacher is doing by talking in wordy monologues about words.)

Composing has to be learned. In *Wally's Stories* Vivian Paley (1981) describes children who are learning to compose oral stories. Such composition is important learning and we must be patient about it. It takes time. Retelling a story is also about composing sentences from your grammar.

The teacher helps the child to write something which that child has a desire to signify, but the teacher must remember what the child dictated, and should make a record for his or her own use.

Writing is a personal activity in which we compose messages which we put down to be read. The writing part of an early literacy intervention is not done just as a service to learning to read; it is not merely an activity engaged in to prepare a child to be a reader. In the end students should move forward with relative independence into any of the writing tasks demanded by the education system. And reading and writing activities should continue to enrich each other.

Parsing and how a sentence might continue

After the child has composed a message for the day, which is one or two sentences long, he or she begins to write it. At first, the writer finds it hard to recapture the sentence beginning, and the first phrased cluster of words. The child composed the sentence and repeated it and began to write it, yet the rereading is often effortful as that 'owned' sentence is pieced together again. This is one example of the child learning how to deliberately fit messages into sentence structures, and how to direct conscious attention to the detail of the task.

In ways that are similar to the writer's building of a sentence, word for word from left to right to create meanings, readers build possible sentence structures as they read; an entry to the book's first sentence must be found, and then word after word must be constructed at each point taking into account all the words so far. Listeners build the possible structured meaning of an utterance as they listen to speakers. What did they say? What did they mean? Upcoming words are influenced by the word order and structure that preceded them. This is sometimes discussed under the heading of 'parsing' (Pinker 1994; see Chapters 2 and 3).

Story production can be a shared activity between child and teacher in which three types of activity occur: at first the teacher writes most of the sentence; then they co-construct the text, interacting in a variety of ways, making good use of the working page; and gradually the teacher helps very little and the child writes.

Composing again, quickly, in the cut-up story

If an early intervention has a writing component in its design (as RR does), children compose a message of appropriate difficulty and write it down as independently as they can, with support from the teacher who has various ways of scaffolding their efforts. Then the teacher can write the same message on a thin card and cut it into word-size pieces. (Sometimes, for a special purpose, a teacher may draw attention to a particular feature like a phrase, or syllable, or rime segment, or single letter by cutting off part of a word, but he or she uses breaks below the word level only rarely — teachers have to resist that temptation.) The child reassembles his or her own sentence in this new puzzle medium. The task is focused on the assembling processes of composing rather than on the breaking down processes of writing. *This is not an optional extra put into the lesson framework for fun.* It is there for serious reasons; it allows the teacher to observe many important aspects of the writing task in more controlled ways.

- *Attending.* It gives the teacher very clear information on things the child is attending to or neglecting.

- *Monitoring.* It shows how the child is monitoring his or her reconstruction of his or her own composed sentence.

- *Self-correcting.* It reveals the processes of self-correction (in the placement of the puzzle pieces) to the child and to the teacher.

- *Shifting attention.* A shift of attention to some new feature of print may be noticed, occurring without explicit teaching.

- *New learning (Aha!).* Something happens which suggests some new awareness, not necessarily raised to consciousness. The child's behaviours may indicate that he or she can work with some new relationship as this familiar story is reconstructed.

- *Assembling messages.* The task reveals *to the writer* how to work strategically across text with assembling sentences — parsing the sentence, word after word, one-to-one correspondence of words spoken and words written, directional behaviours, checking behaviours, monitoring behaviours, sometimes 'segmenting the smallest units behaviour', and word-study of things that 'hearing the sounds' might not teach. The reassembled text is read and the reading is checked against the familiar message which the child composed and wrote.

- *Giving letters minimal attention.* In the cut-up story the problems of finding the letters and sequencing them has been done away with and the child's attention is then on assembling the message from the word level up (most of the time). It focuses more on the assembling processes than on the breaking down processes.

As the children reassemble the cut-up sentence they verbalise their message. They match what they are saying aloud to what they are doing as they search for each appropriate word or part of a word. They keep pace with their voices as they progress with the remaking. At some points children may help their searching or mark time by repeating the word, letter or cluster they are looking for. Sometimes they comment aloud as they search, saying, for example, 'Where is it?'. They make errors and go back and forth to sort these out, occasionally talking about the self-corrections they are making, saying, 'No, it's not that one.' Successful completion may be evaluated with a flourish, 'There!', or a grin of success before rereading and checking.

The cut-up story provides an opportunity to orchestrate strategic behaviours on familiar material, slowed up and deliberately reconstructed. Teachers may notice examples of how the child takes utterances and words apart in this checking task, and the observation may guide further teaching. It helps the teacher to think about what writers do even when they know all the single words. For hard-to-teach RR children this 'reveals' to the teacher how *rereading one's writing calls for working across the knowledge sources word-after-word with increasing speed and flexibility.* The cut-up story reveals what the learner is working on (that is, aware of, or attending to) in text as he or she:

- assembles sentences
- consolidates one-to-one correspondence of words spoken and words written
- co-ordinates directional behaviours
- practises checking behaviours and monitoring behaviours
- breaks oral language into various segments (not just phonemes)
- gives attention to a word among other words in a way that no activity for studying words in isolation can ever teach.

The text used is not unknown or introduced by the teacher. It is a familiar message, composed and owned by the learner, something the child thought up, planned to write, and worked hard to compose and record but in the cut-up story activity the toil of having to form the letters and words is removed.

Some observable changes in sentence writing

In an early intervention of twelve to twenty weeks the lowest-achieving children after a year at school demonstrate most of the changes which occur in children's control over writing in the first two years at school. Their progress should look like a detailed version of what higher achievers are doing more rapidly and earlier. In this one-to-one programme each change in the child's control calls for an adjustment in what the teacher does. It is not possible to describe the infinite range of ways in which a teacher might work with individual children but the following list of changes came from observed lessons and provides a reminder to teachers of how and when they might need to change an emphasis in their teaching. (See Askew and Frasier 1999.)

- Learners master a growing vocabulary of words, and can write an increasing proportion of words independently.

- They shift from laborious writing of these words to fluent production.

- They show changes in the sounds they hear in words, from recording dominant consonants, to recording most consonants, and then to increasing control of vowels.

- They need fewer teacher prompts on how to use what they know to work on a new word, and shift to initiating action for themselves.

- They become comfortable with unusual features like silent letters (as in 'gate' and 'know') and doubled letters (as in 'letter') and hard-to-hear letters (as in 'went' and 'felt').

- They add inflections without having to work on them.

- They gradually gain a working control of the spelling combinations of English vowels, and other common spelling clusters.

- Their ways of working have speeded up so that they write increasingly long and complex sentences.

There is a lot to be learned about how to write down a language and later changes are dependent upon a secure foundation created in the early stages. The list above does not provide a teaching progression: effective early intervention instruction would be working towards many of those changes concurrently throughout the entire series of lessons (Hobsbaum, Peters and Sylva 1996).

Conclusions

The early intervention teacher keeps the child an active participant, who initiates whatever he or she can, but the teacher shares the writing task and demonstrates how a good writer works on challenging words. The teacher anticipates the need for help, and interacts with the child on the practice page where all the risks are taken. The teacher also looks for tutorial opportunities elsewhere in the lesson which can be linked to today's writing, offers rich opportunities to generate correct responses giving minimum assistance, or teaches extensively according to the momentary changes in the needs of the learner. The teacher cannot afford to make assumptions about tacit awareness, but must check that the child has the control which that teacher was assuming.

Every interaction in the daily writing segment is a teaching move — not a memory task, nor a practice attempt, nor an analysis of sounds, but carefully determined and astutely delivered teaching with a target that involves learning how to do something, do it better, do it faster, link it up to something, and prepare it for future independent use. (Those things include much more learning than just attending to the sounds in words.)

When we direct our mind's attention to some object, or some problem, this process can be called 'taking action'. Directing attention to reading print and to writing messages are actions initiated and carried out by the reader or the writer. Hard-to-teach children can become initiators of literacy activities. When a learner has only limited control over literacy he or she can be encouraged to search for information in either reading or writing, establishing reciprocity between these aspects of learning about literacy.

Teachers need to find the right moments to prompt students to use what they know in reading in the service of writing. To do this a teacher must know a student's current repertoire very well, but this is possible when teaching is individual. Once the child has a sense that knowledge can flow in either direction from writing to reading or from reading to writing, the pool of knowledge from which the child can draw is immediately enlarged.

If we 'go behind the scenes' as it were, beyond the surface behaviours of reading and writing, then what is similar about these two activities becomes apparent:

1) the stores of knowledge about letters, sounds and words which they can draw upon, 2) the ways in which known oral language contributes to print activities, 3) some similar processes that learners use to search for the information they need to solve new problems, and 4) the ways in which they pull together or integrate different types of information common to both activities.

Examples of processes common to both reading and writing activities are these:

- controlling serial order
- problem-solving with more than one kind of information
- drawing on stored information and acting on it
- using visual information
- using phonological information
- using the meaning of what was composed
- using the vocabulary and structure of what was composed
- searching, checking and correcting
- categorising, using rules, and estimating probabilities of occurrence.

In other words, some of the aspects of literacy activities which are shared by reading and writing include how to control serial order in print, how to use phonological information, and how to search, monitor, self-correct and make decisions about words.

Another way to reflect upon the reciprocity of these two sets of activities is to think of how learners can continue to extend their control to more demanding texts in either reading or writing. An effective literacy system designed to extend its own competency depends upon:

- how well children can attend to different aspects of print

- how oral language can be linked to print

- how to use prior knowledge

- how to construct texts (talk, retelling, and composing)

- how to explore print detail

- how to detect and correct errors

- how to go beyond the limits of the system and do some untutored things

- and having the independence to strike out alone.

For those who work in early literacy interventions the general recommendations run something like this. Children build their grammar in oral language learning during thousands of conversational exchanges with expert speakers who fail to understand them when they get too far away from standard forms of English. There is no finer tutorial for learning oral language than not being understood. The shaping is done in every interchange, in every attempt that the child makes to convey a message. The feedback is a naturally-occurring event that is highly tutorial. Early writing benefits from similar kinds of rich interactions and the individual tutorial can deliver these.

There is high motivational value in self-composed messages rather than a dictated task or a message drawn from the teacher's mind, and the child can draw upon established speaking competencies to compose messages for writing. At first encourage the composing of natural sentences that are similar to those which children use in speech; the stylistics of storybooks and other genre can be taken aboard as the task becomes easier for the learner. They will surface later in the things children write.

Helping children to construct new words they want to write rather than stressing memory is a productive initial emphasis. This helps them to build a large writing vocabulary, containing many different words which are written quickly and easily. It provides a host of 'letter clusters' in all their variety for generating other words.

Hearing sounds in words is designed to teach the learner to do what traditional 'phonics' fails to do for some children in classrooms. It recognises that a first step in dealing with letter-sound relationships is being able to attend to the sequence of sounds in words, and to come to know the variety of ways in which these can be recorded in print. The tentative and flexible awareness of sound-to-print relationships that results is a workable basis for mastering the vagaries of the language without creating a mindset that stresses regularity and rules. It helps older children to independently approximate things they want to write about, like 'excepet' and 'conpleteley', which are easily sorted out in a brief teaching interaction.

Teacher interactions support and encourage children's attempts to try longer words and more complex sentences, challenging writers to lift their performance. The literacy processing must move forwards towards more complexity. Teaching practices must engage children in authentic reading and writing tasks of wide variety presented with some sort of management over the gradient of difficulty. Engagement in those authentic tasks should be rich enough to provide opportunities for any child *to expand knowledge about any language process at every opportunity.* When teachers select tasks, texts, activities and outcomes they often limit opportunities for new insights to arise, and for new language knowledge to be an outcome. There should be opportunities for learners to discover new things about print that they have not attended to before. If that sounds complex, that is fine because literacy learning *is* complex. But it is easy for learners to keep reading and writing separate from each other when teachers do not see the similarities between these two activities at the early stages of literacy learning *and* keep them separate. Parents and society also treat these as different achievements.

An important collection of academic papers related to the development of writing was published under the title of *Cognitive processes in spelling* edited by Frith (1980). Seventeen years later Perfetti, Rieben and Fayol (1997) edited a book called *Learning to Spell: Research, Theory and Practice Across Languages.* Reviewing this book Goswami (1999) says it investigates how spelling is acquired and how spelling acquisition relates to reading acquisition. As an update to my interest in the reciprocity of learning to read and write in RR and in *Descubriendo la Lectura,* its Spanish equivalent, I noted two comments by Goswami. She wrote:

> One of the important messages for me ... was that the relationship between reading and writing is complex. This makes guidance to teachers about how to teach the two skills in conjunction far from straightforward.

So research interest is mounting in this area. Her second comment is of high current interest for RR because it is an early intervention being taught in both English and Spanish.

> Disentangling exactly how graphemic conventions in different languages affect the representation of phonology and vice versa promises to be an exciting area of future research in psycholinguistics. (Goswami 1999)

At the practical level of delivering an early intervention to two language groups, with a programme in French being constructed for Canada, RR is grappling with just such issues.

The conventions of writing are arbitrary. Children have to be introduced to the conventions for writing down the language which they speak. Control over an arbitrary coding system cannot 'emerge' in a developing child unless there are some cultural processes which help children to learn the links between what they say and how they might create a record of it. To notice a preschool child's changing responses to print is valuable but to believe that writing is going to emerge without the influence of knowledgeable tutors or models is to deny the child access to the arbitrary rules of writing systems. And that belief leads adults to avoid interacting with children in ways that would be helpful. The preschool child's opportunities to construct a knowledge of print for himself or herself are expanded when we interact with the literacy awareness he or she demonstrates. *There has to be opportunity, interaction and assistance. If the child has not had this support the early years of schooling must provide the tutors and the models, and the early intervention teacher has to be exceptionally helpful if the child is to gain control over the writing system. There also has to be an active, constructive child working on the challenges (with an observant teacher at his or her elbow).*

We currently know less about the strategic processing of the child learning to write than we do about early reading but the effects of one upon the other reported in Chapter 2 (Robinson 1973) are compelling. They underline a critical period from six to eighteen months after entry to school when reading contributes to writing progress and vice versa. Studies by Hobsbaum et al. (1996) and Boocock, McNaughton and Parr (1998) have begun the documentation of processing changes that can occur.

Note 1

Penny was 4:11, was at preschool, and had not yet learned to read. She often produced writing using her name, her brother's name and the few letters she knew. Once she made up some names for her favourite dolls using the knowledge she had:

POUUYi   AUUDO   POOiZ

In the post she received an invitation to Mary's party. She whipped the letter out of her mother's hand and retreated to her bedroom with it. Then she brought it back, displaying the writing in the centre of the card and her mother read it to her. For the time being she was satisfied. That night she asked for paper, saying, 'I want to write to Mary' although no one had suggested that a reply was necessary and her mother could not recall that Penny had ever tried to transmit a whole message in print before. She complained about the first piece of paper she was offered. 'Too scrappy,' she said, so obviously this was an important letter. 'How do you write "come"?' she asked when more elegant paper was supplied. 'What do you want to say?' asked her mother. 'I would like to *come* [stress and pause] to your party,' was the answer. 'Don't you want to put "I" and "would"?' said her mother. Penny shrilled with irritation: 'But I will have to write "come".' It was the operative word, the essence of the message, the important thing to write. Completing that task introduced her to how you can put what you say down on paper. She did not yet know how to search for the first word in the sentence, rather than the most significant word (Clay 1991, pp. 91–93). Penny wanted to signify acceptance.

References

Askew, B.J. and D. Frasier. 1999. Early writing: An exploration of literacy opportunities. *Literacy, Teaching and Learning* 4, 1: 43–66.

Bissex, G. 1980. *GNYS AT WRK: A Child Learns To Write and Read.* Cambridge, MA: Harvard University Press.

Boocock, C., S. McNaughton and J.M. Parr. 1998. The early development of a self-extending system in writing. *Literacy Teaching and Learning* 3, 2: 41–59.

Booth, D. 1999. Personal communication, University of Toronto.

Cazden, C.B. 1974. Play with language and meta-linguistic awareness: One dimension of language experience. *Organization Mondiale Pour l'Education Prescolaire* 6: 12–24.

Chomsky, C. 1971. Write first; Read later. *Childhood Education* 1971, 47: 396–399.

———. 1972. Stages in language development and reading exposure. *Harvard Educational Review* 42: 1–33.

———. 1975a. How sister got into the grog. *Early Years*: 36–39.

———. 1975b. Invented spelling in the open classroom. *Word* (Special Issue entitled *Child Language Today*) 27: 499–518.

———. 1979. Approaching reading through invented spelling. In L.B. Resnick and P.A. Weaver, eds, *Theory and Practice of Early Reading*, Vol. 2, pp. 43–64. Hillsdale, NJ: Lawrence Erlbaum.

Clay, M.M. 1975. *What Did I Write?* Auckland: Heinemann.

———. 1987. *Writing Begins At Home.* Auckland: Heinemann.

———. 1991. *Becoming Literate: The Construction of Inner Control.* Auckland: Heinemann.

———. 1993a. *An Observation Survey of Early Literacy Achievement.* Auckland: Heinemann (First Edition 1972; Second Edition 1979; Third Edition 1985; title change 1993).

———. 1993b. *Reading Recovery: A Guidebook for Teachers in Training.* Auckland: Heinemann.

———. 1998. *By Different Paths to Common Outcomes.* York, ME: Stenhouse Publishers.

Dyson, A.H. 1994. Viewpoints: The word and the world — reconceptualizing written language development or do rainbows mean a lot to little girls? In R.B. Ruddell, M.R. Ruddell and H. Singer, eds, 1994, *Theoretical Models and Processes of Reading.* Newark, DE: International Reading Association.

Dyson, A. Haas. 1997. *Writing Superheroes: Contemporary Childhood, Popular Culture, and Classroom Literacy.* New York: Teachers College Press.

Elkonin, D. 1971. Development of speech. In A.V. Zaporozhets and D.B. Elkonin, eds, *The Psychology of Preschool Children.* Cambridge, MA: MIT Press.

———. 1973. USSR. In J. Downing, ed., *Comparative Reading*, pp. 551–580. New York: Macmillan.

Ferreiro, E. and A. Teberosky. 1982. *Literacy Before Schooling.* Portsmouth, NH: Heinemann.

Frith, U. 1980. *Cognitive processes in spelling.* London: Academic Press.

Goodman, Y., ed. 1990. *How Children Construct Literacy: Piagetian Perspectives.* Newark, DE: International Reading Association.

Goswami, U. 1999. Spelling it out …. Book review of *Learning to Spell: Research, Theory and Practice Across Languages*, C.A. Perfetti, L. Rieben and M. Fayot, eds, in *The Psychologist* 12, 7: 360–361.

Harris, T.L. and R.E. Hodges. 1995. *The Literacy Dictionary: The Vocabulary of Reading and Writing.* Newark, DE: International Reading Association.

Hobsbaum, A., S. Peters and K. Sylva. 1996. Scaffolding in Reading Recovery. *Oxford Review of Education* 22, 1: 17–35.

Kress, G. 2000. *Early Spelling: Between Convention and Creativity*. London: Routledge.

Paley, V.G. 1981. *Wally's Stories*. Cambridge, MA: Harvard University Press.

Pearson, P.D. 1990. Foreword. In T. Shanahan, ed., *Reading and Writing Together: New Perspectives for the Classroom*. Norwood, MA: Christopher-Gordon.

Perfetti, C.A., L. Rieben and M. Fayol, eds. 1997. *Learning to Spell: Research, Theory and Practice Across Languages*. Hillsdale, NJ: Lawrence Erlbaum.

Pinker, S. 1994. *The Language Instinct: How the Mind Creates Language*. New York: William Morrow.

Read, C. 1975. *Children's Categorization of Speech Sounds in English*. Urbana, Illinois: National Council of Teachers of English.

———. 1986. *Children's Creative Spelling*. London: Routledge, Kegan Paul.

Robinson, S.E. 1973. Predicting Early Reading Progress. Master of Arts thesis, University of Auckland Library.

Ruddell, R.B., M.R. Ruddell and H. Singer, eds. 1994. *Theoretical Models and Processes of Reading* (Fourth Edition). Newark, DE: International Reading Association.

Rumelhart, D.E. 1994. Toward an interactive model of reading. In R.B. Ruddell, M.R. Ruddell and H. Singer, eds, 1994, *Theoretical Models and Processes of Reading* (Fourth Edition), pp. 864–894. Newark, DE: International Reading Association.

Shanahan, T., ed. 1990. *Reading and Writing Together: New Perspectives for the Classroom*. Norwood, MA: Christopher-Gordon.

Smith, F. 1978. *Understanding Reading* (Second Edition). New York: Holt, Rinehart and Winston.

Spalding, R.B. and W.T. Spalding. 1962. *The Writing Road to Reading*. New York: William Morrow.

Treiman, R. 1993. *Beginning to Spell: A Study of First Grade Children*. New York: Oxford University Press.

Weinberger, J., P. Hannon and C. Nutbrown. 1990. *Ways of Working With Parents to Promote Early Literacy Development*. Sheffield: University of Sheffield Educational Research Centre.

Williams, J. 1995. Phonemic Awareness. In T. Harris and R.E. Hodges, *The Literacy Dictionary: The Vocabulary of Reading and Writing*, pp. 185–186. Newark, DE: International Reading Association.

2   Acts of literacy processing: an unusual lens

2   Acts of literacy processing: an unusual lens

Two views of change over time

This chapter reports a history which the reader may want to ignore. It is not a history of reading theories for it reviews a small body of evidence collected between 1965 and 2000. When I posed the question 'What is possible for children with reading problems?', people accepted my question but paid little attention to the fact that we began using an exceptional lens to find some answers to it. It was not their error; we underestimated the importance of our methodology and did not articulate its implications. Predictably using a different lens produces a non-conformist view which does not displace existing lenses: rather it is used for limited purposes for which it is particularly suited (like viewing distant things in detail or taking a panoramic photograph). I believe that future developments in early literacy intervention may find some direction by revisiting the history of the evidence we collected when we attended to the detail of beginners trying to read and write texts.

This chapter must begin with an explanation of the terms used in its title. 'Literacy' refers to either reading or writing activities considered separately or together. (That arises from my research which began in 1963.) The focus is on behaviours or acts which can be observed and which provide observers with signals. (We began that exploration between 1960 and 1970.) Trained observers can interpret changes in these signals as changes in psychological processes like perceiving, linking and decision-making (for which we use the general term 'processing'). Most but not all literacy processing is language processing (which became an interest from the 1970s to the present time). The phrase 'an unusual lens' refers to any observational or research methodology which gathers detailed data on changes in the literacy behaviours of young children as they learn to read and write continuous texts over a period of time. (Running Records of reading or writing provide one example of an observational lens directed to text processing; see Note 1, p. 82.)

So what are the two views of progress? Typically progress is assessed by studying what teachers are teaching and measuring which parts of that the children are learning. The progress is measured by tests of letters, sounds, words, or graded texts or products in portfolios. The question is 'What have the children learned from my lessons about my curriculum?' The testing approach has a long history and is accepted as indicating benchmarks to be achieved. It is illustrated by a statement like 'This child is on Text Level 18.' I know what level of text this child can work at but nothing about how that child reads the text.

A predominant approach to beginning reading instruction for the past century has been to describe reading and writing acquisition from an array of pre- and post-tests, and statistically derive the important components of early reading from those scores. Instruction is then designed to develop those components. That has worked reasonably well for most children, except that it has generated many different kinds of programmes for children in the first two years of literacy instruction, and surprisingly angry debates. We have come to expect all such programmes to yield literacy difficulties for about 20 per cent of the school population.

This chapter makes an argument for considering an additional and alternative view to be legitimate. It is referred to as the 'literacy processing' view of progress during literacy acquisition. When we study how children work on texts as they read and write irrespective of how teachers are teaching, we arrive at a description of progress which is different. In my opinion it is the collective wisdom from a small set of research studies which provides a justification for calling this an alternative view of progress.

Experienced classroom teachers become very familiar with the ways in which young children's literacy processing changes during the first years of schooling, and such teachers could justifiably become irritated by this chapter because it seems to traverse familiar territory for them. In my defence I believe that it is the processing view of progress that is the main reason why Reading Recovery (RR) teachers consistently get good results with individual tutoring across the world in many different education systems, child after child, year after year. The alternative view enables us to help children who find literacy learning unusually difficult for many different reasons. I have read in some research reports that RR teachers' success has been due to positive reinforcement, to the prompt questions they use, to good teacher training, and other reductionist attributions. We all like to simplify things, but many things must remain complex. (English grammar is a prime example, and it governs every utterance I make, every sentence I write, and almost all of my reading, yet how can I explain what it is?) Those reductionist explanations for RR's success are usually provided by outside evaluators and they disturbed me enough to make me reread many things published around the time that RR was developed. Were there things we knew then which we had forgotten to articulate? This was more than a sense of nostalgia; it was a genuine concern that we might have overlooked things that were important. We had. It was not that any one of the individual studies had been overlooked but rather that the collective outcome of those studies had not been pulled together.

The case I need to make can only be argued from a limited number of research projects which fall clearly within the defining terms described above. If I am looking towards a new set of hypotheses about how literacy processing changes over time which might be used in future research then the original studies must be reviewed carefully in some detail. A reader could be forgiven for skimming to the tables of hypotheses but *I must construct the evidence for its entries.*

A return to old gold mines was profitable. I discovered again how unproductive and unpopular remedial reading was at the time these studies began, that early writing was a neglected area about to be discovered, and that Elkonin's ideas on hearing the sound sequences in words had appeared in English translation. I was lecturing on a range of clinical problems in children, and the possibilities of preventing some of these. As a result of that return journey I now see the origins of the RR intervention for low achievers in better perspective.

A provocative and novel question becomes the prime focus of this chapter. What do *proficient* young readers do as they problem-solve increasingly difficult texts? What evidence do we have of sequential changes in their proficiency? Detailed analyses of how the behaviours of competent readers and writers change over time in the first three years of school might give us a model of what has to be done to read and write well. In what ways do proficient readers and writers make use of information from print as they read? A secondary interest is, of course, whether low achievers who are becoming successful in an early intervention programme move through a somewhat similar succession of changes. Does an overview of what we know provide a useful mapping of change over time in literacy processing that might guide early literacy interventions? I am seeking a new synthesis of what we already know about this alternative processing view of progress.

A record of acts

I selected an illustration of 'acts of processing' from an old research tape made in 1963. It captures some of the earliest processing behaviours that led to the studies reviewed in this chapter. Kay entered school on her fifth birthday in February and was not a reader. Like all her New Zealand classmates she was not in a preparatory programme: she was expected to learn to read and write now that she was 'in school'.

After a month her teacher introduced her to first level reading books, and in her second month at school she was reading at a higher level of the reading series. (See Randell 1999 for discussion of the type of reading material.) This is how she read:

Kay: We've got a tape-recorder.

Me: Have you?

Kay: (*reads the title*) Grandma (*pause*) Comes (*pause*) To Stay. There's 'come' there. It shouldn't have the 's' on the end. (*laughs*) I just write 'come'. (*reads*) ... comes **to** stay.

Me: All right. Go on. Read the book.

p. 1   Kay: 'Here's the plane,' said Father. 'The Viscount,' shouted Bill. 'The Viscount,' shouted Peter.

p. 2   Kay: 'Grandma is in the plane,' said Father. (*long pause*)

Me: Where are you?

Kay: Here. (*pointing; long pause*)

Me: What does it say?

Kay: 'Grandma ...

Me: Yes. Go on.

Kay: ... is ...

Me: Mm.

Kay: ... in ...

Me: Mm.

Kay: ... the plane,' said Bill.

Me: Mm.

p. 3   Kay: Grandma and Father are in the car. 'Bill, Peter. Come here,' said Father.

Me: Now would you read the next page with your finger?

p. 4   Kay: (*pointing word by word*) 'Mother. Mother. Here is Grandma,' shouted Pe- / Bill.

p. 5   A doll for Sally. A ca-/a fire engine for Bill. A car for Peter. 'Oh thank you, Grandma,' said Bill and Peter and Sally.

p. 6   'Bill, Peter, Sally,
come … to … bed,' said Mother.
Bill and the fire engine (*repeats the line*)
Bill, (*repeats*) Bill and the fire engine
is/**are** in bed.
Peter (*repeats*) Peter and the car **are** in bed.

p. 7   The doll is in bed. (*pause*)
    Me: Where are you?
    Kay: Here.
    Me: What is it?
    Kay: Sally is up. (*She moves to close the book, but seems to be uncertain.*)
    Me: Yes. And what about the last part?

p. 8 Kay: (*She turns the page.*) Sally is naughty.

(This example is referred to later in this book as 'Kay'.)

This child was off to a very good start. The record shows a beginner working with information of different kinds on continuous text. She made sense of the story; she studied a word, 'comes', and commented on the 's' she did not expect to see, she lost the thread and read one page slowly, word by word without linking it up. From time to time she paused and studied the print and could not initiate anything until encouraged. Brilliantly, she corrected herself on the run several times — Pe-/Bill, a ca-/a fire engine — and she anticipated the verb 'is', corrected it to 'are' which must have been on visual information, but rolled it very slowly across her tongue, and caught it again a few words later, as if to say 'Okay, you have to look carefully.' She was not satisfied with what seemed to be the end of the story but did not assume that there must be another page. *She used several working systems in the areas of story structure, word structure, the sounds of letters, and language structure. She already knew that reading is complex and if you shift gear and work on the text in different ways it can be figured out.* After two months at school she was moving into a second level book. Nothing in that record tells us that by the end of the school year she will be in the proficient group for literacy; she has a lot to learn.

Such transcriptions of what children said and did developed into what is commonly called today a 'Running Record'. It is one systematic procedure for recording reading behaviours observed during text reading, a tool for recording and then interpreting how children work on texts. It is widely used by classroom teachers and can be a reliable and valid measurement but it is sometimes used in quite unacceptably slipshod ways by educators without the benefit of training, who use shortcuts and idiosyncratic variants. RR teachers use it daily to guide instruction. A Running Record, expertly used by a trained teacher and carefully interpreted, provides a valid view of change over time in children's reading. For several legitimate reasons researchers and educators distrust Running Records: they do not conform to the rules of standardised tests; some of the behaviours observed appear for a time and then disappear as a reader makes progress; and the text material read, while providing a gradient of difficulty, is not laid out in equal steps.

A Running Record is only one example of what I am calling *an unusual lens. Any observational tool or research methodology which gathered detailed data on changes in literacy processing over short time intervals of time from subjects who were reading or writing continuous texts would be such a lens.* It transmits a different kind of information from that provided by scores on phoneme, letter and word tests, or from comprehension questions. So we get an alternative view of progress.

A record of progress

When a child's progress through a series of reading books is listed from first to last along some gradient of difficulty we can record the accuracy with which each book was read (see Figure 1, p. 47) and day by day or week by week we can record the child's increasing control over text reading. It is reassuring to know that progress is being made as time passes. When that kind of record is also backed by an analysis of the literacy processing behaviours of the reader from time to time, teachers in classrooms and early intervention teachers have a tool for monitoring changes in how the reader works on the text, what the reader is noticing, what is easy, what is confusing, and what needs the teacher's attention.

I want to provide an account of progress made by proficient readers and how their problem-solving changes during the first two to three years of literacy instruction. I will start with children at or around eight years of age and then review evidence of how their competency might have been constructed. If, in the manner of the biological and zoological sciences, we document how behaviours pass through several different phases in the first years of instruction, each successive phase of greater complexity than the one which preceded it, then the acquisition sequence to be described will probably be somewhat analogous to the changing states of a developing foetus, and unlike the accumulation of items in a bank account. *What I end up with is not a theory of instruction, but a theory of the construction of an inner control of literacy acts.* The focus is on changes that can be observed in day-to-day reading and writing and on some standard tasks, rather than on responses to experiments, or changes in test scores. Some of the research studies I review have been published; others are theses available in university libraries; most used '*an unusual lens*', making frequent observational records of children over short intervals of time as they engaged in literacy activities.

However, if literacy learning is not a simple process of additive accumulation but is transformed in a sequence of changes from simple processes to more complex processes, then concepts of equal steps or mere arithmetical gains become untenable. Changes in processing which occur over time would probably not proceed by equal interval steps, and small steps of great importance could occur close together in the early stages of learning to read with larger steps taken at greater intervals of time among older readers. This is problematic for literacy researchers whose statistical

Figure 1 Record of books read: accuracy and difficulty rating
(Easy, Instructional, and Hard)

Week	Book title (publisher series) Key: R to R — Ready to Read series PM — Price Milburn series	Level	Accuracy	Rating	Self-correction rate
1	Nick's Glasses (R to R)	10	98%	Easy	1:1.3
2	Breakfast (Young Shorty)	12	94%	Inst.	1:2.5
3	Mark Fox (Young Shorty)	14	96%	Easy	1:2
4	The Hat Trick (Bangers & Mash)	13	98%	Easy	1:1
5	Burglars (Young Shorty)	15	93%	Inst.	1:2
6	Burglars (Young Shorty)	15	96%	Easy	1:1.3
7	Wet Days at School (City Kids)	14	98%	Easy	1:2
8	Buster is Lost (Lang. in Action)	15	94%	Inst.	1:2
9	My Ghost (Mount Gravatt)	15	95%	Easy	1:2
10	A Hat for Pedro (Pedro Books)	14	95%	Easy	1:1.5
11	Pedro and the Cars (Pedro Books)	15	90%	Inst.	1:3
12	Monster Looks for a Friend (Monster Books)	16	98%	Easy	1:1.3
13	Pot of Gold (Scott Foresman)	16	96%	Easy	1:1.5
14	Giant's Hiccups (Open Highways)	17	96%	Easy	1:2
15	Monster and the Magic Umbrella (Monster Books)	18	97%	Easy	1:1.3
16	Chocolate Shop (Young Shorty)	18	94%	Inst.	1:2
17	Beauty and the Bus (Hart-Davis)	18	94%	Inst.	1:2
18	Magpie's Tail (R to R)	19	98%	Easy	1:2
19	Poached Eggs (Hart-Davis)	19	94%	Inst.	1:2
20	Monster at School (Monster Books)	19	97%	Easy	1:1.5
21	Won and Lost (Young Shorty)	20	96%	Easy	1:2
22	The Hairy Boggart (Story Box)	22	98%	Easy	1:1.4
23	Gotham Way of Counting (R to R)	23	93%	Inst.	1:2.6
24	The Greedy Cook and the Hungry Shark (N.F.S. School Journal)	24	97%	Easy	1:1.3
25	Only a Little Fire (PM)	25	97%	Easy	Nil
26	(No record taken)				
27	Having a Haircut (City Kids)	24	94%	Inst.	1:2
28 & 29	The Old Car (PM)	25	95%	Easy	1:1.75

tools require equal intervals, but it is no reason for discarding a useful tool for observing progress. Using 'an unusual lens' forces us to recognise the utility and the limitations of the analyses we typically make.

I assume that we need to know what proficient readers do if we are to enable less proficient readers to become more effective literacy learners. Therefore I have chosen to extract findings from the original research reports *with most emphasis on the proficient readers.*

The research reviewed highlights the opposition between an additive model of reading progress (credit in the bank account or scores for words known), and a transformation model (describing changes in the complexity of the processing system). Progress would be reported in the additive model as quantitative counts or scores, while progress in the transformation model would need to demonstrate changes in crucial variables like:

- mobilising several resources needed for a specific task,

- or integrating different kinds of information,

- or demonstrating alternative ways of using information.

My argument is not that an additive model should be abandoned for a transformation one; to respect both as useful alternatives is merely to recognise that the methods used by science to gather data affect the data available for collection and the kinds of explanation which can be obtained.

After the development of Running Records of text reading (Clay 1966, 1967), through the next two decades several theses and dissertations presented to the University of Auckland plumbed the potential of recording reader behaviour while reading text, and a few explored the more difficult task of recording behaviours while writing texts.

According to Yopp and Singer (1994) teachers exert control over the success or failure of beginning readers by varying the demands that classroom tasks make on the resources that must be activated by the reader, and the level of learning and criteria required for successful progress in learning to read. I am clear that the literacy processing systems that are constructed by learners during beginning literacy are massively influenced by the expectations and opportunities of the school curriculum and by the teaching practices of the schools. The studies could be biased by what was happening in New Zealand classrooms from 1963 to 1996. The New Zealand children discussed in the following synopses of research projects began school instruction in literacy on their fifth birthdays and were expected to read storybooks and write daily in their first year at school. At that time practices for literacy learning followed common curriculum guidelines and instructional emphases; schools made choices about the delivery of instruction and the materials used but the core instructional thrust was similar for all children in all schools, public and private, providing some instructional consistency. Two studies were conducted in the United Kingdom. One emphasis which may be peculiar in New Zealand instruction is *the high demand from the first days of school for children to read and write texts according to their competencies but always as independently as possible.* (Consider Kay's record, proficient at age 5:2 after two months at school.)

To begin this analysis with proficient readers may seem a back-to-front way of relating emerging competencies to later achievements, especially for a developmental psychologist like me, but by attending to the proficient older group I can escape temporarily a) from arguments about beginning reading methods, and b) from an emphasis on the outcome behaviours of adults. From an account of what independent readers do at eight years I want to work carefully through research evidence to identify some components out of which this effective functioning was probably constructed. Many shifts occur in tentative information processing as children construct the cognitive processing resources needed for more advanced literacy activities. Such components are likely to be described differently from those which arise from test score analyses, or pre- and post-test research designs. My task will undoubtedly prove to be difficult if what has to be described passes through kaleidoscopic changes in multidimensional processes, is hidden from view, and is executed at high speed, all of which are viable assumptions.

Successful readers at about eight years and one study of older readers

By definition, successful readers by about eight years of age can work at problem-solving the hard parts of the texts while also rapidly processing most of the messages. They have built effective processing systems which allow them to read and problem-solve known words in new texts and new-to-them words encountered for the first time. They can work aloud or silently. Those successful readers do what needs to be done mainly alone, somewhat analogous to the way every child builds a grammar for speaking. Instruction by teachers will have brought many new things to the readers' attention, but the learners' own contributions to acts of reading have been considerable.

However, these successful readers still have much to learn. They read more slowly than successful older readers but within the next two years as they read silently their reading speeds will increase, they will read more difficult texts, and word-solving and self-corrections will rarely be heard. Change must continue to occur for obviously a proficient reader at eight cannot do what a proficient reader at sixteen can do. It will be necessary to look at how beginning readers begin to build the power system which expands first to the competencies of the beginning silent reader around eight years and then beyond that to those of the older silent reader (Singer 1994).

Because the processing behaviours of the youngest readers are overt and easily observed it is possible to specify in some detail what occurs before most reading becomes silent reading. A theoretical model of successful oral reading before the shift to mostly silent reading could characterise the primitive system out of which the silent reading systems are built. From studies by Williams 1968, Imlach 1971, Clay 1970, and Sue Watson 1975, the description of processing of proficient readers at about eight years of age is extracted.

Williams 1968 (see Clay 1982)

This research study described how successful readers aged 7:10 read five graded paragraphs from a standardised test (Neale 1958).

- They read accurately at a good pace, solved new or difficult words, and detected and self-corrected many of their errors.

- Analysis of those errors showed that, on many occasions, the word selected, though wrong, was typically influenced by 1) syntax, 2) meaning (local and more extensive), 3) letters, and 4) letter-sound relationships.

- When an error occurred the substitute word was close to the text words *on all four types of information,* suggesting that these good readers could be using sub-word, word, syntactic and semantic information when approaching unfamiliar words.

- Self-corrections implied that a mismatch had been detected between the information used in the substitution and other information available to the reader.

Readers read five- to nine-year texts more or less correctly and problem-solved 1) on new words, 2) on miscued known words, and 3) on strings of words which were reworked during self-correction. Analysis of the errors and self-corrections suggested that the readers were working in several different ways with information from the printed page.

This flexible way of working would allow for an ever-increasing control over more difficult texts: *a) increased amounts of problem-solving could be expected to increase problem-solving power, and b) the reading work done could sharpen knowledge of, and access to, new vocabulary.* When the child reads correctly we as observers cannot know precisely what information contributed to his or her decisions, but correct responding would tell *the reader* that the processing undertaken created no dissonance and the words decided upon fitted in every way with the text. On the other hand, as the reader converts difficulties (such as new words, not-yet-familiar words, old words with new meanings, or new groupings of words) into opportunities to 'solve the text' successful processing activity could extend the reading repertoire and/or force the reorganisation of existing processing resources. One might expect to find continuous change over time in such behaviours in a series of longitudinal observations. When the child is reading independently, both the correct reading and the problem-solving at difficulties could contribute to *consolidating and extending* the processing system being used.

Notice that this description is very different from that of an 'additive' model of reading progress in which progress is expressed in scores or counts or enumerated skills. A 'transformation' model of progress describes how different kinds of information in print come to contribute together to a decision and how early primitive decision-making is refined and expanded into more efficient decision-making. This transformation model provides a different view of changes in learning to read, a view which becomes possible with the development of:

- a simple technology for making records of oral reading

- analyses supported by linguistic theories

- a description of behaviours which teachers can observe

- a theory about how an initially simple processing system changes over time to become a complex processing system.

This theory contrasts with two other theoretical assumptions: that reading is driven by a simple processing system or that there is only one reading process and readers differ in the control of that process. A developmental view, involving organismic and experiential factors, describes early literacy responses which are simple, slow and separate changing to later literacy responses which are complex, fast and interactive. Failure to make shifts in processing power is apparent in many cases of literacy difficulties. Juel (1980) provided an example of one girl's writing at Grades 1, 2 and 4, and a recent analysis of reading disability (Spear-Swerling and Sternberg 1996) identifies this as a core problem.

Clay and Imlach 1971 (see Clay 1982)

A second study of the same age group studied pausing, stress, pitch and juncture during text reading (Clay and Imlach 1971). These observable sound signals in oral language are clearly described by linguists. Children read four stories ranging from easy for all to sufficiently difficult for the best children to show the full range of their skills. The texts were not from any standard source such as graded paragraphs but were analysed in various ways to depict a gradient of difficulty. On these texts the *proficient readers*:

- made fewest pauses,

- read an average of seven words between pauses,

- and paused only briefly.

- They read accurately making only one error in 100 running words,

- their substitutions could be analysed for the syntactic, semantic and letter-sound information in the texts,

- their reading speed increased as pause and stress times were reduced,

- and they used a wide range of pitch (although weak stress was high and possibly linked to making a shift to silent reading).

- They usually read the message in syntactic sequences, indicated by pausing and stress,

- and frequently disregarded punctuation signals at the end of clauses or sentences (possibly related to the increase in reading rate and/or to processing information across sentence boundaries, working with larger stretches of discourse).

The results suggest that the processing is complex rather than simple, and affected by the demands of the task. Apparently these successful readers worked sequentially across text giving detailed attention to phrase, word, letter cluster, and letter-sound possibilities, and used information from story, sentence, and between-sentence sources. Such research findings could not be accounted for by a theory of progress in reading which explains the behaviour in terms of increasingly rapid recall of words, or increasing automaticity. No fixed top-down or bottom-up sequence was detected. When the readers switched to problem-solving mode they entered the problem from any one of several information sources (see Rumelhart 1994, and Chapter 3).

In contrast to the proficient readers, less successful groups in Imlach's research worked with short phrases and more often at the word or sub-word level (on letter clusters and single letters). Letter-sound options and word discrimination contributed to the successful reading done by the less successful groups but the fast, accurate, sequential reading of texts by the better readers involved, additionally, linguistic information from large stretches of structure, meaning and discourse, and faster processing times.

Clay 1970

A third study which complements the previous ones involved reading words in isolation. (Reading a list of words deprives the reader of supportive textual information at syntactic, semantic and discourse levels of text analysis and forces the problem-solving to depend on letter, letter-sound, letter cluster and word levels of information in print and memory.) A longitudinal study was conducted with children aged 5:6, 6:0, 7:0 and 8:0 by repeating an experiment on the same children. Children read equivalent lists of fifteen words, all easy for six-year-olds, but printed in normal, reversed and inverted orientations. Howard and Templeton (1966) had predicted that the changes in the orientation of the print *could be more disturbing as the children became more familiar with the normal orientation* of letters and words, and that hypothesis was strongly supported among the proficient readers both in the statistical analysis of word-reading scores and in the behavioural descriptions of how the children read. At 5:6 they scored well for age on all orientations, showing little effect from the changed orientation. Scores dropped significantly on reversed words by 6:0, and on inverted words by 7:0. *By 8:0 years those* proficient *readers were more disturbed by the changes in the print orientation than any of the other three lower-achieving reading groups:*

- they stumbled on reversed and inverted orientations,
- paused for long periods,

- offered no response,

- squinted at the words,

- backed away from the print,

- or tried some strategy for solving the very words which they read so easily in the first year at school.

Statistical and behavioural evidence clearly indicated that the processing systems of the good readers worked well for the kinds of letters and words they heard often and expected to see in print, and reversed or inverted forms of easy words became harder to read as reading accuracy increased. The processing of information in print appeared to have changed markedly following the accumulation of successful reading experience to high expectancy of standard orientation of symbol forms. (Low literacy achievers at eight years approached reading with word-processing strategies that mirrored the performance of the proficient readers at six years. They scored better on reversed and inverted print than the proficient readers.)

Sue Watson and Clay 1975

Although this study falls outside the scope of my review it informs the discussion. It was a study of oral reading of pupils in the first year of high school: most were thirteen years old. Could an 'oral literacy processing analysis' of text reading provide useful information at this level? Cross-national research placed the overall average level of reading among New Zealand high school pupils at that time as satisfactory (Thorndike 1973), but Sue Watson showed that numbers of pupils did not have the processing skills needed to study their texts and source books (Nicholson 1984). Watson formed quartile groups of Low (L), Low Middle (LM), High Middle (HM) and High (H) using the silent reading scores of all Form 3 students on the Progressive Achievement Tests (NZCER). Then the 253 pupils read six graded paragraphs aloud (Neale 1958). *The task was easy for high school entrants and reading accuracy scores were high.* Reading test scores from high- to low-achieving were related to how errors were processed, to reading rate, and to the number and type of self-corrections. The 'literacy processing' findings were these:

- Self correcting behaviour showed how well readers were monitoring their reading.

- Subjects relied heavily on their knowledge of English sentence structure and when they made an error it was likely that the sentence could, grammatically, have continued that way, indicating the use of syntactic information up to the point where the error occurred.

- Students were more often able to conform to the grammatical constraints of the text than to anticipate precisely the words used by the author or the turn of phrase or plot that author introduced.

- Proficient readers substituted equivalent or approximate meaning for text.

- Semantic and syntactic acceptability of the errors fell as text difficulty increased, regardless of the ability of the reader, but the effect on poorer readers was greater than on proficient readers.

- Analysis of errors in oral reading was an aid to discovering the literacy competencies of a particular reader in relation to a particular text or textbook being read.

'An unusual lens' used with proficient thirteen-year-old readers provided important information about low achievers but it had reached its limit of usefulness for the average and proficient readers, and failed to describe their competencies.

(from Table 1, pp. 84–85)

6   Successful readers at about eight years

Any of the following in any order or combination

- Partially silent processing.

- Accurate reading of larger chunks of information on harder texts.

- Knows how to add words to own repertoire.

- Marked shifts in rate of acquiring new words in reading and writing.

- Problem-solves new words, miscued familiar words, and strings of words with self-corrections which occur close to the point of challenge.

- Errors are close to the text words on syntactic, visual, phonological and semantic information.

- Has reduced or refined most subsystems to eliminate unnecessary work.

- Can alter the weighting of attention to different knowledge sources, that is, can give more attention to sub-word information with hardly noticeable effects on pace.

- Has constructed complex structures of processing skills.

- Increased speed coming in part from efficiency in the processing system which does not have to work slowly through earlier processing links.

Combining some of these may lift processing out of this group.

Summary of studies of older independent readers

Williams and Imlach demonstrated accurate reading of increasingly difficult texts in classroom-type activities, and effective processing of larger chunks of language information handled fluently. A reduction of processing time was noted but not measured. Lower levels of accuracy on harder passages were associated with more attention to language detail and increased processing time, but without neglecting any important sources of information. An unusual lens focused on processing behaviours produced rich information for proficient readers at about eight years. They got to the messages of texts in oral reading by selecting and compiling from a wide repertoire of personal resources in order to problem-solve sequences of words with accuracy and fluency. By thirteen years of age, observing and recording oral reading behaviours provided insights into the ways in which the lowest achievers were processing information in print when they read aloud but does not probe the competencies of proficient readers at this level. A tabular summary of some hypotheses derived from this cluster of studies is shown on page 54. (This is the final phase (6) in Table 1 at the end of this chapter, pp. 84–85.)

Early reading and writing: starting school and early progress

Having described what was found at an eight-year-old end-point, can one find evidence of changes that occur between five and eight years?

Starting school

Studies by MacKinnon 1959, Nalder 1984, Barbara Watson 1980 and Clay 1967, 1991 are included in this section.

MacKinnon 1959

The recording of reading behaviours has a long history. In 1959 MacKinnon reported on his experiment in Edinburgh. The children were five years of age, just starting their first year of school. He convinced some experienced teachers to participate in an experiment. They were to use some new and very formal materials (Gibson and Richards 1957) with new entrant children for seven weeks. Children were in groups of three, four days a week; then the normal classroom programme began. Three boys and three girls from one classroom in each of three different schools were selected and a control group of similar numbers read the same materials individually with the teacher when no other child was present. MacKinnon provided excellent descriptions of early attempts to read.

- The children made many mistakes.
- They frequently made guesses at what was written.
- They were often confused by taking the beginnings and ends of similar words as their only means of attack.

- They tended to rely on what was spoken immediately before as the only clue for what they were to read next.

- They substituted, omitted and inserted words to match something about the picture.

- These behaviours recurred even when children were prompted to do otherwise.

- In the early stages children seemed to be limited to one task at a time.

- Teachers reported difficulty in having children recognise when a turn was to begin, and to pay attention to the spot where reading was taking place.

- After 28 meetings children recognised how the sentences were linked together not only on one sheet but from one sheet to the next.

He reported that the children showed great enthusiasm when they solved a word; they said the word with stress, often repeated it aloud and sometimes clapped their hands!

A cluster of three New Zealand studies provide baseline data at the beginning of formal instruction, one in 1963 and two in the early 1980s. Each study showed that a record of attempts to read text can be used even when there is very little literacy behaviour to sample.

Nalder 1984

This research followed the progress of sixteen five-year-old children in four middle-class urban schools and its purpose was to evaluate revisions being made to a reading book series. At entry to school on their fifth birthdays (which is standard New Zealand practice) a wide range of individual differences existed. Children:

- knew a few concepts about print

- understood that print contained the message

- had some understanding of moving left to right and down a page of print

- recognised a few letters in text, and wrote some letters or words

- did not know about the word-by-word nature of language

- did not understand the importance of order when placing words in print

- had difficulty orchestrating looking, pointing and saying into a useful sequence

- could not read emergent texts but most would try to.

A few were ready to read emergent texts relatively independently and Kay, by comparison, was already beyond the emergent level.

In the first six months all children made progress, rates of which varied, *but the range of scores increased on all measures during those six months.* The low-progress children took six months to reach the entry levels of the more proficient new entrants on a test of some of the early concepts needed to read texts, and some of those children still did not understand the word-by-word nature of reading. (See also Clay 1985.)

Text reading was only one of their reading programme activities but how did these children work on a book? Children started with different knowledge, read at different levels on 'emergent level' texts, progressed at different rates, and reached criterion points at different times. Beginning readers were all involved in shared reading (when most help was given by the teacher), guided reading (when most instruction was given by the teacher), and independent reading (when the teacher offered minimal support).

Proficiency was indicated when the teacher introduced a more difficult text but children did not necessarily read the same books at a particular level because books might be selected to suit a class theme or a group or an individual problem. That different children could read different books runs *contrary to a popular assumption that children learn, day by day, the lesson for the day and all move forward together.*

Nalder (1984) described the early directions of change over the first six months of instruction like this.

- At first the non-reading school entrant children 'tell' the story in their own language mixed with some of the language of books. They match a text to a page, and give some evidence of directional skills and line matching.

- Then they begin to try to use the language of the book, to match what they say line by line, and (later) word by word with some attention to occasional visual cues in known words. Language composed by the child supports any processing but can override the printed text.

- Another change is detected when the reader uses the language of the book, matched word to word, and definitely attends to some visual information. There is a lot of searching, checking and self-correcting, with appropriate appeals for help, and some omissions.

- Within about six months fluent accurate reading is achieved by many with some successful solving, and two or more sources of information are used for one decision.

After six months at school, proficient readers can be independent when handling the challenges in appropriately selected easy texts, using several sources of information (semantic, or syntactic, or visual, or sounds in sequence), and knowing how to check one kind of information against another. Somewhere in that sequence the hand and eye movements described by McQueen (pp. 64–65) become controlled and directed to the task. A further study of entry to school behaviours was reported by Clay (1985).

Barbara Watson 1980

What opportunities to learn were teachers providing for beginning readers? Watson (1980) recorded these for the school morning, during reading and non-reading time. She observed teacher and child in alternated rotation, at fifteen-second intervals, for 80 new entrants in ten classrooms in the middle of the school year. Observations covered all curriculum subjects, including activities around a topic for the week, the planning and creating of art and craft constructions or trips undertaken. From this comprehensive sampling it was surprising to find that across the whole morning 53 per cent of teachers' time was directed to learning to read and 20 per cent more was related to learning to write. Teachers worked to make children aware of literacy in many different activities, whenever possible. Reading and writing instruction occurred across the curriculum during the whole morning but the highest proportion occurred during the designated 'reading period'. Watson assessed children's progress on several tasks including Running Records.

'Processing information from print', wrote the author, 'refers to the attention a child gives to the details in the text which will help him or her respond to text with an utterance. In this sense the child is reading.' She categorised the behaviours being taught as:

- visual attention to print
- directional behaviours
- attention to language sounds
- processing information from print
- the production of writing.

The 80 children had different kinds and amounts of literacy knowledge and were responding in different ways to the print in their environment. Most attention was given by the teacher to 'processing information from print' followed by 'the production of writing', and particular attention was paid during the school morning to 'directional behaviours'. There was no scripted programme, and the ten teachers taught differently. They designed their own curriculum activities to achieve the results prescribed in general guidelines; each emphasised the aspects of reading and writing he or she considered to be important, but each of the behaviours listed above received comparable attention within those diverse approaches.

The teachers had probably all been influenced by the Early Reading In-service Programme developed by Penton and Holdaway (1973) and Slane (1979) which was available nationally. The children were getting suitably sequenced opportunities to learn about print within the framework of reading storybooks and writing activities, and the teachers had clear expectations for learning. Watson's categories of processing behaviours could be applied to both what the teachers paid attention to *and* to what the children were learning to do. She described the children as gradually bringing the referents and the sounds of language together with directional and visual information in message-gaining, problem-solving activity.

Clay 1967, 1991

A longitudinal study of the first year of instruction followed a randomly selected group of 100 children from five urban schools at weekly intervals. They started school as described in the previous two studies and evidence available for a proficient group of readers and writers after six months at school confirmed that proficient children already attended to many things:

- they responded to print with a series of utterances
- they checked with pictures for agreement
- they matched pointing and word utterance on 50 per cent of the text
- they increased attention to words using the spaces between words to guide them
- they located one or more words on request.

At the point where the teacher introduced their first reading book:

- they could not read but they used the words of the text with 80 per cent accuracy
- they selected words one after the other to construct viable sentences
- they could reject a response and try a different one
- they began to self-correct
- they knew a few words in reading and/or writing
- they could bring two kinds of behaviours together (for example, verbal and pointing behaviour)
- the separation (juncture) between words was often stressed.

In these first months at school the children were learning to read and write. Correct performances came and went, here today and gone tomorrow, quality fluctuated, but gradually *a quite simple set of responses became controlled, accurate and co-ordinated*, as a result of initial teaching on simple story texts which they were expected to read. (Kay took only a month to match that description; other proficient readers took longer.) A climb through a gradient of difficulty in text began when the child could:

- construct what a line of print might say

- locate pattern by pattern the sequence of information he or she could attend to

- detect some mismatch between seeing and saying.

These were primitive forms of later efficient reading behaviours. They became purposefully directed in some primitively integrated way to the problem of extracting a sequence of cues from a text. Children were attending to letters, and words, and the sounds of letters in reading and writing, and they monitored these activities, while enjoying the story they were composing, in either reading or writing. Singer (see Chapter 3) described reading as recurrent sequences of input, mediation and output, which describes the primitive processing manoeuvres of these children. (Somewhat repetitive structures in texts can support but also limit this early processing.)

The utility of such descriptions is that they refer to changes in processing systems *which are occurring daily.* Teachers' selections of texts can be guided by their daily observations of children. Traditional research analyses do not inform daily instruction in this way. A summary of changes in processing across the whole of the first year at school for Helen who began formal literacy instruction on her fifth birthday tells the same story in case study format. She was the middle child in the high-progress quartile, not as advanced as Kay, but a proficient reader.

Within three weeks she moved her finger across text showing consistent directional behaviours for written English. Her teacher began shared reading with her in a small group of children using a big book so that all the group could see it. The text was short and simple. Such activities continued for five weeks in a print-rich classroom with many other literacy activities, including daily writing.

Then Helen 'read' an unseen text of the same easy level as the shared books of the classroom to me as researcher, using some letter and word knowledge, detecting some errors and using several ways of getting to the message of the text (such as pictures, selected letter or word clues, anticipation of the story, and prior knowledge of how to work with language). She was attending to several different sources of information in print. Her teacher valued these activities as helpful learning.

A group of children with similar achievements was formed by the teacher to begin a challenging climb up a gradient of difficulty provided by many little storybooks. Helen's teacher matched instructional demands to their fast progress, changing the level of texts as required. The teacher's matching of progress with challenge was informed by how well Helen put together new text on approximately the same level of difficulty, and how well she met the challenge when the difficulty level was raised.

After ten weeks at school Helen had moved through several levels of book difficulty, and had read several books on one level (i.e. new encounters with text of similar difficulty) before the difficulty level of text was increased. The pace was steady but not fast and this seemed to be a period of consolidation or integration of some kind. Helen was a reader of simple new texts after six months at school. (Clay 1991)

Summary of this cluster of entry to school studies

These four studies show that it is possible to record children's attempts to engage in literacy processing from the time they enter school, irrespective of the types of programme being used, or the different competencies among school entrants, or the delivery systems designed by different teachers.

(from Table 1, pp. 84–85)

1   **Early reading and writing: starting school and early progress**

Any of the following in any order or combination

- Attends to forms and patterns in print.
- Attempts some visual analysis of pictures, and print.
- Is impressed by arrangements of print signs.
- Knows some letters.
- Picks out one or two words with lapses.
- Has some concepts about print under control.
- Tells the story that could be in the print.
- Writes odd letter forms and primitive texts.
- Faces the first challenges of continuous texts in print.
- Matches a text to a page of a book.

Children attend to separate aspects of reading or writing tasks.

Combining some of these may lift processing out of this group.

It is not uncommon for children to find it easy to attend to separate aspects of reading and writing tasks but quite difficult to bring two aspects to bear on one bit of solving. Also, three sets of early literacy behaviours confirmed widely in English-speaking countries in early intervention research (RR) interest me.

- Many beginning books with labelled pictures do not work well as start-up books. Why? Is it because there is no story to support a sustained conversation, or little scope for bringing prior knowledge to the text?

- Many children who can attempt a one-line text are confused by two lines of text. Why? Is it because earlier texts built up other expectations?

- Many children who are doing well at learning letters and learning words cannot show you just one letter, or just one word? Why?

Are these trivial questions? No reasonable theoretical explanations have been offered in the literature I read. My question to readers is not what is your best guess but rather what research could we do that might explain these things.

Connecting up some aspects of written language: proficient readers after several months at school

Important observations and some shifts in processing have been observed after children have been in school for several months. The next cluster of studies continues with the report of Helen's progress later in the first year at school, then brings in an interesting study by McQueen and Robinson's study of children between six and eighteen months at school. It makes it difficult for my readers that neither the children nor these independent research projects can be pushed into neat blocks of time dictated by age or time at school. I have chosen not to force this issue at this early stage of forming hypotheses. So phase 2 behaviours in Table 1 (pp. 84–85) shift to phase 3 behaviours somewhere between about six months and eighteen months at school.

Clay 1967, 1991 (continued)

Helen's progress continues from the last section.

> Text difficulty was lifted every week or two, and an increased amount of reading came with the increase in difficulty. Her rate of reading increased from less than one word a second to more than one word a second, faster on easy and familiar material. New vocabulary was mastered easily; her preferred approach to a new word was a) rapid search, b) a decision that she did not know and c) a request to be told. Usually the teacher directed her to 'work it out'. She paid close attention to the word on the next two or three encounters, but solved it without further help, i.e. she worked on (analysed or processed) the new words as if this were self-instructive.
>
> When working independently on a new text containing new challenges Helen made one error in every 100 words (a rate averaged over her weekly records throughout the year). She found it easy to detect errors in so much accurate reading, searched for better responses, tried to correct 1 in 2 errors and succeeded in self-correcting 1 in 3 errors. Sometimes errors which 'fitted quite well' were not corrected. Occasionally, after a correct response, she returned to the beginning of a line or repeated a word or sequence of words, as if to confirm a response. Confirming checks accounted for 32% of her problem-solving on text. She was a proficient reader demonstrating self-monitoring and self-correction!
>
> Uncorrected errors agreed syntactically with the text (in 82% of single word errors and 60% of a sequence of errors). Her problem-solving was efficient with quick and correct responses most of the time.

Despite her low error rate she had plenty of opportunities to work on a large corpus of error-correcting because she read so much. She succeeded in reading by detecting and overcoming inefficiencies in the context of quantities of successful processing. A new storybook selected by the teacher was read with 90% accuracy when introduced and more than 95% accuracy within a few days.

Her teacher controlled the difficulty level of the materials ensuring whenever possible that the first reading was above an accuracy level of 90%.

After one year of school, Helen had made high progress through the required gradient of book difficulty and had fast, efficient ways of working on continuous texts. She expected meaningful, linguistically probable utterances, and selected words in the sequence of a text that matched the source word in many ways. Easy and hard texts were approached differently, and her fast self-correcting looked like a primitive version of what Singer described as assembling together the strategies appropriate for the task's challenges. (Clay 1991)

A proficient reader like Helen would possibly build the inner strategic controls whatever her teacher attended to, and would expand her knowledge and skills as she read more texts. She became independent as a reader of texts at her level, building some of the knowledge and skills on her own, and using the wider resources of phrase, sentence and story to support her reading. By the end of her first year at school Helen was well on the way to our eight-year-old end-point and would probably make a smooth transition into silent reading. One could say that she had already laid an appropriate foundation for building a power system to support subsequent literacy learning. The ways in which her perceptual and cognitive strategies are used will obviously change as she encounters more challenging texts. (This is more than a matter of literacy learning: it is complicated by the need for changes in young children's oral language learning as Roger Brown proposed in 1976.)

Clay 1970, 1982

The progress of children selected from four very different language backgrounds was the focus of subsequent study asking similar questions but with a different research design. Each of the four groups, aged 5:0, 5:6, 6:0 and 6:6, was followed, this time for six months. (A useful design feature was that the performance of the 5:0 group at 5:6 could be compared with the performance of the 5:6 group when they entered the study, and so on.) This study confirmed that the four language groups (Advantaged English, Average English, Maori and Samoan families) had significantly different levels of oral language learning. *The beginning readers (5:0–5:6) were constructing messages by drawing on the oral language skills which they already had, and on their prior experiences in their community, however high or low these were.* At this stage children had not learned the close, detailed visual discriminations necessary for the use of much visual information. Gradually during the first year of instruction they began to focus on the detail of print searching and checking print information. This increased receptiveness to visual information is a very important part of the first year of instruction. The child learns to pull different kinds of information in print knowledge together in the ongoing task of reading a message.

McQueen 1975

This researcher identified observable movements (motor responses) exhibited by children aged 5:6 to 6:6 who were being taught to read and were reading orally. He trained a team of 21 student teachers to record specific movements made by children while reading individually to their teacher in a classroom. Descriptions of the trunk, head, eye, mouth and arm movements while reading were vivid and captured images of five-year-olds tussling with a strange task. Such behaviour became minimal as the child learned more about the task in hand and focused attention on it. McQueen warned that the observation of specific motor responses alone would not constitute a method of detecting better or poorer beginning readers but that watching a child over time could provide reliable supplementary information in some cases. He made no assumptions about how and why psychological systems affect or are affected by the motor behaviour of the child.

Merely to read his fine-grained descriptions of the movements conjures up images of the wriggling and jiggling of children as they read aloud, the facial contortions and the movements of even the 'non-involved' arm and hand. Some of the behaviours he isolated were:

Trunk	Stooping forward, straightening up. Dropping one or both shoulders, swaying left, swaying right …
Twist	Twisting of the trunk, left hip and shoulder leading; twisting of the trunk, right hip or shoulder leading; twisting the whole body originating in the legs …
Head	Distractive movement away from the task, inclination or looking from another angle, looking ahead (anticipation), looking back …
Eyes	Fixation on text or a point of the text, wandering off print to an illustration, or elsewhere …

His interpretation of careful statistical analyses of his data was that 'a complex higher-order interaction exists between all the variables' (p. 157) which he had studied. Observable movements by the child who is reading to the teacher point up some obvious and yet interesting things.

- It was easy for McQueen's observers to identify a wide range of motor behaviour in these readers; they were reduced in older and better readers to useful and more controlled movements.

- He identified the total hand movement score as a predictor variable contributing approximately one fifth of the variance in beginning reading. When several hand movements (hand-pointing, mis-matching, search and relocation) were combined as a total hand movement score, they reflected the degree to which using the hand to guide reading was established.

- The observation of wandering eye movements and hand movements especially in young children could provide additional information to teachers on the beginning reading status of the child.

- Children who are better readers may be so due to the development of sound visual habits of scanning or attending to print with controlled and persistent eye movement.

McQueen interpreted his results on eye and hand movements within the 'sub-strata factor model' by Holmes and Singer (1961). That model defines reading as:

> an audio-visual, verbal processing skill of symbolic reasoning, sustained by the inter-facilitation of an intricate hierarchy of sub-strata factors that have been mobilized as a psychological working system and pressed into service in accordance with the purpose of the reader. (See Chapter 3.)

The ability to find what to attend to, to decode symbols and then to understand the meaning of the message are artificially separated in debate but behind these activities there are a myriad of integrated subsystems.

This is an account of the working systems in motor behaviour that are involved in the early stages of acts of reading. McQueen saw the reading process as a multiplicity of interacting parts or as a complex of integrated functions and these conclusions led him to question many assumptions about the psychological systems that mediate between letters, sounds, words, and sentences. He questioned whether it was appropriate to break the reading process down and give instruction on isolated parts of the code. He was impressed by the involvement of the hand and eye movements in early reading. As effective scanning of print became controlled by the reader, hand movement to support the visual system was recorded less often.

What connections might exist between his findings and Robinson's evidence in the next section that writing (a motor activity) is highly related to reading progress?

Robinson 1973

Robinson's research documented the importance of writing in early literacy learning. She put some of Clay's hypotheses to stringent statistical test. She tested the relationship between some descriptors of literacy behaviours, including writing vocabulary and phonemic awareness in writing, and progress in reading. She found that *the main predictor of early reading progress across all groups including the proficient group was writing vocabulary,* namely the number of words a child could generate himself or herself and write correctly given a maximum time of ten minutes. She devised a useful assessment task which is now widely used.

Two samples of children were selected from four suburban schools: 50 children were studied from 5:6 to 6:0, and, concurrently, 45 children from 6:0 to 6:6. This study reported all children and not merely proficient readers and writers. The samples were representative of the Auckland urban area for parent occupation and gender, and initial reading scores at 5:6 were distributed over a wide range. Having gathered her data by observing processing behaviours Robinson selected multiple-regression analysis as a technique to examine change over a six-month period in the two age groups. Reading progress was measured by both monthly observations of text reading and word tests, providing detailed observations of change over time. Twelve pre- and post-tests were administered (covering text reading, concepts about print, visual discrimination of letters, short-term auditory memory, writing vocabulary, dictation and oral language) and the independent contribution of each test to predictions of progress was calculated.

The analysis question was, 'Did the relative contribution of individual component skills of reading increase or decrease in importance over that time period?' This research was exploratory in the following ways.

- The use of multiple-regression analysis to predict short-term reading progress from pre-test variables was exploratory.

- The range of tests used was wider than in previous research, tapping more specific skills and including tests of writing.

The major predictor *of reading progress* from 5:6 to 6:0 was writing vocabulary, contributing predictions above any other variable. A cause and effect relationship was not demonstrated, and this would be expected if a high degree of interdependence between reading words and writing words existed. Word-writing ability and word reading ability may both be the result of many kinds of experiences with letters, numbers, words, stories and drawings which enable the beginning reader to learn many things about print. It should not be assumed from this study that success in the first years of learning to read would be assured by simply teaching children to write words.

There were few directional trends of increasing or decreasing relationship of the other test scores and reading progress, but *visual discrimination and attention to print variables (writing vocabulary, letter identification, Concepts About Print tests) had strong relationships with reading progress for both age groups.* Language skills played a more important role in the prediction of reading progress among the older group of children when they were reading longer books containing more complex language. Despite this, *until eighteen months after beginning literacy instruction, writing was the predominant predictor of reading progress.*

This finding about writing was important but *the contribution of this research to the understanding of change was more important.* Evidence from the data analysis suggested that the period 5:6 to 6:6 was a period of rapid change and proficient readers as a group differed significantly from low-progress groups at 5:6 and 6:0 on four measures, namely writing vocabulary, letter identification, concepts about print, and a word test. *It is probable that proficient readers were already building powerful strategies for using different information sources in some integrated way for problem-solving (see Kay and Helen)* while low-progress readers were more likely to be switching from one information source to another.

All children were making progress but proficient-for-age readers maintained their lead. It seemed as though by 5:6 they could follow the directional rules which low-progress readers were still learning over the period 5:6 to 6:0, and they were attending to print detail in sequence. All children in the study were learning more about print over the six months of the study but some children started further along with higher levels of skills than others. *Robinson demonstrated with a rigorous statistical analysis the major importance of writing after the first six months of learning to read in New Zealand classrooms.* Her development of the Writing Vocabulary test for *An Observation Survey* (Clay 1993) and her membership of the RR development team contributed the writing emphasis in that programme.

In summary

Rapid change occurs over about a twelve-month period for those who are becoming proficient. Two indicators of the construction of useful working systems that support early literacy progress have been described, namely, a control over motor behaviours and a strong contribution to reading from writing. This may well be the peak time for both those reciprocal relationships to occur. When studying the entries in phases 2 and 3 in Table 1, remember that individual children will be changing on different time schedules and in no fixed sequence. A serendipitous change in one kind of behaviour may 'cause' or lead to kaleidoscopic shifts in other factors.

(from Table 1, pp. 84–85)

2 **Connecting up some aspects of written language: proficient readers after several months**

Any of the following in any order or combination

- Attends to shape, size, position and pattern in print.

- Searches in oral language for ways to express the pictures.

- Has an insecure knowledge of direction and order on a page.

- Has some understanding of moving left to right and down the page.

- Usually tries a left before a right page.

- Tries to use the language of the book, but also own spoken dialect.

- Produces many letters, some words and one or two short sentences in writing.

- Points, trying to match word by word in reading or while writing.

Combining some of these may lift processing out of this group.

(from Table 1, pp. 84–85)

3   Proficient beginners negotiating more transitions

Any of the following in any order or combination

- Orients to print, knows where to start and where to move.
- Good control of most related motor behaviours.
- Approaches print word by word in reading and/or writing.
- Knows print gives the message.
- Attends in a focused way to the detail of print.
- Shows awareness that oral language relates closely to print.
- Knows pictures can prompt but not determine the text.
- Copes with several lines of text in a simple book.
- Can focus on and use first or last letters.
- Tries to read simple story texts.

Combining some of these may lift processing out of this group.

Proficient readers in the second year of instruction

Over the next twelve months or so there are pronounced shifts from phase 3 behaviours in Table 1 to another set of descriptions in phase 4. Early literacy intervention educators could find it interesting to consider Ng's data on how proficient readers orchestrate the management of several kinds of information as they read.

Ng Seok Moi 1979

The proficient readers in Ng's study were about halfway along the second year of school. Her research focused on errors and self-corrections made by competent readers in 20 randomly selected primary schools in Auckland. They were at or above the average for their class on a research-based word-reading test. Tests and Running Records of text reading were taken at 6:0, 6:6 and 7:0.

A new feature of this study was the report of processing behaviours on three types of text: texts already read at least once in class, unseen texts, and texts with a regularised decoding emphasis which was unfamiliar to the children. (The seen and unseen texts were from the *Ready to Read* series, Department of Education 1963; and the two passages from texts which regularised the introduction of phonological components of the language, *The Royal Road Readers, Books One and Eight*, were carefully graded to cover all phonic complexities, according to the authors, Daniels and Diack 1954, 1958.) Running Records were taken as each child read text at three levels of difficulty (95 per cent accuracy and above, 90–94 per cent accuracy, and 85–89 per cent accuracy). A database of 14,596 errors and 3078 self-corrections on text reading was analysed under headings like word substitution, substitution of complex word sequences, insertion, omission, and complex changes of letter or word order. A high level of consistency in the coding behaviour of two researchers was achieved. This was an interesting and complex study and I will only draw attention here to three points. Evidence was found to suggest that children shifted their attention across information types according to task demands, and that they gave differential weighting to information sources on regularised text. Changes in self-correcting were noted.

1   *Shifts of attention.* Proficient readers gave more attention to graphemic information on hard texts. They used most sources of information together most of the time and seldom used letter-sound information in isolation. They were able to interweave visual, phonological, cognitive and motor learning into a coherent and efficient problem-solving process, and *the most proficient readers made the fewest changes in processing when the type or difficulty of text changed as if they could allocate additional attention to letter form and sequence but at the same time maintain their attention to language.* This matches the observations of Gibson and Levin (1975) that beginning readers have more difficulty with attending to *language and graphic information together* compared with more advanced readers. In addition, faced with the question 'What might this word be?', proficient readers in Ng's study could switch to alternative processing modes when their usual approach failed with scarcely noticeable changes in behaviour. Children in this study seemed to have gone some way towards acquiring control over the various information sources in print and could tap into these in flexible ways to get the problem solved. They were appropriately tentative in their information processing.

2   *Different weighting to information sources.* Proficient readers could apparently give different weighting to graphic (visual) and language information to help them deal with different levels of text difficulty. At the point where processing was observed, the readers did not take different routes to word recognition as is hypothesised by dual-process theories, but instead they assigned different weighting to different kinds of information. The best readers were able to 'change gear' to use more graphemic information while still attaching importance to using as much contextual information as possible. The readers closer to average levels of achievement were still moving towards that degree of flexibility at seven years. If one held the view that there was only one path to becoming an effective reader, or at the most two alternate paths, then this interesting variable of shifting the weight of attention paid to different sources of information could easily be overlooked.

When processing text which had been regularised for a decoding emphasis proficient readers were more likely to use language and letter-sound information together than to attend to either separately. Increased attention to graphic information occurred together with increased attention to language information, negating any set sequence in their learning of how to process printed messages.

3 *Self-correction while reading.* Self-correction indicates that the children have learnt something about the range of behaviours which are acceptable in reading, and have developed ways of monitoring their own responding. In the second year of school overt self-corrections decreased for the total group of proficient readers and particularly for the most proficient. It was as if self-corrections were becoming covert rather than overt. (See also Goodman and Burke 1972 and Clay 1991.) Changes in the incidence and nature of overt self-corrections are indicators of change in the reading process (see Chapter 5).

Boocock 1991; Boocock, McNaughton and Parr 1998

The Boocock, McNaughton and Parr (1998) study of writing processes was hard to place as it spans four years of school but because it reports some rapid changes during this period it is included here.

Christine Boocock completed a study of what children wrote in New Zealand classrooms in the first four years of school but attention here is paid to the proficient writers in the second and third years. Could processing be captured by observing and analysing writing behaviours in a manner comparable to the taking of a Running Record in reading? Boocock recorded each child's behaviour while writing for a five-minute period. Categories used to codify the writing behaviours were:

- generating messages
- word or sub-word repetition before and during writing
- rereading the written text
- writing and editing of text
- child-initiated search for help
- uninitiated interruptions by other children
- other behaviours.

The result was something like a running record of writing behaviours.

Individual differences by the end of the first year of school were vast, ranging from those who still had no concept of a word and wrote strings of letters, to those who could control the writing system enough to form messages into paragraph-length stories with the most common words and many sounds recorded correctly. Children learned to effectively monitor their work, and search for ways to take their own learning further. Changes were noted in rereading, editing, resource use, and oral language use. A panel of experts judged the children to be better writers as they moved up the school.

There were some recordable shifts between the second and third year. One shift was the sudden increase in the writing of words in isolation correctly without assistance. There was a three-fold increase in the mean number of words written per five-minute period from the first to the third year of school, and in the total number of different words written correctly without assistance. This shift occurred after the descriptions of reading behaviours reported by Ng (above) and before the end-point we have been considering. Boocock concluded that each child had a personal vocabulary of words he or she could write, and had gained control of the most frequently used words in daily writing. These 'known' words, usually recurring with high frequency, became progressively easier to write quickly. In learning how to write a vocabulary of words accurately and quickly children had also learned powerful generative strategies. They had been able to develop behaviours that enabled them to attend more quickly to key features of words, to bring new words rapidly under similar fast processing, and give more time to longer words and less frequently used words.

> The rereading behaviour suggested shifts in the amount of text children had to monitor overtly to keep control of the task … the [older] children were able to write more words in the same time and keep control over what they were saying before rereading their text. We could assume they were monitoring more in their heads as they wrote [because] their edits increased over time whereas their overt reading did not. They would be potentially able to notice more and learn more by themselves. (Boocock 1991, pp. 52–53)

The children seemed to have processing strategies which enabled them to expand their writing vocabularies significantly. Learning 'how to [do certain things]' created ways of going beyond what was known, towards a self-extending system. Rereading by children of what they had written changed as competence increased and older competent children were able to write more words in a sequence and keep control over their planning better than younger, less competent children. There was a trend away from the intermediary use of verbalising in oral language before writing, to recording thoughts directly in written language. Oral behaviour was important both for phonemic analysis and for oral composition of text when children first began to write but such reference to an oral language resource became less frequent. However, children who did not appear to use oral language or overt phonemic analysis still made the same gains in numbers of words and the generative use of known words as the children who offered overt analysis of their own language (Boocock, McNaughton and Parr 1998).

(from Table 1, pp. 84–85)

4 Proficient readers/writers use subsystems to support each other

Any of the following in any order or combination

• The reader works across print, parsing word by word, using oral language, or syntax or meaning as a guide. Temporarily it may sound laboured.

(continues over page)

(continues from p. 71)

- Prompted by visual information, scanning print left to right, most attention to single letters, beginning to use clusters of letters or chunks of words. Temporarily it may sound laboured.

- Prompted and then unprompted re-runs, with cross-checking not always successful.

- Increase in self-correction; notices gross discrepancies.

- Shifts processing from one approach to another on words.

- Selection of 'next words' often led by oral language knowledge, or an expected order in the real world.

- Works with short phrases but more often at the word or sub-word level.

- Surface features (spaces and punctuation) in writing getting attention.

- Using some phonemic segmentation in reading and writing (sounding out but using chunks and clusters as well as single letters).

- Gathering more concepts about print, more letter knowledge with many capital/lower case distinctions.

Combining some of these may lift processing out of this group.

Phase 4 in Table 1 reports on children who are quite proficient, who use many subsystems to support their current reading and increasingly lift their level of performance. From the same studies phase 5 reports children who are doing fast processing with accuracy on more advanced texts. Both groups are proficient and will be readers and writers. The crucial question is this: will the first group become the fast readers like the second group? Or are the tables describing two kind of processing systems — one which learned rapidly to work effectively and the other which constructed itself a little less effectively? A feature of the fast-processing group is probably that they got there in a short period of time as change followed change rapidly. Even RR children can join this group (see Nicholas in O'Leary 1997).

(from Table 1, pp. 84–85)

5 Fast processing with accuracy on more advanced texts

Any of the following in any order or combination

- Takes ownership for solving new words.

- Problem-solving new and difficult words, and correcting many errors.

(continues over page)

(continues from p. 72)

- Integrates information from different knowledge sources: visual, phonological, meaning and structure information.
- Uses any information sources effectively on well-chosen texts but easily thrown by a challenging text.
- What is read is processed quickly and is mostly correct.
- Effective processing deals with chunks of information.
- Has reached high scores on knowledge sources (or *An Observation Survey*).
- Controls links between visual/aural, left/right, first/last, semantic/syntactic, picture/story information.

Combining some of these may lift processing out of this group.

If early intervention drags out the treatment, and gives unduly elongated 'practice' rather than a series of lessons where change follows change in rapid succession, there may be a danger that teachers are creating processing systems which work but not all that well. This is a question about the pace of change, not a call for speed from the teacher. I hope my suspicion is unfounded. Many people would explain the differences in terms of ability but my experience with RR suggests that a treatment variable could be involved. A 'stretched' series of lessons, interrupted teaching, failure to get early movement, a teacher–child pair who do not work well together — these things impede a steady pace of change. It may be important to find out whether, once one begins to learn how to work with a code, it is advantageous to be consistently challenged to drive in a higher gear. Immersion courses in learning a new language provide an example in which the 'pace of change' is an important factor.

Turning 'an unusual lens' on low achievers

Many published case studies

Running Records of text reading taken by class teachers enable them to respond contingently to a reader's current instructional challenges (Clay 2000a, 2000b). RR teachers attend to children's acts of processing *daily* in order to plan the next lesson and select a new book. Their daily records will contain evidence of processing and published case studies of RR children's progress will report changes in processing over a series of lessons, provided the author has been observant and articulate about such changes. However, for reasons of cost effectiveness RR typically ends when readers reach the average band of their age group so any illustrative extracts from published case studies will only have aimed to have them reach average band performance.

I selected two examples of such reports from Susan O'Leary's book entitled *Five Kids* (1997). Nicholas was from a highly literate family with high expectations. He was the lowest achiever in literacy in his class. (I added the italics to highlight processing behaviours.)

Nicholas

When we started working together, Nicholas had good skills, but he couldn't apply them. He knew all his ABCs. He could write several words but couldn't read them back. He corrected errors well on easy books (a self-correction for every error) but when the books became a little more difficult, his self-corrections all but stopped. He made only one correction for every twenty-seven errors. Books became like a Lewis Carroll poem for him but *he trudged on even so, speaking nonsense.* (p. 68)

As he became more aware of the importance of looking at the whole word, his errors and *his reading switched briefly to being based mainly on reading the word in isolation;* he forgot the importance of meaning as he read. He read "be-tord-torger-toeger-togther-toe-toegeether-torger" for together. (pp. 77–78)

In his final lessons Nicholas read a harder book each time, still making some errors, but also making visible progress in applying what he had learned. *If he reached a point where what he said didn't make sense, he would back up in the sentence and start again,* a clear sign that he was *using meaning and structure in approaching words.* He was confident, he was independent; he was relieved. (p. 81)

Nkauj Hli

Nkauj Hli (Go-Lee) monitored letters in order across unknown words and *began to confirm for meaning,* making nonsense errors but then correcting them as she read. (p. 149) [By about lesson 14] Nkauj Hli was even *starting to use syntax coupled with meaning* in her predictions of what a word would be. (p. 151)

She wrote "Monkeys eat bananas. So do gorillas." In two sentences with twenty-six sounds, she heard and correctly wrote all six words. This is excellent writing for a struggling student at this stage. (pp. 146–147)

After making each error she corrected it … looking closely at the page. That day she wrote "I bet I can find your tail," *hearing every sound in order as she wrote.* (p. 152)

She wrote about a fable: "He pointed his gun at the dove." She consciously *generated words: his* from *is, gun* from *fun, dove* from *love* and felt very confident about her writing. (p. 156)

In her last lessons her errors were generally on unknown words probably requiring expert input) and she learned to try to bring meaning to reading difficult words. She read 'auncles' for *Aunty* — showing she had started to read the word visually and knew *aunts* were like *uncles*, but she couldn't remember the word for the female. (p. 156)

The two studies with low achievers I want to report are about writing.

Glynn, McNaughton and Wotherspoon 1975

A study which used a behaviour analysis research model (see Church in Chapter 7) was conducted in 1974 when two research students jointly observed changes in the reading and writing behaviours of nine intellectually challenged children aged between seven and nine and with IQs in the 60–75 range. This study is reported by Smith and Elley (1997) under the heading 'Can everyone be taught to write?'

> By the end of the study, all nine pupils were able to generate sentences on their own, yet none could produce single words at the beginning. During the early stages of the intervention the children's sentences were very simple, e.g. 'I am a boy. My name is Terry.' However, towards the end the researchers noted a number of complex sentences appearing amongst the simpler ones, e.g. 'If a bee comes along and there was a boy standing there, the boy would run away.' (p. 78)

Smith and Elley concluded from this research that intellectually challenged pupils can learn to write if teachers respond appropriately to their efforts; a system of positive feedback produces greater improvements than a system which emphasises negative comments; that if children are given credit for approximations to the correct forms, they will gradually improve; and that as children progress they seem to depend less on an external feedback system (p. 79).

At a time when interest in writing was low, and when the idea that both reading and writing should be considered together as literacy learning was very new, McNaughton (1974) and Wotherspoon (1974) clearly captured change over time in both reading and writing behaviours.

Hobsbaum, Peters and Sylva 1996

These authors studied the teaching interactions of seven teachers working with seventeen RR children during the writing segment of their RR lessons in the United Kingdom. (These were not proficient writers but they were becoming quite good writers in an early intervention.) The children composed sentences to be written and from their records the researchers marked off talk cycles, which were made up of several teacher–child interactions about a word being written, moving on to another cycle until the sentence was complete. One part of this research looked at how these interactions changed over time in a series of lessons.

Data from one child illuminates that changes occur in the content and the context of the word cycles as the teacher structures the internal setting so the child develops increasingly more complex actions independently.

Phase 1   *Close monitoring and intervention*
Features — heavily dominated by teacher leading transitions
— child verbalizes letters before writing in order to check or confirm with the teacher

Phase 2   *Teacher acts as prompt or 'memory amplifier'*
Features — child can identify need but requires help to achieve
— child makes overt connections of knowledge
— child verbalizes letters while writing
— child begins to operate teacher-modelled strategies

Phase 3   *Teacher is essentially reactive*
Features — child acts more, vocalizes less
— evidence that child has internalized the teacher's prompts
— child writes silently or with few utterances of letters
— child monitors own writing (p. 18)

Children over time primarily take control of:

- *Strategy monitoring*:   holding the message in working memory and rereading independently in order to locate the next move.

- *Whole word recall*:   identifying the word and writing it immediately without apparent searching or use of phonemic information.

- *Surface feature control*:   self-regulates spacing and handwriting and shows understanding of punctuation.

- *Phonemic segmentation*:   where a phoneme is articulated, the child goes straight to the written letter without the need to say the name or sound of that letter before or in the process of writing it.

Scaffolded interventions in the writing episode showed how teachers helped children to connect what they knew to information they encountered in new experiences (p. 21). The authors pointed out the difference between a tutor or teacher scaffolding one brief task (Wood, Bruner and Ross 1976; Rogoff 1990) and the cyclic nature of scaffolded teaching which occurs in response to growing curricular demands to lift the level of performance and take the activity on with less and less help, becoming eventually independent. (See also Clay and Cazden 1990.)

Changes in literacy processing over time

If I stay with my hypothesis that the outcome of proficient reading and writing can be achieved by taking different paths then it would be an utter waste of time to try to create a table of stages to be achieved at set ages. Nothing so systematic was intended nor is it likely to be found. It is more important that this analysis open up questions and discussions, and generates some well-designed research that could lead to more valid descriptions of changes that occur and of the conditions under which these occur. RR professionals could assemble data to show that children who are among the low-achieving 20 per cent of their age group in literacy achievement can make processing shifts similar to those described in this chapter. The purpose would be to provide good descriptions to guide contingent teaching. Such work would also establish a theoretical value for watching children.

A reader of an early draft of this book asked, 'Does she intend to leave things open and not to discuss each of the subsystems and how they change?' Yes, that is so. We have enough data to consider a theoretical description of change over time to be feasible but we have insufficient detailed research to construct more than a skeleton built up from fragments. Books on a gradient of difficulty are the successive markers of progress which classroom teachers can use (Figure 1, p. 47), and words in sentences written without assistance can be counted (Figure 2, p. 78). Such monitoring reveals when a child is marking time and not moving forward, but the records do not tell the teacher what aspects of the reading or writing processing that teacher should give attention to. A theory of the changes that occur in literacy processing is needed to reveal to the teacher how well the recalling, linking and checking are being carried out as the child problem-solves the words in the text.

What would such theory look like? The changes would necessarily look different under different teaching and curricula prescriptions because those conditions provide or preclude particular opportunities to learn. The tentative, hypothetical set of changes over time that has been derived from the limited research evidence in this chapter offers a framework of hypotheses about how literacy processing is likely to change over time in the early years at school. Teachers need theory at two levels: a theory of what occurs which would put flesh on this skeleton, and a theory of how to interact with what occurs which could lead to improved teaching interactions.

Evidence reviewed in this chapter leads to several conclusions. Proficient readers use language and visual and motor information from the beginning of their formal schooling. They pay close attention when new and different texts present new challenges. While not relinquishing their hold on the support of meaning and structure, proficient readers become able to give increased attention to the detail of new words, near-new words or unexpected words during the second year in formal instruction. It suggests that our understanding of how children are constructing literacy processing systems is informed by knowing what occurred immediately prior to the famous 'one second of reading' (Gough 1985) and what

Figure 2 Weekly samples of writing showing progress

Week	Key:	unmarked — D.B.'s writing underlined — used for sound analysis print in grey screen — given by teacher

Week	
1	The dog we know was standing by our place.
2	The pirates ran back to the ship and they paddled back to the other island.
3	The big monster went to look for houses to live. He said "This house is too small for me and too long."
4	Trog went to the Quickerwits to see how to make fire.
5	Ann goes to a new school. Chris said She is too small to go to a new school.
6	The New Doctor. We went to the doctor. We think we going to get an injection.
7	Tom and Sam were friends. Tom made a nice garage and all the people says "What a clever man you are Tom."
8	The Yukadoos. The Yukadoos eat up the flowers and mess up the garden. They sing in the shower and dance in the shower.
9	Anna said "Your porridge is ready Mum and Dad." Mother said "it looks nice my dear."
10	Godfrey and Wendy and Bart went to the shop. They saw Mr Fisher and Mrs Davis. Bart called out "Mr Fisher and Mrs Davis I got a goat."
11	Sophies mother sings sad songs and low songs. Mother and Sophie went outside and it was Christmas.
12	The Three Little Pigs. The three little pigs was big and Mother said "you are big grown up boys." Mother said "Be careful of the wolf." "Yes Mum."
13	Tom and Sam. Tom and Sam were the best friends of all. But Tom was busy building a tower in his garden.
14	"We are going to the shop" said mother to Helen and Baby. Ta ta Baby called.
15	When the gingerbread man came along the road I said "Come here I want to eat you up."
16	Supper for a Troll. In a dark dark woods was a old troll. He was hungry.
17	The Cake. Mary's mother made a cake for Mary's birthday. And her mother made a nice birthday cake. Mary's friends came at her house. She was happy at her birthday.
18	The Kuia and the Spider. "Hey old lady my web is nicer than your weaving." "Oh yeah my weaving is nicer than your web."
19	The Frog. The frog sat by the stream and cried and all the water fell on his feet.
20	The Fat Cat ate people. Once there was a little cat and a old lady and the old lady said to his cat to look after the washing. The little cat said "Yes" "Oh good" he said and ate it up. When the lady came back she said "Oh my, where is my washing?"

went on in the second and third seconds afterwards. It also helps to know whether the reader is a beginner with a primitive processing system or an accomplished reader.

In the research studies reviewed proficient readers responded to a double demand as they became more proficient — they mobilised processing systems to suit the challenges of particular texts, and they gave more weight to the graphemic (visual) sources of information while also considering new syntactic structures, or new content and vocabulary. This calls for tentativeness and flexibility in using prior literacy learning and a willingness to venture into unknown territory.

Of course it is necessary to know 'the words' but is that enough? Reading words in isolation makes it clear whether a learner knows the word or not; teaching words in isolation is systematic and orderly; testing words in isolation is quick and simple, and reading non-words has provided good experimental data on one aspect of reading processing. So why should we not just deal in single words and make the learning, the teaching, and the testing and the explanations less complicated?

It is hard to ignore the intriguing data that is currently available in the detailed recording of children's responses during text reading. Descriptive research on what happens during text reading has revealed some of the mysteries of how young readers actively work on the information in texts. Proficient readers seem to compile complex processing in flexible ways very early and yet changes in what they do can be recorded over the first three years in school.

What on the surface looks like simple word-by-word reading of a short and simple story involves children in linking many things they know from different sources (visual, auditory/phonological, movement, speaking/articulating, and knowledge of the language). When they problem-solve texts they dip into these 'different ways of knowing something' and make a series of decisions as they work across text. To look only at letters and words, or how comprehension questions are answered, is to ignore the problems faced by the reader to sequentially 'solve the parts within the wholes' to get the precise message. Unquestionably what has gone before in reading or writing influences the next decision. (The sequencing of these decisions is like the steps in making perceptual decisions described by psychologists like Solley and Murphy 1960 and Lynn 1966, see Chapter 4, p. 157.) Reading or writing text involves a string of sequential decisions. It is clearly more complicated than identifying a word by recalling it from a memory bank, and it is important to explain what triggered the recall, and why some of the possible words recalled were rejected.

Unfortunately making a list of things a reader must be able to do to show they are competent is like laying a set of precision tools out on a table. Teachers need better models explaining how the novice reader uses the tools, and how that use (in processing) changes the system that will be used next time. We cannot yet describe precisely what these changes would look like because the different prescriptions and practices in education systems have such a massive impact on what children are permitted to learn. However, somewhere in that sequence the hand and eye movements described by McQueen become controlled and directed to the task (probably between phases 2 and 3 in Table 1). Further changes include:

- some strategic behaviours which become very rapid

- others which are no longer observed (like directional confusion)

- substitutions which combine visual, phonemic, structural and semantic information but remain as errors, for using all these sources of information together is a marked shift in processing efficiency

- less repetition

- returning back along text for shorter distances

- improvements in error rates and self-correction rates

- increases in speed of processing

- self-correction begins to occur close to the point of error, as when, after uttering the wrong sound for the first letter of a word, the reader self-corrects.

A few available research studies provided glimpses of the progressive construction of a system which works on some texts and breaks down on others. Reading behaviours (and the processing system being used) shift up or down an effectiveness scale dependent on:

- level of a text's difficulty

- how the teacher introduced it

- familiarity with similar texts.

Young proficient readers build effective, monitored, self-corrected and self-extending networks of minimally conscious strategies for making letter and word decisions in controlled sequences that are consistent with the preceding text. They must do this if they are to read text efficiently. They assemble a complex processing system which attends to word processing (letters and words), and to sentence processing (including what has gone before, possible upcoming structures and meanings at several levels). Processing refers to getting access to and working with several different types of information to arrive at a decision. These two activities, word processing and sentence processing, are legitimate domains of study in the psychology of reading in mature readers (McKoon and Ratcliff 1998).

The literacy processing systems mobilised by the young reader or writer during the years of literacy acquisition must remain open to change if the reader/writer is building a self-extending system. A critical question hardly ever mentioned in literacy literature is how should initial knowledge be acquired and organised to facilitate the flexibility needed for a wide range of future applications? Spiro and his co-authors suggest that 'from the perspective of the learner, well-structured domains are ill-structured until the principles of well-structuredness are discovered'. That sounds remarkably like the situation that beginning readers find themselves in. These authors recommend that becoming flexible should increase the chances of noticing new ways to connect and organise things while still allowing old information to be available (Spiro et al. 1987, pp. 196–198). In a later article Spiro et al. (1994) contend that, in many real-world situations when knowledge cannot be routinised, mechanised or automatised, it must be controlled flexibly so that transfer of something known to something unknown can occur.

Another psychologist agrees with them:

> … the task is to learn how to soft-assemble adaptive behaviours in ways that respond to local context and exploit intrinsic dynamics. Mind, body and world thus emerge as equal partners in the construction of robust, flexible behaviours. (Clark 1996, p. 45)

Again, that sounds to me very like a description of what is needed for change over time to occur in early literacy processing behaviours. I have not found relevant research evidence to fill an immense gap between the acts of processing described in this chapter and the ideas put forward in the quotations above. However, notice the potential of this early acquisition of literacy theory for crossing the artificial boundary that has been drawn between learning to read and reading to learn. With more data we may be able to link up with the theoretical models of reading processes previously reserved for 'advanced readers'. Theories of literacy acquisition which stress broad-band competencies and flexibility provide a likely framework within which to search for self-extending systems. Meanwhile the provocative view discussed in this chapter is grounded in records of daily progress with thousands of readers and writers.

This review and the tables could generate a host of hypotheses for exploration and discussion. If we were to search for the integrations that occur and how readers learn to weight the attention that they allocate to different processes at different times, we would not be short of research topics.

If my readers have tired of so many new hypotheses asking for discussion and thought, and so few directives of what to teach tomorrow, you should know that I intend to take the advice of the great ethologist Konrad Lorenz who advised that every research scientist who wanted to keep young should discard one pet hypothesis every day before breakfast. Maybe it is time to do that.

Note 1
Tools for observation
In Jane Hurry's (1996) paper 'What is so special about Reading Recovery?' she provided an account of how RR teachers capture detailed evidence in Running Records to monitor progress in specific ways.

> The principal method of formal assessment is the Running Record, made on a new graded book every day throughout the programme ... The teacher records the child's repetitions, self-corrections and errors (noting down the apparent strategy being relied on when the error occurred — meaning, syntax and/or the appearance of the word). This record allows the RR teacher both to assess the appropriate level of text difficulty for each child on a daily basis, and also to monitor the strategies that the child is employing during reading. The teacher encourages pupils to recognize their own mistakes (self-monitor) and to use a range of strategies to correct those mistakes. Clearly, a good understanding of each pupil's approach to reading is invaluable ... It must be one of the major strengths of individual tuition that the teacher can be aware of a particular child's level of attainment and approach to learning. (p. 97)

Running Records are also used by teachers in classrooms to guide a child's approach to learning as and when needed at frequent intervals, but not daily.

Making records of text reading to guide instruction is discussed in a book on assessment (Johnston 1997, 2000).

> Running Records are not perfect reflections of children's oral reading ... However they do provide some extremely useful data that can both document change and direct instruction ... Increases in self-correction alone, given a comparable error rate, suggest a greater degree of understanding ... We can look at changes in readers' cue use and integration, range and flexibility of strategy use, persistence, fluency, book difficulty, expression, and confidence. Some of these are not recorded in the Running Record per se but can be important annotations on the record. (pp. 230–231)

The Hurry and Johnston appraisals suggest how this tool can provide a clear account of a child's processing which the teacher can use to improve the performance of low achievers by adjusting day-to-day instruction in early literacy interventions. Classrooms teachers also use this tool to inform their teaching from time to time when they want to monitor the progress of individual children.

A Running Record should be thought of as one tool among others that might yet be developed to describe how children work on continuous text (a tool yielding reliable and valid measurements). *An unusual lens would be any observational tool or research methodology which gathered detailed data on changes in literacy processing over short time intervals while the subjects were reading or writing continuous texts.* It would be an instrument or procedure that could capture how the learner works at learning, and how those ways of working change. It stands in contrast to word tests and comprehension questions which assess what the learner has already learned. There are two parts to the teacher's training on Running Records: first the teacher must learn to take quality records, and second there is need for a theory, or at least a framework like that provided in Table 1, which allows the teacher to interpret the behaviours that are recorded.

Note 2

The extensive review of miscue analysis (Brown, Goodman and Marek 1996) describes it as a technique focused on reading as a language process. Should it have been included in this chapter? Is it a methodology one could call an unusual lens? I think it is, and it has provided the methodology for extensive research. I decided against inclusion because theoretically, the theories used to interpret the data are different. One theory, simplified for conciseness, sees reading as a language process which is basically the same at any level of performance; the other sees it as complex neural processes which initially work together in simple systems and which gradually undertake increasingly complex activities. Because I work with children who have difficulty learning to read for a multiplicity of different reasons I want to describe and explain changes which a Goodman theory might want to claim do not exist.

Note 3

'Acts of Processing' studies benefited from many concurrent studies which used behavioural analysis research methodologies. Among those studies were the following: McNaughton 1974, 1978, 1983; McNaughton, Glynn and Robinson 1981, 1987; Wotherspoon 1974; and Wong and McNaughton 1980. Wheldall and Glynn (1988) provided a useful list of ten characteristics of a behavioural interactional perspective and suggest the behaviour analysis has much to offer education if contingencies in contexts are to be considered.

Table 1 Hypotheses about possible progressions in acts of processing occurring in early reading and writing for tentative and flexible discussion

1 Early reading and writing: starting school and very early progress
Any of the following in any order or combination
- Attends to forms and patterns in print.
- Attempts some visual analysis of pictures, and print.
- Is impressed by arrangements of print signs.
- Knows some letters.
- Picks out one or two words with lapses.
- Has some concepts about print under control.
- Tells the story that could be in the print.
- Writes odd letter forms and primitive texts.
- Faces the first challenges of continuous texts in print.
- Matches a text to a page of a book.

Children attend to separate aspects of reading or writing tasks.
Combining some of these may lift processing out of this group.

2 Connecting up some aspects of written language: proficient readers after several months
Any of the following in any order or combination
- Attends to shape, size, position and pattern in print.
- Searches in oral language for ways to express the pictures.
- Has an insecure knowledge of direction and order on a page.
- Has some understanding of moving left to right and down the page.
- Usually tries a left before a right page.
- Tries to use the language of the book, but also own spoken dialect.
- Produces many letters, some words and one or two short sentences in writing.
- Points, trying to match word by word in reading or while writing.

Combining some of these may lift processing out of this group.

3 Proficient beginners negotiating more transitions
Any of the following in any order or combination
- Orients to print, knows where to start and where to move.
- Good control of most related motor behaviours.
- Approaches print word by word in reading and/or writing.
- Knows print gives the message.
- Attends in a focused way to the detail of print.
- Shows awareness that oral language relates closely to print.
- Knows pictures can prompt but not determine the text.
- Copes with two lines of text in a simple book.
- Can focus on and use first or last letters.
- Tries to read simple story texts.

Combining some of these may lift processing out of this group.

4 Proficient readers/writers use subsystems to support each other
Any of the following in any order or combination
- The reader works across print, parsing word by word, using oral language, or syntax or meaning as a guide. Temporarily it may sound laboured.

These possible changes from simple to complex processing should *not* be seen as stages.

- Prompted by visual information, scanning print left to right, most attention to single letters, beginning to use clusters of letters or chunks of words. Temporarily it may sound laboured.
- Prompted and then unprompted re-runs, with cross-checking not always successful.
- Increase in self-correction; notices gross discrepancies.
- Shifts processing from one approach to another on words.
- Selection of 'next words' often led by oral language knowledge, or an expected order in the real world.
- Works with short phrases but more often at the word or sub-word level.
- Surface features (spaces and punctuation) in writing getting attention.
- Using some phonemic segmentation in reading and writing (sounding out but using chunks and clusters as well as single letters).
- Gathering more concepts about print, more letter knowledge with many capital/lower case distinctions.

Combining some of these may lift processing out of this group.

5 Fast processing with accuracy on more advanced texts
Any of the following in any order or combination
- Takes ownership for solving new words.
- Problem-solving new and difficult words, and correcting many errors.
- Integrates information from different knowledge sources: visual, phonological, meaning and structure information.
- Uses any information sources effectively on well-chosen texts but easily thrown by a challenging text.
- What is read is processed quickly and is mostly correct.
- Effective processing deals with chunks of information.
- Has reached high scores on knowledge sources (or *An Observation Survey*).
- Controls links between visual/aural, left/right, first/last, semantic/syntactic, picture/story information.

Combining some of these may lift processing out of this group.

6 Successful readers at about eight years
Any of the following in any order or combination
- Partially silent processing.
- Accurate reading of larger chunks of information on harder texts.
- Knows how to add words to own repertoire.
- Marked shifts in rate of acquiring new words in reading and writing.
- Problem-solves new words, miscued familiar words, and strings of words with self-corrections which occur close to the point of challenge.
- Errors are close to the text words on syntactic, visual, phonological and semantic information.
- Has reduced or refined most subsystems to eliminate unnecessary work.
- Can alter the weighting of attention to different knowledge sources, that is, can give more attention to sub-word information with hardly noticeable effects on pace.
- Has constructed complex structures of processing skills.
- Increased speed coming in part from efficiency in the processing system which does not have to work slowly through earlier processing links.

Combining some of these may lift processing out of this group.

References

Boocock, C. 1991. Observing Children Write in the First Four Years of School. Master of Arts thesis, University of Auckland Library.

Boocock, C., S. McNaughton and J.M. Parr. 1998. The early development of a self-extending system in writing. *Literacy, Teaching and Learning* 3, 2: 41–59.

Brown, J., K.S. Goodman and A.M. Marek. 1996. *Studies in Miscue Analysis*. Newark, DE: International Reading Association.

Brown, R. 1976. *A First Language: The Early Stages*. Harmondsworth, England: Penguin Education.

Clark, A. 1996. *Being There: Putting Brain, Body, and World Together Again*. Cambridge, MA: MIT Press.

Clay, M.M. 1966. Emergent Reading Behaviour. Doctoral dissertation, University of Auckland Library.

———. 1967. The reading behaviour of five-year-old children: A research report. *New Zealand Journal of Educational Studies* 2, 1: 11–31.

———. 1970. An increasing effect of disorientation on the discrimination of print: a developmental study. *Journal of Experimental Child Psychology* 9: 297–306.

———. 1982. *Observing Young Readers: Selected Papers*. Portsmouth, NH: Heinemann.

———. 1985. Engaging with the school system: A study of new entrant classrooms. *New Zealand Journal of Educational Studies* 20, 1: 20–38.

———. 1991. *Becoming Literate: The Construction of Inner Control*. Auckland: Heinemann.

———. 1993. *An Observation Survey of Early Literacy Achievement*. Auckland: Heinemann (First Edition 1972; Second Edition 1979; Third Edition 1985; title change 1993).

———. 2000a. *Running Records for Classroom Teachers*. Auckland: Heinemann.

———. 2000b. *Concepts About Print For Teachers of Young Children*. Auckland: Heinemann.

Clay, M.M. and C. Cazden. 1990. A Vygotskyan interpretation of Reading Recovery. In L. Moll, ed., *Vygotsky and Education*. Cambridge, UK: Cambridge University Press.

Clay, M.M. and R.H. Imlach. 1971. Juncture, pitch and stress as reading behaviour variables. *Journal of Verbal Behaviour and Verbal Learning* 10: 133–139.

Daniels, J.C. and H. Diack. 1954, 1958. *The Royal Road Readers*. London: Chatto and Windus.

Department of Education. 1963. The *Ready to Read* series. Wellington: School Publications (now Learning Media).

Gibson, C.M. and I.A. Richards. 1957. *First Steps in Reading English: A Book for Beginning Readers of All Ages*. New York: Pocket Books.

Gibson, E.J. and H. Levin. 1975. *The Psychology of Reading*. Cambridge, MA: MIT Press.

Glynn, T., S. McNaughton and A. Wotherspoon. 1975. Modification of reading, writing and attending behaviour in a special class for retarded children. Unpublished research paper, Department of Education, University of Auckland.

Goodman, Y.M. and C. Burke. 1972. *The Reading Miscue Inventory*. New York: Macmillan.

Gough, P.B. 1985. One second of reading. In H. Singer and R.B. Ruddell, eds, *Theoretical Models and Processes of Reading* (Third Edition), pp. 661–689. Newark, DE: International Reading Association.

Hobsbaum, A., S. Peters and K. Sylva. 1996. Scaffolding in Reading Recovery. *Oxford Review of Education* 22, 1: pp. 17–35.

Holmes, J. and H. Singer. 1961. The substrata-factor theory: Substrata-factor differences underlying reading ability in known groups. US Office of Education, Final Report No. 538, SAE 8176.

Howard, I.P. and W.B. Templeton. 1966. *Human Spatial Orientation.* London: Wiley.

Hurry, J. 1996. What is so special about Reading Recovery? *The Curriculum Journal* 7, 1: 93–108.

Johnston, P.H. 1997. *Knowing Literacy: Constructive Literacy Assessment.* York, ME: Stenhouse Publishers.

Johnston, P.H. 2000. *Running Records: A Self-tutoring Guide.* York, ME: Stenhouse Publishers.

Juel, C. 1980. Longitudinal research on learning to read and write with at-risk students. In M.J. Dreyer and W.H. Slater, eds, *Elementary School Literacy: Critical Issues.* Norwood, MA: Christopher-Gordon.

————. 1988. Learning to read and write: a longitudinal study of 54 children from first through fourth grades. *Journal of Educational Psychology* 4: 437–447.

————. 1991. Beginning Reading. In R. Barr, M.L. Kamil, P.B. Mosenthal and D. Pearson, eds, *Handbook of Reading Research*, Vol. 2, pp. 759–788. London: Longman.

Lynn, R. 1966. *Attention, Arousal and the Orientation Reaction.* London: Pergamon.

MacKinnon, A.R. 1959. *How Do Children Learn to Read?* Toronto: Copp Clark Publishing.

McKoon, G. and R. Ratcliff. 1998. Memory-based language processing: Psycholinguistic research in the 1990s. *Annual Review of Psychology* 1998, 49: 25–42.

McNaughton, S. 1974. Behaviour Modification and Reading in a Special Class. Unpublished Master of Arts thesis, University of Auckland Library.

————. 1978. Instructor Attention to Oral Reading Errors: A Functional Analysis. Unpublished doctoral dissertation, University of Auckland.

————. 1981. Becoming an independent reader: Problem-solving during oral reading. *New Zealand Journal of Educational Studies* 16: 172–185.

McNaughton, S., T. Glynn and V. Robinson. 1981. *Parents as Remedial Reading Tutors: Issues for Home and School.* Wellington: New Zealand Council for Educational Research. Reprinted 1987 as *Pause, Prompt and Praise: Effective Tutoring for Remedial Reading.* Birmingham: Positive Products.

McQueen, P.J. 1975. Motor Responses Associated with Beginning Reading. Master of Arts thesis, University of Auckland Library.

Nalder, S. 1984. Emergent Reading: A Development Year Project. Report distributed by the Reading Advisory Service, Ministry of Education. Author address, 10B Nea Place, Glenfield, Auckland, New Zealand.

Neale, M. 1958. *The Neale Analysis of Reading Ability.* London: Macmillan.

Ng, S.M. 1979. Error and Self-correction in Reading and Oral Language. Doctoral dissertation, University of Auckland Library.

Nicholson, T. 1984. Experts and novices. *Reading Research Quarterly* 19, 4: 436–450.

O'Leary, S. 1997. *Five Kids: Stories of Children Learning to Read.* Bothell, WA: The Wright Group/ McGraw-Hill.

Penton, J. and D. Holdaway, 1973. *The Early Reading In-Service Course.* Report to the Director-General of Education. Wellington: Department of Education.

Randell, B. 1999. Shaping the PM story books. *The Running Record*, RRCNA 11, 2: 1–12.

Robinson, S.E. 1973. Predicting Early Reading Progress. Master of Arts thesis, University of Auckland Library.

Rogoff, B. 1990. *Apprenticeship in Thinking — Cognitive Development in Social Context.* New York: Oxford University Press.

Rumelhart, D.E. 1994. Toward an interactive model of reading. In R.B. Ruddell, M.R. Ruddell and H. Singer, eds, *Theoretical Models and Processes of Reading* (Fourth Edition), pp. 864–894. Newark, DE: International Reading Association,

Singer, H. 1994. The substrata-factor theory of reading. In R.B. Ruddell, M.R. Ruddell and H. Singer, eds, *Theoretical Models and Processes of Reading* (Fourth Edition), pp. 895–927. Newark, DE: International Reading Association.

Slane, J. 1979. An individual audiovisual in-service course for teachers: The Early Reading In-service Course. *Programmed Learning and Educational Technology* 16, 1: 38–45.

Smith, J.W.A. and W.B. Elley. 1997. *How Children Learn to Write.* Auckland: Addison Wesley Longman.

Solley, C.M. and G. Murphy. 1960. *Development of the Perceptual World.* New York: Basic Books.

Spear-Swerling, L. and R.J. Sternberg. 1996. *Off-Track: When Poor Readers Become "Learning Disabled".* Boulder, Colorado: Westview Press.

Spiro, R.J., R.L. Coulson, P.J. Feltovich and D.K. Anderson. 1994. Cognitive flexibility theory: Advanced knowledge acquisition in ill-structured domains. In R.B. Ruddell, M.R. Ruddell, and H. Singer, eds, *Theoretical Models and Processes of Reading* (Fourth Edition), pp. 895– 927. Newark, DE: International Reading Association.

Spiro, R.J., W.L. Vispoel, J.G. Schmitz, A. Samarapungavan, and A.E. Boerger. 1987. Knowledge acquisition for application: Cognitive flexibility and transfer in complex content domains. In B.K. Britton and S.M. Glynn, eds, *Executive Control Processes in Reading.* Hillsdale, NJ: Lawrence Erlbaum.

Thorndike, R.L. 1973. *Reading Comprehension Education in Fifteen Countries.* Uppsala: Almqvist and Wiksell.

Watson, B. 1980. An Observation Study of Teaching Beginning Reading to New Entrant Children. Master of Arts thesis, University of Auckland Library.

Watson, S. and M.M. Clay. 1975. Oral reading strategies of third form students. *New Zealand Journal of Educational Studies* 1, May: 43–51.

Wheldall, K. and T. Glynn. 1988. Contingencies in contexts: A behavioural interactionist perspective in education. *International Journal of Educational Psychology* 8, 1 and 2: 5–20.

Williams, B. 1968. The Oral Reading Behaviour of Standard One Children. Master of Arts thesis, University of Auckland Library.

Wong, P. and S.S. McNaughton. 1980. The effects of prior provision of content on the oral reading proficiency of a low progress reader. *New Zealand Journal of Educational Studies* 15, 2: 159–175.

Wood, D., J.S. Bruner and G. Ross. 1976. The role of tutoring in problem-solving. *Journal of Child Psychology and Child Psychiatry* 17, 2: 89–100.

Wotherspoon, T. 1974. Modification of Writing Behaviour in a Special Class. Master of Arts thesis, University of Auckland Library.

Yopp, H.K, and H. Singer. 1994. Toward an interactive reading instruction model: Explanation of activation of linguistic awareness and meta-linguistic ability in learning to read. In R.B. Ruddell, M.R. Ruddell and H. Singer, eds, *Theoretical Models and Processes of Reading* (Fourth Edition), pp. 381–390. Newark, DE: International Reading Association.

3   Assembling working systems: how young children begin to read and write texts

3 Assembling working systems: how young children begin to read and write texts

First, some assumptions

The provocative hypothesis in this chapter is that several kinds of perceptual/cognitive systems are critical for extending literacy processing power, and that they enable us to learn to read by reading, and learn to write by writing. The first section of this chapter reviews some of the special demands of reading continuous texts and how children meet the challenges. Two reading theories are then reviewed briefly because they are helpful for conceptualising the changes over time that occur in text reading behaviours. Some important early learning about literacy which is not covered by the two theorists is proposed as 'a missing knowledge source' in most beginning reading theories, and the primitive working systems used while knowledge is very limited are discussed. Some issues around the term 'literacy processing' are revisited and research questions about reading continuous texts are raised.

Literacy learning as reading and writing

Almost every child learns to read print and write print at the same time. Paying attention to print in these two activities surely has reciprocal effects, one affecting the other, whether we plan for this to occur or not. When writing we attend to every feature of every letter in correct sequence and to words in text, one after the other, and to composing language (just as we do in reading). The reciprocity of early reading and writing has been obvious to some theorists but neglectfully avoided by most.

I assume that when children are introduced to reading and writing at the same time in their schooling they will be drawing on the same knowledge sources and somewhat the same perceptual/cognitive processing networks in both activities. However, there is little in this chapter on writing because little research is yet published about the processing of writing at the early stages of literacy learning.

If my hypothesis is worth pursuing then research and debate would need to be directed a) to the kinds of perceptual/cognitive working systems behind the behavioural evidence which young learners exhibit, b) to how these change rapidly over time in both beginning readers and writers, and c) to how they operate independently or jointly to extend the neural networks which underpin advanced types of processing.

When reading without any problems

When adults focus on their own reading they usually ask, 'How do I read an unknown word?', to which they answer, 'I sound it out'. This leads them to the conclusion that reading is a process of breaking down in which the sound sequence is articulated by the reader. Research shows that after two years at school, children have learned to say that this is how they read (Clay and Williams 1973). Proficient readers also explain reading as recognising words, which is an important outcome of successful reading.

Surely the most important thing to be explained by reading theory is how I am able to read when everything is going well! So I intend to explore a counter-argument which claims that children who are learning to read and write continuous texts use those texts to help them build the effective neural processing systems which successful readers use as they read without problems.

Eye movement research (Rayner, Raney and Pollatsek 1995) shows convincingly that readers attend to almost every word, and to the sequence of letters within words in order to distinguish similar words one from another. They say that young fluent readers work in this way also. The same authors use eye movement technology to investigate how readers read texts when it is not the single words that count but the particular clustering of words that can change the message of the phrase, the sentence or the discourse. Omit the word 'not' in a sentence and the message goes awry. Sounds, letter-sound relationships, letter clusters and words can be practised in isolation; but the groupings of words become critical when we are reading and writing continuous text.

When reading without problems it seems as if we are juggling many things simultaneously. An extensive repertoire of item knowledge learned and practised in isolation, and a single technique of sounding out the phonemes in words is a skimpy preparation for understanding the messages in texts.

In the first years of school, learners read and write continuous texts. Too frequently teaching attends to learning the words, or learning letter-sound relationships. What else do young children need to know to read their simple texts? Some viable hypotheses are these.

- Proficient readers build complex reading processes from the beginning.

- Descriptions of what it is that proficient readers do during acquisition help teachers to understand what low achievers need to learn.

- There may be several routes to proficiency.

- Teaching letters, sounds, words and isolated skills first, while downplaying the need to work at understanding messages, does not seem to impede the progress of proficient learners but could make it harder for some learners to incorporate the (hidden) linguistic relationships into the patterning of processing at some later time.

Oral language as resource and beneficiary

Consider how oral language is learned. Between the toddler's one-word utterances and a six-year-old's account of a story he or she has read, children become adept at communicating and they reformulate their phrases and sentences to ensure that they are understood. The school entrant has much more to learn about oral language but has already organised for himself or herself a remarkable control of communicating as a speaker. How did we ever come to think of literacy as simply governed by letter-sound relationships or by the size of the vocabulary of known words? When we think of a child learning to speak we do not think of oral language learning in such limited ways; we pay little attention to learning phonemes or words and we do not insist that things about oral language be learned in a set sequence. *Reading and writing are at least as complex as oral language, with some extra challenges thrown in.*

Debates on 'reading methods' have a long history. Once upon a time, when children entered school, they were given contrived texts. A set of letters and short words were built into highly contrived sentences which were unlike the language spoken by the children. (The genre was sometimes called 'primerese' or 'basalese'.) A small set of letters was taught, then children read two- and three-letter words made up from that limited set, and they read these highly selected words in awkward sentences, repeated in a contrived text according to a deliberate plan. I clearly remember from my fifth birthday that:

Pat can run and jump. May can skip.

And I suppose the text continued with:

Run, Pat, run and jump.
1, 2, 3, go.
Skip, May, skip.

(I can thank Whitcombe and Tombs Publishers and Kelburn Normal School for giving me that memory back in 1931.) This approach produced sentences which were a poor match for children's remarkable control of the language. This type of manipulation reappeared recently as 'decodable text'. When I rewrote some decodable text trying to get closer to language that young children might use I did not produce language which a young child would utter spontaneously.

Text published 1996	Less artificial rewrite	Rewrite in more child-like language
This is Tig's big tin bin.	Tig is a pig.	Tig the Pig was **very** hungry.
Tig is in the big tin.	Jim put crisps in a bin.	Jim filled a tin with crisps
Jim sits by the tin bin.	Tig gets in the bin.	and Tig jumped in the bin.

The task in decodable texts is to learn letters, sounds, letter-sound relationships, and clusters like 'ig' and 'in'. Learners attend to sounds in almost unpronounceable tongue-twisters, and the words are in an order that the children would rarely hear in speech. The sentences offer little support to young children who are not finding it easy to learn to read and write. On the other hand literacy activities can be designed to enlist the language competencies which children already have, rather than put those competencies on hold while contrived tasks are introduced. Texts can make it easy for children to do what they do as speakers of a language. Why not tap into this existing language strength when children begin to read?

Some theorists justify the 'basalese' with the argument that reading and speaking are different activities (which of course they are) but to go from that statement to claim that how we understand the language we speak does not influence literacy acquisition is mischievous hyperbole. We should not ignore these facts:

- Oral language is a coded activity learned by toddlers and preschoolers.

- Reading and writing is a second coded activity acquired by children who already control the easy-to-learn parts of a language.

- As literacy is learned it is a great advantage to be able to monitor what you think you see in print through a set of oral language competencies.

- Reading and writing will enrich a child's understanding of what one can do with language.

Children who read and write texts can get unlimited exposure to learning letters, sounds and words, and teachers can extract suitable examples from the texts around the classroom at any time in any lesson, at any time of the day (see Watson 1980, Chapter 2). Teachers can be trusted to monitor that essential item learning is being learned; monitoring detail in item learning is merely a matter of organisation for teachers in schools and it is easy to arrange for it. A distrust of teachers leads administrators to produce detailed curricula, prescribing what shall be taught before what, and when it shall be tested, and specifying benchmarks in terms of the number and type of items known. Standardised sequences of learning may confuse the low achievers and hold back the proficient children.

An end-goal for the acquisition phase of literacy learning is for children to become efficient readers of texts. After about three years at school they read long texts at speed with few errors, dealing with different kinds of information in print silently and apparently simultaneously. By that time the language activities of their classrooms will place heavy demands on knowledge of sentence structure and shades of meaning. If we harness the established power of children's oral language to literacy learning from the beginning, *so that literacy knowledge and oral language processing power move forward together, linked and patterned from the start,* that will surely be more powerful.

If children have access to interesting stories in small books arranged in a gradient of difficulty, they have plenty of opportunity to gain control over three hidden types of information in texts, the phonological, syntactic and semantic. In texts written in childlike language the features of language which teachers need to bring to their attention will occur in beginning texts as frequently as they do in the children's spoken language; some features will occur often and be learned earlier and others will occur less often and be learned later. An appropriate ratio of opportunities for teaching letters, for letter clusters and for words will occur in those texts, and the grammar (structure or syntax) and vocabulary which children already use when speaking will support their attempts to read and write.

Stories read to children introduce them to new language forms. How could a four-year-old, telling a story to a favourite bear, ever come up with, 'Kangaroo was born on the 95th of May' (White 1984), if her language had not been influenced by stories she had heard? Reading to children from books beyond their reading level is helpful and two reasons for this are because it contributes to incidental learning of new vocabulary (Elley 1989) and increases exposure to literary language. It is powerful to harness the established power of children's oral language to literacy learning from the beginning, so that new literacy knowledge and new oral language powers are linked and patterned from the start. *Children with the least preparation for literacy learning need such an integrated approach if they are to catch up to their classmates.*

So my discussion proceeds on these assumptions: that literacy learning includes reading and writing, that the aim is to have children reading a variety of texts using a range of flexible strategies (including but not restricted to attacking unknown words phoneme by phoneme), and composing simple messages in writing. As children work towards this end-goal, oral language is both a resource and a beneficiary.

From acts of processing

Some special demands of reading and writing continuous texts

Knowing what it is that proficient readers do as they work on texts provides teachers with ideas about how to scaffold opportunities for less proficient children to learn during their first three years of school.

Reading text involves working with a string of sequential decisions, and so does writing, and when we record how proficient readers work on a text it is unquestionable that what has gone before influences the current decision. It is more complicated than recognising a word recalled from a memory bank. It is helpful to ask, 'What triggered that recall? And why was that other word recalled and then rejected?' (see Chapter 5).

Secondly, proficient readers appear to make decisions during text reading which imply that they are choosing how to process a particular text.

> When reading a text a reader … is faced with a number of activities, all of which compete for time and resources. Different sets of activities are consequent upon the decision of whether to read for gist or for detail. In essence the crucial problem is deciding where to go next. Should one plough on remorselessly? should one skip ahead? should one ignore a particular figure for the time being? (Britton and Glynn 1987, p. xii)

One theory of learning to read generated by Holmes (1953, 1960) and developed by Singer (1994) describes this as assembling the processing system needed to complete a particular task. A key concept from the Holmes/Singer theory referred to here is that the processing systems of the brain which solve the new word or phrase or text message are assembled to do a particular job. On another occasion, or on a different text, the working system assembled could be different (see Table 2, p. 113, and Singer 1994, p. 913). What literacy learners do between five and eight years of age fits very well within that concept although for beginning readers the options of what to do and how to do it are severely limited.

Putting such views alongside research on acts of literacy processing I came to a fresh synthesis of what I think happens. Children begin to read or write using very simple 'working systems' borrowed at first from different kinds of learning prior to school which have to be adapted for these novel activities. Over three to four years they construct a vast range of complex processing activities, finely tuned to the requirements of literacy learning. As they read across a sentence, word after word, they pull together the processes they need to make a decision about a fragment of text, trying to take into account the immediately preceding items in that sentence or story. This suggests that observant teachers could select texts for a particular child which not only draw upon working systems which that child has in place, but also challenge these to change. This would explain what 'matching text to a child' could really mean! What on the surface looks like a simple word-by-word reading of a short story involves children in linking many things they know from different sources.

When they problem-solve text they dip into these 'different ways of knowing something' and make a series of decisions as they work across the text. To only look at this in terms of letters and words attended to is to ignore much of what readers do, sequentially, 'to solve the parts within wholes' as they work across messages.

Day by day teachers move children up a gradient of difficulty in texts asking them to lift their level of functioning, and encouraging them to attempt more complex decisions. Teachers are most effective when they are available to respond to a child who is making one of those decisions close to the moment when it is occurring. (Did you listen to children reading today?) A description of what shifts in processing to look for, and a theory to explain the kinds of shifts in processing which are likely to occur would assist teachers to scaffold instruction. Collecting evidence of those shifts and searching for theoretical explanations of any sequences of change in reading behaviours could result in excellent practical guidance for teaching in classrooms.

Some special demands of text reading are:

- that readers need to select a way to process a particular text

- that as they read across a sentence solving word after word they pull together the processes they need to make decisions about fragments of text

- that what has gone before influences the current decision

- that even the reading of a simple story involves the linking of many processes like visual perceptions, auditory/phonological analysis, movement, speaking/articulating, and knowledge of language use and reference. Fortunately beginning readers externalise much of their decision-making and we have learned how to keep Running Records of the changes over time in early literacy behaviours in some detail.

Processing in early writing makes analogous demands (see Chapter 1).

When children are expected to read texts

Building a literacy processing system only begins when a child is expected to compose and write a simple message or read a simple continuous text. The coming together takes place early, as soon as society and the school expect it. The expectation that messages exist in continuous text calls together the first working systems. Given rich opportunities to read text, children work slowly at first but gradually learn to work rapidly and to use more complex sets of information. Some of the information is visible in the print and its layout, and some of it involves language information which is supplied by the reader.

Current descriptions of what amounts to 'progress' in reading and writing are very different. Typically researchers 'measure' a precondition and an outcome condition in a sample of children, and then statistically derive components from the averaged changes in text scores. From those components, curricula are designed. This approach does not document change in fine detail and produces gross approximations to the changes which occur in individuals. More critical is the fact that the significance of individual diversity in sequences of learning is averaged out. This is why instructional programmes derived from such research have no chance of solving the problems of literacy learning difficulties which have many different origins. Research studies are needed which go beyond the exploratory studies of text reading discussed in the last chapter. For example, O'Leary's (1997) reference to 'the re-running start' as a powerful thing to learn because it produces evidence of what is being integrated, suggests a question waiting for an answer. Is she right, and if so, in what way?

Information gained from studying acts of processing would lead to different descriptions of progress from those currently popular.

Teachers contribute to the shifts in the processing which children are able to carry out, by:

- altering the learning opportunities provided

- prompting to influence the choices made by the constructive learner

- altering the interactions between teacher and learner.

Novel sentences not encountered before

In every message I read, in the sequence of words in a newspaper report and in my current bedside reading, I have to put novel sentences together. The items of language in print are encountered again and again but the message is always different.

> Virtually every sentence that a person utters or understands is a brand-new combination of words, appearing for the first time in the history of the universe. (Chomsky 1957; Pinker 1994)

The quote refers to speaking but applies to reading also.

Visible items and invisible relationships

In the past the teaching of reading has paid particular attention to controlling the frequency with which items occur — the printed letters, clusters of letters, and words. When publishers and their authors specified repetition and practice of words as essential for teaching literacy they altered the natural frequencies with which visible words recur in writing and reading.

Most of the information we use as readers is invisible information (phonological, structural and semantic), brought to the text by the reader on the run in the sequential activity of reading novel messages: a) the sounds which can be associated with visible items in quasi-regular ways, b) the rules for stringing words together in sentences, and c) the meanings transmitted not only by the word but also by its placement in the sentence and text. We can 'read' four or more different meanings into the six words, 'It is too hot to eat' (DeStephano 1978, p. 31), and we can bring meaning to the sentence, 'May May be here in May?', which is a meaningful question which my friend might answer but which my computer has just judged to be illegal.

There is some regularity in the sounds represented by consonants in English but some letters represent more than one sound and some sounds can be spelt in more than one way (Dewey 1970). The reader of English must cope with this but the reader of German escapes this problem (Wimmer and Goswami 1994). Knowing such things about the sounds of letters and letter clusters is *essential but not sufficient* for successful reading of texts.

The visible features of punctuation and layout show that small changes can signal big differences in the interrelationships between words, as in:

' … go in the car when … '

' … go in the car. When … '

We can teach children to 'read' things in isolation — letters, words, common labels or phrases — but very soon children have to use these 'items' in texts in which prior words have specific implications for subsequent words. Clusters of letters can often be heard as distinct patterns of sounds but there are exceptions for which the reader must be ready. So the links of form-to-sound or sound-to-form must not be taught in ways which monopolise attention and deny the processing system the flexibility to deal with exceptions.

Teachers can prompt children to attend to invisible relationships with simple questions like, 'Would that make sense?' for meaning, or 'Can we say it that way?' for structure, or 'Can you "hear" this letter?' for auditory input, and 'Does it look right?' for visual input. At first children may not distinguish the questions well but five-year-old children know a great deal about 'making sense' and also about what can be said and what cannot be said in the language. Teachers work on visible features every day. Readers have to rapidly access visible information as the first step in processing and quickly match it up with information from language knowledge which is not represented visibly.

Texts provide the opportunities to build up experience with the mixing of visible and invisible information, including the ways in which one word influences another in a message. The call to 'read to children at home and in school' has contributed greatly to the understanding that children can learn many things about texts, especially about the invisible features, as they listen to stories told and stories read to them. Margaret Meek made a valuable analysis of *How Texts Teach What Readers Learn* (1988). She pointed to ways in which rich literary texts could teach new readers how to work with texts. Her reference was more towards the invisible semantic themes in print and less towards the structure of language as a hidden support system but her title and arguments brought to our notice features of language which do not, on the surface, have an obvious representation in print. Other researchers have studied how readers acquire a sense of story, the ways in which the reader must bring meaning to the texts from their experiences using schemas of what the world is like, termed 'scripts' (Anderson 1985; Anderson and Pearson 1984), and how readers carry information across sentence boundaries (Chapman 1981).

Adults reading aloud initiate a range of adaptive and self-correcting actions as they work to produce an acceptable message from a hard text and young competent readers can be heard pulling things together 'in some integrated way' on text. Children need opportunities to learn to read various types of texts efficiently. Depriving them of this adds risk to literacy learning. Special programmes for children who have extreme difficulty with literacy learning cannot afford to ignore or over-emphasise either visible items or invisible features of texts without seriously limiting their effectiveness.

Repetition in reading is a special case. It occurs when I decide to reread a text, or when an author intentionally repeats a text (as in poetry or in some children's stories), or if the phrase is a cliché or a very common item like 'a ton of bricks' or 'for the life of me'. Frequently-used phrases do occur in text, but mostly the sentences, the stories, the meanings in texts will have a singular message. As readers we expect to find a 'new' message in every text, and repetition can be irksome. Repetition is helpful with beginning readers but an early escape must be made from its misleading message of 'sameness'.

Most theories assume that children read and write continuous texts

Discussions which imply that readers are reading continuous texts have been provided by most theorists: Rumelhart (1994) with his multiple knowledge sources used simultaneously; Haber (1978) and Smith (1978) with their analysis of many kinds of redundancy; Miller (1981) who spent a lifetime of work on communication and language; Goodman and Goodman (1979) who assumed that in some ways the process was the same at all stages of reading; Meek (1988) who argued that texts teach what readers learn; Rosenblatt (1994) who stressed that reading was a transaction between the text and the reader; Anderson (1985) and Anderson and Pearson (1984) who introduced the concepts of schemas or scripts; Singer (1994) who developed a complex model sensitive to changes from early reading to mature reading; and many others. Different theories flourish because each can point to what has been neglected by other theories in the complex world of literacy processing.

It is the professional role of linguists to analyse languages at many levels, such as:

- discourse including stories

- the sentence patterns of a language

- the syntactic or phrase structures (permissible rules for grouping words)

- the words or lexicon collected in dictionaries

- morphological components (the smallest units of meaning)

- phonological units, including onsets and rimes and phonemes.

Any item on the above list may become the focus of attention in a theory of reading. To illustrate how theorists can stress some parts of a language hierarchy we might point to Frank Smith (1978) on features of letters; Gough (1985) on phonology and the order of letters in letter clusters and words; Goswami (1998) on letter clusters as 'rimes' in relation to analogy; Ehri (1991) on word learning; Rumelhart (1994) on the simple phrase or syntactic level; Goodman (1994) giving foremost importance to semantics; and Brown, Palincsar and Armbruster (1994) on the cognitive aspects of making links in discourse. Interactive theorists (including some of the above) argue that each of these levels of language yields useful information for the reader who may start on any level and draw on any other level simultaneously or successively. The Holmes/Singer theory discussed later in this chapter (Singer 1994) presupposes that a competent reader will control a range of processes and adapt flexibly to the demands of a specific literacy task by assembling a temporary system from among those available to deal with the literacy task in hand.

Young speakers entering school already control linguistic processing strategies in oral language. An interactive theory sees the reader as a decision-maker using existing implicit awareness of different kinds of information to get messages from texts. The interactions between learner and teacher about the texts bring about the early changes in processing. Well-trained teachers who lift the performance of individuals through some gradient of difficulty in texts, prompt the reader to search for this or that type of information.

A hierarchical concept of levels of language information gave us the unfortunate terms top-down and bottom-up as a classification of theories. I find a concept of assembling the working systems for a specific task in hand allows more scope for knowledge sources and neurological networks to be used flexibly and effectively by readers. *The Holmes/Singer theoretical position does not require one to assume a hierarchical order of importance among different kinds of linguistic awareness, nor a separation of writing from reading.*

Combining or integrating different processes

To speak we must bring different kinds of information, different mental activities, and different choices together as we put thoughts into words. A remarkably clear example of a three and a half year old's attempts to construct the meaning he needed to convey was provided in this message: 'Markie me … Markie me pushed … Markie pushed me … falled me.' Even adult speakers will stumble over a sentence construction from time to time. Much of the knowledge that we pull together for speaking can be used in either reading or writing.

As speakers we monitor our own speaking and sometimes go back to select a different word or touch up the grammar of the utterance. A listener tries to follow a speaker and *parse* the sentence so far to make sure that he or she is receiving a 'possible' message. This *parsing* involves correctly relating particular sounds and words to the spoken words that surround them (Pinker 1994).

Average readers in their first year of instruction are slow readers; they spend about one second on each word, whereas proficient readers take less than a second. Both groups construct a sentence or text sequentially from beginning to end, using whatever activity they can muster to yield a good message. At each point in the sequential reading final decisions are usually made at the word level, but getting to that is more complex than merely recalling a word. Like speakers, readers parse as they go, and from time to time they discover a need to revise the reading just as they would do when speaking. Writers reread their texts to ensure that these grouped relationships are acceptable so far. We pull words together for literacy acts constrained by the invisible relationships and roles which words have within a simple sentence.

Parsing a sentence can lead readers 'up the garden path', wrote Pinker (1994, p. 212), when they expect a sentence to proceed in one way and it does not. Three of his many examples are:

Fat people eat accumulates.
The cotton clothing is usually made of grows in Mississippi.
The horse raced past the barn fell.

Notice how strong one's syntactic anticipation is! Probably the re-running of a piece of reading text, which young children do without prompting, had its origin in the young speaker's experience with parsing spoken language. Pinker's sentences point us to things readers of text must do which are hard to explain with word-reading theories.

Research which followed children through the changes of their first year in literacy instruction led me to this working definition of reading during the acquisition stage. *Reading is a message-getting, problem-solving activity, which increases in power and flexibility the more it is practised (Clay 1979) and it is complex because 1) within the directional constraints of written language attention to 2) verbal and 3) perceptual behaviours is 4) purposefully directed 5) in some integrated way 6) to the problem of extracting a sequence of cues from a text 7) to yield a meaningful and specific communication (Clay 1966, 1991, p. 243).* The phrase 'in some integrated way' was intentionally vague in 1966, to acknowledge the 'unseen nature of the in-the-head processing of the reader', and the state of research. This chapter (and book) are part of a further exploration into the nature of that 'integration'. The search involves trying to understand 'the perspective of the developing organism' (Campbell 1993), an internal focus on the inner control being constructed by the learner, but also how the reader uses the text as an external resource for decision-taking (A. Clark 1996). The cognitive domain being explored is literacy learning and the intention is to consider learning to read and write as they emerge together during the first three years of formal instruction.

When I use the words 'construct' or 'constructive' to refer to children building reading and writing processes, I cannot assume that children will construct the sources of knowledge about the arbitrary written code entirely alone but that co-construction occurs in interaction with knowledgeable adults (McNaughton 1995). (The adults cannot do the learning for the child but must enlist the child's attention and effort, and provide helpful information in response to what the learner is able to do.) However, I am concerned that discussion of co-construction often stops short of a description of what occurs, for it omits part of the process described by Vygotsky (1962). Supported at first by social contacts the literacy learner gradually has less need of the scaffolded support of the expert, and the reader begins to perform alone *but improves his or her reading and writing processing as those activities are pursued, learning more on his or her own.* Silent reading is a classical example of this and the transition from mainly oral to mainly silent reading is worthy of detailed study in this respect. Meek would possibly argue that it is the reader and author who co-construct in acts of silent reading: the silent reader learns more from reading more difficult texts, with the help of the author.

How the learner works across continuous texts becomes more obvious if detailed observational records are kept of young readers reading aloud, especially when such records are repeated from time to time to capture change over time in what learners are becoming able to do. In such records we can see evidence in self-corrections of how *the previous text influenced the reader's decisions about the subsequent text.* The reader's decision-making about what a text says is referred to in this book as 'literacy processing', and that term includes all the levels or aspects of language that linguists have described but does not imply that the cognitive processes which the young reader constructs conform to the order or structure of the linguists' hierarchy.

Simple and complex theories of reading will co-exist

Changes in the ways in which children make decisions about print can be recorded between five and eight years. At these ages the reading is slow enough for some of these changes to be observed in real time, whatever instruction is being delivered. In whatever way we conceptualise the processing systems (as cell assemblies, or networks, or strategies, or working systems), they *must be infinitely flexible and temporarily tentative* during the acquisition of literacy. Such flexibility must be important for young learners because they do not yet understand the nature of the problems (see Spiro et al. 1987). Anything set in stone could become an impediment.

Child readers around the world get to common outcomes by different instructional routes, and this suggests that no specific piece of learning is essentially prior, except perhaps that one's speaking becomes linked to literacy activities. (This is true for both a fluent speaker of the language and for the learner of a new language.) Singer wrote that the young child has to learn three major types of operation, namely:

1) how to get different kinds of information (in the technical sense of information theory) from print by actively searching for *input*

2) how to use one or more kinds of information to form hypotheses and evaluate a possible response (carried out in the head, which Singer called '*mediation*')

3) how to confirm a selected response or reject it (*response formulation*).

(This general description will also be found in accounts of what occurs in oral language processing and in the visual perception in print.)

The first primitive indicators of in-the-head processing about literacy are detectable, recordable and quantifiable when formal instruction begins (see 'Literacy

Awareness', Clay 1998), or soon after (see Kay, Chapter 2). Early recordable behaviours point to changes in knowing:

- where to attend

- where to search

- what information to use

- what to relate it to

- how to monitor its acceptability

- what to do in the face of a dissonant result.

All these activities call for in-the-head decisions and problem-solving in milliseconds of time.

The learner orally produces word sequences that fit the matrix of information within and between each word in the text. Being successful *consolidates the ways of working that were used to get the message, and allows familiar words to become recognised rapidly.* Young readers use both familiar and new information in much the same way although their first responses are primitive attempts. Singer warns that the processing systems of young learners are 'under construction' and undergoing rapid change as oral reading shifts towards silent reading under the influence of many factors such as:

- teachers who gradually increase the difficulty of texts

- changes in the ways in which texts are printed (the most obvious change being the late introduction of justified print)

- the need to solve multi-syllabic words in more difficult texts at speed, working with clusters of letters.

The work done by the processing system may appear similar over time, but marked changes in the reader's interaction with the printed page have been recorded. Literacy learning theory must become interested in such changes. A series of Running Records from children reading texts can provide evidence of change in reading behaviours. Teachers can take these records, observe the behaviours and support the idiosyncratic processing of a particular child in ways which advance the effectiveness of the reading or writing. Children need slightly different prods and prompts to keep them on a trajectory of progress. It is tempting to use simple, shorthand explanations of learning to read such as:

- learning a vocabulary of words,

- or doing intensive analysis at the sub-word level to 'attack' unknown words,

- or recognising many words rapidly, and stringing them together to understand a message.

But the goals of literacy instruction are *clearly not to produce readers and writers of words one at a time but rather to read words as interconnected, in phrases, in language structures, and across discourse. Words are placed together in studied ways by authors intending to communicate fine differences.* The miraculous emergence of two-word structures in the utterances of two-year-old toddlers produces extremely ambiguous sentences: that example reminds us that reading words two or three at a time may not result in receiving a clear message either. Interconnectedness in the language of reading and writing is so obviously crucial.

The authors of instructional programmes select the things they want children to attend to; the best of those programmes are driven by a particular theory *and each programme emphasises and neglects different aspects of literacy processes.* These are their selling points. Once children have learned the practical tricks of '*the selected method*' on 'the selected texts', progress is thought to be assured. Children who are active, constructive thinkers do learn from different approaches. It is the constructive children who make most programmes work. An alternative approach, designed especially for children who have pronounced difficulty learning, assumes that a watchful teacher must assist the learner to develop and integrate a complex set of neural processes from the beginning. This is the approach taken in Reading Recovery (M.M. Clark 1992; Adams 1990).

To put this briefly, complex theories about complex literacy activities are usually applied only to older children. *If literacy teaching only brings a simple theory to a set of complex activities, then the learner has to bridge the gaps created by the theoretical simplification. The lowest literacy achievers will have extreme difficulty bridging any gaps in the teaching programme and linking together things that have been taught separately.* They require a watchful teacher who shares the complex task and knows when to withdraw his or her help, bit by bit, as the low achievers construct necessary literacy processes. The teachers create the supporting structure within which the low achievers can be appropriately constructive. There has to be a plan for providing additional support briefly, and, following a temporary intervention, a plan for taking away the support when the literacy processing itself can ensure subsequent progress.

However, in the year 2001 if we choose a complex theory to guide young children's literacy learning we are likely to encounter gaps in our own knowledge for there will be areas where there is no relevant research.

For a long time education systems have delivered to low achievers curricula made up of item learning and/or skills relating to how to 'attack' new items. In contrast I suspect that what really matters is how quickly the young learner works out how to engage with continuous text, *for the richer texts themselves provide supporting structures. Many remedial materials do not.* If the acquisition of reading takes a long time on sparse texts (as it often does with low achievers), or if the pace of learning is slowed for any reason, the risk of literacy learning difficulties is probably increased. Reading Recovery (RR) experiences suggest the need to keep learners moving along with a sense of pace and change. Today's new learning should settle quickly into what is already known, freeing attention to go to more 'newness'. Such movement, and rearranging, and spotting new differences are the signs that process-building is occurring in milliseconds of time.

Theory-building from the results of carefully controlled research studies becomes difficult as soon as we accept that major variables have reciprocal effects on each other. Attending to and using even one type of information within print gives the reader access to other types as a consequence. A theory of operating on several sources of information allows the reader to confirm or reject an hypothesis about a decision by using any of several different kinds of information (Rumelhart 1994).

As beginning readers work with different kinds of information their processing is laboured, observable and clearly sequential. They make perceptual and cognitive decisions like those described in 'On perceptual readiness' (Bruner 1957), a theory in which cognitive and perceptual processing share a common decision-making process. It is possible to place most acts of literacy text processing in Bruner's framework even though he did not discuss literacy learning. After an early period of orientation to print, the young reader constructs some message-getting activities, such as:

- the conscious search for, and analysis of, different types of information in print,

- the necessary monitoring and error detection processes,

- together with highly practised and fast perceptual responding.

(Kay, in Chapter 2, in the first weeks of learning to read did some fast processing and some slower searching.) Subsequently these processes seem to require little conscious attention (Rumelhart 1994).

What is it about working on continuous texts that children might have to learn to do? Many working systems are described in different branches of psychological research. For example, studies of 'sentence processing' in the text reading of older readers has raised questions about how the reader works on the syntactic structures of sentences, and how a listener or reader knows which of several different meanings to extract from a sentence like 'It's too hot to eat.' A different body of research on 'text processing' has raised questions to do with how the meanings of larger units of text are understood, focusing on how the words and ideas of a text link with long-term memories (McKoon and Ratcliff 1998 discuss both these types of processing). And under the topic of executive control systems which manage reading activities a wide variety of working systems is proposed (Britton and Glynn 1987). Later in this chapter and the next two, attention will be given to working systems which are important for the very simple processing done by beginning readers.

Is a theory about working across continuous text, taking relationships between words into account, a theory of comprehension in an unfamiliar guise? No. We probably want to reserve the terms 'comprehension' and 'understanding' for some overarching processes but at least the word-by-word decision-making (as in parsing) marks out a path towards comprehension. A comparable situation arises as a writer composes. Sequential decision-making depends on tentative understanding of the message so far, while allowing the language user to change direction en route. Early effective reading and writing of continuous texts places high demand on understanding groupings of words in the messages read or written so far.

I am discussing a simple level of comprehension, a word by word, sentence by sentence, and page by page understanding of a very simple story such that an ending could be anticipated by the young reader who has comprehended the strings of words for their collective meaning.

> The bird sat in the tree.
> The cat sat in the tree.
> The dog sat under the tree.
> I watched them
>   And watched them
>   And watched them.

The young reader works across text taking letters, sounds, words and inter-word relationships into account, but also working with groupings of words and their inter-relationships. A listener can sometimes sense when the child reader is relating the current page to what has happened so far in the story. When I discover ambiguity in my own writing I have usually reread the text only to discover it could mean more than one thing. As both reader and writer I hasten to reduce the ambiguity and reconstruct the word sequences. Comprehension is involved in all reading and writing of continuous text, even a one-sentence message. It is often reserved in educational writing for the text or discourse level of understanding.

A brief review of two existing theories

The phrase 'in some integrated way' in my early definition masked unknown territory. So did some early titles I used like *The Patterning of Complex Behaviour* and *The Construction of Inner Control*. If the phrase 'in some integrated way' needs explication in a developmental account of literacy processing, how far forward could the two theories discussed in this section take us? As I explore some developmental aspects of that integration I find both Rumelhart's (1994) *interactive processing using multiple knowledge sources* and Singer's (1994) *tentative and flexible mobilisation of systems for particular tasks* are extremely valuable conceptualisations. Both theories describe complex literacy processes used by independent readers which might be applicable to young learners but neither provides a full account of acquisition in the first years of schooling. Neither theorist assumes that the reader's knowledge about his or her own cognitive processes (meta-cognition or hyper-cognition) is essential. Neither theorist assumes that problem identification or problem-solving is necessarily conscious or necessarily reflective of one's memory, comprehension or prior problem solutions (Campbell 1993, p. 178). Therefore these two theories might be relevant for understanding the efforts of beginning readers and writers who are not sure what it is they are doing because they are working with a code and they cannot grasp its structure (Spiro et al. 1987; Downing and Leong 1982). From the theories of David Rumelhart and Harry Singer, extracts are presented which may throw light upon these complex issues; for extensive accounts of the theories read *Theoretical Models and Processes of Reading* (Ruddell, Ruddell and Singer 1994).

Rumelhart's interactive theory

Reading is the process of understanding written language. It begins with a flutter of patterns on the retina and ends (when successful) with a definite idea about the author's intended message. Thus reading is at once a 'perceptual' and a 'cognitive' process. It blurs and bridges these two traditional distinctions. Moreover a skilled reader must be able to make use of sensory, syntactic, semantic and pragmatic information to accomplish his task. These various sources of information appear to interact in many complex ways during the process of reading. The theorist faced with the task of accounting for reading must devise a formalism rich enough to represent all of these different kinds of information and their interactions. (Rumelhart 1994, p. 864)

Rumelhart considered an accurate representation of the act of reading a text called for hypothesis generating and evaluating across different kinds of knowledge. But a full explanation of reading would have to go beyond the mere listing of information sources to hypothesise about how they interact. *It is important for the reader to keep in mind that Rumelhart's knowledge sources are not storage facilities, but they are decision-taking activities.* Each actively scans messages coming in or going out, and actively sifts, sorts and contributes to decisions. A brief summary of Rumelhart's sources of knowledge (pp. 886–889) is presented with many direct quotes from that article.

1. Symbols and their features
The particular pattern of features of any letter distinguishes it from all other letters. These patterns must be learned. Features distinguish similar letters one from another. Feature distinctions are challenging when a child knows only a few features and a few letters.

2. Letter knowledge
'This knowledge source scans the feature inputs and whenever it finds a close match to a known letter it posits a letter hypothesis. In addition, whenever a letter hypothesis appears [it is evaluated] against feature information.' (p. 886) Early knowledge based on visual forms is rapidly enriched during reading with additional phonological information, so that hypotheses and decisions come to include the combined visual-with-sound information. ' … the letter-level knowledge source presumably takes into account the probabilities of letters in the language.' (p. 887)

Successful beginning readers have letter knowledge prior to entry to school (Durrell 1958); letter discrimination is necessary but not sufficient for reading (Gibson 1969); learning to identify as distinct entities all letter forms used in English is a large set of visual perception learning and takes place slowly as new forms are successively distinguished from known ones (Clay 1966, 1991). Known letters provide footholds of one kind in continuous text once children begin to read and write, and before they have mastered the entire set of letter knowledge. Mature readers (and theorists) find it hard to think how a child can 'read' simple texts accurately when the child 'knows' only some of the letters. In early reading when children 'read' text correctly they may be using only some of the letter information in the text.

3. Letter cluster knowledge

'This knowledge source scans the incoming letter-level hypothesis looking for letter sequences which are likely to occur and which form units in the language or for single letters which are frequently followed or preceded by another letter.' (p. 887)

Children's oral phonemic representations include strong evidence of how sequences of phonemes 'stick together' forming cohesive units within the syllable and 'children treat some sequences of phonemes as units' (Treiman 1993, pp. 282–284). Bryant and Bradley's (1985) research on 'rime' provides evidence of how early children use an aural 'clustering' of sounds within a word, and spontaneously play with rhyming and sounds. This suggests that readers can search for and use chunks quite easily. Many teaching programmes use drill or workbook exercises which have children circling letter clusters or building lists of words with similar beginnings and endings, but that is unnecessary busy work because clusters should receive attention during any reading and writing activity. Attention at the letter-cluster level allows children to get to new words in reading or writing with early attempts at finding analogies — the cluster is part of something else they know. It probably saves effort or processing time to get quickly to something new using a chunk of something already well known. If the literacy learner has both a sizeable reading vocabulary and sizeable writing vocabulary, these provide two resources for noticing and using letter clusters which the learner can draw upon when faced with new words.

4. Word knowledge

In this source of information the brain 'scans the letter-cluster and letter sources for sequences of letters which form lexical items or which are close to lexical items. When it finds such information it posits the appropriate lexical hypothesis ... In addition whenever a lexical item is postulated from either semantic or syntactic sources the lexical knowledge source evaluates that hypothesis by postulating those letter cluster and letter-hypotheses that are not present. Those letter and letter-cluster hypotheses that are present are strengthened due to the convergence of the lines of evidence. Other alternatives without such convergent information are relatively weakened.' (p. 888) Tentative decisions are made which may be changed as more information comes to hand, later in the text.

The words read are the vehicles for using letter-feature, letter-sound, and letter-cluster knowledge to clinch decisions, but we are often puzzled by the competent readers who fail the discrimination test of what is a letter and what is a word. This is something of a developmental puzzle.

5. Syntactic knowledge

This knowledge source operates with any of the other sources of knowledge. '… whenever a lexical (vocabulary) hypothesis is suggested one or more syntactic category hypotheses are entered into the message center, … categories which are most probable, given the lexical item, would be entered first. Similarly sequences of lexical category hypotheses would be scanned looking for phrase possibilities.' (p. 888) The decision-making process is strengthened by information from both smaller or larger stretches of language.

The phrases children construct in their conversations lead to more awareness of language structures within sentences in their writing and reading. Syntax refers to the structure of language which governs how words are ordered in particular sequences, and syntactical rules change the inflections of words used in those sequences. Syntax clearly demonstrates the linkages of words in continuous texts. Some error behaviour of beginning readers reveals the extent to which children allow the syntax of language to influence their responding. In a linguistic analysis of 10,000 errors made by 100 children while reading continuous text in the first year of instruction, it was possible to see how often readers' errors anticipated a permissible syntax for the upcoming word sequence (Clay 1968; see also Weber 1970) and how the syntax of the child's own spoken language could make its contribution to the reading of continuous texts. Syntax is also complexly involved in decisions about sentence beginnings, noticing and 'reading' punctuation, reading fluently with phrasing, and using expression and intonation. Observant teachers notice how the texts children read *draw upon and extend their existing syntactic knowledge.*

There are even (unspecified) rules for the order in which certain qualifiers and adjectives precede the noun in the noun phrase. So:

one/ very/ large,/ newly painted,/red/ Ford/ truck

becomes unacceptable to speakers of English when the rules are ignored, as in:

one/ Ford,/ red,/ newly painted/ very large/ truck,

which produces an urge to reorder the words.

It is apparent that the development of syntactic awareness and an effective reception of the messages of authors would be less satisfactory if the young learner were reading contrived texts. One justification offered by defenders of the old-style basal readers was that by the time children were in the middle of Grade 2 they would be reading rich continuous text anyway. This would not be true of children with low achievement who needed the help most.

6. Semantic and discourse knowledge

'This is perhaps the most difficult source of information to characterize. Nevertheless its operation is essentially the same as the others.' (p. 889)

It is now widely accepted that reading to children is valuable for learners from preschool through high school, and that all readers have to construct meaning to comprehend text. Preschool bedtime stories have children reacting to the characters, and to the plot which sometimes children want rewritten. (One child rewrote Joy Cowley's *Ratty-Tatty* story because she was unable to accept that the rat rather than the elderly couple became the victor!) When children develop a sense of story this supports their reading of stories. Meek (1988) wrote of the ways in which an author (through the text) teaches children about reading. An example of rich semantic sources of information to support reading and writing activities would be found in a topic approach, where a theme of interest is studied in many different ways and reading about it becomes easier as knowledge about it increases. Genre theorists have demonstrated that a diet solely of stories can leave a beginning reader with expertise for story reading that does not work well on information texts. Knowledge about texts and genres beyond the sentence level assists the reader.

Rumelhart has provided us with a view of a reader operating multiple scanning systems at different levels in a printed text — feature, letter, letter-cluster, word, syntactic, semantic, sentence and discourse levels. In the beginning reader each knowledge source is limited and still accumulating new knowledge. When teachers are alerted to the different sources of knowledge which can be used by the reader, they begin to notice examples of this use as children read to them. *Supported by the teacher the learner comes gradually to know how and when each kind of information can help with decisions.*

The Holmes/Singer theory of subsystems which power the surface behaviours

Another theory which deals with how the brain is making decisions during reading was called a 'substrata factor theory of reading' by its author, Jack Holmes. In 1960 in the *Proceedings of the Fifth Annual Conference of the International Reading Association,* Holmes asked, 'Just how complex is this ability we call reading?' and he argued that it is supported by an intricate hierarchy of substrata factors that have been mobilised as a psychological working system and pressed into service in accordance with the purposes of the reader (reprinted in Singer and Ruddell 1970, pp. 187–188). In a *Review of Educational Research* he wrote:

> All signs indicate that the psychology of reading is on the threshold of ... a forward thrust and that both stimulating and disturbing days lie immediately ahead. In this new atmosphere, cherished ideas are bound to be challenged, and new ones will contend for their places when the old ones fall. (Holmes and Singer 1964)

In the following decade when I joined different discussion groups of theorist-researchers at two conferences, Holmes' prediction had come true. We had entered an era in which 'theoretical models and processes of reading' (Ruddell et al. 1994) have flourished.

Holmes' theory and its research base are not familiar to many teachers today but it provides a powerful metaphor for those teachers who work with children in early intervention programmes and it deserves their attention. It provides a theoretical basis for a serious discussion of prevention (see Chapter 6), and for hypothesising how the inner control of strategic behaviours and self-extending systems must be constructed by the learner over time. *If the long-term aim of an early intervention programme is to prevent subsequent difficulties, then teachers in such programmes will have to help children develop a power system of the kind Holmes described.*

For thirty years Singer conducted a research programme applying these ideas to old and young learners, and he reviewed these in 1994. He proposed that ' … as individuals learn to read, they develop brain systems which can be sequentially and hierarchically organized [by the learner] to perform a particular literacy task. Such systems are related to improvement in the speed and power of reading.' (p. 913) He described the reader as having to draw on cell assemblies in the brain and organise them into different working systems according to moment-by-moment changes in the tasks or purposes of the reader.

> As a reader's purposes change, or the difficulty of material alters, or the content to be read changes, the reader mobilizes, organizes, and reorganizes substrata factors into momentary working systems in response to each change … Through these changing working systems an individual is able to attain speed and power in reading.' (Singer 1994, pp. 906–907)

Holmes had described reading in a similar way.

> … appropriate, but diverse, subsets of information, learned under different circumstances at different times and therefore stored in different parts of the brain are brought simultaneously into awareness when triggered by appropriate symbols on the printed page. These substrata factors are tied together in a working system, and as their inter-facilitation in the working system increases, the efficiency of the child's reading also increases. Here is an explanation, then, of what may take place when the child learns to read better, by reading. (1970, p. 188)

Holmes defined a working system and explained its neurological status.

> A working system may be described as a dynamic set of sub-abilities which have been mobilized for the purpose of solving a particular problem. Neurologically, a working system is conceived of as a nerve-net pattern in the brain that functionally links together the various substrata factors that have been mobilized into a working communications system. (1970, p. 189)

Reformulation of that definition in terms of advances in neurological science would be enlightening.

McQueen (see Chapter 2) used this theory to link motor behaviour to early reading progress. It would be interesting to study how his account of the changes in literacy processing over time could be related to recent developments in neurological psychology.

Table 2 is a brief summary of Singer's formulation of this theory.

Table 2   A summary of part of Singer's theory which applies to young learners (refer 1994, pp. 909–913)

1)   Over time, as one learns to read, one constructs complex problem-solving structures which are complexly interwoven and functionally organised.

2)   The working systems or mental structures, or functional neural communication networks, are at least three hierarchical assemblies of cells or neurological subsystems for:
- interrelated input (sensation and perception of stimuli)
- mediation (interpreting, inferring and integrating ideas)
- output (response formulation) systems.

3)   The components can be mobilised at any one moment and organised to recognise a word, to associate meaning with a word, and to integrate and transform ideas into an overt response, switching gears according to the demands of the task.

4)   Working systems are being organised and reorganised constantly according to the reader's changing purposes, the shifting demands of the perceived task, and, over time, the increasing competencies.

5)   This explanation of the mental structures and dynamics involved in reading tells of constructing sub-systems from which the individual can compile a functional system required to complete specific literacy tasks at any one moment.

6)   With continued development, with instruction, and with the experience of reading progressively more challenging material, changes occur in the working systems so that the increased speed and power of reading is related to a) changes in available substrata factors, b) increase in the variety of available substrata factors, and c) increase in their integration and consequent inter-facilitation.

There could be more than one route to successful reading, so that two individuals may attain the same level of achievement but by means of different compilations of working systems (p 913)

Yopp and Singer (1994) highlighted change over time in a first grader's reading system and suggested how teachers could facilitate its formation.

Although the teacher can, and tends to, assume [responsibility for] the linguistic and cognitive requirements in the initial period of learning to read, a teacher phase-out from this responsibility and a phase-in of students as they become ready to develop and mobilize their own resources and interact with more demanding stimulus tasks on their own is necessary in order to pace their reading development at an appropriate rate. In short, an inverse relationship exists between the contribution of the teachers' resources and the demands that can be placed on students as their resources develop. The role of the teacher is to control this shift. (p. 388)

When teachers take records of children reading texts those teachers record children searching for particular information, finding it, associating it, linking it to prior experience, moving across visual, phonological, language and semantic information, checking how it is going together, backing up and looking for new hypotheses, self-correcting, reading on, using peripheral vision and syntactic anticipation.

Here is a simple example of how complex these assemblies of working systems must be. After a year in kindergarten (in the United States) a low-achieving boy, about six years of age, was reading *All By Myself* by Mercer Mayer to his teacher. She found him 'absolutely delightful to work with' and said, 'Each day he amazes me.'

Child: I can brush my hair.
Text: I can brush my fur.
Child: That's a funny-looking word for 'hair'. I'll go back and figure it out.

After reading the entire text he turned back as fast as he could to the earlier page, pointed to 'fur', said 'fur' loudly, and slammed the book closed, smiling from ear to ear. Mission accomplished!

This young reader could not put a word-solving system together so he put the solving on hold until the book was finished, made a delayed but correct decision, and seemed proud of his achievement! In the end he assembled a working system to do the job. He was working at a very primitive level of reading but at that level he got the job done. Although I cannot tell precisely what systems contributed to his 'reading' I can record his responses to text and capture evidence of his complex problem-solving. I have some idea of how to increase the efficiency of his problem-solving in upcoming lessons. Average readers in their second year of school really work hard at finding and using systems that solve the challenges of integrating information in texts. And yes, the teacher might have prompted this child to look hard at the first letter, or to analyse 'fur' into its sounds, but when he was allowed to try to solve his own problem he showed he was ready to use his existing 'working systems' to reach a perfect solution, and learn a new word on his own initiative. Rereading the book tomorrow he may well be looking for the 'f'. Finding a route in his existing rudimentary processing system and operating with flexibility, he showed the teacher that he was ready for some more traditional approach to sub-word analysis. The episode was a prompt to the teacher to teach him something new.

This hypothetical construct of working systems broadens our explanation of individual differences, wrote Holmes (1960).

Two children … may read quite differently not only because one child has more and better information stored in this or that particular substrata factor, but also because, for reading, one has a working system that is superior to [or different from] that of the other. (p. 188)

Literacy awareness and orienting to print: formative origins of later working systems

The two theories described above capture many of the features of proficient seven- and eight-year-old reading but how do the theories relate to beginning reading? What is proposed for discussion in this section is an account of primitive working systems involved in orienting the learner to a new kind of task (Clay 1998). Theorists have too often searched for components of major importance for reading after a year or more of instruction, and so have not observed the formative stages of some significant working systems. A concept of 'readiness', or of a preparatory period of confusion before 'real' literacy learning, masked the need to look closely at certain foundational literacy behaviours in their earliest stages.

To briefly review what we know of the origins of the earliest working systems for literacy learning, I have drawn illustrative examples from a well-known account of Paul's reading and writing progress (Bissex 1980). This detailed case study has four advantages: it was a research study; the observations were home-based; it focused particularly on writing; and it reported change over time during this period when a child works on creating the earliest working systems. This is one individual child's record, but my claim is that children take different paths to common outcomes. For example in Paul's case he avoided the complications of text at first until he had some hand-holds on a number of labels and words. (I am not suggesting that this is a standard account of what children do, for it demonstrates an idiosyncratic choice which Paul made.)

Oral language systems are in place

The tapestry of five-year-old oral language was documented in many publications after 1960. The fabric is intricately woven from the articulation and use of phonemes, times heard in songs and verses, vocabulary learned in different environments, conversations which require the construction and reconstruction of sentences in order to be understood, statements turned into negatives and questions, the shape of stories told, and stories read. *The range and depth of oral language knowledge varies greatly from child to child, creating the inevitability of individual differences.*

Children draw upon this oral language which they brought to school as they learn to read and write but at the same time the tasks of literacy learning direct their attention back to units within their own speech of which they were not previously aware. Children's vague ideas about a completed 'utterance', or the breaks between words (word juncture) become more explicit as they learn to read and write continuous texts. The sounds of language become more apparent in their exchanges with texts, particularly when they are trying to write texts. Knowledge stores for oral language structures become more varied and more complex as young talkers talk (Hart and Risley 1999).

Knowledge of the world, a culture, people and books

The cultures of home and community will have created for children very different stores of knowledge about the world and what can happen in it. There may be only a small overlap in the experiences, references and values of any three particular children. Teachers of new entrants astutely search for the knowledge base which an individual child can bring to a text. The individual differences in knowledge about literacy are multiplied when we consider the further differences in knowledge of the world that the reader must bring to the reading and comprehension of texts.

A working system for assembling stories

At two and a half years Paul sat down with a *Curious George* book that had been read to him many times and, turning the pages, told a story that went with the picture. This was not a memorisation of what he had heard but a kind of reconstruction. It was not simply telling the story because it was done in the context of looking at the book and turning the pages, saying aloud sentences that went with the picture on each of those pages. Bissex reports Paul's earliest, most global attempt to give verbal responses to a book full of print (1980, p. 120), *Curious George Gets a Medal* by H.A. Rey.

> He saw some pigs. He saw some pigs. Saw some other pigs.
> (*Turns the page*) They run out.
> (*Turns the page*) But Curious George had gone — gone on a cow.
> He had gone on a cow with a lawnmower.
> (*Turns the page*) Can't find Curious George.
> (*Turns the page*) Can't find Curious George. He had gone.
> (*Turns the page*) They took him on a truck.

Storytelling and storybook reading provide many kinds of preparation for learning to read and write.

First encounters with a visual code and how it works

A major challenge for the young child entering formal instruction is finding out what the marks on paper stand for. A code is many things — laws, regulations, rules, a cipher, secret language, signals, or sign-system. To the novice, print and writing are a set of signs that adults seem to understand. Initially the marks have no sound. Very slowly as preschool children explore the shapes of printed forms (notably in their attempts to write) they come to understand that the marks have something to do with the language they speak. In fact what we say can be put down in print, and what is in print can be spoken by adults. They also learn that print stands for something, usually through names, perhaps their own (Kress 2000). They have yet to find out how this all works. Their early writing tells us what they are exploring.

> At 5:6 (and not yet in first grade) Paul demonstrated his ability to decode with no context cues simple words like baby, stop, yes, duck, and join (Bissex 1980, p. 124) … but he avoided continuous text.

The code knowledge of children starting school will range from none to very extensive. New things are learned quite rapidly in a good school programme but some children will begin school with almost no literacy knowledge and each of the children will know different things. These individual differences result from a lifetime of prior experiences which have been different.

School entrants begin to store a few items in a few knowledge sources

Usually children develop some literacy awareness before they come to school (Clay 1998); they notice a few bits of printed language. Children can select what to attend to, and some children choose to avoid and ignore print. Paul's first reading words were his name and 'Exit', from turnpike travel.

> At 5:3 he was still reading too slowly and uncertainly to get much from continuous text … he tended to focus on captions … He read labels, titles, signs, and writing on … commercial packages, especially cereal boxes. (Bissex 1980, p. 123)

Once children begin formal literacy learning knowledge increases rapidly. At first the young reader works with just a few items and searches for these in the environment. He or she distinguishes print from pictures, letters from words, and has vague notions about texts. Here are examples of children making distinctions.

- A few letters are learned and primitive categories are formed:
  It's got two Timmies (T's) *and no Stephens* (S's).

- Letter clusters are discovered as repeatable 'bits':
  Look! There it is again! ('and' in 'landed' and later in 'sandwiches')

- Word sequences recur in books or in the classroom labels:
  Bill and his car is/are in bed … (stressed in the next line) *are in bed.*

- New encounters call for some rearrangements of ideas:
  I said 'come' but it's 'come-s'.
  It shouldn't have the 's' on there.

Notice the last statement which might be reinterpreted to mean, 'In my reading system at this time, "come" has no "s" on it.' Children comment on things that make two books the same or different, and rich experiences come from being read to. New items capture a child's attention as a result of three things: environmental encounters, self-initiated activities and instruction.

Directing attention outwards: directional, motor and spatial learning

The learner directs attention *outwards* to the print in books. The arbitrary rules used for writing down a language determine the order in which the reader should attend to the print, a set of rules not needed until one tries to read or write. These particular directional constraints are not needed by the child until someone decides the child will become a reader. Learning about the directional rules and the layout of print in books; the first primitive approximations of 'where to begin' reading or writing; selecting a starting point, moving left to right and returning down left; being consistent in this irrespective of which page is being read or the placement of the text on the page; with all these things to learn it is a long journey, and it includes 'reading the spaces'.

The difference in time taken for this journey by identical quadruplets of similar intelligence was six months (Clay 1974). This period of apparent directional 'muddlement' is not part of reading theories and is not addressed in them (except for Downing and Leong's (1982) theory of confusion). Directional behaviours manage the order in which readers and writers attend to anything in print. Gaining control of them is a foundational step in literacy as oral language is matched to written language. Yet most reading theories begin after this has happened. A publisher recently asked me whether directional behaviour was a part of literacy learning!

The teaching implications are clear. The teacher reads texts to small groups of children — stories, news, songs and poems — and demonstrates directional behaviours. The teacher also circulates around small groups of children, helping them to write. Slowly they begin to attend to print within the directional constraints of printed matter and to actively produce print within those same constraints in writing. Items in isolation (rather than texts) do not provide the same opportunities to learn how to direct attention to print in appropriate ways.

Switching attention from oral to written to oral language

Probably the difficulties of co-ordinating oral utterances with language laid out in a book are underestimated (Clay 1991, pp. 113–140). Reading becomes word-controlled as the words in speech are matched to the words in print (Clay 1967; Biemiller 1970; Chall 1983; Ehri 1991), but there is a period of time in early reading when how to co-ordinate these two kinds of behaviours challenges the learner.

> The same month [5:1] Paul brought a book over to me and read the title word by word, pointing to the words as he said them … He seemed aware of word

boundaries in reading before he started indicating them in his writing. (Bissex 1980, p. 122)

Children will try to reread easy stories independently. Group activities with charts for the simplest stories, songs or poems help them to work out how to do this switching from thinking about oral language to thinking about printed language.

Directing attention inwards

The active learner trying to operate on print begins to develop some vague *expectancies* about print.

> On a chapter title of *The House at Pooh Corner*, 'Tiggers don't climb trees', Paul read:
> Tigger don't — Tiggers don't — clim trees — climb trees. (Bissex 1980, p. 126)

Did he think that 'the message of print can be like spoken language', and there is one exact verbal rendering? Or was it some other hunch like:

- it must not disagree with a total context including pictures,

- or it is laid out left to right and top to bottom on the page,

- or it contains groups of marks separated by spaces and stops,

- or it is somehow related to spoken words separated by juncture,

- or it contains patterns constructed out of smaller units,

- or it contains units probably related to sounds in other words?

Fortunately we do not need to programme exercises to teach these things. Most can be developed in a schoolroom version of the bedtime story in which very simple texts are introduced, read and reread in small group situations where children can see large print, watch the teacher's movements which demonstrate where to focus, where and when to move, or isolating bits of text and putting bits together. The novice tries to join in with other children who are reading aloud. Some of this learning will be begun in these groups and will be shaped up in one-to-one reading sessions with a teacher. When a young reader pauses, goes back, reads again, and says, 'Oh! I see how it goes', that reader has possibly just worked out one of those things, and we possibly would not know which one it was.

> Paul noticed an effect of these challenges on him. He told his mother, 'You know what sometimes happens to me when I'm reading? It's so difficult I read backwards.' (Bissex 1980, p. 125) She noticed that about this time he had read 'clol' for 'cool', 'crad' for 'card', and 'push to' for 'push out'.

Attending to several knowledge sources to find one solution

Any correct word in a text fits a matrix of relationships like a piece in a jigsaw puzzle, and any kind of information which is dissonant with a selected response will potentially trigger an awareness of error. Even early attempts to read and write can involve more than one knowledge source. Children give evidence of trying to choose between alternative possibilities quite early in learning to read when there is disagreement between what they say and what is in the text. The reader has a vague awareness that he or she must employ self-instructions (M. Vernon), modes of processing (MacKinnon), strategies (Bruner), operations (Piaget), information processing (Gibson), orienting-exploratory actions (Zaporozhets), probability estimates (Cherry), or problem-solving (Downing) to discover a best-fitting response. (I judge that this bouquet of alternative terms need not be referenced.)

This 'willingness to choose between alternatives' appears before or soon after children enter school and begin to work with familiar, easy texts, often before they move into book reading (Clay 1966, 1967). From willingness to choose the young reader moves quickly to complex error detection and correction behaviours but the first occurrences are noticed by the reader *before* he or she can resolve the difficulty (see the 'fur' example, p. 114). Children act as if aware of some conflict of their response with something in the text. The experience of revising utterances (see Chapter 5) had its origins in the preschool world when children tried to tell something, and had to recast what they said before they could make others understand. The willingness to choose between alternatives foreshadows the developing processing systems which will monitor, correct and control advanced literacy behaviours. A willingness to choose between alternatives leads to a search for more information and this can potentially take processing to new levels of complexity.

Rumelhart (1994) proposed that a (neurological) message centre receives hypotheses from each knowledge source. This centre keeps a running list of hypotheses about the nature of the text so far. Each different knowledge source constantly scans the message centre for the appearance of an hypothesis relevant to its own type of knowledge. Hypotheses are confirmed, disconfirmed and replaced by new hypotheses, and the process continues until some decision is accepted. The most probable hypothesis is determined to be the correct one. Even beginning readers do this checking, as the next example shows. It came from a child who verbalised what she was thinking.

After six months at school this girl was trying to read the phrase 'look after' in the text 'Look after Timothy'. The story was about Mother buying a hat, so 'look at' and 'hats' could have been appropriate in the general context of the story. Unprompted the reader worked aloud, sorting through her possible choices:

> It wouldn't be 'at', it's too long.
> It wouldn't be 'hats'.
> It wouldn't be 'are' [getting closer to the letter sequence], it's too long.

She was willing to choose between alternatives but the problem was not resolved. She left the word 'after' out, read 'Look Timothy' and three pages later she read the word effortlessly. The two language alternatives 'to look at' and 'to look after' could not be 'processed' the first time around, but her efforts at processing were close to the target.

In Rumelhart's explanation the message centre took care of such processing. He said it monitored position along a line of text, the knowledge source of the hypothesis (letter, sound, word or phrase), and alternative hypotheses from other knowledge sources. Rumelhart illustrated how this would work if the reader were reading the noun phrase 'the car'. An hypothesis that the first word in the string is the word 'the' is supported by the hypothesis that the first letter of the string is 't', and supports the hypothesis that the string begins with a noun phrase. *An hypothesis can be generated by any knowledge source (and possibly from more than one source simultaneously).* The processing system makes a decision and checks out its implications. If the attempt seems to be a misfit with the information available it will take a bit longer but the system will eventually settle for an hypothesis that it can accept. Deciding between hypotheses will depend upon what is stored in the various knowledge sources, and how well they are linked up for this crucial decision. (Singer would call this 'assembling working systems'.)

In this example Paul provides a demonstration of trying to 'read' but without the benefit of structure or meaning.

> I was reading a paperback novel. Paul leaned over my shoulder and from some distance began reading the top line of tiny print. The text was:
>> 'one's nerves but finally so familiar ... '
> Paul read: 'one's never but ...' (made several attempts and triumphantly figured out) 'finally so' (and after a struggle) 'family-air'. (Bissex 1980, p. 128)

That attempt contrasts with another record which captures thinking aloud while reading alone, and trying to link word-solving strategies with semantic and syntactic information. In the text which challenged another child, something was eating '... the fresh green leaves'. The child said:

> '... the f-fish ... fresh
> Now what could be fresh?'
> She looked carefully at the illustration.
> Returning to the print and sounding out the letters she said, 'gr ... ee ... green leaves.'
> Returning to the beginning of the phrase she combined her findings:
> '... the fresh green leaves.'

To describe this reading as a left to right sounding out of the phonemes in words is to ignore how the reader used different kinds of information to get the message from that text.

Cycles of parsing from print to message to print to …

By the time they have been at school for six to twelve months most children demonstrate clearly a halting model of reading. It helps if they have some idea of what the story is about gained from an introduction by the teacher, from the illustrations, and/or from a look through the book from beginning to end. They focus on the beginning of sentences, attend to print, get a sentence starter and then work through the sentence from print to message to print to message, word after word. When a word requires problem-solving they will shift quickly among meaning, letters, sounds and structure, choosing between alternatives. They move from print to message and back recursively at each decision point, word after word, as the 'fresh green leaves' example showed. Proficient readers at this stage work left to right across a line, word by word, parsing the word groups, getting meaning to aid the solving and using solving to clinch the meaning. They are making links within and across the linear text using different kinds of stored knowledge. Rumelhart proposed that information from more than one source is needed to confirm and reject hypotheses arising from any single source.

A teacher's urging to 'Have a go' or 'You try it' or 'What do you think it could be?' is an invitation to form some hypothesis somewhere in the processing system and make a decision. In contrast if the child is only expected to respond to isolated items like letters, or sounds, or words from a vocabulary list (and this happens when children are not expected or allowed to read texts), these activities might add items to some knowledge sources without necessarily creating links across knowledge sources. After only a brief time at school, children can establish many ways of checking upon the words in the text they are reading, if they are allowed to.

Important learning which supports the decision-taking has to do with layout, position and the orientation of signs and symbols, movement left to right across words and lines of print, and matching oral and visual patterns.

At this stage as the children write or read they are doing two things well: 1) they are making up stories, and 2) they are checking them in detail against what they have learned about print. Then a slow gradual process of change occurs as substitutions made for text words (errors) come to match most of the visible information, and the sentence makes sense and could have continued that way. The child will rapidly make a self-correction if he or she notices some detail that does not fit. Making substitutions (which match on visual, structure and meaning features) and self-corrections, and rapid processing, are features of assembling effective working systems early in literacy acquisition. On familiar (easy) material this work is carried out quite quickly and smoothly; on harder text (more difficult for any of a number of reasons), the back and forth processing of print to message to print to message can be observed again.

Two different extremes of behaviour can be observed on the same page of reading by an observant teacher. Figure 3 represents the initial slow responding when the reader is building a processing system in Example A and rapid reading of what is known in Example B.

Figure 3   The processing system may be under construction (A) or already exist (B)

Example A	Example B
Processing system under construction	**Processing system is available**
• Slow working, linking and deciding	• Rapid processing
• Attention given to:	• Attention given to:
— learning how to pick up information	
— learning how to link information	— rapid parallel processing
— learning how to check a decision	
• Action	• Action

If teachers want to see the rapid recognition that is represented in Example B they have to help the learner to build the working system that is represented in Example A. They have to know that, with opportunities to problem-solve text, the effortful processing on the left gives way to the fast recognition of the right example. The payoff is that the working system for solving on the left remains available for any new text challenges. The figure represents literacy processing in a grossly simplified form.

Change over time is recognised by teachers who can judge a word read or written to be:

- new

- only just known

- successfully problem-solved

- easily produced but easily thrown

- well-known (recognised in most contexts)

- known in many variant forms.

The first changes occur quickly, as this example shows.

> When Paul was 5:10 [Bissex] noticed a good example of several ways of 'knowing'. Paul read his first whole book *Go, Dog, Go!* which he first attempted at 5:7. 'And I only needed one word,' he remarked proudly afterwards. The word he needed was 'those'. After [Bissex] supplied it, [Paul] recognized it the next time it appeared, but the time after that he hesitated and then finally sounded it out 'th-oh-ss' and then 'th-oh-z', correcting according to his knowledge of real (spoken) words. (Bissex 1980, p. 129)

Paul had established the network of strategic behaviours needed to do all the correct reading plus the required word-solving in that example and this may well be thought of as a satisfactory foundation for constructing a self-extending system.

Most theoretical models of reading begin their descriptions about acquisition from the point where children have already created links between language and print, meaning and print, visual perception and print, have caught on to the directional rules of print, and have learned to work in primitive ways with some parts of these essential working systems. The existing models give little attention to the early formative period, even though entry to formal schooling should force our attention to much of this learning. People question whether things like directional behaviour are really part of learning to read, and assume that merely teaching letter-sound relationships can stand in lieu of helping a child to bring into existence the broad range of working systems or neural networks needed for being able to deal with print.

Processing activities and processing changes

There is great relief for the teacher, the child, the parent and the administrator or psychologist-assessor when the child consistently reads or writes a new word rapidly and accurately (as in the rapid processing example in Figure 3). There seems no need to ask how or why it went well, or what changed to bring about this effective responding on text. However, teachers of young learners find the concept of in-the-head processing comprehensible; it allows them to relate the behaviours they can observe to their assumptions about what the child knows and needs to know.

Processing

One of the explanations of RR's success with the professional development of its teachers is that its theory provides them with a language for discussing the changes involved in early literacy progress. Teachers talk about shifts in processing, referring to all the activities happening in the learner's head, brain, mind or neural networks! Processing is also analysed in the error and self-correction analysis of Running Records. We found that it did not help teachers to talk about perceptual or cognitive activities as these require some background in psychology. It would be premature and probably unhelpful to develop a model of neural networks with aroused and interactive functional circuits changing themselves as more complex circuits are activated. It is important for teachers to note that psychologists have developed two different bodies of knowledge around word processing and sentence processing (see p. 80 or McKoon and Ratcliff 1998). Pending future research a concept of processing, though irritatingly vague, is currently utilitarian.

Parallel processing during word-solving

In Rumelhart's (1994) model of processing, the skilled brain can apparently work on different kinds of information simultaneously, which he described as a highly interactive parallel processing system (pp. 886–889). Like Bruner (1957) he assumed a continuity between perception and cognitive processing, but unlike Bruner he used the word 'perception' to cover the entire process (p. 893). Competent adults faced with signing a legal document provide an example of highly complex processing. They may say they are 'reading the fine print' or 'reading between the lines' when they are probably checking two things meticulously: 1) that they have understood all the precise but invisible relationships between the words, and 2) that they are not inventing relationships that are not there.

Successive processing

In published accounts of preschool learning, different children are described as attending to different facets of literacy activities (Ferreiro and Teberovsky 1982; Weinberger, Hannon and Nutbrown 1990) and sometimes they are observed actively combining knowledge in interesting ways. Studies of children who have just come to school show them moving across print, selecting some letters or words for attention, or making up sentences to match the pictures. As they try to read and write they go through a process of discovery of how what they know relates to anything about the print on a page or in a book.

Research reports of young children reading produce evidence of beginning readers picking up different kinds of information in sequence. A child might attend to the first letter, then glance at the picture, return to the word, and reread the line. They find it easier to focus on one type of information but can be prompted to take another kind of information into account.

Gradually young children come to act like readers and attend to more than one kind of information to solve words and phrases (pictures, story, schema, letters, words, catchy stretches of language, novel ideas and new names for new objects). The proficient reader selects a response to a particular word and seems to take visual, phonological and structural information and meanings into account, even when the solving fails. Even a proficient child can be caught attending to 'this before that' when the text is hard, rather than pulling all the information into the decision. This is probably related to how fast the knowledge sources can identify information and have it accepted by the message centre.

Quite early children can be observed to check one kind of information with another and when two sources of information produce competing alternatives the reader often notices that something is not right. For familiar words on easy text the processing becomes rapid and it appears to arise simultaneously from several different features at once. Young children mix slow sequential processing on 'harder words' with faster processing on 'easy words'.

Searching, choosing and rejecting processes appear in records of young children's reading behaviours. Knowing a few letters or words allows a child to actively search for identity, similarity or difference between what he or she says and the text. Differences are easy to detect because they need only occur in one detail or knowledge source whereas identity must be established as correspondence in every respect. Young readers after one year at school already adjust their processing to the demands of the task, processing differently when reading easy, instructional and challenging texts.

The illustrations in books may 'teach' the beginner to combine messages from the pictures with the messages in print, a preliminary to understanding that his or her own prior knowledge relates to print. Rereading is an act of monitoring and a versatile strategy used either to confirm responses or to search for new input. It allows the reader to pay more attention to invisible relationships between words or to more of the visible features of letters or words, in order to gather up necessary information for solving the problem that was not activated on the first run (Clay 1966, p. 275). I recorded young readers doing this; O'Leary (1997, p. 35) described this as a 're-running start'.

Studies of self-correcting behaviours show how beginning readers of texts operate sequentially when solving errors. The fact that readers self-monitor and self-correct is signalled by their verbal protests, repetition, revised attempts, and going back to a previous part of the text. Self-monitoring and self-correcting appear early, in the first attempts at text reading, and they persist as good indicators of changes in inner control in oral reading for two or three years (Clay 1991; MacKinnon 1957).

Word level problem-solving uses information from both invisible phonological, semantic and syntactic links between words, and visible sub-word features. The ultimate check for establishing the identity of a word may be in terms of either smaller units, such as sounds, letters or clusters, or larger units of language such as sentence, text or discourse units.

A sentence constructed word after word sets readers the task of finding a 'next word' which could continue the sentence grammatically, hold the meaning, and fit with the story. These higher level checks must be combined with visible information in the print. (This means that the same message may be signalled in several ways.) Different kinds of information will converge on a correct response or, conversely, produce dissonance at an error. The child learns to detect errors, to correct them, and to make decisions.

According to a Holmes/Singer theory the task of early readers would be to build a power system:

- which allows at first for successive processing

- which constructs and expands Rumelhart's knowledge sources, actively forming hypotheses and making decisions

- which searches for different kinds of information in print and chooses between alternatives

- which tries to work with speed and fluency whenever possible.

There are few signs of successive processing as decision-making becomes more rapid and substitutions for words match the text word closely on several criteria. Successive processing usually appears when the input is new, and in younger children, but fast processing of known letters and words can be recorded when the neurological network is still quite primitive, and even simple literacy responses can arise from using several knowledge sources.

Strategic control over processing

Unfortunately the term 'strategy' has several meanings in educational literature, and one of these refers to directing oneself verbally (which implies also verbalising about what one is doing). While this might be conceptually valid when discussing the reading of older children, my studies of proficient young readers suggest that it is not appropriate to teach for that type of meta-cognitive awareness in five- to six-year-old children. Most things we do as readers need to operate below the conscious level most of the time so that fast and effective processing of the print is achieved and attention is paid to the messages rather than to the work done to get to the message. How this comes about must be probed in future research.

Bruner (1957) defined a strategy as a decision process which involved the search for discriminatory cues that will code the stimulus into appropriate categories. Some psychologists call activities 'strategic' when there is a programmatic assembly of operations aimed at a common goal (Wood 1978). A simple example would be when a) directional behaviours, b) visual recognition, and c) letter-sound knowledge have to be combined to respond to a teacher's simple demand to 'Sound out that word.' It is as complicated as that! It calls for assembling a system across three disparate processes: how does the child come to direct attention to visual features in the text, and the phonological possibilities, and search, link, decide and respond. The term 'strategic' is used in this book in the limited sense of knowing how to work on words, sentences and texts to extract the messages they convey.

To learn to act strategically the learner must find some input information and act upon it. A vague sense of success may lead to similar activity being used again on other words with similar features. Knowledge of letters, sounds and words plus some strategic management will allow the reader to go beyond the known to respond effectively to novel items in a text. Young children who learn a few past tense verbs ending in 'ed' — 'played', 'mowed', 'tipped', 'stopped' — can be heard taking the risk of adding similar endings to novel words. We notice their attempts on irregular words — 'throwed', 'satted', 'drinkded'. The children have a way of getting to past tense verb endings and the behaviour has been called rule-governed. No rule is articulated. The solving is not a conscious activity; nobody verbalised it, and no one made the children say it to themselves.

Such descriptions of strategic behaviour are close to Singer's concept of assembling input-mediation-output systems which pick up, integrate, interpret and infer in the head. Behavioural records usually only capture combined behaviours and do not reveal the separate input-mediation-output systems which produce those behaviours. I have used the term 'strategic activity' to refer to what goes on in any of the aspects of processing which Singer proposes, when the brain:

- picks up information,

- works on it,

- makes a decision

- and evaluates the response,

as well as to the overarching execution of that sequence. The young learner attends to external information in the printed text, initiates mental activities, and reads aloud. I reserve the word 'strategy' for in-the-head neural activity initiated by the learner, and hidden from the teacher's view. Given this gloss of 'strategy', teachers cannot teach or demonstrate strategies; they can infer them from the behaviours they record, and they can encourage learners to be strategic by the ways in which they teach.

In waking hours we work assiduously to overcome uncertainty. If we look at an object which was specially designed to create a sense of uncertainty (like a photograph of a magnified, well-known object which shows only a small part of it), the eye and brain scan the object and its context searching for cues that will reduce that uncertainty. We try some cognitive activity, like verbalising its characteristics, or searching our memories, and we choose between the possibilities, discarding some. 'In-the-head strategies' work something like that.

We may never have definitive descriptions of what a child needs to do while learning to read; all we can observe is the work children do as they read continuous texts aloud, and how they go back and alter their decisions, correcting themselves. This is the evidence teachers work with and one reason why early reading has to be a read-aloud activity. Control systems are developed to manage the different types of information and to manage the assembly of working systems needed to get the solving done. Records of behaviour taken over time can be analysed to map the changes in how children are monitoring their own reading and the ways in which they are using syntactic, semantic, visual and phonological information.

The operations carried out when we attend, remember, link and recall information, deliberately or (almost) automatically, tend to be highly practised. We solve anagrams and mentally fit shapes into a geometric space. A verbal puzzle about travelling east for 40 km, and south for another 40 km, challenges us, so that after several more turns we can still describe a position in relation to the starting point. People manipulate information in different ways.

Young children are usually confused if we try to put these mental activities into words. Teachers cannot teach the learner how to orchestrate this complexity but they can support the child who is constructing effective reading processes, pointing up relevant information with direct or indirect prompts. If the teacher does not understand literacy processing, prompting will be hit or miss.

'Reading work' is a neutral term I have used with teachers for talking about activity within and across Singer's three systems when the reader directs attention, picks up and uses information, monitors the 'reading', makes decisions, and activates self-correcting to revise a prior decision. Some of this reading work is signalled by behaviours teachers can observe and record. Effective processing should not be laboured, even when the reader is highly focused on problem-solving; it must become faster and more efficient, and for the most part covert and not observable. A mature reader continues to problem-solve texts, using analogies, personal rules, hypotheses and tentative solutions awaiting further information later in this or other texts.

Learning 'how to do something' (to work with input, mediation and output) is powerful learning. A couple of new items read correctly ('then', 'there') is a small gain when compared with consolidating the strategy of knowing how to cross-check the letters in sequential order with an analysis of their phonemic structure, checking each move, and all unprompted and in your head.

The processing necessary for reading texts can bring the novice reader into contact with new items in print, new links to known features, new features of grammar, new vocabulary, or new ways of expressing things, grist for the mill of knowledge sources. Readers of texts are drawn into new ways of solving and gain new insights about solving by the challenges of new texts. The young proficient reader is soon able to make fast, hardly-noticeable decisions and change direction at any point in the processing path (Helen in Chapter 2), and is doing what I do as a reader of texts which challenge me.

A few items and a few powerful strategies can set a beginning reader on a path towards a self-extending system quite early. Theoretically I assume that it is not the items that lift the children to new levels of text difficulty but the strategic power to use what is known in the service of problem-solving the unknown.

Chapter 5 focuses on the special case of self-correction as one executive or controlling process to illustrate processing in some detail. The act of self-correcting seems to create more awareness in learners of perceptual and cognitive processing. Some examples illustrate how this might happen.

1) Child: The   boy/SC
    Text: The   big   boy took his bag.

The attempt was a good fit for meaning, syntax, first letter and size of word but the self-correction restructured the noun phrase to fit with the visual information. Sophisticated? Not necessarily. The child may merely have skipped the word 'big' and attended to 'boy'! We cannot know.

2) Child: Mum got out her k———
                 to knit a woolly jacket.
                 That should be n-nitting. Is it?
    Teacher: What do you think?
    Child: It is.

The child protests about the conflict of phonemic and visual information, *is forced by the teacher to make a decision*, accepts congruence except for the first letter in the word, and is left with something to resolve. The child learns that things are not always predictable! The reading problem is temporarily solved, but the reading processing system has received a jolt at the phonemic level. A change in the processing system is imminent. The teacher at that moment in scaffolding the child's processing, chose to prompt the child to make a decision rather than launch into explanations about silent letters. Having succeeded in reinforcing the child's attempts at processing by reaching a solution, the teacher could handle the silent letter in a throwaway comment like, 'That's a letter we don't sound. Some words are like that.'

3) Child: Don't/SC   open the door   when   I'm   away
    Text : Do not   open the door   while   I'm   away

    Child: or the   wolf   comes/R/SC   come   in
    Text: or the   wolf   will   come   in.

The reader restructures the verb phrase to match with the visual information.

In early reading and writing it is probably no more than a sense that something is wrong that triggers a self-correction but by the second year some children can become articulate about some of their self-corrections. What happens at self-corrections, and over time to self-correcting, needs to be part of an explanation of early reading progress. (See Chapter 5.)

I recommend to teachers of young children that they use the word 'strategic' to refer to the directing of in-the-head activities which are initiated by the learner. These are hidden from the teacher's view and only inferred. Teachers tentatively infer from behaviours how the child is processing the information. They cannot teach or demonstrate a strategy for the learner.

There are many things we have yet to find out

What is the developmental build-up of the processing activities described in this chapter or the tentative table of processing behaviours in Chapter 2?

At entry to school the new learner uses existing processing systems:

- for syntax (including parsing a spoken sentence word by word)

- for the meanings of words and larger stretches of language

- for the visual forms of objects, scenes and pictures

- for making sense of all the activities in a preschool child's world

- for understanding stories.

Talking, understanding, looking and storying involve the child in processing information from the environment. It would be sensible and economical for school systems to adopt curricula and practices which capitalise on that prior learning.

At entry to school new processing competencies have to be developed to deal with written language. This raises many questions.

- Does the school allow a new learner to bring what he or she already knows to what he or she now has to do, to become a reader and a writer?

- How does a learner learn to work on the different kinds of information in the text? Separately, at first; and then in some integrated way?

- How does a reader learn to search, cross-check, link, make decisions and evaluate those decisions while working across print?

- How and when does a learner initiate problem-solving from context and meaning at several levels? From oral language knowledge? From analogy with known words? From breaking the word apart in some way? From using letter-sound knowledge?

- What makes the learner cluster letters and work on chunks of words?

- Does the learner learn to deal with these possibilities one before the other, or at one and the same time?

- How does the learner avoid the dominance of any type of information and keep the processing flexible?

Most theories and recommended practices neglect the earliest phase of literacy achievement described here. They jumpstart the child into learning a prescribed curriculum of items sequenced arbitrarily, or a list of skills. Such approaches ignore existing competencies. Could we work with a curriculum of competencies?

For decades a concept of readiness shrouded the earliest phase of literacy acquisition in a haze and it was displaced more recently by the ambiguous term 'emergent literacy' which now has enough multiple meanings for me to abandon the term. There are still many things we must study to enhance our understanding of the earliest working systems which support literacy learning, and we need to find out more about how the demands of continuous texts aid early literacy learning. When research described children's actual behaviours in new entrant classrooms, the concept of readiness was useless as an explanatory concept.

What successive integrations of early behaviours occur?

When we give a child a simple book expecting him or her to 'read' it, or ask the child to compose a message which the teacher will scribe, such deliberate attempts to teach literacy must coax several literacy processes into action all at the same time.

Children enter school with individual histories which are different, and schools must provide for children whose prior competencies are different. A prescribed sequence of learning will not engage all children. Qualitative changes occur over the first six months of school, and all children must learn to problem-solve texts by bringing very different kinds of information together. The shifts they make to bring different systems together are signalled in their behaviours and I suggest three examples.

1) They make unstable newly-learned responses to print (locating, or looking, sounding parts and making letters), and these occur erratically, make unpredictable appearances and gradually become consistent.

2) New integrations appear, such as when the teacher notices that most error substitutions have an appropriate initial sound.

3) Observable behaviours (like pointing or self-correction) once used, disappear into some other integration, no longer needed as props most of the time but still available if there is a need to draw them into the solving process, momentarily.

This RR teacher observing a teacher she had trained came close to observing 'integration' if that is possible.

Belinda was reading a new book early in her RR sessions. Her teacher had a clear theme for the lesson, to encourage Belinda to monitor her reading by checking visually the words she knew well. She usually relied on the pictures, the meaning and the language structures but did not look carefully at the printed words. Her inner battle to reorganise her way of working and take on this new learning became apparent when she said thoughtfully, 'My head is so full of things I can't read hardly.' She did not seem to be frustrated but rather to be thinking aloud about the struggle going on in her head.

Phonemic awareness (Elkonin 1973) might be traced developmentally from weak beginnings, through clear awareness and use, to its shift into more sophisticated kinds of mediation of letter clusters and chunks, and later, to solving multi-syllabic words at speed. Successful readers and silent readers give no observable evidence of the phonemic awareness of almost every word they read correctly. The type and timing of such shifts across languages differ because the characteristics of languages differ: teaching procedures for RR in Spanish emphasise different components at different times from the procedures used for English. Astute observation over time is necessary to capture the emergent integrations being exhibited by individual learners, and to notice the fade-out periods which occur as early primitive systems become part of more efficient processing. The phrase 'in some integrated way' is a valuable concept in search of a thorough analysis.

Can a gradient of text difficulty induce change?

Children can use their control of oral language and knowledge of the world, and as-yet-limited literacy knowledge to move up through a gradient of difficulty in texts. They are aided by teachers who arrange their opportunities and support their efforts. As texts are read and written different kinds of learning are drawn together, coupled, integrated or changed. New items of vocabulary are added, frequently constructed from familiar bits, roots, prefixes, patterns, clusters, chunks and analogies. In the short time it takes a budding reader to read through many texts on an increasing gradient of difficulty (see Figure 1 in Chapter 2), the network of strategic activity gets massive use, expands in range of experience, and increases in efficiency. This happens providing the reader is not struggling.

We might then predict that poor readers do not merely have lower cumulative scores of phonemic awareness, letter-sound knowledge or words recognised: they are failing to build a network of perceptual and cognitive strategies for decision-making as they work across texts; they are failing to pull together separate processing activities into smooth, integrated sequences (Bruner 1974); and they are failing to develop cognitive control mechanisms. If they do not have opportunities to do successful processing, such changes will not occur.

How can learners extend their own knowledge sources?

Children begin literacy learning with limited ways of making decisions in each knowledge source (Rumelhart's list extended by other early working systems described on pp. 115–124 of this chapter). As the child actively works at reading and writing, content builds in each knowledge source because massive opportunities are provided to read and write stories pitched at an appropriate difficulty level. A broad-band curriculum will have a higher likelihood of connecting with a particular child's competencies than a narrow curriculum prescription. Narrowing the focus will narrow the range of individual differences for which the programme will be successful.

Inevitably, new literacy learners work with limited and inaccurate knowledge of letter forms, of letter-sound associations, or of words, and their awareness of the hidden relationships in texts is being aroused by exposure to activities which allow for this. They can be observed extending their own knowledge, going beyond the information given (Wood 1998). Children who actively participate in literacy activities become exposed to more and more perceptual comparisons and pay attention to more hidden relationships in texts.

How can learners extend their own working systems?

What mediates the changes? What is it that teachers need to support? Studies of change might be undertaken in a myriad of ways and I do not want to point in any particular direction. The examples below are intended to capture how varied this search might be.

- Self-correction changes before observers' eyes from a return to the beginning of the line (or sentence), to a return along several words, to a return along the word being processed, to articulating only the first sound of a word, before it disappears altogether. These shifts can occur in proficient readers in the first year of school. The response system no longer has to make a fresh start, but makes a targeted, momentary adjustment, and continues. The processing is very 'together'; re-running is not extended back along the line but has become restricted to solving parts of words. It looks like the local parsing that is common in speech as we choose our words carefully.

- Changes in speed of reading between familiar and new texts are marked at first but before long proficient readers maintain much the same speed on most of their reading, with only slight changes of speed at a puzzling encounter (see Ng, Chapter 2).

- Changes occur from single-word and single-letter processing to using parts of words in clusters/chunks/syllables/roots. Pieces from 'known items' are used to construct 'new knowns' as children build up their word knowledge and letter-cluster knowledge sources. If that is not occurring the system cannot readily extend itself.

- The change from word-by-word reading to smoother phrasing with intonation is observed, not just on easy books but on novel material.

- Multi-syllabic words are probably processed differently from single-syllable words. How and when do these changes occur? Perhaps two processes develop side by side, one for word-by-word reading which is noticeable early, and one for longer words which does not have many opportunities to show itself early because of the texts used.

- Could we study the subsequent learning that follows in individual subjects for whom we record a new insight (Kay's 'come'/'comes'; the 'nitting' solution; or an 'and, landed, sandwiches' discovery of chunks)? Where did each of these insights go next? In what form is the discovery settled into the processing system?

Shifts in mediation which children verbalise should make us think about other changes in mediation to look for. At an imaginary level, the primitive network which solves an early problem is probably extended in two ways: first, frequent successful problem-solving would strengthen accessibility of that specific kind of processing, but solutions found to new challenges should add to the entire neural network aroused to complete the solving.

How can learners sustain flexibility across the systems?

The high-progress child acquires a variety of approaches and develops versatility in dealing with the different aspects of knowledge (for example letter forms, or word forms). A recent study of how a teacher scaffolds writing opportunities (Hobsbaum, Peters and Sylva 1996; see Chapter 2, p. 75ff) describes change over time in writing in one-to-one teaching and illustrates the variety and flexibility needed in a writing processing system. The authors reported that, over time, children take some control of:

- a monitoring strategy that holds the message in working memory and rereads it in order to locate the next move

- some kind of word recall such as (a) identifying the oral word without searching, with no obvious use of phonetic cues, or (b) applying reading knowledge to writing with no apparent analysis

- the regulating of surface features like spacing and letter formation and punctuation (and later, handwriting)

- the search for phonemes in speech, articulating and going straight to the written letter without the need to name that letter or sound in the process of writing it.

The authors described how, when and in what manner children took control of aspects of the literacy task and how the adult control was 'faded' leaving the learner to work on the sub-components of the task. The teacher retained responsibility for getting the task completed and for increasing the challenge of the subsequent task. The study discussed how flexibility is supported and teacher control faded.

It is the teachers' role to take children up into more difficult material, but they need to remember that widening the range of text types is also necessary to encourage the flexibility which the system needs. When children can return to reread a wide variety of familiar material, this provides two types of learning opportunities: firstly, there is the opportunity to orchestrate alternative ways of processing information in print; and secondly, there is the opportunity to read those texts with increasing levels of independence (Clay 1991). Integration, independence and flexibility are possible when children have wide-ranging chances to read texts which are well within their competency, in addition to working on unfamiliar texts at the edge of their working knowledge. Studies of how processing seems to change across the first, second, third and fourth (spaced) readings are informative (Askew 1993). A flexible processing system allows learners to mobilise or construct assemblies of working systems which could be different for different activities, in both reading and writing. Two things have to increase in efficiency: a) using what is known, and knowing how to find it, and b) taking on the new, and knowing how to use it to solve more problems, and where to store it among existing knowledge so that it can be retrieved when needed.

Many of the features highlighted in Singer's theory and research analyses were captured at a primitive and formative stage within the first years of learning to read in the 'processing research studies' of five- to eight-year-old children (Chapter 2).

Research on older readers (Guthrie 1973) suggested that a goal of reading instruction was to help the reader build a knowledge of components of reading into a single process so that the components become mutually facilitating. There are two alternate ways to reach that goal. Advocacy in the past has encouraged teachers to focus first on the components to be learned, the items like sounds and words and the skills needed to work with the items. It was thought to be satisfactory to teach children component skills, and leave them to go through some combining, reshuffling, remodelling or transforming processes later. Many authorities would now consider it unfortunate that educators ever came to believe that they could first attend to establishing decoding and years later bring comprehension to centre stage. Today many authorities would recommend that different competencies should be fostered together from the beginning of literacy learning.

There is much for us to learn about from future research. While these different theories are studied in depth, the pragmatic approach has been to conceptualise progress as represented by a gradient of difficulty in the texts read, stretching from the earliest simple stories to high school texts. Progressive lifts in difficulty level of texts challenge readers to access a wider range of working systems. To sustain successive change the system must work tentatively and change flexibly.

The self-extending system

A self-extending system can be thought of as bringing about new forms of mediation, or altering an existing working system to become more effective, or compiling more effective assemblies of systems. Such changes would come from powerful interactions with teachers, from building larger reading vocabularies, from comparing and evaluating decisions, from extending a network of strategies for problem-solving, and from increasing the range of texts read and therefore the opportunities to work the system. Singer's theory begins with an assumption of simple neural networks which expand and cell assemblies which become more complex. A commonly observed example of how an early primitive processing system can develop itself may be observed in those readers who quickly shift to reading levels far beyond the average of their classes, seven-year-old students who sound as if they read like those who are eleven years old and get similar test scores but often do not have the language or world knowledge to understand all that they can seem to read quite well.

> A self-organizing system is one in which some kind of higher-level pattern emerges from the interactions of multiple simple components without the benefit of a leader, controller or orchestrator. (A. Clark 1996, p. 73)

Or as Williams (1968) reported:

> When a child is reading independently, both reading correctly and problem-solving at difficulties this would contribute to a self-extending system. (p. 50–51, Chapter 2)

In an extensive psychological review of research on self-regulatory mechanisms Karoly (1993) is highly critical of the achievements in psychology to date relating to a concept of self-regulation. He issued this warning:

> In its modern cast, the topic of self-regulation has captured the creative imagination of a variety of researchers. The empirical results of their work, however satisfying, should be viewed with an appreciation of their recency, their loose ends or unfinished agenda, their restricted phenomenal range, and their limited pragmatic yield to date.

It is a little too soon to be making this a major explanatory concept for how children learn to read by reading. Apparently some very careful research work needs to be undertaken.

Conclusion

Assuming that classroom tasks are predominantly directed to reading continuous texts, and that all of Rumelhart's knowledge sources contribute to progress, then changes over time reported in studies of high progress readers in the early years of school, in different languages, countries, educational settings and instructional programmes, can be accommodated at the highest level within a Holmes/Singer-like theory. We need further refinement of the general explanations in their writings together with *a heightened respect for the critical factor of individual difference* when we conceptualise the progress of young children in the early years of formal instruction.

Rumelhart's list of knowledge sources are conceptually helpful but must be supplemented. A body of early learning essential for literacy development falls under the collective heading of 'Literacy awareness and orientation to print', and includes knowing:

- how to assemble stories

- that print can be written

- that attention must follow the rules of direction

- that symbols have only one orientation

- how to switch attention out to the page and back into the head

- how to work with complex information and come to decisions.

Children have to adapt their preschool working systems to make them work on the written code, learn some new skills, lay down the foundational knowledge sources and learn how knowledge from very different sources can be found, assembled and integrated.

My account arises from my use of theory as a tool to help me think about what could power the progress from beginning reading to independent silent reading, a tool to be honed and sharpened, and in due course replaced by a better-crafted tool. It is possible to relate an acquisition model of changing competencies to a Holmes/Singer substrata-factor theory. Acts of reading are acts of construction rather than instruction. Most instruction, defined as the adopted curriculum plus the craft of teaching, serves to fill out children's knowledge sources. Just as adults know how to talk with preschoolers in ways that enable them to master oral language, so teachers hearing children read or sharing their attempts to write are somehow able to reinforce progress for most children. Because continuous texts of increasing difficulty are used much of the time, the reader is pushed to develop new strategies. Teachers hear it 'all coming together' and they reinforce and scaffold this. Perhaps this accounts for why 80–90 per cent of children learn to read in any reading programme. Perhaps some major variable theories make it harder for some children.

If the reader thinks that a complex theory of literacy learning is too difficult for the classroom teacher, it gives pause for thought that classroom teachers across the world have become RR teachers who work with such a complex theory because it helps them to accelerate the progress of the children who are being left behind by their classmates for any of a number of reasons. Even though a simpler theory may suffice for most children, *I am certain that a view of complexity is the kind of understanding required to deliver results in an early intervention programme aiming to prevent subsequent literacy difficulties in as many children as possible.*

Whether teaching in classrooms might be driven by a complex theory to foster these changes over time would be a topic for another paper. For now I must side with Holdaway (1979) when he wrote about 'self-regulation' and agree that 'There is no better system to control the complexities and intricacies of each person's learning than that person's own system operating with genuine motivation and self-determination within reach of humane and informed help.' (p. 170)

References

Anderson, R.C. 1985. The role of reader's schema in comprehension, learning and memory. In H. Singer and R.B. Ruddell, eds, *Theoretical Models and Processes of Reading* (Third Edition). Newark, DE: International Reading Association.

Anderson, R.C. and P.D. Pearson. 1984. A schema-theoretic view of basic processes in reading comprehension. In P.D. Pearson, ed., *Handbook of Reading Research.* New York: Longman.

Askew, B.J. 1993. The effect of multiple readings on the behaviors of children and teachers in an early intervention program. *Reading and Writing Quarterly: Overcoming Learning Difficulties* 9: 307–315.

Biemiller, A. 1970. The development of the use of graphic and contextual information as children learn to read. *Reading Research Quarterly* 6: 75–96.

Bissex, G. 1980. *GNYS AT WRK: A Child Learns To Write and Read.* Cambridge, MA: Harvard University Press.

Britton, B.K. and S.M. Glynn. 1987. *Executive Control Processes in Reading.* Hillsdale, NJ: Lawrence Erlbaum.

Brown, A.L., A.S. Palincsar and B.B. Armbruster. 1994. Instructing comprehension-fostering activities in interactive learning situations. In R.B. Ruddell, M.R. Ruddell and H. Singer, eds, *Theoretical Models and Processes of Reading* (Fourth Edition), pp. 757–787. Newark, DE: International Reading Association.

Bruner, J. 1957. On perceptual readiness. *Psychological Review* 64: 123–152.

———. 1974. Organization of early skilled action. In M.P.M. Richard, ed., *The Integration of the Child into the Social World*, pp. 167–184. London: Cambridge University Press.

Bryant, P. and L. Bradley. 1985. *Children's Reading Problems.* Oxford: Blackwell.

Campbell, R.L. 1993. Commentary. In A. Demetriou, A. Efklides and M. Platsidou, *The Architecture and Dynamics of Developing Mind. Monographs of the Society for Research in Child Development*, No. 234, 58: 168–191.

Chall, J.S. 1983. *Stages of Reading Development.* New York: McGraw-Hill.

Chapman, J. 1981. *The Reader and the Text.* London: Heinemann.

Chomsky, N. 1957. *Syntactic Structures.* The Hague: Mouton.

Clark, A. 1996. *Being There: Putting Brain, Body, and World Together Again.* Cambridge, MA: MIT Press.

Clark, M.M. 1992. Sensitive observation and the development of literacy. *Educational Psychology* 12, 3–4: 216–223.

Clay, M.M. 1966. Emergent Reading Behaviour. Doctoral dissertation, University of Auckland Library.

———. 1967. The reading behaviour of five-year-old children: A research report. *New Zealand Journal of Educational Studies* 2, 1: 11–31.

———. 1968. A syntactic analysis of reading errors. *Visible Language* 8, 3: 275–282.

———. 1974. The spatial characteristics of the open book. *British Journal of Educational Psychology* 39, 1: 47–56.

———. 1979. *The Early Detection of Reading Difficulties: A Diagnostic Survey with Recovery Procedures* (Second Edition). Auckland: Heinemann.

———. 1991. *Becoming Literate: The Construction of Inner Control.* Auckland: Heinemann.

———. 1998. *By Different Paths to Common Outcomes.* York, ME: Stenhouse Publishers.

Clay, M.M. and B. Williams. 1973. The reading behaviour of Standard One children. *Education (New Zealand)* 2: 13–17.

DeStephano, J. 1978. *Language, the Learner and the School.* New York: John Wiley and Sons.

Dewey, G. 1970. *English Spelling: Roadblock to Reading.* New York: Teachers College Press, Columbia University.

Downing, J. and C.K. Leong. 1982. *Psychology of Reading.* New York: Macmillan.

Durrell, D. 1958. First grade reading success study. *Journal of Education* 140, February.

Ehri, L.C. 1991. Development of the ability to read words. In R. Barr, M.L. Kamil, P. Mosenthal, and P.D. Pearson, eds, *Handbook of Reading Research*, Vol. II, pp. 383–417. White Plains, NY: Longman.

Elkonin, D.B. 1973. USSR. In J. Downing, ed., *Comparative Reading,* pp. 551–580. New York: Macmillan.

Elley, W.B. 1989. Vocabulary acquisition from listening to stories. *Reading Research Quarterly* 24, 2: 174–187.

Ferreiro, E. and A. Teberosky. 1982. *Literacy Before Schooling.* Portsmouth, NH: Heinemann.

Gibson, E.J. 1969. *Principles of Perceptual Learning and Development.* New York: Appleton, Century, Crofts.

Goodman, K.S. 1994. Reading, writing, and written texts: A transactional-sociopsycholinguistic view. In R.B. Ruddell, M.R. Ruddell and H. Singer, eds, *Theoretical Models and Processes of Reading* (Fourth Edition), pp. 1057–1093. Newark, DE: International Reading Association.

Goodman, K.S. and Y.M. Goodman. 1979. Learning to read is natural. In L.B. Resnick and P.A. Weaver, eds, *Theory and Practice in Early Reading*, Vol. 1, pp. 137–154. Hillsdale, NJ: Lawrence Erlbaum.

Goswami, U. 1998. The role of analogies in the development of word recognition. In J.L. Metsala and L.C. Ehri, eds, *Word Recognition in Beginning Literacy*, pp. 41–63. Mahwah, NJ: Lawrence Erlbaum.

Gough, P.B. 1985. One second of reading. In H. Singer and R.B. Ruddell, eds, *Theoretical Models and Processes of Reading* (Third Edition), pp. 661–689. Newark, DE: International Reading Association.

Guthrie, J.T. 1973. Reading comprehension and syntactic responses in good and poor readers. *Journal of Educational Psychology* 65: 294–299.

Haber, R.N. 1978. Visual perception. *Annual Review of Psychology* 29: 31–59.

Hart, B. and T.R. Risley. 1999. *The Social World of Children Learning to Talk.* Baltimore: Paul Brookes Publishing.

Hobsbaum, A., S. Peters and K. Sylva. 1996. Scaffolding in Reading Recovery. *Oxford Review of Education*, 22, 1: 17–35.

Holdaway, D. 1979. *The Foundations of Learning.* Sydney: Ashton Scholastic.

Holmes. J.A. 1953. *The Substrata-factor Theory of Reading.* Berkeley, CA: California Book.

———. 1960. The substrata-factor theory of reading: Some experimental evidence. In the *Proceedings of the Fifth Annual Conference of the International Reading Association New Frontiers in Reading*, and reprinted in H. Singer and R.B. Ruddell, eds, 1970, *Theoretical Models and Processes of Reading* (First Edition), pp. 187–197. Newark, DE: International Reading Association.

Holmes, J. and H. Singer. 1964. Theoretical models and trends toward more basic research in reading. *Review of Educational Research* 34, April: 127–155.

Johnston, P.H. 1997. *Knowing Literacy: Constructive Literacy Assessment.* York, ME: Stenhouse Publishers.

Juel, C. 1988. Learning to read and write: a longitudinal study of 54 children from first through fourth grades. *Journal of Educational Psychology* 4: 437–447.

Karoly, P. 1993. Mechanisms of self-regulation: A systems view. *Annual Review of Psychology*, 44: 23–52.

Kress, G. 2000. *Early Spelling: Between Convention and Creativity.* London: Routledge.

MacKinnon, A.R. 1959. *How Do Children Learn to Read?* Toronto: Copp Clark Publishing.

McKoon, G. and Ratcliff, R. 1998. Memory-based language processing: Psycholinguistic Research in the 1990's. *Annual Review of Psychology* 1998, 49: 25–42.

McNaughton, S. 1985. Beyond teaching: The development of independence in learning to read. Conference address, 11th Annual Australian Reading Association, Brisbane.

———. 1995. *Patterns of Emergent Literacy: Processes of Development and Transition.* Auckland: Oxford University Press.

McQueen, P.J. 1975. Motor responses associated with beginning reading. Master of Arts thesis, University of Auckland Library.

Meek, M. 1988. *How Texts Teach What Readers Learn.* South Woodchester, Stroud: The Thimble Press.

Miller. G.A. 1981. *Language and Speech.* San Francisco: S.F. and W.H. Freeman.

Morais, J. 1995. Do orthographic and phonological peculiarities of alphabetically written languages influence the course of literacy acquisition? *Reading and Writing: An Interdisciplinary Journal* 7: 1–7.

Ng, S.M. 1979. Error and Self-correction in Reading and Oral Language. Doctoral dissertation, University of Auckland Library.

O'Leary, S. 1997. *Five Kids: Stories of Children Learning to Read.* Bothell, WA: The Wright Group/ McGraw-Hill.

Pinker, S. 1994. *The Language Instinct: How the Mind Creates Language,* p. 22. New York: William Morrow.

Rayner, K., G.E. Raney and A. Pollatsek. 1995. Eye movements and discourse processing. In R.F. Lorch and E.J. O'Brien, eds, *Sources of Coherence in Reading.* Hillsdale, NJ: Lawrence Erlbaum.

Recht, D.R. 1976. The self-correction process in reading. *The Reading Teacher*, April: 633 ff.

Rosenblatt, L. 1994. The transactional theory of reading and writing. In R.B. Ruddell, M.R. Ruddell and H. Singer, eds, 1994, *Theoretical Models and Processes of Reading* (Fourth Edition), pp. 1057–1093. Newark, DE: International Reading Association.

Ruddell, R.B., M.R. Ruddell and H. Singer, eds. 1994. *Theoretical Models and Processes of Reading* (Fourth Edition). Newark, DE: International Reading Association.

Rumelhart, D.E. 1994. Toward an interactive model of reading. In R.B. Ruddell, M.R. Ruddell and H. Singer, eds, 1994, *Theoretical Models and Processes of Reading* (Fourth Edition), pp. 864–894. Newark, DE: International Reading Association.

Singer, H. 1994. The substrata-factor theory of reading. In R.B. Ruddell, M.R. Ruddell and H. Singer, eds, *Theoretical Models and Processes of Reading* (Fourth Edition), pp. 895–927. Newark, DE: International Reading Association.

Singer, H. and R.B. Ruddell, eds. 1970. *Theoretical Models and Processes of Reading* (First Edition). Newark, DE: International Reading Association.

Smith, F. 1978. *Understanding Reading* (Second Edition). New York: Holt, Rinehart and Winston.

Spiro, R.J., R.L. Coulson, P.J. Feltovich and D.K. Anderson. 1994. Cognitive flexibility theory: Advanced knowledge acquisition in ill-structured domains. In R.B. Ruddell, M.R. Ruddell and H. Singer, eds, *Theoretical Models and Processes of Reading* (Fourth Edition), pp. 602–615. Newark, DE: International Reading Association.

Spiro, R.J., W.L. Vispoel, J.G. Schmitz, A. Samarapungavan and A.E. Boerger. 1987. Knowledge acquisition for application: Cognitive flexibility and transfer in complex content domains. In B.K. Britton and S.M. Glynn, eds, *Executive Control Processes in Reading*. Hillsdale, NJ: Lawrence Erlbaum.

Treiman, R. 1993. *Beginning to Spell: A Study of First Grade Children.* New York: Oxford University Press.

Vygotsky, L.S. 1962. *Thought and Language.* Cambridge, MA: MIT Press.

Weber, R. 1970. A linguistic analysis of first grade reading errors. *Reading Research Quarterly* 5: 427–451.

Weinberger, J., P. Hannon and C. Nutbrown. 1990. *Ways of Working with Parents to Promote Early Literacy Development.* Sheffield: University of Sheffield Educational Research Centre.

White, D.N. 1984. *Books Before Five.* Portsmouth, NH: Heinemann.

Williams, B. 1968. The Oral Reading Behaviour of Standard One Children. Master of Arts thesis, University of Auckland Library.

Wimmer, H. and U. Goswami. 1994. The influence of orthographic consistency on reading development: word recognition in English and German children. *Cognition* 51: 91–103.

Wood, D. 1978. Problem-solving: the nature and development of strategies. In A. Underwood, ed., *Strategies of Information Processing.* London: Academic Press.

———. 1998. *How Children Think and Learn* (Second Edition). Oxford: Blackwell.

Yopp, H.K, and H. Singer. 1994. Toward an interactive reading instruction model: Explanation of activation of linguistic awareness and meta-linguistic ability in learning to read. In R.B. Ruddell, M.R. Ruddell and H. Singer, eds, *Theoretical Models and Processes of Reading* (Fourth Edition), pp. 381–390. Newark, DE: International Reading Association.

4 Adjusting the visual working system for literacy: learning to look at print

4 Adjusting the visual working system for literacy: learning to look at print

Chapter 3 outlined the concept of reading and writing being supported by working systems which are assembled to carry out particular literacy tasks. This chapter provides one example of how available research on various important working systems might be reviewed with practitioners in mind. Up-to-date reviews of psychological and educational research could become a resource for those who train early intervention teachers to understand what some of the working systems might be. In this chapter, research and authorities on the processing of visual information are reviewed with early intervention teachers in mind.

When visual perception is poorly organised the child's classroom learning is massively muddled. Dion had been at school with good classroom teaching for two years. He had supplementary teaching (not Reading Recovery (RR)) beyond the classroom programme on two occasions, but it did not overcome his problems. At seven years he was given the Concepts About Print test. After 'doing' reading and writing every day for two years at school, he could not find the first letter in a word, nor locate 'just one letter' or 'just one word', nor detect an alteration of word order in printed text, nor detect an alteration of letter order. How confusing those two years of literacy experiences must have been just because he had no organised way of attending to the visual information in print. He did not have any deficit in visual perception; no one had helped him to learn how to look at the written code and what to look for.

How to look at a code and what to look for

Educators will agree that children have to learn how the sounds of spoken language relate to printed language, but they too often overlook the obvious, that children must be able to find out which visual hooks to hang their phonemic awareness on. Teachers often give too little thought to how we perceive the things around us in our world; how we see the printed page, and how we hear the spoken word. In many classrooms everyday assumptions about looking at print are sufficient for teachers to teach most children effectively. For children who need supplementary teaching in early intervention programmes everyday assumptions have not been enough; their teachers have to think very carefully about learning to look at print. Visual information is picked up at high speed by the brain; we perceive objects directly. However, perceiving the symbols of language is different. The event symbolised is arbitrary, ruled by conventions and not naturally given (Gibson 1969). Learning to look at language symbols and knowing what to look for is a beginning task for the literacy learner. There is a critical time when a child is beginning to look seriously at print and direct his or her prior visual learning and prior oral language learning to working out how the things he or she can say are coded in print. Adults devise props and procedures to 'help' children with this learning but many of these have arisen from a superficial analysis of what the challenges actually are.

A part of the visual learning involves how to recognise each of those arbitrary symbols used in written language. Every symbol has to be discriminated at speed from all possible and impossible symbols. That learning takes a stretch of time, perhaps six to twelve months of classroom instruction. To a child the relationship is arbitrary — the letter 's' makes the sound /s/ because adults say it does, and there is no 'real world' reason why a particular symbol should represent a certain sound. Many classroom teachers pay little attention to this; they go straight to the assumption that they must teach the sounds of the letters, and design activities to help children link sounds to letters. Most of those children have yet to learn how to distinguish one letter from the other. Teachers overlook the huge task of learning to discriminate 54 letter symbols one from another, and learning to attend to those symbols in a particular order, one after the other, while only moving from left to right. Teachers have to be sure that wandering eyes become disciplined and notice the features of letters, and the detail of print. The order of inspection is critical.

The co-ordination of body, hand and eye movements is involved when children are learning to pay visual attention to print. The learning is gradual, not sudden (McQueen 1975; in Chapter 2), and occurs as children are reading their first books and writing simple messages.

Preschool children show us what they can visually attend to. They notice only a few letters, but also things like a hyphen in a name, or a curly comma, the dot over the 'i' and the horizontal lines in the capital 'E'. Adults often do not notice how captivated, or puzzled, some young readers and writers are by these things. Adults tell us that they had to rediscover that capital letters and lower case pairs are sometimes different in form (dD, eE., rR). Consider the differences in letter font forms and how we ignore them.

Young children may treat the things we group together to be different letters. One child was sure that the word IAN was different from another word written as Ian.

So the visual learning of letters over time becomes a matter of learning which variants can be categorised together as 'the same letter', and which variants cannot be included in the category. (Readers might like to construct a series of variants which turn an 'S' into a '5'.)

Experienced readers are surprised by children's confusions. To the child who is not yet sure of which way up letters have to be, the e/a pair may look similar; to a child confused by angles the k/y pair might seem more or less the same. Teachers are familiar with b/d/p/q confusions and with the n/m/u/h/r group, and obviously letters in the set I, i, l, L plus number 1 are very easy to confuse. At first glance it may seem a simple task to remember all the letters and produce a response in reading and writing to each of them but we underestimate our own achievements. At the most abstract and flexible level a single letter form can be written and recognised as 'the same thing' when it has a variety of visual forms.

a *a* *a* ɑ A **A** *A* A

Experienced readers forget how easily, for reading purposes, they group forms into categories all of which have the same value. Such differences catch the interest of some young children making discoveries about print, but they confuse others.

In recent years printers have been persuaded to alter some features of print in beginning reading books to reduce some of the challenges that children face, and some features which have been varied in different reading series include:

- the spacing between lines

- the spacing between letters

- the spacing between words

- the font, some judged to be clearer than others

- special forms of the letters ɑ, a and g, g.

From time to time alterations to beginning-reading books have been initiated to exclude upper case letters or lower case letters, or omit punctuation, but such alterations have not been supported by research evidence and have not lasted.

One letter may signal several things

It is an achievement of beginning readers that they learn these visual discriminations easily and are able to look at print and link other kinds of information to those visual forms. They read, adding to their letter knowledge as they do so. As competent readers they will know implicitly that one letter may signal several different things, and different letters may signal the same thing, and sometimes letters do not signal any sound.

Evidence of changes in visual learning

In Chapter 2 I reported on an experiment exploring some visual discrimination tasks during the first three years of school. I concluded that proficient readers rapidly became used to the printer's conventions: they learned about the letters and their orientations and variations, and they habitually and rapidly scanned print in ways which facilitated their reading. *After three years of instruction the lowest achievers were not as efficient as the proficient readers had been at the end of their first year at school.* The low achievers were moving forward too slowly, and their slow rate of sorting out this visual learning must have impacted on their literacy learning in general. The proficient readers at eight years provide an excellent example of perceptual learning as it was described in a recent psychological review.

> Perceptual learning involves relatively long-standing changes to an organism's perceptual system that improve its ability to respond to its environment. (Goldstone 1998)

What kinds of long-standing changes had my low achievers learned in their first three years at school?

Print information must pass through the visual sense for reading to occur and children have to learn what visual information in print is usable, and how to use it. But the visual code of written language must also give access to the sounds of language and all other facets of the language code.

I introduce the topic with caution. If my simplifications in this chapter lead the reader to believe that he or she now understands this topic then I have created a problem. Any 'bright ideas' or 'new solutions' which arise in readers' minds as a result of reading this discussion should be treated with studied skepticism. Hopefully teachers will seek a new awareness of the challenges for children, but not standardise their teaching solutions.

Visual perception is hard to think about because it occurs very fast, and it is hidden from sight! Psychologists can design controlled experiments to probe this area; observant teachers can only try to understand:

- how perception enters into their own activities
- and how it enters into the acts of reading and writing of their students.

Teachers are not trying to develop visual perception; that began in infancy. Becoming literate involves making the processes of visual perception operate under a new set of arbitrary constraints which apply only to the written code of a language. Some of the simpler concepts about the visual perception of print are discussed in this chapter.

Many of the important theorists quoted in reading research were visual perception psychologists who, at one time or another, applied their theory building to reading and reading problems — Bruner, although he did not study literacy behaviours, Philip Gough, Frank Smith, Eleanor Gibson, Paul Kolers, Ralph Haber, and Magdalen Vernon to name a few. It was a topic of high interest in the 1960s and 1970s, and Goldstone's (1998) valuable review of 'Perceptual learning' points to a revival of that interest.

Complex perceptual decision-making

Observing your own visual behaviour

Driving involves giving visual attention to things out there, picking up information quickly, in a thousandth of a second, linking up with prior experience stored in the head, and producing a correct decision! Driving is an experience which many of us have every day, and it is massively involved with taking in visual information and acting upon it every minute the car is moving. Reduce the driver's visual perception — with rain or snow, or a shattered windscreen or a mud-shower, or a drunken state of mind — and that driver is in trouble.

Not everyone realises how much drivers depend on what they hear when they drive (auditory perception) and how much hearing enters into our judgements. Reflect on how you process visual or auditory information as you drive. Observe what kinds of information you take in while you are waiting for traffic lights to change. Ask yourself some of these questions about the information you gathered with your eyes.

- What changed in your visual environment before you stopped?
- What did you notice immediately afterwards?
- What did your eyes attend to first?
- Then what did you do?

You will have to take yourself by surprise if you want to observe your own behaviour; if you plan ahead you will change what you see!

Many of us can recall one or two driving experiences vividly. We might remember clearly when our brains did amazing things in an emergency. We also know that brains work on more than one level, keeping our driving safe on the one hand while allowing us to have a vital conversation with our passenger. Or we may recall completing some planning or a problem-solving task in our heads before we arrive, a little surprised, at our destination. If driving conditions get bad we slow down, we become more deliberate in searching for the necessary visual information and we ask the children in the back seat to 'keep quiet' while we concentrate on processing that information into appropriate driving decisions!

Driving does *not* provide us with a model of what happens in literacy processing, but it does provide opportunities to observe and think about the complexity and the speed with which the brain takes in and uses information and arrives at decisions. *The beginning reader is a little like the novice driver out in the car on the road for the third or fourth time, unsure of what to attend to first and wondering how he will ever get all the information into the right decision-making sequence.* Driving and literacy processing both involve complex processing of sequences of information leading to fast decisions. The activities are alike in that they are complex and require us to combine looking, hearing, deciding, moving and taking action. The big difference is that driving takes in sensory messages from the real world directly; reading, on the other hand, takes in messages that have been coded first into an oral language, and then coded again into the printed symbols of written language. Coding, twice over, complicates the initial learning task immensely.

Discuss this with colleagues. A particular focus could be to try to give examples of how the brain acts on information it receives from 'out there', first examining your own experience with driving and then examining your own experience with reading. The next two or three sections might prompt such discussions.

Going in search of information

Our brains go in search of information when we direct them to, but brains also go in search of information when we do not recall sending them to get it!

- In your car, when you slowed down what might be some of the different kinds of information that made you do that? Visual? auditory? or mental calculation of some kind? Think of actual experiences you can remember.

- Were you conscious of the decisions you were making at the time?

- Were you responding to one kind of stimulus? or a pattern? or a sequence of things?

- Do you sometimes anticipate things that do not then occur?

- Talk about what a driver has to anticipate.

- Why is anticipation necessary? or helpful?

Inside or outside?

Where does the problem-solving begin? To observe visual perception we need to slow things down. Think of these activities.

- You sense something, like a flash of light or a sound, which you noticed when you went in search of it, or which forced you to attend to it. (You need to bring a specific personal experience to mind.) Did the activity start outside or inside your head?

- How did you work on that experience in your head?

- What decision did you come to about that thing you encountered through your visual sense?

- What action did you take? What response did you make?

Suppose that we are viewing a large painting on the far wall of an art gallery and think about these things.

- The forms and colours created by the artist reach our visual sense and it is likely that, although we are standing still, 'we go in search of further information' scanning the canvas. (Each of us would choose our own starting point and scan the forms along our own pathway, pausing and shifting idiosyncratically.)

- Tentatively we may think about features of the painting (oil or water, landscape or portrait, ancient or modern, dark or light, likeable or not likeable).

- We think we have picked the possible artist and the subject, a tentative decision.

- We move forward to do some close-up scanning and read the title and confirm the artist's name.

Working on some examples can help teachers to separate out three parts of brain activity — input, processing and response.

- Suppose you are about to be involved in an imaginary phone call. Where does this activity begin when *you* initiate this phone call? Usually it begins *inside your head* with a thought. This is an 'inside' trigger to action, what some would call 'central processing' in the brain.

- What happens when you answer a phone call? It begins with a ringing in your ear which you respond to, coming from outside your brain and you take action. If you stop the sequence with a malicious little thought about not answering it, then taking that decision (thinking) may be the only action that you take.

- What happens when you begin to send a postcard to someone? Where does that action start? (Think of the decision to do it rather than what you saw that made you think of doing it. The sequences in our active lives quickly get complicated.) Your decision to send the postcard results in the production of writing; the messages you could have spoken are now coded into visual forms which you put on paper. You check it visually, rereading.

- On the other hand what happens when you find a card from the Greek Islands in your mailbox which you read eagerly? The visual forms are a stimulus to your brain which you use to get to the messages. You may read them taking no outward action but if they are exciting you may shout them aloud.

It is not easy to talk about a simple act, or a simple stimulus, or a simple response: the brain connects them up so easily to other experience we have had, they quickly become complex. Discussions can help you clarify your thinking.

- Talk about the perception of sound. What auditory experiences can you talk about? All talking involves auditory perception, and that means listening to yourself and to others.

- Talk about the feel of movements. What messages go to your arm and hand as you move to lift a block of cheese from the refrigerator? Talk about directional behaviours, and order and sequence when the rules for scanning print are not the same as they are in English.

- Define visual perception in an utterly simple way.

Everyday activities and perception

The examples asking you to think about the role of perception in viewing a painting, answering the phone, sending a postcard and driving a car were intended to make you think about using perception in everyday life. Thinking about driving as a familiar complex activity *which human beings have to learn* involves us in thinking about:

- visual perception
- auditory perception
- movement and motor perception
- linking and thinking
- integrating different messages or making them work together

- coming to a decision quickly
- sending messages to feet or hands to take appropriate action.

Reading and writing are more complex, and it is not so useful to observe one's own literacy behaviours because they are so highly practised. When we take notice of some public sign it is interesting to think analytically about how and why we did what we did. One day I was being driven through the 'leafy glades of Surrey' and at 50 kph I 'saw' a notice in English that had the sequence 'aaa' in one of its words. I know I saw it but it cannot happen in English so what did I do wrong? Or was it a unique encounter? I believe it was an advertiser's trick to capture my attention but I have never been able to go back and check that visual perception.

Adding more psychological ideas

How do we get visual information from objects?

Here is a helpful exercise.

Describe how you perceive an orange.
What nonverbal processes are involved?
You see shape, colour, markings, stalk or leaf.
You smell, taste, feel, use several senses, and receive sensations.
Would you ever use different kinds of information for one decision?
How do you combine different kinds of information?
How do you exclude some possibilities?
Can you mention any other processes you used?
Convince me that what I am holding is an orange.

So, identifying an object can be quite complex, especially in poor light, and we combine different kinds of information in order to discriminate one thing from another: several possible answers call for decisions between them. What does 'information' mean when used in this technical sense? Distinguish this from the common everyday meaning of 'information'. Here are some explanations given by authorities.

Information is any property of the physical environment that reduces uncertainty, eliminating or reducing the probability of alternatives among which a perceiver must decide. (F. Smith in his 'Glossary of Terms', 1971)

Information in perception [is] that aspect of stimulation that specifies the properties of things and events. Information in information theory is an indication of the number of possible alternative messages that may be sent and received. (Harris and Hodges used this explanation in *The Literacy Dictionary* in 1995.)

The visual perception of an object involves getting some information and doing something with it. We use information of different kinds to decide that this is fruit, a real orange and not an artificial one, quite clearly distinguishable from other alternatives (Bruner 1971).

Sometimes sights and sounds force us to pay attention to them because they are bright, or loud, or startling. Most of the time our brains are actively searching for information, and car-driving provides an example you can analyse. The brain is not just receiving sensory information. From all the possible things out there it is actively selecting a few to attend to, and making a crucial link between incoming stimuli and an appropriate response. When the information passes through the eyes, then identifying the object is the visual perception of the object.

Any one of your senses might lead you to the same interpretation — the colour of the orange or the smell — but information from more than one sense could make the identification easier. Imagine exploring the orange blindfolded or in the dark. How could you decide what it was?

Visual perception is going on most of our waking moments, and this psychologist's definition suggests this continuity.

> ... perception is ... an irregular cycle of recurring events which is reinforced by sensory stimulation and by the appropriate eye movements. (Hebb 1949, pp. 101–102)

It usually helps early intervention teachers to discuss clear examples from their personal perception experiences, and from their reading and writing experiences. Trying to recount these experiences often clarifies one's thinking.

Here is an example which helps us to think about 'what goes on in the head' after perceiving. I took an unexpected letter out of my letterbox. I immediately thought 'A card? an invitation? a thank-you note?' What triggered those responses? I glanced at the print, read my name and the first line of my own address and I knew who had sent the letter and what it contained. All I had read was my own name and my own address! Through the print I got a message and with my brain I assembled a scenario; a 'thank you' for a gift at a recent farewell celebration. The slightly different forms of the handwritten letters were perceived and processed by my brain which went straight to a meaning on the basis of minimal clues. I could have been wrong but I had a high degree of certainty as to who the writer was. To clinch the decision my eyes went straight to the signature of the open card, and my certainty was justified. Undirected my brain had sifted and sorted contexts and options, discrediting large bodies of alternatives into which the minimal clues fitted. My brain is highly practised: it has been identifying things for decades.

Teachers with active minds will ask themselves questions about children's reading. 'How did he get to that response? What was he looking at? or thinking about?' We cannot know what our own brain is doing much of the time, and we certainly cannot expect to know what a pupil is doing 'in-the-head'. We can only infer from behaviours that something might be happening and we must be tentative and flexible about our guesses.

Using the visual sense in reading and writing

There is no reading in any language without first having some visual input (with the exception of Braille which lets you read by using the sense of touch, or a technology allowing a machine to read print to blind people). Frank Smith stressed that you cannot read if the lights go out. I have a new and up-to-date image. My talk to be delivered the next day was in my computer. The power was on. The computer was working. I punched the correct key to bring up the file and probably the file was accessed. However, I could not read the script because the screen was black. There was no reading. Worse than that, there was no talk! There is nothing to read without the visual input.

Early intervention teachers must think carefully about children who find it difficult to locate the visual information they need in the printed code and this is more difficult than object identification. Both teachers and children have to pay particular attention *to the complex sequences* of symbols which occur in words and in lines of print.

Accurate sensory processing transfers information to the brain, not as pictures or forms but as impulses in the nervous system. Every time we read, every time our eyes fixate (that is, focus and pause before jumping forward again), visual information of some kind is available to the brain, and we know from carefully conducted experiments that competent readers fixate close to once on every word. We may find that hard to believe. It is hard to observe our own visual perception because it all happens so fast. That is why we cannot really trust our own observing. We know from experiments that certain things happen which we are unable to observe in our own experiences.

In a study of the *physical movements* that young children made when they were reading to a teacher (McQueen 1975), it was not surprising that one of the factors highly related to reading progress was whether the eyes were seen to be 'wandering' or whether the reader could focus attention on the print. Where to look and what to look for, how to fixate and move the eyes across print are among the first things a novice reader learns.

What happens in writing? First there is a message in the head that needs to be formulated. We find and use information that is stored in the brain and we compose a message and put it into print through handwriting, or typing or by using a computer keyboard. But when writers are producing printed forms they check features of the text as they make them. (It is a visual check which may be rapid and rough but which is essential to keeping the production on track.)

Think of your personal experiences of using the visual sense in some recent literacy activity and analyse the task into its three phases of input, central activity in the brain, and response. (Try this on auditory perception too.) Avoid the exceptional, the cute, or the complex examples and go for the simple everyday ones.

Input, processing and output

Let's think about brains. What does the word 'brain' make you think of? Be very specific.

- Was it some words, a definition of something like intelligence, or perhaps a visual image of one or two hemispheres, with complex folds? or a CAT scan?

- Think of what a brain looks like and draw it (motor output).

- Think of a brain and define it (verbal output).

- Now talk about the different activities that went on in your brain so you could a) do the drawing and b) construct a definition.

- What input did I provide?

- What output did you provide?

- Describe the central processing, that is, what went on in your head that led to the output (your response)?

Teachers often think that 'a good memory' is responsible for the recall of words. That explanation will not enable them to solve the problems of children who find literacy learning difficult. They need to ask themselves about the input, the acts of processing, the 'going in search of' helpful information and deciding on a satisfactory response. Teachers in effective early intervention programmes must try to think about the activities occurring in the brain, some of which we direct and some of which seem to go on by themselves and surprise us. Central processing is a useful term for this.

There are only two general kinds of behaviour going from inside the brain to the outside world. Either we can move, or we use language, and sometimes we do both those things at the same time. It sounds too simple but it is true. It is easy to see that writing is both movement and language but what about reading? For young children reading is also movement and language as they learn to direct their attention to the directional conventions of the print, and get the sequence of visual attention working without having to pay attention to it. When the reader becomes more expert most of the movement is automatic and eventually even the language becomes an in-the-head activity.

Getting more technical about visual information

How do we get to visual information while we are reading? Television producers and designers of advertisements use eye-catching gimmicks to control from the outside what you will perceive. Something 'catches your eye', or 'catches your attention'. Newspaper headlines and book jackets are designed to catch the attention and the printer can 'call your attention' to things in print by layout and design features.

The reader initiates a visual search for information. The first glance may be merely to find out whether there is anything worth attending to. Then the reader must go in search of visual detail which is then referred to some central processing system. If the brain needs more visual information it will direct more searches until a decision can be made (Lynn 1966).

It may help you to think about what you do when you try to read print that has been degraded in some way, as in hard-to-read handwriting, or smudged print, or text with missing letters, or in very poor light. Alternatively, what do you do when print is highly decorative? It would be useful to try this out and talk about what you do as you go in search of more information.

Perception psychologists who have made an analysis of perception describe several stages in this searching and deciding what you are looking at. In the beginning:

- there is an *expectancy*,

- which leads to *directing attention or orienting towards something*,

- which leads to *looking, searching, comparing and discriminating*.

- Several alternative possibilities seem to be lurking around, and the brain seems to *test them out*. They compete one with the other and some have to be discarded or rejected.

- One or two highly probable responses are *trialled or checked*.

- A decision is made and checked.

The reader asks himself or herself, 'Do I have enough information?' or 'Am I satisfied with my decision?' or 'Do I need to get more information?'

An easily remembered general way to summarise this sequence of events has been proposed by several psychologists, and early intervention teachers have found it a useful reminder of what children are trying to cope with.

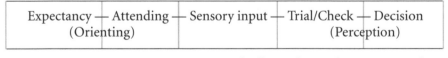

Expectancy — Attending — (Orienting)	Sensory input —	Trial/Check — Decision (Perception)

(Solley and Murphy 1960, p. 320)

This figure analyses each act of perception in the following way:

- the preparatory stage of expectancy,

- giving rise to attending,

- a sensory reception stage,

- a trial and check stage,

- and a final decision stage.

It is not as clear as that because these stages do not exist as isolated units. They merge and intertwine in the process of deciding, cycling back, making other decisions. They are hard to observe, and are rarely clear-cut. Yet we often see spectacular examples of parts of this total process in the early stages of literacy acquisition among children who are having difficulty learning to go in search of visual information in print. They are having more difficulty than most in finding the important distinctions between letters, and between words. To become aware of what is challenging a child teachers may need to think more analytically about those stages, and a first step towards this is to adopt the language of the figure above.

Expectancy, orienting, turning towards and initial attending

As something interesting or relevant comes into the field of vision the observer makes an orienting movement to bring the image into clear focus. For example, as you bring out a reading book the child turns towards it and initiates some searching, scanning the object. At the earliest stage the teacher may open the book and point to the beginning of the print but soon children can do this for themselves. If we borrow a term from psychologists who experiment with animals, this first and important stage at the beginning of a new act of perception is the orientation. When a child is about to learn to recognise a new letter it must be in an obvious and easily seen place and the child must direct his or her attention towards it.

Several tentative encounters lead the beginning reader to attend to this object. Some visual features of the print are recognised. More encounters contribute recognisable information, and identification of the letters or words comes more quickly.

If these sensory experiences flow fast and chaotically this does not become productive, so teachers must introduce new learning under conditions which make the orienting encounter clear, rather than confusing. This is difficult because as an observer you can rarely tell:

- what the perceiver is attending to

- or in what order he or she is attending to things.

For children having difficulty with literacy, new learning should be presented with visual clarity. The introduction of new visual information should be clear and distinct from what the child already knows, with no opportunity to generate or practise confusions. Then as the child begins to recognise a new letter or word it is important that the visual decision-making gradually becomes fast, and accurate.

And if conditions for learning are not like this, what happens? Imagine what a camera would see if it were set for multiple exposures of a certain object passing in front of it at irregular intervals. We probably create situations like this for the children we teach.

Under normal circumstances, and for most children, learning to go in search of visual information in order to recognise something is so easy that it seems to the observer as if the brain were 'snapping' the image into place as if taking a picture. Usually teachers will not need to make any analysis which involves thinking about the stages of perception. When beginning readers become more competent there is little need for the teacher to consider these perceptual issues at all.

For a few children, and in the early stages of letter and word discrimination, the emergent reader and writer is learning:

- how to orient to print,

- how to search for information in print,

- how to work with the written language code,

- how to make decisions,

- and how to do these things quickly.

Once children have learnt how to apply their vast experience from early childhood to the new challenges of perceiving the code of written language the things I an writing about here require little further attention even in early intervention programmes. For a few children teachers need more understanding of perception.

Goldstone (1998), in his review of perceptual learning, recommended some topics to watch for in future research. I think three of these will be significant for literacy learning.

- *Attention weighting.* Increasing the attention paid to important dimensions and features. (See Ng in Chapter 2.)

- *Differentiation.* Stimuli that were once indistinguishable must become psychologically separated.

- *Unitisation.* Tasks that originally required detection by several parts are accomplished by detecting a single constructed unit representing a complex configuration.

Teachers of literacy to young children will have no difficulty in finding examples of those three perceptual mechanisms.

Attending to visual input

How would you try to learn a new symbol system?

Go back to observing your own behaviour. Scan the visual features of the two front pages of *The Snow Maiden* and describe what you attended to on each page.

An English and Russian edition of *The Snow Maiden*.

Teachers learn a little more about the visual perception of a printed code when they begin to examine a language written with rules for coding a different language into print. In the days of basal readers interested adults were sometimes given something that looked like a basal reader, but in a different code, and they were asked to 'break the code'. That exercise focused them on the word recognition and/or letter-sound relationships of the coding system.

A more realistic challenge comes from having a text for teachers written in a different script, as in Hebrew or Arabic, using different directional rules. I chose an example from a children's reading book written in Burmese, a script I had never seen before. I found it very difficult to discriminate the different letters because they seemed so similar.

ကျီးနှင့်ဇီးကွက်

တနေ့သန္နိုက် ကျောင်းဝင်းထဲတွင် ဇီးကွက်တကောင်ကို မြင်ရ၏။ ဇီးကွက်ကို ကျီးကန်းများက လိုက်ဆိတ်နေကြသည်။ ထိုအခါ ဆရာကြီးက အောက်ပါပုံကို ပြောပြပါ၏။

ကမ္ဘာဦး အခါက ငှက်တို့သည် စည်းဝေးကြ၏။ အစည်းအဝေးတွင် ငှက်တကောင်က ဆို၏။ အချင်းတို့။ လူတို့တွင် မင်းရှိသည်။ ငါတို့တွင် မင်းမရှိသေး။ မင်းမြှောက်ထိုက်သော ငှက်ကို ကြည့်ကြကုန်ဟု ဆို၏။

ထိုအခါ ငှက်အများက ပြော၏။ ငါတို့သည် ဇီးကွက်ကို နှစ်သက်၏။ သူ့ကို မင်းမြှောက်ကြကုန်အံ့ဟု ပြော၏။

ထိုအခါ ကျီးတကောင်သည် ထ၍ ဆို၏။ အချင်းတို့။ ဤဇီးကွက်၏ မျက်နှာကို ကြည့်ကြပါကုန်လော့။ မင်းမဖြစ်မီက ဤမျှ ကြောက်ဖွယ်ကောင်းလျှင် မင်းဖြစ်သောအခါ မည်သို့ ဖြစ်မည်နည်း။ စိတ်မဆိုးပဲနှင့် ဤမျှကြောက်ဖွယ်ကောင်းလျှင် စိတ်ဆိုးသောအခါ မည်သို့ ဖြစ်မည်နည်း။ ဤဇီးကွက်ကို မင်းမြှောက်ရန် ငါသဘောမတူဟုဆို၍ ပြင်းထန်စွာ ကန့်ကွက်ပြီးလျှင် ကောင်းကင်သို့ ပျံလေ၏။ ဇီးကွက်လည်း ပြင်းစွာအမျက်ထွက်၍ ကျီးနောက်သို့လိုက်လေ၏။ ထိုအခါမှစ၍ ကျီးနှင့် ဇီးကွက်တို့သည် ကမ္ဘာရန် ဖြစ်ကြလေသတည်း။

၆၇

An early-reading book in Burmese.

It is useful for teachers in early literacy intervention programmes to briefly but seriously explore learning another script. As they study an unfamiliar script written responses to questions like these could be discussed.

How do I explore this?
What am I looking for?
What processing am I doing?
Can I describe how I perceive the symbols?
How can I remember four of them?
Would it help to write them?
How did my looking change on the second or third attempt?
What other kinds of changes occur as the symbols become more familiar?

Noting our own reactions to a new script and how we overcome our problems can help us understand more about how children come to grips with a symbol system.

What do you know about your old symbol system?

Teachers are such expert readers and writers that their expertise makes it difficult for them to understand a child's challenge. How the teacher perceives print has changed massively with practice over the years, and how he or she learned to perceive print cannot be observed. (This is why the 'new script' of Burmese was introduced.) To sharpen your awareness of how you process information, study the following interesting example of a child's Christmas story, called *Mary had a baby*.

MERE Ad A DIBE Tusif
Ad A dokE Tish was
Bon in A stibl An d thE
SEphs shEhErds Pnd thE ᵍ
wosmEn clm To siy im A
stAr LEd dE~~mdEaftiAN~~
tEY ~~But~~ Bug im sum
PRESEnts foR im A
Kimg SEd hE wud cL
Tish iust And mErE
mud tum BEthiEhEm
dEY WET to sim
wiy ES thE Ll
of thE Kim thE
Klm SET is omE
thE omE cL Tis
thE NET miwl
A iTL wus
dE thE iTL sEd
BuT . Tis wus
A LAf iwi
BEthiEhm

Mary had a baby Joseph
had a donkey. Jesus was
born in a stable and the
shepherds and the 3
wise men came to see him. A
star led them and
they brought him some
presents for him. A
King said he would kill
Jesus. Joseph and Mary
moved from Bethlehem.
They went to some
where else. The …
of the king. The
king sent his army.
The army killed Jesus.
The next morning
an angel was
there. The angel said
but Jesus was
alive in
Bethlehem.

What an amazing story composed by a young child! The story is articulate and well-formed, and yet teachers have great difficulty reading the original child-written text. It is not because the writer invented some unusual spellings (although that occurs) but rather something which clashes with our own highly practised visual perception of print. We are looking for perceptual cues that are not there. We expect a text to support our typical ways of carrying out visual search. The difficulty we have as readers in this example is not about what the child cannot do but what we as readers have difficulty doing. As highly efficient readers we are expecting letter and word forms to fit with our existing categories in our heads. When they do not, we say the script is unreadable. This example gives us a sense of how *expectancy* operates. Usually expectancy is helpful; in this case it interferes with our reading.

When a child needs help with learning to look at print

An early intervention teacher who judged that some of his or her children might need more help with attending to the visual information in print would begin to observe those children more carefully and ask himself or herself some questions. There are dangers in even beginning to do such an analysis because teachers as observers are constructing an explanation of something which they cannot see.

- They observe some behaviour.
- They interpret this response, asking themselves, 'What could be the difficulty behind this?'
- Their hunches accumulate towards one solution.
- There is no way to confirm the 'suspicions'.

This is one of many reasons why early intervention teachers must be tentative, and questioning, and must consult others in their networks and ask for second opinions. It does no good if the teacher's observations only result in labelling the learner. The teacher's questioning should eventually lead to changes in his or her teaching. If nothing is observed which allows a teacher to confirm the hunch then that teacher must drop it and remain tentative and cautious. *Give those hunches enough thought to open new possibilities for the learners but remember that any strong conclusions are likely to close out new learning opportunities. Always get a second opinion from your peers and tutors or teacher leaders.*

It is important to remember that children may be having difficulties for two reasons:

- they may be paying *superficial attention* to print,
- or they may be paying *devoted attention* to print blotting out access to other necessary information.

Analyse how a low achiever attends to input

The hair/fur example (p. 114, Chapter 3) describes the reading of a boy selected as a low achiever, responding to his early intervention lesson as his teacher provides him with opportunities to use what he already knows. Discuss the ways that interaction with a text involved learning about using visual information.

Is the next example a confusion over visual information? Nolan was also at the beginning of an early intervention, also in the first two weeks, and his teacher was trying to work only with what he already knew. Nolan was older than most early intervention children: he was eight years old and was bilingual in Japanese and English. He spent much time with grandparents in Hawaii. In his small book entitled *Blackberries* the author Trussell-Cullen provided a picture in place of the word 'bucket' (on what theoretical basis? one might ask). Nolan read only the words.

Father Bear's blackberries went into this

Mother Bear's blackberries went into this

Baby Bear's blackberries went into this

The teacher said, as she pointed, 'You can say bucket here if you like.' Nolan read it again as she had suggested. Then he said, knowingly, 'You could say it that way but you could say it this way', and he read the page again omitting the words for 'bucket'. It made sense, sounded right, and matched the text! Then he found an explanation to settle doubts. 'Perhaps the writer of this book can't write "bucket" ', for Nolan knew about words which you know but cannot write. So how does visual information fit into this example?

Talk about visual information with teachers, a little at a time

In an act of perception the brain has to be active. Early intervention teachers should have discussions among themselves about this. It is possible to discuss visual information, talking about how children find it and how they use it. Throughout a training year, bring some discussions back to the following.

- *Auditory perception.* Talk about non-language sounds first, and then about using oral language. Talk about hearing, hearing language, ears, auditory sense, and auditory perception. What things make speaking on the phone difficult?

- *Hearing structure or grammar.* Have a brief discussion on the final 's' on words; verbs, plurals and possessives. What do you notice? That final 's' transmits so much information and we are usually blissfully unaware of it. Talk about grouping words, regrouping and the difference this makes to meaning.

- *Talk about direction and layout.* This is arbitrary and it changes in other languages. It must be learned. Use these questions to analyse some of the things the brain has to do.

Be on the lookout for any puzzling confusions that arise in training group discussions. This set of questions may help.

- What behaviour is involved?

- What senses are involved? (Visual, auditory, movement, other?)

- How can we make it easier for the learner?

- How do we get the child actively participating?

- What is the learning we are aiming for?

- What activities are being constructed?

- What is the final outcome?

- Where must the reader's attention be?

Those eight questions can now be used to examine *the visual side* of literacy. Then:

- Talk about 'Locating responses'.

- Talk about 'Learning to look at print'.

- Talk about 'Letter identification'.

- Talk about 'Taking words apart while reading'.

- Talk about 'Making and breaking, which sharpens perception'.

Such discussions will hopefully raise awareness of some simple visual aspects of literacy tasks.

Some apparently 'simple' activities are actually quite complex

Things become more challenging when the brain becomes involved in visual activity linked to something else like movement or language. Talk about the part *played by visual activity* in the following activities:

- pointing while reading

- assembling cut-up stories

- reading stories

- writing stories.

Complexity can easily turn our attention *away* from the visual perception aspects of literacy towards other things.

A challenge to teachers' thinking about how the brain works on getting messages from print could now be offered. How, precisely, does learning to hear the sounds in words (as in using Elkonin boxes) involve auditory perception and visual perception? How does slow articulation of a word help auditory perception and visual perception?

Literacy activities call for fast visual processing

It is imperative that the brain goes in search of visual information on the printed page. There needs to be fast and accurate processing of visual information by an active mind, and the reader is not conscious of directing attention when things are going well. Conscious attention is not primarily on visual things when the reader is:

- phrasing in fluent reading,

- solving words while reading continuous text, or

- writing stories independently.

The practised responses appear to need less conscious attention to visual detail but the attention to visual features is directed by the brain.

Proficient readers have learned to work with larger units (like clusters, chunks and words or short phrases) much of the time but they rapidly shift to smaller units of information like letters to make a necessary distinction without being consciously aware that they are doing this. Frank Smith (1971, pp. 70–79) discussed this. Recently, Goldstone (1998) discussed working with clusters of letters or short words under the heading of 'unitization'.

> Unitization involves the construction of single functional units … a task that originally required detection of several parts can be accomplished by detecting a single unit … (p. 602)

Clusters of features are 'chunked' together so that they are perceived as a single unit or pattern. We have to think carefully about this. Before the features of a word are recognised in all their detail the rough pattern may lead the child to a good guess. Goldstone is referring to something different. After the fine detail of the word has been learned, and can be recovered if necessary, then presumably faster responding is achieved by responding to larger units, chunks or patterns. One suspects that the effort needed to 'read' a friend's illegible handwriting occurs because we have to give away our usual reliance on larger units and search the fine detail of the letter features.

Useful things to remember about the visual perception of print

Two of the journeys each percept makes

Recall your decision-making in the *Mary had a baby* example. At first we reject the stimulus and accept that we do not know what has been written; our practised recognition makes us reject it at the first, fast glance. But then we find that we can read it once we have 'tuned in' (that is, we can tutor our visual perception and make it 'see' the text by reading it two or three times).

We can see then that a visual percept takes at least two journeys. The visual perception of print:

- becomes more detailed, more differentiated, and then more richly patterned (chunked or clustered or unitised), and we may be conscious or not conscious of the patterning,

- and it becomes faster as we have more encounters with print.

We need to think of an initial orientation to new visual percepts followed by several encounters in which what is known is known tentatively, leading to picking up more detailed information, being more sure, more speedy, and more economical in the processing. If teachers try to increase the speed when the rich patterning is not occurring, this will not work!

Visual perception is affected by situations or conditions

Talk to colleagues in a group about the conditions under which children find it difficult to get information from print, to find and focus on important detail. I have room for only one illustrative example, but it is an important one. Teachers have asked what their tutors/teacher leaders mean when they call for 'crisp and clear work with letters on the magnetic board'. Think how helpful it would be:

- if magnetic letters were stored away from the working space and out of direct view of the learner

- if the child worked at his or her eye level

- if the working space was clear and not cluttered, especially when a new task begins

- if things to be compared were placed close together, with big spaces to separate things not being considered together.

The background space should throw up a clear image of what is to be looked at. Teachers must ensure that the child's visual attention is directed where it needs to be, and must find ways to prevent 'wandering eye' behaviour. For beginning readers, publishers and illustrators of books often violate this. They pepper the beginners' field of vision with competing images making the print harder to read.

In a discussion group it would be useful to select any task involving visual perception which you might give to a five- or six-year-old, such as distinguishing letters or words in some way, and then talk about the challenges for the learner who has to work under any of the following conditions:

- at first encounter
- among easy choices
- among difficult choices
- given plenty of time
- at speed
- with minimal attention
- with intense effort to learn
- with recurrent opportunities.

How could a teacher make it easier for a learner to visually search for an answer on a magnetic board task or in a text when:

- selecting from a group of letters?
- following along a line of print, and on to a second line?
- attempting any visual item on the Concepts About Print task?
- reading a long stretch of print?
- reading text overprinted on the pictures?

Learning to deal with a sequence of symbols

In print, there are many sequences — sequences of letters, of words, of phrases, and of sentences. Visual information is stored in print in a particular order and going in search of helpful information *must somehow take account of order*. We have to learn to scan the symbols in a visual sequence in an unalterable order. In the preschool years children learned that objects remain the same even when they are reordered or turned upside-down. At school this is still true of the objects around them but they are faced with the linear code of written language and have to learn about letter order and orientation and word order! *In spite of what they have learned about objects in the world they now have to respect minute changes of order in printed language.*

The sequence of words in a printed sentence cannot be checked by a child until the child can also separate out the words in the language he or she speaks. When children get better at doing this and with keeping to the directional rules of the language, they have some control over word sequence. Similarly there is no way they can check a sequence of letters until they can separate out (articulate) the sounds of a letter sequence within a word. However, something as simple as writing one's own name can establish many features about coding, but particularly letter sequence. On the other hand if the teacher tried to explain this in words, this could be utterly confusing.

Some children have difficulty accepting that the order of letters left to right must be respected. They have difficulty attending to the words in order and they find it difficult to differentiate words containing almost the same letters, or the same letters but in a different order. They come slowly to notice the transpositions of letters placed in different positions. (See the 'name puzzle' in *Becoming Literate*, Clay 1991, p. 227, or the rearranged letters in words in the Concepts About Print task, Clay 1993.)

Saying and reading just a few words across a line helps the learner to work with order. Writing a few words helps establish both letter and word order, and more generally establishes the importance of sequence.

The orientation of letters

Preschool children observe and remember the orientations of shapes with difficulty. They may be unable to see the difference between a shape and its mirror image even when this is pointed out. They change the position of letters they know rather easily, rotating them in various ways, and some children continue to do this at school. Ignoring the orientation of letter symbols may persist in reading and writing. Most children quickly get this under control but if this jumbled learning is not replaced in the earliest months of school, confusions may become firmly established. Magdalen Vernon (1957) did not consider reversals to be of great importance in reading as all beginners show them, but correct orientation must be learned before too long and without pressure. One simply has to learn that in the world of print, orientation is of critical importance.

Coded symbols and coded messages

When reading about young children exploring a printed code for themselves it is interesting to ask, 'Which features of a printed code is this child attending to, or playing with or perhaps coming to understand?' It is surprising that many preschool children make a distinction between drawing and writing quite early and quite easily. The distinction between pictured objects and coded signs is one of the first steps towards handling coded symbols.

Many things make a coded system difficult to understand. The meaning of the word 'pretty' is not carried in the visual stimulus. It must be associated with the word. It could just as well be associated with the word 'belle'. Similarly, the graphic character 'P' in English is given a different phonemic assignment in the Russian alphabet (see *The Snow Maiden* example on page 160). Two-dimensional shapes which do not pictorially represent anything are not at first easy to learn. Even when children can perceive shapes, so that they can match them or pick out one that is like another, they may not be able to reproduce them in drawings. For some reason they have considerable difficulty in forming angles and copying angular shapes.

What are the units of the code?

What should the child treat as a unit? The letter, the word or a whole phrase? These things are not obvious and learning them takes time. In print the young reader has to locate letters, and words, and groupings of words. The words are signalled by spaces, but children's writing tells us that some are slow to catch on to the function of the spaces between words.

It is probably fortunate that early reading and early writing are introduced at the same time; reading provides some opportunities to work with the larger units, and writing forces you to work with the features of letters and the detail of letter discrimination and letter order. This is one aspect of the reciprocity between the two literacy activities.

Differentiation divides wholes into separated parts. Unitisation occurs when known parts which consistently occur together are processed as a functional unit. For example, letter units are identified but they also form a cluster, syllable or word unit.

Without giving them a thought adults respond to many spatial features of text that create units, some of them aesthetic and some coding a message. (Consider what the spatial features of the following paragraph break and the change in print size signal to you.)

Learning to read using chunks of print

Linguists and psychologists write about the sequential constraints within and between the strings of sounds in spoken language and consequently the written symbols in written language. At five years children already know how to inflect new words such as three different plural endings ('wheels', /z/; 'bikes', /s/; and 'watches', /əz/) from their implicit knowledge of sound sequences in speech. Readers have implicit knowledge of which letters are likely to follow other letters; they have learnt which sound sequences can be pronounced together ('ing', 'and'); they read with the help of word order rules dictated by the phrase structure of the language and they string words together trying to find the acceptable phrasing. They are aware of some of the probabilities of what kinds of words or letter sequences tend to occur in print. Such implicit awareness is what the young reader has yet to accumulate.

Readers transfer all the regularities they are familiar with in speech to print and they soon learn new regularities that occur in books but rarely in speech (like 'said Mother' or 'Once upon a time'). It is disturbing to think of the distorted expectancies of word and letter occurrence which a child might be learning from some contrived texts designed by well-intentioned adults. A child's reading from a 1960s book using a strict control over vocabulary ran like this.

Child:	Come here.	Red, come.	Bill, Bill.	Come here
Text:	Here, Red.	Here, Bill.	Come here.	Come here.

While this child could 'read' nothing on the page, he had learned to produce utterances that sounded very like the style of his reading books.

The relation of speech to the code

The abstract symbols we call 'letters' make words; they are the means by which we put our speech into print. We use letters to encode our messages. Language codes differ in the number of sounds they use and the number of letters they need.

In English spelling there are different ways to spell a particular vowel sound, and a particular letter may represent more than one vowel phoneme. This is true of some consonants also. Often there will be no clues as to which of two or three sounds is represented. Sometimes there are clues in letter order (the letter's environment), or the context within which the letter symbol occurs.

It would be unusual to find a child splitting the 'Th' to 'T' and 'h' at the beginning of a sentence. There is a huge possibility that an initial letter 'T' at a sentence beginning will be part of a 'Th' phoneme. Which of the two 'Th' phonemes in English this represents is another matter; for most people, an unimportant matter.

In beginning reading books children are highly likely to encounter the letter 'a' signalling five different phonemes — 'cat', 'gate', 'what', 'car', and the indefinite article.

A fairly expert perception of speech is helpful when beginning to learn to decode a written symbol system into speech. It is not enough to comprehend the meaning of a spoken message; the child must be able to break it into segments and combine these according to some rules about order (Gibson 1969).

Children need experience with words in texts and words in isolation; words in continuous text favours learning about word probabilities while words in isolation favours learning about letter sequences.

Any child of five to six years can remember some forms without difficulty but it takes a while to discriminate accurately the differences between all the letters in the whole alphabet. How fortunate the child whose alphabet only has fifteen letters! And how challenged the child whose code has 60 or more! This entire set of knowledge must be mastered quickly by all children. If children are given a little time they come to differentiate most letters within the first year in which they learn to read, whatever kind of programme they learn from. The residual difficulty lies in remembering which of the easily confused letter shapes corresponds to which sound; and this difficulty persists even in normal readers, probably due to an inability to learn about orientations.

Letters which stand out in some particular way are noticed. Initial and final letters in words are marked off by the spaces between them. It is harder (and takes longer) to observe and distinguish the sequences of letters in the middle of words. This is something to be learned! Sometimes but not always shortness in a word makes for easy recognition. 'Alexandria' was advantaged as a literacy learner when she eventually learned to read and write her name!

Control over directional behaviour in reading, supplemented by practice in writing messages, compels children to observe each letter in turn and makes them attend to order. Until this is learnt reading is extremely unsystematic, consisting of a hit-or-miss recognition of a few letters within a few words (Vernon 1957).

Learning to visually discriminate coded language

Children will differentiate letters slowly, *each one from all the others already known.* They begin with a few known letters. If you introduce a new word when the child only knows two of the five letters in that word, what do you expect the child to attend to visually? The two letters he or she knows?

A great deal of information of different kinds is embedded within lines of text, information that must be picked up visually:

- the letters of the alphabet

- the words of the dictionary

- new words the reader has never heard spoken

- the spatial signals of layout and print forms.

What is easy and hard to see? Discrimination performance can be improved by an easy-to-hard procedure in which learners are first exposed to easy, highly separated discriminations and then asked to make successively more difficult discriminations, according to Goldstone (1998, p. 578). When designing an 'easy to hard' sequence for a particular child the following should be kept in mind.

- Children begin with easy-to-see letters.

- Letters will be easy to see in isolation.

- They are harder to see when embedded within words or within text.

- A new letter introduced along with known letters will be easy to see; two or three new letters will make the learning much harder.

- Forms that differ most are easier to discriminate.

- Ask the child to group what he or she sees as similar.

- Match, pair and group things that are similar.

- *Later,* ask the child to find what is different; this is the harder task. It calls for many comparisons.

If you ask the child to pick one letter or word from a set, that odd-one-out choice is hard because it calls for visual perception of each member of the whole set and a decision.

In the letter identification section of RR a magnetic board and plastic letters are useful for teaching the child *how to work with letters and with words and with the relationships between them.* The purpose should never become merely teaching letters, or teaching sounds, or teaching words. The question is, 'How can I get this child to work with letters and sounds and words making tentative and flexible decisions about them?'

Visual information (features, letters, chunks, clusters, syllables, words, phrases and punctuation) gives the reader access to all the other sources of information and all the alternative predictions, from which a selection is made.

Things which might improve the child's visual discrimination

Teachers will be well-equipped to observe beginning reader behaviours if they understand most of this chapter. They should be equipped to work out ways to approach the learning or relearning for which a particular pupil is ready. The following summary gathers some of these things together.

- In learning to read, the visual perception learning of greatest importance occurs in a child's first introductions to 'language in print'. How to access visual information in print is learning upon which all literacy is built.

- In one second of reading, divided into a thousand parts, the visual perception response occurs during the first one to two hundred milliseconds, and is accompanied or rapidly followed by a phonological response if required. It takes the average beginning reader another 600 milliseconds to get the word together and give a response.

- Overt behaviour is easier to teach than a decision made in the head. The teacher will find it easier to help the learner control specific external behaviours than to help the reader control perceptual learning.

- Set out to make sure that the learner is visually attending to what he or she needs to attend to. Check this. Telling is never enough.

- In initial learning do not leave wild, alternative responses open to the reader. Keep the stimulus and correct response close together in place and close in time. When necessary, intervene to prevent wandering attention, or to interfere with an habitual unwanted response.

- An observant teacher will be at the ready to make very sure that an old habit lurking behind successful responding is not allowed to surface. (That means that teachers should control for regression to a less effective habit. Do not leave an old bad habit open to chance at any time when you are trying to eliminate it.)

- Once the child seems to be attending to some new item, vary the places in which it occurs. This helps to curb the chance that the child is responding only to the position, or the particular text, rather than the visual form. The child needs to be able to carry the learning to somewhere else on another occasion.

- Improvement can then occur through directional training and a small amount of verbal directing (such as, 'Where is the first letter?' and 'Where do we start?').

- Verbal instructions almost always get in the way of a fast visual response. If the emphasis needs to be on fast perception then limit instructions to simple imperatives such as 'Do this!' or 'Cover the end!' synchronised with what is happening.

The tutoring of discrimination is gradual, a bit-by-bit continuing activity throughout a whole lesson series. It follows the child's prior learning in a sequence something like this (but never necessarily so!):

- Orient to any features at first.

- Bring attention later to fine detail.

- Sharpen attention.

- Shape towards a more decisive response.

- Speed up.

- Fade the attention given by the learner towards effective choices with *little conscious attention.*

Every teaching move should bring several gains and the teacher should aim for higher goals than mere repetition or practice.

If the child is finding some things hard to learn, write down what the changes over time are that you might expect to see, and monitor for these. The changes involve:

- going from a first encounter,

- to an obvious effort to learn among easy choices,

- to choosing from among difficult choices,

- and to working at speed with very little attention.

It is not easy to make simple concluding statements about visual perception but these are some things to bear in mind.

1) Children make the print-to-language link only when they work from visual features in the print in reading text.

2) Children learn the print-to-sound link easily when they try to write words and texts from the language they use in their own speech. This early implicit knowledge can be used during reading and should be prompted by the teacher.

3) Children show that they understand that 'letters make words' when they have worked in both reading and writing and begin to make analogies saying 'this is like that'.

Phonics programmes can lead to 1) or 2) or 3) and text reading and writing programmes can also lead to 1) or 2) or 3).

The beginning reader and writer is a long way from having anything under perfect control, and each of the things the child is learning about — letter knowledge, letter production, letter-sound possibilities, word knowledge, writing vocabulary — is on at least two journeys, one of coming to know the differentiated detail and then regrouping some of this in some unitised chunks, and the other of responding to it faster and faster with minimal attention unless detail is a task requirement.

Beginning readers form implicit hypotheses about what happens in print and these hypotheses should be changing almost daily. Children have to withstand rapid changes in their understanding in the early stages of literacy learning, and for this the steadying support of a teacher is essential. As each facet of literacy processing becomes stronger, better known, more rapidly perceived, the learner is expected to deal with more complexity, at faster speeds. There are always new units of written language moving from:

- new
- to only just known,
- to successfully problem-solved,
- to well-known (recognised in most contexts),
- and finally to any variant form, or in a surprising context.

The old established responses can be tripped up when, at one particular moment, the rapid pick up of visual information was not good enough. (The child was tired, unwell, distracted, or having an off-day.)

Four summaries

Clark (1996) foreshadowed massive reshaping of our understanding of perception in the future, as theories of body and mind in context continue to evolve. For the present these summaries may have utility for practitioners.

1.   Goldstone (1998) set many things about visual perception in perspective in this statement from his review.

> Perceptual learning exerts a profound influence on behaviour precisely because it occurs early during information processing and thus shifts the foundation for all subsequent processes in the sequence. (1998, p. 606).

2.   Magdalen Vernon (1957) wrote:

> The general conclusion to be drawn from studies of [visual] form and word perception in little children is that below a certain age they are unable to perceive and remember small details of shape with great accuracy. In particular they do not realize which details are significant and which are comparatively irrelevant in defining the essential structure of a shape; nor do they understand the relationship of parts to the whole. They are also ignorant of the orientation of shapes in space. Thus they may be capable of perceiving and recognizing rather unsystematically certain letters and certain words by means of their general shape or from some of their letters. But they have not acquired the ability to understand the importance of particular details in letter shapes, their spatial position, and their relationship to one another within the total word shape. Even if they can perceive these details they do not remember their significance ... this ability seems to develop rapidly ... though recognition of the importance of correct order of letters in the word may come considerably later. (pp. 29–30)

3.   Another summary was provided by Eleanor Gibson.

> Perceiving by means of symbols was compared with perceiving by means of representations. It is mediated perception ... of a different kind, because the mapping of a symbol to the thing or event is arbitrary or conventional, not naturally given. Learning enters into the perception of symbols in three important ways. First the symbols themselves, such as speech sounds and letters, must be perceptually differentiated from one another. Second, invariants of mapping from the symbol set to the set symbolized, must be learned. This may be a matter of paired associate learning of a code, but it is also possible that the correspondences are abstracted from the stimulus flux. A letter-sound correspondence, for instance, may be induced from a larger context where a recurrent regularity can be detected. Third, a set of symbols has rules for how they may be put together in a sequence. These rules constitute structure and man must learn to perceive the structural constraints in the sequence for the information in even the simplest sentence to be transmitted. (Gibson 1969, p. 443)

4.   The same Eleanor Gibson in her summing up of perceptual development apologised to Lewis Carroll for this account.

> The time has come, the author said
> To sum up many things:
> Of features learned for face and space
> And rules for letter strings —
> Of structure found and noise reduced
> That reinforcement brings.

Note 1

A chapter on 'Eye movements and discourse processing' by Rayner, Raney and Pollatsek (1995) outlines these basic characteristics of eye movements in reading.

> During reading, we make a series of *fixations* and *saccades* as our eyes move from one location in the text to another. Eye movements are necessary because of acuity limitations in the visual system. In order to process a new part of the text, we move our eyes so as to place the fovea (or central region of vision) over that part of the text we wish to process next. Fixations which average around 250 milliseconds, are the periods of time when we acquire new information from the text. Separating the fixations are rapid movements of the eyes (called saccades) from one place to another in the text: on average, the eyes move about 8-9 character spaces with each saccade ... During saccades no useful information is acquired from the text because the eyes are moving so rapidly. Although the majority of eye movements during reading are in the forward direction (or from left-to-right for readers of English), about 10 per cent to 15 per cent of the time we move our eyes back to look at text that our eyes have already passed over; these movements back in the text are referred to as regressions. (p. 10)

Note 2

Eleanor and James Gibson's ecological approach to perception has had a profound influence on the study of visual perception (Clark 1996; Goldstone 1998). This approach emphasises direct perception of information from the world picked up by the learner who goes in search of previously unused information. Goldstone set Gibson's views in current perspective in his recent review.

> In her 1991 preface to her 1963 *Annual Review of Psychology* article, Gibson laments, 'I wound up pointing out the need for a theory and the prediction that more specific theories of perceptual learning are on the way. I was wrong there — the cognitive psychologists have seldom concerned themselves with perceptual learning'. (Gibson 1991, p. 322) The reviewed research suggests that this quote is too pessimistic; there has been much progress on theories of the sort predicted by Gibson in 1963. These theories are receiving convergent support from several disciplines ... Traditional disciplinary boundaries will have to be crossed for a complete account.

References

Bruner, J. 1971. *Going Beyond the Information Given: Studies in the Psychology of Knowing*. New York: W.W. Norton.

Clark, A. 1996. *Being There: Putting Brain, Body, and World Together Again*. Cambridge, MA: MIT Press.

Clay, M.M. 1982. *Observing Young Readers: Selected Papers*. Portsmouth, NH: Heinemann.

———. 1991. *Becoming Literate: The Construction of Inner Control*. Auckland: Heinemann.

———. 1993. *An Observation Survey of Early Literacy Achievement*. Auckland: Heinemann (First Edition 1972; Second Edition 1979; Third Edition 1985; title change 1993).

Gibson, E.J. 1969. *Principles of Perceptual Learning and Development*. New York: Appleton, Century, Crofts.

———. 1991. *An Odyssey in Learning and Perception*. Cambridge, MA: MIT Press.

Gibson, E.J. and H. Levin. 1975. *The Psychology of Reading*. Cambridge, MA: MIT Press.

Goldstone, R.L. 1998. Perceptual learning. *Annual Review of Psychology* 49: 585–612.

Harris, T.L. and R.E. Hodges. 1995. *The Literacy Dictionary: The Vocabulary of Reading and Writing*. Newark, DE: International Reading Association.

Hebb, D.O. 1949. *The Organization of Behaviour*, pp. 101–102. New York: Wiley.

Lynn, R. 1966. *Attention, Arousal and the Orientation Reaction*. London: Pergamon.

McQueen, P.J. 1975. Motor Responses Associated with Beginning Reading. Master of Arts thesis, University of Auckland Library.

Rayner, K., G.E. Raney and A. Pollatsek. 1995. Eye movements and discourse processing. In R.F. Lorch and E.J. O'Brien, eds, *Sources of Coherence in Reading*, Chapter 1. Hillsdale, NJ: Lawrence Erlbaum.

Smith, F. 1971. *Understanding Reading* (First Edition). New York: Holt, Rinehart and Winston.

———. 1978. *Understanding Reading* (Second Edition). New York: Holt, Rinehart and Winston.

Solley, C.M. and G. Murphy. 1960. *Development of the Perceptual World*. New York: Basic Books.

Vernon, M.D. 1957. *Backwardness in Reading: a Study of its Nature and Origin*. Cambridge: Cambridge University Press.

5   Self-correction in text reading: research and theory

5 Self-correction in text reading: research and theory

This chapter also relates back to Chapter 3 and assembling working systems. It explores the appearance and disappearance of self-correcting behaviours and raises the question as to whether these could be considered an early form of executive control mechanisms being used to manage the process of assembling working systems. The review raises more questions than it gives answers at this time.

Introduction

A teacher's observation of an active reader after a few weeks of Reading Recovery (RR)

The teacher listened as the child began to read some books that were familiar. The teacher prompted her to 'Read it with your finger', because she sometimes had difficulty matching a spoken word with the printed word. 'Now it came out right,' said the child. 'I had enough words each time I pointed.' Later the teacher offered no assistance as the child reread the book introduced the day before, a book which the teacher and child had worked on together about some new learning. The child read until, puzzled, she stopped. 'That didn't make sense,' she observed, repeating the beginning of the sentence and taking another look. Then after a moment the child reflected aloud, 'Oh, it says *away. That makes sense.*'

A researcher's observation

At entry to school no child could read any book although within two weeks some 10–15 per cent were responsive to their own names in print. One year later, at six years of age, the children were located all along the *Ready to Read* book series from the first to the fifteenth book level, and three children were still on preliminary material. So how and when were children promoted to their first 'reading book'? Promising children were promoted to one-line-per-page books rather quickly. In five different schools with from average to disadvantaged populations, all children were working on some simple books by their seventh week at school. A number of behaviours were monitored by teachers *prior to children being placed on books,* but no teacher mentioned self-correction or speech repairs back in 1963. The five schools had similar promotion policies and promotion to more challenging reading books depended, not on a calendar date, but on the teacher's judgement of individual children's preparedness. Under these conditions my records showed self-correction (repair or revision) appearing about three weeks prior to their promotion to the books of the reading series. This happened although self-correction was not something their teachers could have talked about. Teachers had a tacit awareness of some change in children's responses to texts.

The children's revision of what they said could have occurred because of awareness of letter and word forms, or some directional rules for attending to print, or some sense of position and movement on the page, or sound links in the speech response, or a mismatch between spoken and written word. To decide about promotion to book-reading teachers might have noticed some movement towards a 'willingness to choose between alternatives' in responses to print. Watching their progress over the rest of the school year it was concluded from this study that children become more attentive to the different kinds of information in print as they try to confirm decisions made, and correct any errors. If they meet with sufficient success they are reinforced for the effort. Problem-solving and self-correction are most tutorial for the learner when there is a large amount of correct responding and not more than 10 per cent of the words involved in error, word-solving or self-correction. (Extracted from Clay 1966, pp. 46–86.)

Description

Self-correction is observed during the oral reading of texts. It is an outcome of trying to read texts. It occurs when a reader misreads a text and, without prompts or signals from another reader, stops and corrects the error. Self-correcting from a child *reading to himself* on his first attempt at a simple book called *The Bear Family* was recorded like this.

Child: Here is Father Bear.
Text: Here is Father Bear.

Child: Mother/SC   is Mother Bear.
Text: Here   is Mother Bear.

That example is simple but when extensive records are analysed such behaviour is very interesting. Why does spontaneous correction of reading errors occur? Presumably it stems from an awareness, however vague, that there is supposed to be a neat fit between the reader's knowledge and the words in print, and as readers work on the several messages of the text — the story, and semantic, syntactic, visual or phonological information — they discover things that do not fit with what they have just read. Sometimes the child follows an error with a protest but does not succeed in making the self-correction.

Child: Dad, let me paint you.   Hey! You can't paint you!
Text: Dad, let me paint too.

Child: ... said the children.   It hasn't got the letters for 'said'.
Text: ... shouted the children.

Child: Country School.   What's 'bus' doing there?
Text: *The School Bus* (book title)

The child's knowledge of the world, or some aspect of reading knowledge, or illustrations probably signalled that something was not quite right in these examples.

Children learn to monitor themselves to keep their correct reading on track, and when something seems to be wrong they usually search for a way to get rid of the dissonance (Schwartz 1997). It is important for teachers to notice self-monitoring because the process is a general one required in all reading, and because the child's half-right–half-wrong behaviours help the teacher to decide what to teach next.

If the child resolves the problem we call this self-correction. Self-correcting can be heard in young readers when the way they are being taught does not discourage this. It is overt and recordable in everyday reading (Clay 1966; Goodman and Goodman 1994). Good readers of five to eight years reading aloud can be heard to follow an error with a self-correction of one in two to five errors (Clay 1967, 1969; Ng 1979; Donald 1981; Singh, Winton and Singh 1984; McNaughton 1988). Self-correction is of interest to researchers because it is more reliably observed than self-monitoring and provides good information of how the reader is making decisions at a) the error and b) the correction. Because its value has been challenged in theoretical debate part of this chapter will focus on the uses and limitations of self-correction as a research variable.

Self-correction: an early form of an executive control process

The main argument of this chapter is that self-correction behaviours are evidence of one kind of executive control developed and mobilised by readers to keep them on track. The term 'executive control' in reading has been applied to several different ways in which readers control their reading. For example, the choices that readers make to read a text in a particular order or at a particular pace, to start reading and to stop, to skip or skim, have been examined. Wagner and Sternberg (1987) identified one of three constituent parts of the executive control of reading as '*monitoring the success of one's strategy implementation, which may lead to revision or outright replacement of the strategy*'. So not only is the rendering of the text corrected but also the process by which the error substitution was selected may have changed.

A close look at self-correcting during the first three years of literacy learning reveals some early indicators of this type of control system which change over time from the first overt occurrences on simple text (the examples given above) through to its disappearance as reading becomes proficient. During that time a teacher has a window of opportunity to observe self-correction as children gradually become able to process the messages in print.

The literature on executive control systems does not imply that the reader or writer knowingly or consciously directs or manages some activity. Most executive control systems proceed at high speeds, and verbalising would get in the way and slow the process. Having students explain why they did something may provide the teacher with more insight into how a child worked, which means that it may help the teacher to scaffold his or her instruction appropriately, but it may interfere with fast integrated solving with minimal attention.

A wider view of self-correction

Self-repair in speech

Self-correction in reading looks like what is called self-repair in oral language, a term which began to appear in the oral language research literature in the 1970s (Frompkin 1971, 1973, 1980; Karmiloff-Smith 1979). The need for this term in oral language was obvious; self-repair refers to the speaker's revising behaviour while generating an utterance. It results in a change to the structure or the message of the utterance (Marshall and Morton 1978; Levy 1999). Self-repair seems to be cognitively similar to self-correcting which occurs in reading, except that a written text requires a visual stimulus to be matched with a verbal one. Self-repair in children's speech has been studied:

- as they produce utterances

- when they act as listeners monitoring and evaluating the messages of others

- as they reformulate their speech in response to listener feedback such as not being understood

- when they are planning and anticipating what to say.

For example, Evans (1985) studied self-initiated repairs in the speech of eighteen kindergarten and eighteen second-grade children in fifteen sessions of 'show and tell' in the classroom. The records were scored for self-correction or repetition, word choice, reference and syntax, postponements and abandonments. Seven per cent of the utterances of children aged five were self-repairs rising to 19 per cent in the older children. Children did detect and repair their own speech errors, but it was not clear whether the repairs were made a) to adjust to perceived listener needs, or b) to meet personal standards of the children for communicating effectively.

David Wood also wrote about children's self-corrections:

The frequent pauses, 'hms', repetitions, backtracking and attempts at self-correction evidenced in the child's talk suggest both that he is aware of, and that he is *working on*, the many problems he has yet to solve in order to make what he says sensible to another person. (Wood 1998, p. 152)

In a research study of children's oral narratives Hickman (1985) reported that children who are learning to speak correct themselves yet seem seldom to be corrected by others. Her four-year-old children seldom attempted to correct their own ambiguous referring expressions, whereas the stories of seven-year-olds contained many examples of pauses, hazes, false starts, reformulations and repetitions: evidence that the children knew that they had work to do in order to achieve coherent, intelligible narratives. Ten-year-olds also frequently paused, hesitated and attempted to correct what they said but their attempts at self-correction usually resulted in effective utterances whereas, more often than not, the seven-year-olds' attempts resulted in ineffective or mixed cases (Wood 1998, pp. 153–157). *Wood suggested that children teach themselves how to use and understand complex aspects of language structure* (p. 136) *and that self-correction in oral language and in problem-solving were signs of self-instruction.* They know more than they can currently say and therefore can solve some of their language-learning problems themselves (p. 135).

The disposition to correct oneself is not an attribute of personality or ability. When children know, albeit intuitively, what looks, sounds or feels right, we have reason to be confident that they will self-correct and self-instruct. Children who do not show signs of self-correction, as many do not in mathematics, are, I suggest, offering mute testimony to the fact that they do not know what they are doing or where they are supposed to be going. (Wood 1988, p. 199)

When Karmiloff-Smith (1992) was explaining how children lift their language competence and progressively change or reformulate how to put ideas into speech, she asked whether working on self-repairs in oral language contributed to these lifts.

She rejected an early model, the Marshall/Morton conclusion that reformulation occurred when speakers noticed they had not been understood, and she concluded from her research on children that being aware of some language forms followed at some distance in time *after* children had used those forms efficiently in their own language. She argued for a success-based theory of acquisition.

An example of a task she used to test children's awareness of particular linguistic features provides an illustration of self-repair. Karmiloff-Smith created a context for language by placing two pens, one eraser, one earring and the child's own watch on the table. She hid the child's watch and then asked, 'What did I do?' Sometimes children made lexical repairs: 'You hid the pe … no, the watch.' At other times they made referential repairs: 'You hid the blue pe … the red pen.' And sometimes they made grammatical or systemic repairs: 'You hid my wat … the watch.' One of her ten-year-olds showed how complicated this last repair is to explain, even though the child explained it very well. The exchange went like this.

Child: You hid the watch.
Observer: Why did you say '*the* watch?'
Child: Well, '*my* watch' because it belongs to me, but I said, 'You hid the watch' because there are no other watches there. If you'd put yours out, I would have had to say 'You hid my watch' because it could have been confusing, but this way it is better for me to say 'You hid the watch' so someone does not think that yours was there too.
            (Karmiloff-Smith 1992, p. 50)

This child explained very clearly the hidden rules we use as we construct utterances.

Self-regulation

There is common ground in the arguments of several theorists which might contribute to understanding self-corrections in reading.

- Noam Chomsky (1957) claimed that every sentence we utter is novel and has to be constructed.

- Self-repairs in oral language occur as we produce utterances which are orchestrated but never automatic, according to Karmiloff-Smith (1992).

- Wood (1978) described strategic behaviour as a programmatic assembly of operations aimed at a common goal. (Reading and writing can be thought of as programmatic assemblies of operations.)

- Rumelhart (1994) described reading as the co-ordination of complex actions and the interaction of several hypotheses across multiple knowledge sources.

- Singer (1994) described reading as assembling working systems to suit the task, which implies that the regulatory hierarchy itself may not be fixed but fluid and changing.

- Singer's (1994) overarching organisation involving input, mediation and response postulates a more general yet simplified image of assembling a solving process within which the potential for self-correction exists.

It seems to follow from such theoretical hypotheses about constructing and orchestrating, building working systems, working across networks and assembling operations, that all such processes leave scope for inefficiencies and error. Young children's self-corrections on literacy tasks demonstrate in a simple way how their inarticulate sense that *'something needs to be done because something is not quite right'* develops into efficient and useful overt behaviour and can become clearly articulated. It then seems to become shaped by successful reading experience into an implicit executive control mechanism operating in silent reading.

Karoly (1993) synthesised many of these discussions when he reviewed recent work on self-regulation for psychologists. He described research on this topic as a healthy and growing enterprise in developmental psychology. Self-regulation, he explained, refers to those processes, internal and/or transactional, that enable the individual to guide his or her goal-directed activities over time and across changing circumstances. Human self-regulation denotes 'staying on-course against obstacles, or recalculating that course' (which is exactly what the term 'recovery' means in 'Reading Recovery'). At some mismatch things that may change are the allocation of attention, the mobilising of effort, planning or problem-solving, verbal cueing and expectations.

The apparent simplicity of the situation is misleading. Karoly warned that when a complex embedded stream of events (like reading a sentence of text) is analysed in research, the risk is that only a portion of the regulatory cycle may be examined. This happens because the seamless integration of causal mechanisms cannot be traced with prevailing analytic techniques. However, we now have more than twenty years of experience with Running Records of text reading which document that when the practising teacher keeps the reading task at 90 per cent accuracy or above, apparently this controls enough of the reading and self-correction situation to reveal to the learner the structure of the task he or she is working on. It also provides teachers with evidence of processing for a period until self-correction disappears and becomes silent processing.

Signalling the same message in more than one way

There are features of texts which increase the possibility of detecting errors. First, there may be three or four different ways of sending the same signal to a listener or reader. For example, there are several signals used to show that a question is being asked. 'What am I talking about?' is clearly a question, a) because it begins with a question word, b) because the order of words has been altered, and c) because it sometimes is said with rising intonation. In print it is written with the question word, the altered verb, a question mark and perhaps speech marks. This multiple signalling in language is called redundancy. In this case redundancy does not mean unnecessary, but rather it indicates there is more than one signal, and if we are uncertain about the first signal we can confirm it by checking another signal. Such redundancy in written language (discussed by Smith 1971 and Haber 1978) is an important concept for understanding how self-correction can arise.

Second, there is another kind of redundancy in the words we read. Each word in print carries several kinds of information — semantic, syntactic, visual, phonological, orthographic and even layout and positioning in texts — and that provides more than one entry to solving a problem. It also means that information from one source can be checked against another (Rumelhart 1994). Alternate routes to information on a piece of text might arise from:

- using the meaning of the story,

- predicting from syntax and checking the letters,

- working out the word from other words by analogy,

- sounding out the word or parts of it,

to name a few options used singly or in combination. Any one of these sources may give the reader information which conflicts with a chosen response. Redundancy exists in speech but in literacy activities there are the added sources of visual information and the layout of text. Redundancy and multiple information sources are important for understanding how a reader begins to self-correct in reading aloud or reading silently.

When the child is learning how to read, information from any of these sources will be fragmentary because the child is still building up the knowledge sources from a zero base. ('He does not know a single word!' is a common lament of children's first teachers.) Prior language knowledge may enable the young reader to 'say what the book says' correctly without knowing much about print. However, by doing this pairing the reader can learn more about the phonological or visual features in print. The process noted in the mature reader is different. He or she:

> … may be seen as selecting, within the available redundant information, those cues that are necessary to message identification. Clearly, in this process, some errors must occur. That efficient readers would develop an effective strategy for recognising when a substantive error has been made and for correcting that error (re-selecting from the available information) is a likely hypothesis and constitutes a strong theoretical basis for regarding self-correcting as a central strategy in reading development. (Donald 1981)

Meeting the 'known' under slightly different conditions

It is common in language to come across something known (as in old and familiar) in a new setting. Its occurrence suddenly makes us think. The element of surprise keeps us flexible and tentative, adjusting our categories and hypotheses, and adding to our knowledge sources. I have assumed in other chapters that any feature of print could pass through several phases of 'knowing' from new to barely known, to easy to get right or wrong, to well-known, and to known in a wide variety of forms. The learner of literacy will always have features of print 'becoming known'. When something is 'becoming known' there will be potential for self-correction to occur, and it is easy to observe this during text reading.

Another important type of 'knowing' for reading text is being familiar enough with the 'form' in sentences, or phrases, or word sequences, to be able to manipulate them (change your response, as in come/comes, Chapter 2, or look at/look after, Chapter 3), or even think of shifting to a different way of putting the sentence together. This can involve grouping our understanding of the string of words in a different way. For example, regrouping may be necessary even though you read the next sentence without error.

We will sell gas to anyone in a glass container. (Pinker 1994, p. 102)

When I first observed young children 're-running' in reading (Clay 1967) I described it as an efficient tactic, going back to the beginning of a sentence or line, clearing the mind of all the false attempts and taking a fresh run at the text. It is probably time to re-examine such repetitions with another theory in mind. In addition to clearing the decks, and providing the reader with scope to pull more information into the solving, I suspect that something else is occurring when we observe this ubiquitous behaviour.

When researchers studied what happened to re-runs or repetitions in records of 'acts of processing', they reported a clear sequence from the early days of learning to read, up through the first and second years of instruction, related to how far back along a line children return. Repetitions get closer and closer to the point of difficulty in this order:

- line beginning
- phrase(s)
- word
- initial letter(s).

If novice readers must parse the printed sentence as they read it word by word (that is, collect up the structure and meaning so far), they fall readily into the most effective way to reconstruct the sentence, the syntax and the meaning by starting the sentence again. In the act of doing this they discover implicitly that 'it is like it is in oral language', although they are not aware that they parse speech. Beginning readers test out whether the grouping of words so far is secure enough to proceed further. Probably we should not give undue weight to this because it is untutored and not conscious. It is interesting, however, to think about what is occurring in re-running and self-correcting; the parsing of an oral language, something already established, is becoming linked to reading.

Repetition of this kind may indicate that the reader is calling upon some established type of processing to contribute to the problem-solving, a signal that working systems are being assembled.

Self-correcting remains in the reading repertoire of mature readers, and is something that television newsreaders try to avoid! It undoubtedly occurs for many reasons but a possible link by beginning readers to the parsing they do as they construct utterances or comprehend them is highly likely.

Descriptive research evidence

On occurrence

In descriptive research of *change over time* in early literacy (Clay 1966, 1967) I studied reading errors and self-correcting behaviours (Clay 1969). Weekly observations of 100 children throughout their first year of instruction yielded 2700 self-corrections for analysis. I plotted error ratios against self-correction ratios for the child who was the median case of each quartile group to illustrate ways in which their progress differed. An interpretation of that data, representing accumulated experience for a child over the first year at school, was that:

- the high-progress readers made few errors and many self-corrections which led to efficient processing of information in print

- the middle to high group produced many errors and many self-corrections; their efforts to resolve inconsistencies worked but the process they used did not operate very efficiently

- the children in the middle to low group were trying to self-correct but there did not seem to be enough good-quality processing for the reader to know whether things were going well or not

- the low-achievement group produced fewer attempts of any kind, had high error rates, made hardly any self-corrections, and showed little effort to construct reading responses. This happened for many different reasons.

(These were quartile groups with 25 children in each. They were not reading similar texts, but were reading texts selected by teachers as appropriate for their presumed level of achievement. Therefore the best performances were recorded on the more difficult and elaborated texts, and the poorest performances on the simplest texts. This is a methodological problem in studying early reading in general and self-correction in particular.)

Overt self-correction behaviour emerges early

Teachers can observe and record self-correction early in instruction; it changes in several ways during the first two or three years of literacy acquisition and disappears in good readers between seven to nine years when a transition is being made to silent reading. If children are required to read orally and if text difficulty is substantially increased, it can be observed in older readers (Williams 1968; Watson and Clay 1975; Ng 1979).

Self-correction ratios relate to progress

Rank correlations of self-corrections summed over weekly observations in the first year of instruction, and expressed as error to self-correction ratios, were moderately correlated with reading progress, measured by standardised word reading tests (Clay 1969) at six, seven and eight years of age (r = 0.67, 0.61, 0.60).

Self-correction appears when correct responding is high

Thompson (1981) made this clarification arguing that some other variable such as the amount of correct responding may bring about this relationship. It is true that a high level of accuracy (90 per cent or higher) is a prerequisite for self-correction to be a positive manoeuvre; the instructional consequence of this is that teachers need to select reading material along a gradient of difficulty to get the balance of correct response to error and to self-correction right (see Figure 1 in Chapter 2). Teachers do not find it hard to select texts that children can read at or above 90 per cent accuracy. *Teaching interactions at self-corrections, as distinct from following correct or incorrect responding, are timely and can capitalise on the learner's shift in attending.*

Self-correction can be increased or decreased by teacher response

This was demonstrated in several studies within a theoretical framework of behavioural analysis, which reported that when teachers give or deny time for pausing, or vary their levels of verbal reinforcement for self-correcting, their interactions appear to alter the amount of self-correcting that occurs (Glynn, McNaughton and Wotherspoon 1975; McNaughton and Glynn 1981; Singh, Winton and Singh 1984; McNaughton 1987; Wheldall and Glynn 1988).

Do proficient readers self-correct?

Ng (1979) studied 52 proficient readers in their second year of school in New Zealand (aged 6:0, 6:6 and 7:0), and ratios of one self-correction to one to five errors were found in all four proficient groups from average to very high progress. However she controlled the text difficulty to 90 per cent or above for each reader. On identical texts the self-correction rates would probably have varied.

Self-correction behaviour is dependent on many things

Obviously text difficulty determines whether self-correction occurs because self-correction ratios depend upon the prior occurrence of error. When a text is easy there is little need and little opportunity to self-correct. When the text is hard there is little problem-solving of errors or unknown words and therefore little self-correction. However, if the text is around the child's instructional level, neither too easy nor too hard (which can be operationally defined as reading at or above 90 per cent accuracy) then readers produce self-corrections which are very informative for reinforcing and shaping processing behaviours.

From research reports and from practical use of self-correction in classroom assessments of reading progress by teachers, it is clear that this behaviour varies depending upon:

- the occurrence of error
- the level of error
- the difficulty level of the text for the reader
- the type of text being read
- the interactions of the teacher and reader
- the characteristics of the instructional programme
- the stage in strategy formation reached by the reader.

Having due regard for those interrelationships it has still been possible for researchers to describe, and for teachers to create, the conditions under which self-correction rather than teacher correction of children's errors in reading can occur (Learning Media 1985). Teachers are encouraged to compare error and self-correction ratios to guide their judgements about readers and texts (using Running Records in reliable ways) but not to depend on one or the other, and not to engage in quantitative analyses of these ratios (Clay 1993a, 1993b).

In summary

Observable, overt self-correction in language productions occurs during the first two to three years of school in oral reading instruction and raises questions about how a reader is interacting with a particular text. It does not have a linear relationship with progress because although it arises early, fewer self-corrections are observed as reading becomes increasingly well-orchestrated. To force older readers to make self-corrections one has to find texts that are artificially difficult for them (such as text with invented words as in science fiction or written in the style of Lewis Carroll). During early literacy learning self-correction may alert teachers to how readers are learning to use sequences of information in text (Rumelhart 1994). Observing self-correction may provide teachers with important information for scaffolding instruction for individual needs.

Silent readers obviously regulate how they read but self-regulation begins early, and self-correcting is one observable activity among a range of self-monitoring and problem-solving strategies that teachers of young children can watch for. Young readers notice that things are not quite right, and become aware of mismatches. They search for more information and this can result in corrections. The reader is not always successful, and is often prompted by a teacher to take another look. Self-correcting actions arise unprompted when learners find that something they see, or think of, conflicts with something else. Here are three examples.

	1	2	3
Child:	I/(Repeat)/Nope!/R/SC	meet/mak/SC	and she said/(Pause)/(Repeat)/SC
Text:	It	make	and she did

Beginning readers and writers probably have no more than a vague sense that something is wrong but by the second year some children can become spontaneously articulate about some of their self-corrections. This should not surprise us because ever since they learned to speak they have been monitoring messages in oral language. Researchers find it difficult to record all the self-correcting behaviours of second and third year readers for two different reasons:

- the speed of processing increases,

- and self-correcting seems to become covert and begins to take place before the reader makes a response we can hear.

When a reader half-articulates the initial consonant of one word and quickly switches to another word, recorders find it hard to agree about what happened.

Self-correction must contribute to the forward thrust of reading competency. At each substitution the child initiates a search for more information, generates and evaluates hypotheses, and makes decisions. By definition a decision that ends in a self-correction is a correct decision and the reader may have attended to features ignored in the first attempt. We cannot know what information the reader used to reach a correct response which fits perfectly into its textual slot, but when an error is corrected we can ask, 'What information was absent in the error that was subsequently present in the self-correction?' What happens over time to self-correcting needs to be part of an explanation of early reading progress.

Self-corrections help researchers to make inferences about how the reader makes use of those hidden interrelationships that exist in stretches of text. In the error/self-correction couplet we could explore changes over time in the reader's use of Rumelhart's (1994) knowledge sources, noting which are available to the reader — the letter features and forms, phonological information, visual clustering of letters, words, phrases, word groups, syntax or grammar, local meaning (words, sentence, page), story and plot, world knowledge of a wider kind, direction, layout, and print conventions. There will be a large measure of inference and hypothesis in how a teacher interprets self-corrections but we are particularly informed by children who expose their thinking to us, commenting on how they are carrying out the self-correcting. However, if a researcher induces the learner to focus on, or talk about, the processing (that is, how he is working), then this changes the nature of the processing.

Self-correction is mostly observed when young children are trying to read texts. A theory of reading words in isolation cannot provide a satisfactory model for understanding texts since it cannot deal with the hidden syntactic and semantic interrelationships between words that occur in texts, or with the sequential dependencies between prior and subsequent parts of texts. *Although self-correction could be said to occur in most cognitive activity, when observed in language activities it is related in important ways to sequence and time, for what has occurred so far in a sentence or story constrains what can then occur.*

In some instances self-correction appears to arise by a more 'direct memory for words' process, but this does not characterise what *young* learners do most of the time.

Theoretical utility

From behavioural analysis research

Behavioural analysis research has contributed to discussions of self-correction (see Note 3, p. 83) and McNaughton's arguments around the issues of learning new words in context (1985), and the role of errors in literacy acquisition (1988), and learning to read independently (1981, 1987) are presented to illustrate this.

He asked, 'How can the reader go beyond what has been directly taught when faced with the unfamiliar?', and found that successive encounters with, and solutions of, unknown words can produce learning. His research showed that at least a quarter of the unknown words encountered during reading were learned sufficiently well by average and high progress readers while reading texts to be identified in isolation in a subsequent test. The readers could identify some words in context which they had not previously identified in isolation. Having identified them once, they continued to do so across successive encounters in different sentence contexts. He concluded that the solving in context was an impressive display of independence by relative novices (1985).

In a paper entitled 'A history of errors in the analysis of oral reading behaviour' (1988), he argued for two possible interpretations of behavioural data on errors while reading.

> Behavioural analyses of oral reading behaviour have ascribed different functions to errors and the correction of errors. Two positions are discussed. One is the legacy of Skinner which viewed errors as problematic and which advocates near error-less learning. The other position views errors and potential errors as providing opportunities for self-regulation and enhanced feedback. On the basis of recent research this paper argues that errors can have generative and inhibiting effects on oral reading, depending on the instructional context and the literacy goals of the classroom. (McNaughton 1988, p. 21)

He also argued that readers who learn from instructional interactions with teachers must eventually become proficient and independent of the teacher's instruction. This contrasts with seeing the teacher as 'the informed one' who transmits learning to the child. He cited studies of learners actively solving problems and argued that idiosyncratic but independent strategies used in this problem-solving must become increasingly effective and independent of the situations in which they were developed. Relative independence is present when the child controls the performance and is therefore actively engaged in learning. Such independence does not just 'arise'; it is an outcome of the learning events created by teachers, and of negotiations between teachers and learners which foster and make room for such independence. So readers learn to go beyond what they can at present do, and go beyond the teaching they receive. He claimed that independent learning as he defined it 'is more robust and generally more effective than learning which is cued and controlled by someone else'. Self-correction is one indicator of independent problem-solving.

He proposed that the opportunity to monitor, evaluate and modify performance creates performance-directed regulation, arising from one's own performance. The existence of a low but significant rate of potential and actual error may facilitate the acquisition of reading skill. The setting events which increase the probability of interactions between reader and text and reader and teacher are:

- the types of texts

- the difficulty levels in the sequencing of texts

- the dialogue events which characterise group instruction, and the characteristics of one-to-one settings.

A cognitive theory of developing inner controls

Self-repairs appear early in the preschooler's speech. The beginning reader demonstrates self-correction, not only on language but also on matching verbal behaviours with directional movements (see the example which opens this chapter). When children read texts of appropriate difficulty level for their present reading skills (that is, at or above 90 per cent accuracy levels), this gives enough support from familiar features in text to allow attention to shift to novel features of text, without losing the support of language. Language provides the context within which the word is embedded; the meaning and language structures provide some basis for deciding about the challenge; story and text so far may trigger a checking process; and printed letters and words contribute learned phonological associations. Active constructing and checking processes ensure that readers will learn more every time they read, independent of instruction. That is one way new learning occurs.

Self-correcting provides a window on processing

At this time children are building an inner control capable of generating appropriate responses to texts of ever-increasing difficulty, but as the competent reader becomes more competent that behaviour is observed less often by teachers.

Correct or silent reading provides no such window on the processing that is occurring. Self-correcting provides an example of how and when a self-correcting network of strategies for generating responses to texts might be observed or studied. The behaviour sequence tells what is ignored in the error response and the self-correction tells what extra information could have been attended to, in order to get to the correction. So an error response with a mismatch of information is noticed by the reader (conflict) and self-correcting activity is initiated. By definition the result of the self-correction is agreement between all sources of information in the text (success).

The observer cannot tell precisely what information the reader used to generate the error or the self-correction but comparisons between the two can generate explanations of the processing being attempted.

Learning to read takes place over time and reading behaviour can be observed from the onset of formal instruction until a stage of relative independence when the reader learns more about reading by reading. The reader making good progress during this period gradually constructs:

- a network of strategic behaviours
- or action systems
- or cell assemblies
- or hierarchical structures
- or assembled components

(and there are many theoretical accounts of these, each slightly different from the other). The reader is seen to be searching for information in print that supports correct responding. These cognitive terms describe what readers do as they work sequentially on the information sources in print to get to the author's message.

Children have to learn ways of operating on print using what they know to check their estimations of what the novel features of text say. They have to learn how and where to search for information, how to cross-check information, how to go back and get more information, and how to get confirmation. They cannot do this within a narrow strategy of sounding out words or mere memory for known words but must go beyond this if they are to be able to check for themselves whether they are correct. *They learn to work with what they know to get to what they do not know, and to confirm what they are unsure of.*

An efficient system of behaviours for reading texts of increasing difficulty includes many kinds of strategic behaviours such as:

- controlling serial order according to the directional rules for the script being read, across lines and within words

- using what you know about in reading to help writing and vice versa

- problem-solving with more than one kind of information

- actively searching for various types of information in print

- using visual information

- using language information

- drawing on stored information

- using phonological information

- working on categories, rules or probabilities about features in print

- using strategies which maintain fluency

- using strategies which problem-solve new features of printed words and meanings

- using strategies which detect and correct error.

(The 'fresh green leaves' example in Chapter 3, p. 121, illustrates some of this reading work.)

Behaviours that signal the assembling of working systems

As each paper in this volume has been developed independently a problem has emerged. 'Assembling working systems' has created a demand for identifying how self-correction can be aligned with its hypotheses. I see this task as one for the future, and urge my readers at this point to consider a more detailed account of self-correction as one active part of the assembling of early working systems, linked tightly with developing executive control mechanisms.

The practical utility of self-correction

Signals of processing for teachers to look for

Usually in correct reading we do not know when a reader notices new features of print because the response fits perfectly into its textual slot, but if that reader makes an error and then corrects it (and the teacher is recording the behaviour in detail) then the teacher can prompt, demonstrate, or teach immediately to adjust the processing or after reviewing her records of the lesson can analyse what kinds of information are being ignored to produce the error. Knowing the progressions that typically occur the teacher can judge whether the processing is becoming more effective. Her teaching is towards 'how to do the solving' rather than towards being correct and accurate. Prior to a major shift to silent reading teachers can check on whether appropriate processing systems are in place. If, on the other hand, reliance is placed only on correct responding as the indicator of progress in reading, teachers do not have access to this inside view of preparedness for what is ahead. The two approaches yield different explanations of the self-extending competencies of the processing system in silent readers.

Analysis of self-corrections

When the reader stops, tries again, and corrects the original error, a teacher has some evidence about the kind of information in print being used to problem-solve the text. The teacher needs to take a record of this behaviour as it occurs (Clay 2000). An analysis of both error and self-correction behaviour, separately and in relation to each other, tells the teacher:

- what the child was attending to at the point where error occurred

- whether the child was aware of mismatches between the text and the first selected response

- what the child was attending to in resolving the error

- when the child was relating 'external' information out there in the text to prior 'internal' information that child already had.

The teacher can analyse the errors for the kind of information that was neglected, and the self-corrections for the information subsequently included, and can tune his or her interactions with the child accordingly.
   If teachers:

- record the original error behaviour,

- and the problem-solving of the error,

- and the subsequent self-correction,

this provides them with a window on that child's current reading processes for reading that particular text. Too much attention to accuracy draws teacher attention to errors but not to solutions. Attention to self-corrections provides the teacher with a way of observing what information the child is using or neglecting to use at the point where an error is made and what initiatives the child makes to overcome the problem.

A check on teacher inference

Teachers make assumptions about pupils at every turn in the working day. Some assumptions prove to be valid and useful and some are false. Teachers need ways of checking on their everyday assumptions about children. Taking records of children's reading and writing provides information against which to check one's assumptions.

Teachers are encouraged to select text to achieve accuracy at or above the 90 per cent accuracy level. Within the 90–100 per cent accuracy level they watch for the subgroup of behaviours classed as self-corrections. These provide the signals that 'reading work' is being done.

Absence of such behaviour can mark two opposing possibilities — either successful, accurate reading or errors occurring with no successful error-correction. The teacher's solution to the first phenomenon is to lift the level of text difficulty and observe again. The second phenomenon should be cause for concern and should turn the teacher's attention to the child's problem-solving strategies on novel text. Perhaps the reader is unable to engage in a search for more information and bring information together from several sources.

The inferences teachers make from observations of a more general kind can be checked by:

- taking records of a reading
- analysing a Running Record
- checking the results of teaching and intervention studies.

There is an important role in the beginning stages of a complex constructed activity like reading for teachers to check on whether their inferences about what children need are close to what is actually needed.

Contributions to teaching interactions

Does self-correcting behaviour provide for quality learning opportunities? Probably, in at least two ways.

1.   There is an opportunity for children to notice their own reading processing. By definition self-correction is initiated by the reader. So, reading along a line of story text the child becomes aware without prompting that something is awry. Young children often go back to the beginning of the sentence taking a fresh run at the text. Older children return only a few words or perhaps stop and work at the troublesome word. This is a moment of close attention. An error response has occurred, is momentarily doubted, and a new search for alternatives takes place. The need to find and use information of various kinds in print is apparent to the reader, and the need to choose between alternatives is the task in hand.

A new response is tried. At this point a self-correction reinforces the reader for several activities he or she has carried out. The reader is reinforced:

- for monitoring his or her own reading and detecting a mismatch

- for searching and finding further information

- for selecting a word which best fits the information he or she can work with

- for making the self-correction which fits well with the message so far.

By definition self-corrections reinforce all the reading work and searching and selecting that was done to find the correct response.

2. There is an opportunity for teaching interaction. The self-correction provides the teacher with an interactive opportunity, to talk about what occurred, and what the child noticed, to link this to other features of print, with a focus on successful problem-solving.

3. When a reader notices an error but is not able to correct it some strong signals are being sent to the teacher. When children sense an error has occurred, give it attention, try another response but do not solve the problem it is as if two hypotheses are up and running together and a decision between them cannot be made. What might a teacher say? Partial attempts are where we can observe whether the teaching is being directed to the need which the child is demonstrating (contingent teaching).

Signals of changes in processing over time

These signals can be observed. The presence of error and the absence of self-correction in the text reading of beginning readers can signal to a teacher that a child is not actively responding to mismatches of what he or she is saying with various sources of information in the text (meaning, syntax, visual or phonological information). If a child is merely inventing text he or she will not notice a mismatch between any two sources of information; the child has to be monitoring closely to notice conflict between a word which retains the meaning with what he or she sees in print, or a syntactic prediction which conflicts with the sound of the first letter of the word he or she is looking at. Good readers take action to try to problem-solve conflicts and this sometimes leads to successful self-corrections. On the first page of a new book a child reads 'Here is spring.' for 'Spring is here.' and corrects himself. Less able readers can be prompted by their teachers to search for, and to become aware of, mismatches (Wong, Groth and O'Flahaven 1994).

At the classroom level the teacher needs markers of change over time in children's reading behaviours. On page 191 there is a list of how far the reader returns along the text to make a self-correction, and that list provides markers of progress which teachers can rely on. There is little variation across that sequence among high or low progress children. A child who typically corrects after the initial letter/phoneme group will only rarely make a longer return. The exceptions would occur on difficult texts. If teachers are encouraged to sensitively observe change over time in the development of a reading process, they will notice the emergence, operation and disappearance of self-correction behaviour as markers of change over time.

Those observations may not be of much importance to classroom teachers in programmes where the curriculum dictates what the teacher must introduce, and would be more significant in programmes that were theoretically based on children's construction of reading processes. They are particularly helpful for observing progress in children taking different paths to an effective reading process.

So an absence of self-correcting on an appropriate level of text difficulty should be a signal to any teacher to prompt the child to 'work it out' acknowledging that this is an acceptable thing to do when things do not seem to be 'a good fit'.

It expands the learner's control over word-solving

When a reader does not yet know:

- all the features of letters,

- or all the letters of the alphabet,

- or most letter-sound relationships,

this novice reader is nevertheless able to read stories in his or her reading books supported by what he or she does know, by the texts themselves and by the teacher.

Even at entry into formal literacy instruction reading is self-regulated in this sense.

A range of self-monitoring and problem-solving strategies

Self-correcting is only one kind of processing activity but it is a general strategy, applied in each area of text information, to relationships across language sources like reading and writing, to other language activities, and to other cognitive activities. It is a sign of effective reading processing initiated by the reader. It is an explicit example of Singer's (1994) idea of a subroutine called momentarily into action when the text features demand that it be assembled into the ongoing processing (see Chapter 3).

We access the self-correction subroutine as easily as I call on a spell-check on my computer and correct my erroneous spelling. Something unknown initiates a search and self-correcting is not the only possible outcome. An absence of self-correcting reduces the learner's opportunities for initiating, forming, practising, extending and refining a network of strategies. Although this cannot be the only route to strategy formation self-correction has features which make it particularly helpful a) to the teacher and b) to the learner who is constructing different ways to get to a response, to affirm a decision, and to correct the response if it is not 'a good fit'.

- What happens during self-corrections calls for explanation because behaviours suggest a potential shift in cognitive processing from what occurred at the uncorrected error.

- Self-correction occurs in perceptual and cognitive types of processing, starting with a vague awareness that something is wrong (Rumelhart 1994; Bruner 1957).

- Self-correcting is important in the study of text processing, rather than in word-reading theories, because it includes information on the use being made by the reader of invisible interrelationships between text features, across sentences, and across discourse.

Successful problem-solving confirms the strategies by which it was carried out, as well as the decisions made. *It is self-congratulatory.* Success will be confirmed by the solving of the problem, the strategies will be reinforced, new information or new links to stored knowledge will be highlighted, new discriminations will be made, and a check with an outside frame of reference — meaningfulness or common practice in the real world — will have been made. The system generating the reading behaviour can be enhanced in two ways: a) by the addition of new data, and/or b) by the strengthening of the strategies that were used. Success not only improves performances on text of the same level of difficulty but also could extend the capacity of the system so that the strategies can be applied to a text that is more difficult. It is my contention that the strong processing systems of proficient readers began the development of these complex word-solving strategies during their first formal lessons or self-initiated attempts to read (see Kay, Chapter 2).

Self-correction probably tutors us to be more explicit in thinking about other processes which may occur as the child reads text correctly when, for example, he or she may not have direct access to a word, uses covert processing and reads the word correctly. Or the child may read correctly and be aware that the correct responses still do not make sense to him or her.

However, self-corrections after errors cannot logically be seen as the agent of such change (as distinct from merely a signal) because successful reading responses will also be the result of problem-solving and checking, and the active reader has much more daily experience with such successful processing than records of error plus self-correction behaviours alone will show. Those records show only the processing at a point where the reading behaviour system has failed to achieve a correct response. There would be more reinforcement to the reader's behaviour system in the masses of correct reading that successfully gets to meaning.

How readers expand the strategic network

When children can work in this way on texts selected at an appropriate level of difficulty the gain is not merely that correct words have been reinforced and practised but that children have opportunities to expand their literacy processing systems. They search for information, pick up new information, cross-relate different types of information, and make decisions using different text-solving strategies.

Opportunities to self-correct allow children to push out the boundaries of their own text knowledge and expand their strategies for doing this. Self-corrections provide excellent opportunities for self-instruction. Because of the interdependent relationships between error and text difficulty it would be difficult to demonstrate that self-correction by itself is a significant determinant of any change which occurs. Group data and averaged scores make little sense when considering self-corrections. However, that does not mean that we can ignore its occurrence and concentrate on variables which have been described as causative. *It is one logical possibility that using phonological information while reading, given the ill-fitting match between sound clusters and text clusters in English (Dewey 1970), only facilitates reading providing some monitoring or self-regulatory self-correction processes are operating.*

A theory for teaching or a theory for explanation: must we choose?

Having come to understand the practical utility and importance of recording self-correction for teaching purposes as the above discussion suggests, I am uncomfortable with the argument that it cannot be parsimoniously incorporated into reading theory, as Thompson (1981) and Share (1990) have suggested. Can models derived from scientific research ignore, discredit or discard a real world variable like this? Grounded theory must incorporate what occurs in the real world as part of the explanation, and this may be precisely why it is useful to have grounded theory around; it acts as a self-correcting opportunity for other theoretical models.

Descriptive developmental research, and behavioural analysis studies of interventions or treatments, and studies of teaching interactions all pay close attention to how the processing of information changes over time in learners. Research designs which make synchronous studies of outcome scores for groups of children produce information which does not tell us how teaching should proceed if we want to change those learners a little at a time over an extended period of time.

Is there a cognitive payoff during literacy acquisition because of the ways in which the learner problem-solves literacy challenges? This is an important supposition in a theory which assumes that there are multiple types of information available in texts; and that little children have to discover what the problem is that they are trying to solve and what kinds of information to search for. *Any theory of how to access various kinds of information and how to search for and pick up the appropriate information while orchestrating the sequential behaviours of text reading will be difficult to test because of the complexity of such a theory.* Yet self-correction could provide a manipulable research variable of what Clark (1996) described as the way we utilise environments to enhance our cognitive functioning.

The selection of an appropriate text in early reading provides the challenge for the reader to engage with novel features of text. *It is both the opportunity for error behaviour and the control of the amount of error behaviour which provide the opportunities for self-corrections.* These in turn provide opportunities to pay closer attention or rearrange categories or shift rules so that the system takes in more information and extends its capacity by doing so. And it is probably important that this occurs as a fairly rapid sequence of changes, day by day in quick succession. In the past we have given slow learners time to learn slowly, and that may have made it harder for them.

These ideas are a challenge to research design. It is fortunate that a literacy processing theory used in the RR intervention has been able to produce successful results with most of the lowest achievers among six-year-old children in English-speaking countries. Perhaps some validity for the concept of self-correction discussed above derives from the massive size of the RR intervention populations. The 'Acts of processing' studies (Chapter 2) have traced a path in the normal development of proficient readers which is consistent with this view of self-correction, and longitudinal studies of subsequent progress following RR interventions show sustained progress. Bryant and Bradley (1985) recommend the triangulation of evidence from experimentation, cross-sectional and longitudinal studies, claiming that this is logically required to confirm research results in developmental psychology. We could now design the third kind of the validation in the triangle, the experiments, to give self-correction theoretical status.

Does research on causation guide or mislead instruction?

The complex patterned stimuli in texts provide many sources of information, which are intricately interdependent, and which are used to select a single solution in which all the sources of input agree. There are presumably:

* several alternative routes to the same solution

* several contributing causes of the same solution

* several alternative sequences of attention or focus

- several optional ways to analyse inputs like phonological analysis or direct perception and relate these to the outcomes.

With such a view it is an understatement to claim that the search for causation in achievement learning is inevitably problematic (Karoly 1993).

School learning consists of several complex sets of learning each of which involves different kinds of psychological functioning, and all of which depend on what the learner has learned so far. In literacy learning children must deal with language structure and meanings, visual perception learning, motor skill of hand and eye movements, knowledge of the world and of the world of books, estimates of the way things can be and can be expected to be, and many of these are stored as memories derived from successful and unsuccessful experience so far. A study of any indicator of early achievements prior to school in any contributing area should correlate in well-designed experimental studies with subsequent progress. Each and every one of the contributing areas of prior achievement may be considered in one sense causative.

Another feature of complex school learning is that programmes expect children to learn aspects of the achievement in certain sequences, and opportunities are provided and withheld in terms of curriculum sequences in the delivery of instruction. So, in this case, a cause may be the cultural opportunity (or lack of it) to get the necessary prior experience, say, a sense of story, which the mandated curriculum requires the child to have.

Suppose as a particular child begins to put ways of working with printed text together to extract messages (reading) or produce messages (writing), and the child attends to messages and structure of language when the programme attends to letter-sound relationships, then his or her hypotheses about the task will be working at odds with those of the teacher. And the emphases could be the other way around. In the interactive situation where the assumptions of teacher and child are mismatched I am not sure where causation fits. Being low in reading skills is a product of facing a programme opportunity you were unable to use. Some survive and others stumble (Stanovich 1986).

The texts which a teacher chooses for a child can facilitate or constrain the opportunities that a child gets to process text information, and the difficulty level of those texts relative to the child's current skills will create or constrain the opportunities for the child to use what he or she knows in the service of independently learning more through reading, making errors and self-correcting. One can say that in this sense the programme and its materials combined with the teacher's decisions cause many of the errors in the child's reading behaviour.

If, on the other hand, one sees reading behaviour as generated by a range of text-reading strategies which teachers may foster by activities like:

- accepting self-corrections as valuable activities rather than 'messy reading' (and note that the result is a correct response),

- allowing time for children to self-correct instead of jumping in and telling or prompting,

- reinforcing the child with comments directed towards the processing behaviours such as 'I liked the way you did that',

all of which lead to appropriate strategic problem-solving, then self-corrections are markers of such processing and do not create or cause it. Dissonance might be seen as the cause of a search, and the hunch or discomfort is not something we know much about although all readers have experienced it.

A network of strategies makes up an action system the creation of which allows for independent learning. The important question is, 'What causes the action system for literacy to come into existence?' There are prior systems like an oral language generating system and knowledge of the world, both of which can create dissonance at an error. However, it is a function of brains that they note and work on dissonant information until it becomes consonant with what the brain knows from a variety of sources (or until we give up on trying to solve the problem which Bruner (1957) called 'gating').

Research may help us to understand causes which occur prior to or during a series of events. Teachers are not able to control the learners' prior exposure to learning, so they must focus on the interactive option; they have management control over that. *The interactive option offers the greatest payoff for teaching even though focus on the prior opportunities might produce the best explanation.* We may be investing tremendous research effort in a research paradigm which can explain but not improve literacy learning because it does not deal with change over time in individuals.

Share (1990) questioned the attention paid by New Zealand teachers of junior classes to self-correction in oral reading. I think he assumed that because teachers record children's self-correction behaviour in their monitoring of children's reading that those teachers were making interpretations that this behaviour caused progress. From a research study he claimed that text difficulty could be considered to be the cause and explanation of inter-individual differences. Given the usual interpretation of causation in experimental research using inferential statistics I could agree with him. However, I would not describe self-correction as a cause of reading progress for things are not as simple as that, especially when one studies change over time in a complex processing system which is still developing! If engaging in self-monitoring is part of the formation of feedback loops essential for message-getting in text reading, and if Singer's concept that a subroutine can be momentarily called into action is applied to self-correction, and if teachers are attending to self-monitoring and self-corrections, then the surface manifestation of self-correction behaviour is one reliable marker of processing when a child is learning to read. If the teacher selects the text difficulty so that self-correcting occurs (which means that the text is read by the child with 90 per cent accuracy or better) and if the teacher provides appropriate teaching interactions, it may follow that the teacher can steadily lift the text difficulty level. The issue that Share and I disagree upon is this. He attributes progress to the rise in text difficulty while I attribute it to the cognitive constructing engaged in by the child who is reading that text. Those attributions are viewing the same event but from different perspectives. We start with different assumptions and arrive at much the same conclusion. I suspect that it was our methodologies for collecting data that got in the way and made a virtual consensus look like a protagonists' debate.

A problem for me with a causal variable approach is that it does not contribute to understanding *in fine detail the changing nature of the interactions that should occur between learners and teachers over time* while a processing system is being constructed. The questions about reading and writing processes to be addressed by self-correction research are whether feedback loops (or Clark's (1996) soft-assembled action loops) involving self-monitoring and self-regulation are essential:

- for reading and/or writing continuous text

- for error detection and correction

- for focusing the learner's attention on the fine detail in print

- for refining teaching responses when working with individual learners

- for silent reading when the teacher cannot prompt the process.

If self-regulation of these complex sequential activities is important, then self-correction in its overt form in beginning reading may be an early sign of the emergence of effective acts of processing of the multiple messages within written texts.

Undirected monitoring

I have just self-corrected the spelling of 'acquisition' while proof-reading this text, not consciously looking for or noting spelling errors, but some visual search outside my conscious direction hovered over the problem area until I finally went back, took notice of it, and corrected it.

References

Britton, B.K. and S.M. Glynn, eds. 1967. *Executive Control Processes in Reading.* Hillsdale, NJ: Lawrence Erlbaum.

Bruner, J.S. 1957. On perceptual readiness. *Psychological Review* 64: 123–152.

Bryant, P. and L. Bradley. 1985. *Children's Reading Problems.* Oxford: Blackwell.

Chomsky, N. 1957. *Syntactic Structures.* The Hague: Mouton.

Clark, A. 1996. *Being There: Putting Brain, Body, and World Together Again.* Cambridge, MA: MIT Press.

Clay, M.M. 1966. Emergent Reading Behaviour. Doctoral dissertation, University of Auckland Library.

———. 1967. The reading behaviour of five-year-old children: A research report. *New Zealand Journal of Educational Studies* 2, 1: 11–31.

———. 1969. Reading errors and self-correction behaviour. *British Journal of Educational Psychology* 39: 47–56.

———. 1993a. *An Observation Survey of Early Literacy Achievement.* Auckland: Heinemann (First Edition 1972; Second Edition 1979; Third Edition 1985; title change 1993).

———. 1993b. *Reading Recovery: A Guidebook for Teachers in Training.* Auckland: Heinemann.

———. 2000. *Running Records for Classroom Teachers.* Auckland: Heinemann.

Dewey, G. 1970. *English Spelling: Roadblock to Reading.* New York: Teachers College Press, Columbia University.

Donald, D. 1981. The role of illustrations in children's oral reading accuracy, strategies and comprehension at different developmental and progress levels: A psycholinguistic guessing game. Unpublished doctoral dissertation, University of Cape Town Library.

Evans, M.A. 1985. Self-initiated repairs: A reflection of communicative monitoring in young children. *Developmental Psychology* 21, 2: 365–371.

Frompkin, V.A. 1971. The non-anomalous nature of anomalous utterances. *Language* 47, 1: 27–52.

———, ed. 1973. *Speech Errors as Linguistic Evidence.* The Hague: Mouton.

———, ed. 1980. *Errors in Linguistic Performance: Slips of the Tongue, Ear, Pen, and Hand.* New York: Academic Press.

Glynn, T., S. McNaughton and A. Wotherspoon. 1975. Modification of reading, writing and attending behaviour in a special class for retarded children. Unpublished research paper, Department of Education, University of Auckland.

Goodman, Y.M. and K.S. Goodman. 1994. To err is human: Learning about language processes by analysing miscues. In R.B. Ruddell, M.R. Ruddell and H. Singer, eds, *Theoretical Models and Processes of Reading,* pp. 104–123. Newark, DE: International Reading Association.

Haber, R.N. 1978. Visual perception. *Annual Review of Psychology* 29: 31–59.

Hickman, M.E. 1985. The implications of discourse skills in Vygotsky's developmental theory. In J.V. Wertsch, ed., *Culture, Communication and Cognition: Vygotskian perspectives.* Cambridge: Cambridge University Press.

Karmiloff-Smith, A. 1979. *A Functional Approach to Child Language.* Cambridge: Cambridge University Press.

———. 1992. *Beyond Modularity: A Developmental Perspective on Cognitive Science.* Cambridge, MA: MIT Press.

Karoly, P. 1993. Mechanisms of self-regulation: A systems view. *Annual Review of Psychology* 44: 23–52.

Learning Media. 1985. *Reading in the Junior Classes.* Wellington: Ministry of Education.

Levy, Y. 1999. Early metalinguistic competence: Speech monitoring and repair behavior. *Developmental Psychology* 35, 3: 822–834.

Marshall, J.C. and J. Morton. 1978. On the mechanics of EMMA. In A. Sinclair, R.J. Javella and W. Klein, eds, *The Child's Conception of Language*, pp. 225–239. Berlin: Springer-Verlag.

McNaughton, S. 1981. Becoming an independent reader: Problem-solving during oral reading. *New Zealand Journal of Educational Studies* 16: 172–185.

———. 1985. Beyond teaching: The development of independence in learning to read. Conference address, 11th Annual Australian Reading Association, Brisbane.

———. 1987. *Being Skilled: The Socialization of Learning to Read.* London: Methuen.

———. 1988. A history of errors in the analysis of oral reading behaviour. *International Journal of Experimental Educational Psychology* 8, 1 and 2: 21–30.

McNaughton, S. and T. Glynn. 1981. Delayed versus immediate attention to reading errors: effects on accuracy and self-correction. *Educational Psychology* 1: 57–65.

Ng, S.M. 1979. Error and Self correction in Reading and Oral Language. Doctoral dissertation, University of Auckland Library.

O'Leary, S. 1997. *Five Kids: Stories of Children Learning to Read.* Bothell, WA: The Wright Group/ McGraw-Hill.

Pinker, S. 1994. *The Language Instinct: How the Mind Creates Language.* New York: William Morrow.

Rumelhart, D.E. 1994. Toward an interactive model of reading. In R.B. Ruddell, M.R. Ruddell and H. Singer, eds, *Theoretical Models and Processes of Reading* (Fourth Edition), pp. 864–894. Newark, DE: International Reading Association.

Schwartz, R.M. 1997. Self-monitoring in beginning reading. *The Reading Teacher* 51, 1: 40–48.

Share, D.J. 1990. Self-correction rates in oral reading: Indices of efficient reading or artefact of text difficulty? Research Note, c/o the author, Haifa University, Haifa, Israel.

Singer, H. 1994. The substrata-factor theory of reading. In R.B. Ruddell, M.R. Ruddell and H. Singer, eds, *Theoretical Models and Processes of Reading* (Fourth Edition), pp. 895–927. Newark, DE: International Reading Association.

Singh, N.N., A.S.W. Winton and J. Singh. 1984. Effects of delayed versus immediate attention to oral reading errors on the reading proficiency of mentally retarded children. *Applied Research in Mental Retardation* 6: 295–305.

Smith, F. 1971. *Understanding Reading* (First Edition). New York: Holt, Rinehart and Winston.

Stanovich, K.E. 1986. Matthew effects in reading: Some consequences of individual differences in the acquisition of literacy. *Reading Research Quarterly* 21, 4. 360–406.

Thompson, G. 1981. Individual differences attributed to self-correction in reading. *British Journal of Educational Psychology* 51: 228–229.

Wagner, R.K. and R.J. Sternberg. 1987. Executive control in reading comprehension. In B.K. Britton and S.M. Glynn, eds, *Executive Control Processes in Reading.* Hillsdale, NJ: Lawrence Erlbaum.

Watson, S. and M.M. Clay. 1975. Oral reading strategies of third form students. *New Zealand Journal of Educational Studies* 1, May: 43–51.

Wheldall, K. and T. Glynn. 1988. Contingencies in contexts: A behavioural interactionist perspective in education. *International Journal of Educational Psychology* 8, 1 and 2: 5–19.

Williams, B. 1968. The Oral Reading Behaviour of Standard One Children. Master of Arts thesis, University of Auckland Library.

Wong, S., L. Groth and J. O'Flahaven. 1994. *Characterizing teacher-student interaction in Reading Recovery lessons.* Reading Research Report No. 17, National Reading Research Center, Universities of Georgia and Maryland.

Wood, D. 1978. Problem-solving: the nature and development of strategies. In A. Underwood, ed., *Strategies of Information Processing.* London: Academic Press.

———. 1988. *How Children Think and Learn* (First Edition). Oxford: Blackwell.

———. 1998. *How Children Think and Learn* (Second Edition). Oxford: Blackwell.

6   Lessons in becoming constructive and the link with prevention

6   Lessons in becoming constructive and the link with prevention

Introduction

Constructive children engage in learning literacy in very different education systems. Formal instruction begins between four and eight years, materials and practices are different from country to country, literacy programmes compete commercially for acceptance, and teachers are trained in different theoretical perspectives. Most are successful. I take the pragmatic view that children as readers and writers, like children as speakers, learn through quality interactions with expert adults. Slight adjustments are made for the age of starting formal instruction in different countries. *A small number of children in each country must be given expert help to get to a kind of survival status in literacy learning, and this chapter is directed to the teaching of those who need such supplementary help.*

For young children who are finding it difficult to engage with reading and writing in classrooms, an early intervention treatment is necessary. The programmes currently available draw on different theories relating to literacy difficulties. From the arguments put forward by advocates for early intervention we can choose which interventions are more likely to have long-term effects. Instruction could, hypothetically, build up the item banks of letter, sound and word knowledge (Rumelhart 1994) and yet the learners may fail to construct the links between them that are essential for reading harder texts later in their schooling. Or the intervention might help learners to construct only certain links selected as 'important' or major variables, deemed by the curriculum designer to be the most critical learning for progress but which could limit performance at higher levels. Can we distinguish between early intervention programmes from their goals and/or long-term outcomes? Are there theoretical arguments which could be considered?

History records that remedial literacy programmes have tended to focus on letter, sound and word learning to the exclusion of other aspects; this learning of items has been so hard to teach that it has dominated the teaching time, and progress has been slow. *To have learned to read and write in only specific ways on a limited range of tasks could not be considered to be preventive of subsequent difficulties but rather to virtually predict subsequent difficulties because the foundation was not broad enough or flexible enough to support later changes.* On the other hand to have learned how to extend one's processing capacity by using it with success on texts of varying difficulty and genre is to have gone through a door which has closed behind one. It makes learners somewhat independent of teachers so that some of their progress results from them advancing their own competencies. When an early intervention builds effective reading and writing processing systems which can handle texts of different kinds (and Singer's model of what these might look like was discussed in Chapter 3), then that early intervention provides the learner with the potential for subsequent successful progress. Whether that potential is realised depends on whether the early intervention programme has prepared the learner sufficiently well to engage with instruction several years later on, or whether, alternatively, the subsequent classroom instruction has been good enough to allow the reader to build upon the foundation laid by the intervention.

It is important to think clearly about today's school improvement programmes which aim to raise the general level of achievement. *Lifting the average scores in schools will increase rather than decrease the need for early intervention.* School improvement programmes designed for success will unquestionably create larger gaps between those who can easily meet the challenges and those who have several counts against them when it comes to school learning. Higher general levels of achievement will create larger gaps between the average and the lowest achievers in literacy acquisition unless special measures are put in place.

In a review of research on reading processes, Stanovich (1986) discussed the possibility of identifying the causes of literacy learning difficulties. He raised developmental questions which are critical for the design and interpretation of research if later outcomes depend upon earlier learning. He discussed:

a) variables which have a continuing high input for both skilled and less skilled readers

b) variables which have reciprocal effects, one upon the other, such as cognitive variables affecting reading and vice versa

c) variables which are important early in acquisition but have developmentally limited effects on later progress (like concepts about print and letter knowledge)

d) variables which are assumed to arise from developmental lags which slow the potential rate of learning.

Theorising of this kind would be needed to probe the potential for the long-term effects of projected treatments.

A brief description of Reading Recovery

Data from studies of one early intervention (Reading Recovery, abbreviated hereafter to RR but more correctly named Reading and Writing Recovery) support a number of unexpected claims like:

- text reading *supports* the progress of low achievers

- learning to write contributes to learning to read

- phonological awareness can be learned concurrently with other literacy learning especially when reciprocity of reading and writing are stressed

- later effects of developmental lags can be minimised in a series of lessons designed and delivered individually (Askew et al. 1998).

RR has been delivered as an early intervention, monitored and researched in most English-speaking countries, and among Spanish-speakers in the United States, after children have had some formal teaching, and by the middle of their second year at school (Clay 1997; Pinnell 1996; Askew et al. 1998).

A brief outline of RR's complexities provides background to the subsequent arguments about prevention. RR is an early intervention designed to reduce the incidence of reading difficulties. It requires three levels of professional training (teachers, tutors or teacher leaders who train teachers, and trainers who train tutors in a year-long tertiary course), and it requires a quality implementation. Twenty years after the programme was developed in New Zealand the lowest achievers after one year at school (that is, 18 per cent of the birth cohort of nearly 60,000 children, Kerslake 1998) were given individual instruction and a second chance at initial literacy learning. In twelve to twenty weeks of special instruction supplementary to classroom instruction, the goals were:

- to temporarily lift their pace of learning

- to permanently lift their levels of achievement

- to build a sound foundation for subsequent literacy learning.

The children are selected on achievement criteria only: they are the lowest achievers in the age group for whatever reason. They have already had one year of good quality classroom instruction, as a result of which they are beginning to get left behind by their faster-moving classmates on the curriculum of that classroom, that school, and that education system. The differences are measurable and significantly different from the average band of the age cohort. No child in ordinary classrooms is passed over for any other reason; there is no selection out because of such variables as low intelligence, poor motor co-ordination or low oral language scores.* In New Zealand in the year of selection two-thirds of children receiving this supplementary instruction reach the outcome criterion of average band performance for their classes, which is the required criterion for ending their supplementary programme. The average time in programme ranges from twelve to fifteen weeks and an arbitrary upper limit to treatment of about twenty weeks is usually applied, capping the level of progress in the interests of cost effectiveness. A third of the children are in a roll-over group (those who enter late in the school year, and complete their programme to criterion levels in the next school year but within the twenty weeks across two school years). The supplementary programme is withdrawn (or discontinued) when teachers judge that the children have basic reading and writing competencies which they are unlikely to lose.

It was never expected that every child could reach an average level of independence in classroom lessons in this time-limited intervention but initially it was not expected that as few as 1 per cent of the age group would need to be referred for further specialist instruction. This has been the case in New Zealand, reported annually by the Ministry of Education. Children needing further help should not be higher than 2 per cent of the age group in a quality school programme. Referred children have made remarkable progress (they are halfway up the mountain, as it were) but they do not demonstrate a self-extending system that could prevent later literacy learning difficulties. Research shows that under favourable conditions many referred children can still achieve this status and in a short period of time with more specialist help (Phillips and Smith 1997). Help for a longer period of time is required for the referred children who are hard to teach (Clay and Tuck 1993).

RR aims to identify a few children for continuing specialist help following one year of good classroom instruction and about twenty weeks of individually designed diagnostic teaching. That is a positive outcome for both the child and the education system. From a longitudinal perspective, after a full programme of RR lessons one of two predictions is made. Either a) the learner will be able to continue his or her learning satisfactorily supported by the classroom programme (that is, he or she will be discontinued), or b) the learner is unlikely to succeed even in small group instruction without a longer period of individual help (that is, referred or recommended, which are alternative terms). This approach is workable; at this time it stands as a viable and tried alternative to proposals which seek to identify the children who will fail before they have been exposed to instruction. It is 'a bird in the hand' approach which is extremely effective. While scientific studies are funded

---

* If a policy of mainstreaming or inclusion for children with pronounced handicaps is operated and a specialist report is available, special conditions may be arranged, over and above the normal preventive thrust of the early intervention using the same theoretical and instructional model, under a label like 'literacy processing theory' but *not* labelled as RR. Work with such children proceeds for longer according to need with different rules for implementation and delivery, and the lower outcomes predicted are accepted as worthwhile. *This then becomes a treatment intervention for individuals, not a preventive intervention which is adopted by an education system*; it involves longer-term treatments delivered to individuals but it uses the same literacy processing theory as RR to guide instruction for individuals who have a cluster of individual handicaps.

lavishly to find alternative early interventions, RR gets good results and avoids a longstanding problem of over-identification for remedial treatment. It also supports the expectation that schools will try to succeed with all children in one way or another.

The researched success of RR *provides a view of what is possible*. For an excellent summary of research studies see Askew et al. (1998). *Pretests select the lowest achievers after one year at school* in several countries and in different educational systems *and post-tests place high numbers of them in the average band for class three to five years later*. In some education systems many of these children would have been categorised as children with specific learning difficulties.

However, because advocacy for early interventions has increased it would be helpful to be able to choose between them on some sound basis. Given the inevitability that classroom programmes will stress some aspects of literacy processes more than others, that teachers will differ in their professional training, and that interventions will differ in the care with which they are implemented and delivered, criteria for choosing within a range of options among early interventions are needed.

Literacy processing and assembling working systems

When we search for early interventions which have sound theoretical arguments for claiming *to prevent subsequent failure we are taking a developmental point of view*. They must place importance on early experience as a foundation for later experience, as the seed from which complex systems develop, and they must pay close attention to the rapid day-to-day changes over time in children's ways of processing information in print.

It would not be enough to plan for accumulating skills and banks of item knowledge in a particular aspect of literacy performance in the hope that later integrations would emerge. Merely accumulating good test scores showing a knowledge of letters, or letter-sound relationships, or an extensive vocabulary of words read, or a fine repertoire of phonological analysis strategies, or reasonable performance on reading a narrow range of texts, would not provide the required insurance for subsequent progress. Learners would need to be able *to read and write texts relatively independently in ways that could lead to the learner taking on new competencies through his or her own efforts in the classroom*. Item knowledge may be acquired by gradual differentiation of new from known items held in memory, but what is critical is:

a) *knowing how to use this knowledge to read and write new messages, and*

b) *knowing how to expand the literacy processing system while doing this*.

The aim is to enable eight-year-old readers to develop the strategic base for the complex literacy processing with which they will need to engage as ten-, twelve- or sixteen-year-old readers. To avoid subsequent limitations an early intervention has to produce learners who do more than accumulate item knowledge and specific skills. It must ensure that readers and writers become competent independent processors of new information and that they have ways of going beyond the known when necessary. A treatment programme must create a broad-based foundation of cognitive competencies with the potential to be self-extending at some later time.

Independent activity is an important feature of this preparation. In RR independent work in reading and writing is passed to the child in the first week of the programme for any part of the child's tasks that he or she already controls. During independent processing much of the activity that could increase reading and writing occurs. To support this the teacher will use meaning as an external guidance mechanism. Meaning is one source of error detection, telling the learner that all is not well because responses do not make sense and calling for active, constructive, independent problem-solving. It is certainly not the only source of error detection. The irritation or dissonance produced by a recognised error, miscue or mismatch, calls for the best available information processing with minimum waste of attention. Even when an incorrect response is given, the teacher can indicate that 'I think you worked well on that but there's another thing to notice.' When the child works independently this also allows the teacher to make many of his or her teaching points on correct reading using examples of successful processing completed by the child. It is particularly important to provide such a learning context if the goal is to develop processing strategies and interactive competencies.

Some instructional implications of a complex model

By way of illustration some of the instructional implications of adopting a complex constructive model of literacy learning are proposed. I start with this prior assumption of complex interacting processes but add *a second assumption that the low achievers, collectively, are a group encountering different sources of difficulty*:

- some due to internal limitations of functioning, for example, if children are partially sighted, partially deaf, have motor disabilities or have suffered accident trauma,

- others due to lack of experiential opportunities in life so far,

- and others having constructed a system of interacting deficits as a product of their learning experiences.

An early intervention would need to provide learners with individually designed and individually delivered instruction which could find ways around a child's limitations in some functions, and which could break a cycle of interacting deficits, whatever those limitations might be. RR's delivery system is designed to do this, using:

- one-to-one instruction,

- with teaching activities selected to meet individual needs,

- paced and sequenced individually,

- delivered by a well-trained teacher

- who keeps good records,

- is alert to all aspects of the pupil's learning history during this second chance to learn,

- and adapts daily to ensure the construction of effective processing at all times despite the not-so-balanced repertoire of the struggling learner.

Such a specially-trained teacher would be scaffolding the learning despite the unevenness of performance and despite the slumps, slides and unforeseen casualties (like interruptions to lessons or the accidental selection of three or four unsuitable texts in a row).

In RR a standard framework for a lesson was designed to ensure daily coverage of necessary sub-component skills or strategies in a literacy processing model. (Sub-components would be identified differently in other early interventions according to the theoretical explanation preferred — they are called 'skills' in a surface behaviour model, 'strategies' in some cognitive models, and 'working systems' in a Holmes/Singer model.) The type, order and sequence of the activities in the lesson keep both teachers and low achievers interested and can be completed in the daily 30-minute lesson in a brisk yet unhurried teaching session (Clay 1985). Surprisingly, they accommodate the changes in teaching that are needed as the children become more competent. Enquirers expect RR to use set texts designed to deliver a sequence of items to be learned. People are puzzled by the set activities required in each lesson, activities designed to elicit, demand and support a broad-based range of strategic behaviours which comes from knowing how to problem-solve in a variety of ways in both reading and writing.

The basis of selection of pupils is an inclusive one, specifying low achievement whatever the cause, so pupils admitted to RR differ greatly one from the other on entry and would have different strengths. If the learning is to proceed out of the reader's current competencies, instruction must allow for very different patterns of strengths and weaknesses in early lessons. A one-to-one teaching format allows the teacher to match the style and content of his or her interactions to the needs of a particular child at a particular time on a particular text. These needs would change during twelve to twenty weeks of lessons because as the demand for new strategies occurs on harder texts, new difficulties become apparent.

Teaching does not necessarily start hard and become easier: in fact the reverse can be the case. Teaching becomes harder because reading must become faster while it is also becoming more complex. The learning must be accompanied by unexpected leaps made by constructive learners whose rate of progress in RR must temporarily accelerate. A new hurdle may be encountered at any time, probably requiring innovative scaffolding by the teacher who failed to anticipate it but then quickly provided for it. For example, the teacher increases opportunities for conversation about the texts when language limitations create a hurdle but decreases them when that is no longer needed. Time is allocated as needed according to the strengths or weaknesses in a particular child's processing systems at any time in his or her lesson series. Things are moving and changing: shifts are occurring, lifts in dealing with complexity are required by the texts selected for the individual learner, and by increasing demands in writing. Precious minutes in the 30-minute lessons are given to producing oral language, comprehending story issues, interacting on cultural meanings, increasing vocabularies, dragging a particular skill into the complexity or helping the learner to drop a prop no longer needed, supporting the reader to orchestrate or bring together behaviours, pausing long enough to let the reader a) monitor his or her own efforts and b) 'fix things up', which means initiating self-correcting. Whatever aspect of the complex processing system is presently challenging a pupil the lesson format allows for daily adjustments. The learner achieves success on a task of appropriate difficulty with teacher support, but the teacher at the same time works on ways to achieve learner success by drawing on his or her most competent responses. *A new way of working is drawn into the well-functioning network, and tentative responding is supported until new strengths become established.*

All but one of the reading and writing activities in RR lessons take place at the level of intact text messages. Sounds, words or letters receive focused attention in one part of the lesson that must appear to the learner as a temporary change of pace from the text activities. The teacher keeps the emphasis on reading and writing continuous texts, and what is learned in isolation is located and worked with in text on the same day if possible.

The teacher aims to develop effective working systems for texts, from which the learner can extract sub-components for attention. If possible texts are used as the context for meeting new challenges and increasing competencies. At any time in an observed lesson, the teacher may be seen teaching items, but only briefly. As and when needed, letters, sounds, clusters and words are drawn from the context of text reading and writing and dealt with. What is unusual is that the teacher chooses to do this knowing precisely what this child knows well, knows tentatively, and does not know. The teacher knows when in text reading this child can tolerate such interference, and importantly, when to let it go. He or she is not driven by a curriculum prescription. The teacher tries not to dismember the text reading task, and not to destroy existing effective response systems. He or she is constantly thinking about the quickest way to move the child on with the fewest teaching moves, the least explanation, and an economic use of examples.

To avoid a cycle of interacting skill deficits

A cycle of interacting skill deficits described by Stanovich (1986) clearly identifies a state of literacy learning in low achievers often apparent by their second year in literacy instruction. Probably how we intervene to change this state of affairs depends on how we think children came to be in that state. Before instruction began these children were not easily distinguished from their peers. Two years in instruction has taken them into a negative learning cycle.

It is quite easy to think of reading and writing activities as involving letters and words, and phonemes and spellings, and reading and writing vocabularies. It is common to refer to what literacy learners do as committing to memory, storing in memory, and recalling from memory these various types of items of knowledge. Teachers over many decades have successfully taught millions of children to read and write with these conceptualisations in mind. My explanation for this success is that when we pair teachers with active child learners whose brains are working constructively on making some sense of their worlds, this can result in successful learning much of the time. The constructive learners come to work with a code which initially seemed unstructured, and by 'doing' the reading and writing successfully in complex and purposeful activities they continue to fine-tune their knowledge of how to play the game, and how this task is structured and how you can approach it.

Many literacy theorists arrive at more complex theories than those which involve committing items to memory. Most theories today assume that reading acquisition involves learning interacting strategies which the reader can use to deal with texts. Low achievers:

- demonstrate fewer strategies and less efficient use of strategies

- avoid reading and do less of it

- act passively in print situations (Johnston and Allington 1991)

- stop trying to use cognitive strategies on text problems

- avoid phonological discriminations if these do not work for them, and try to depend on some other mode of word-solving.

One approach to breaking the cycle of deficits which interact to bring about a downward rather than an upward spiral in learning has been to select some variable which has been shown to be developmentally important and through interventions of small magnitude try to establish the genesis of large differences. Stanovich (1986) suggested that phonological awareness was such a variable; Bradley and Bryant (1983) used a simple task to demonstrate the links between letters and sounds and achieved important gains in reading scores with advantages sustained at follow-up years later. In 1985 these authors suggested raising the phonological skills of all children as if a threshold effect in this area could reduce the incidence of reading difficulties. Such an approach to the problem of reading difficulties allows research to explore single-variable causation with an experimental methodology, or to design paths of progress from analysis of group statistics.

Another approach has been to devise a particular instruction package and to deliver this to children selected according to a particular definition of reading failure, commonly excluding children of low intelligence. The research design of choice is a control group comparison design and the programme would be considered to be supported if significantly greater progress were made by the treatment group than by the control group. There are very few reports of such studies (Gittleman 1985). If significant gains are found when a treatment of a more or less standard type involving a single variable is delivered to children with diverse difficulties, they are often lost at follow-up a few months later (Gittleman and Feingold 1983).

A third approach to breaking the cycle might be called constructive because it seeks to engage readers in operating effectively at a simpler level of text reading and take them through an interacting cycle of skills expanding their effectiveness at text levels of increasing complexity. This approach begins with an assumption that the child is at first constructing very simple action systems which become more complex. As more complicated systems are temporarily assembled to solve a local and immediate problem (Singer 1994), the reader finds new ways to solve problems. Teachers observe that readers extract increasingly more information on texts of gradually increasing difficulty. Such a reader can become aware of new items of knowledge, of new ways of checking on himself or herself, and of new strategic behaviours. In a complex model of interacting competencies in reading and writing the reader can potentially draw from all his or her current understanding, and all his or her language competencies, and visual information, and phonological information, and knowledge of printing conventions, in ways which *extend both the searching and linking processes as well as the item knowledge repertoires.* Learners pull together necessary information from print in simple ways at first (crudely imaged as several blocks of competencies connected by weak links), but as opportunities to read and write accumulate over time the learner becomes able to quickly and momentarily construct a somewhat complex operating system which might solve the problem.

There is no simplified way to engage in the complex activities, but teachers and the public are typically presented with patently untrue simplifications in new commercial instruction kits.

As readers become competent the strategies that make up the linking and decision-making systems encounter new problems and novel features, and these become 'known' and available in the repertoire of problem-solving strategies after one, two, three or more encounters. This is the independent learning engaged in by the 'system in use', the processing carried out by the brain for the reading and writing to occur. I equate the formulation of such a system to what Stanovich (1986) called the positive Matthew effect in reading, and attribute it to a complexity of interacting competencies. The competent reader is constructing a self-extending system (Clay 1979) which is underdescribed as a bootstrapping effect (Stanovich 1986). I am clear that low-achieving readers need to learn to work in ways which foster a gradual expansion of an independent, self-extending processing system and that they do that by successfully engaging with increasingly more complex texts. Their problem is *unlikely* to be a blackout in one sector of the complex system requiring the installation of a single component, such as phonemic awareness (O'Leary 1997; Wong, Groth and O'Flahaven 1994).

My problem with a theoretical approach which identifies 'a major variable' to be emphasised is that I would not expect to break a cycle of interacting deficits with a single emphasis treatment programme for all children at risk, or even for a subgroup. Because we are dealing with complex learning and the learner is constructing neurological networks for doing the task effectively, I propose that the learner would need to drop to a low and simple level of near faultless functioning, move for a second time through the construction of an effective processing system for simple texts, link up each and every component into an effective complex processing system this second time around, and prevent old circuits of association from operating. This can be done even by children who have disabilities. I have watched lessons in which a deaf child used manual signing while reading, and a partially-sighted child picked up a narrow span of visual input with a magnifying device held to one eye, and another child with motor movements limited by cerebral palsy, each individually quite successfully building a complex literacy processing system despite extreme limitations in one or more of the participating functions of the system.

Drawing the arguments together

A theoretical model, grounded in field research on successful learners (see Acts of Literacy Processing, Chapter 2), arose for, and alongside, an intervention for young children critically in need of special scaffolding to build a literacy processing system. At the time RR was developed the following were deemed to be necessary features of instruction.

- The teacher would make maximum use of the existing response repertoire of each child, and hence every child's lessons would be different.

- The teacher would support the development of literacy processing by astute selection of tasks, judicious sharing of tasks, and by varying the time, difficulty, content, interest and method of instruction, and type and amount of conversation within the standard lesson activities.

- The teacher would foster and support active constructive problem-solving, self-monitoring and self-correction from the first lesson, helping learners to understand that they must take over the expansion of their own competencies. To do this the teacher would focus on process variables (how to get and use information) rather than on mere correctness and habitual responses, and would temporarily value responses that were partially correct for whatever they contributed towards correctness.

- The teacher would set the level of task difficulty to ensure high rates of correct responding plus appropriate challenge so that the active processing system could learn from its own attempts to go beyond current knowledge.

To claim that such an intervention could be effective the designers would need to produce evidence that teachers could be trained for this intensive contingent teaching. The RR intervention has given much thought to this; across the world in many countries teachers have been trained to teach in this way.

Lessons in being constructive: the 30-minute daily lesson

Table 3A, column 1 provides a list of activities which must occur in every RR lesson. Critics have called this a regimented inflexible straitjacket. Others would argue that it is a flexible structure into which teachers can feed what is appropriate for different children, in any sequence, and at any time in their twelve- to twenty-week lesson series. Teachers design lessons for individual children and that must be the acme of flexibility. What cannot be reported in this table format are the extremely important changes that occur within each activity during a lesson series; those changes are noted in the guidebook for teachers in training (Clay 1993) as teaching shifts which occur but which were not explicitly formulated in terms of cognitive issues.

Table 3A   Lessons in becoming constructive: some issues
(*Note:* This standard lesson format cannot show the vast changes in processing from the beginning to end of a child's lesson series.)

Activity	Lesson requirements	Issues	Lesson records
Rereading several familiar texts	Books read before, still allowing some processing challenges.	Allows reading volume and compiling, orchestrating and successful processing. Meaning, structure and print guide self-correction and decision-making.	Word recognition. Use of meaning. Phrasing. Enjoying the story. Attention to print detail. Speeded recognition.
Yesterday's new book and Running Record	Second reading. Behaviour record for analysis. No teaching until task has been completed.	Independent use of what was introduced yesterday. Problem-solving alone, monitoring, choosing, confirming or revising and making appropriate links.	Independent reconstruction of a near-novel experience. Successful problem-solving. Teach on both successful reading and errors.
Letter identification	Manipulate magnetic letters. Known range extended in 'compare and contrast' tasks. Speeded perception.	Linked to fast recognition of upcoming new text, and rapid link of letter to sound. Use of letter-to-sound consistencies, and forming letters in readable ways.	Speeded recognition of any form or feature in isolation, among many, and embedded in words.
Shift to include making and breaking, taking words apart in isolation	Take known words apart and construct new from old. Avoid word families or prescriptive sequences. Maximise *the child's* construction opportunities. Prompt and assist.	Prompting for attention to detail in print; segmenting syllables, clusters and phonemes; using what is known to get to unknown. Stresses order and constructing.	Learners notice/use previously taught cluster components during reading and writing. Learning to use these and commenting.

Composing and writing own sentence/story	Child composing a story. Shared production, child or teacher or both. Change over time, lift amount, complexity and increase independence.	How language is constructed and texts are compiled from letters and words. Writing is segmentation. What is written is read.	Produce print versions of words and messages one can speak. Able to get to new words.
	Hearing and recording the sounds in words.	Sound-to-letter consistencies. Using known to get to unknown.	Phonological analysis, by letters and by clusters. Looking for more known and more independence.
	High-frequency words written quickly. Known words written quickly.	Known in every respect. Operates on phonological or spelling knowledge.	Speeded recognition and production.
	Read and reread the composition as necessary.	Self-monitoring feedback, and feed-forward processes.	Self-correcting while writing — noticing, rereading, composing again, referring back. Examples of initiating word-solving.
Cut-up story	Reconstruction of teacher's copy of the child's story cut up.	Self-monitoring, checking, self-correction. Searching for verbal and visual matches.	Monitoring and correcting behaviour, verbal and in movements, and comments on these.
Introduce carefully selected new book	Text not read. Teacher and child discuss sense, plot, vocabulary. Use and emphasise new language terms and language structures.	Model of how to orient to a text, that is, how to prepare to access knowledge, using context, print information and questions.	Participation with the teacher orienting to a new text. Record child's comments and questions.
First reading of carefully selected new book	Not interrupted by too much teaching. Read with the help of the introduction, some prompting to support reading of continuous text. Analysis at sub-word level usually after successful word- or text-solving. A teaching opportunity may occur because some new difficulties arise.	Complicated unseen inter-actions. New opportunities for linking and making connections and going beyond the information given. Testing ground for emerging strategies, consolidating some and opportunity for learning others.	Independent on novel text, reads easily, and mainly correct. Problem-solves the hard bits, pauses, tries and tests. Sounds good.

Some of the lesson activities

The lesson activities and the records to be kept of children's responses and teachers' moves are outlined in *Reading Recovery: A Guidebook for Teachers in Training* (Clay 1993) and are not repeated here. The following is a brief account of the kinds of cognitive payoffs *from only four of the lesson activities* outlined in Table 3A.

1. Rereading familiar books

Rereading allows a child to return to familiar books which still offer some processing challenges. This may mean consolidating learning that is not yet secure and it may be reading in a well-paced way. Memory for text or words is not the goal; a memorised text does not offer processing challenges. The readings provide the child with opportunities to compile the reading across working systems and orchestrate the processing (that is, put it all together). (Conceptually it would not be necessary to compile the same system for each reading and thus rereading would be an opportunity to 'compile again' a little differently rather than repeat the performance.) Print and language both guide the readings, and self-correction and decision-making are at their most effective. This is where RR increases the volume of reading, reducing the advantage that good readers have been reported to have over poor readers.

Casual observers suggest many hypotheses for including familiar reading such as children enjoying rereading several partially familiar stories or making a good start to the lesson or providing a warm-up period at the beginning of the lesson, calling working systems into action. RR professionals have a more serious and functional justification; for them this is the time when readers orchestrate (pull together in appropriate sequences) their strategies, decision-making, problem-solving and executive control sensitivities and responsibilities.

While the complexity of that orchestration occurring in milliseconds of time is not something teachers can observe directly, psychologists like Masson (1987) have provided evidence for the importance of familiar reading.

He considered differences in the first and last readings of mature readers, and asked these interesting questions: Why were successive readings faster? And what does the improvement in reading speed imply about possible changes in processing? Are processing operations applied at the first reading represented in memory and reapplied on later readings? Do second and successive readings put less demand on problem-solving and decision-making (executive control mechanisms) so that attention may be given to other tasks such as detecting error in the text? Are operations which were not yet under the control of executive control mechanisms being gradually brought under their control? It is possible that improved reading speed may be due to certain perceptual operations (fluency of letter and word identification) and that these may contribute to the speed of problem-solving and decision-making. The apparent ease of reading a sentence may be attributed by teachers to the beneficial effects of a previous encounter but they will not know whether the fluency is coming from faster perceptual operations, better memory operations, more efficient strategies for cross-relating information, or more effective control mechanisms for managing 'the reading'.

2. Yesterday's new book

This is the second reading of a new book introduced the previous day. No teacher help will be given until after the whole reading has been accomplished and recorded by the teacher. The teacher makes some teaching points which arise from that second reading; he or she selects for attention those which will contribute most to a lift in the child's competencies. The reader works independently, problem-solving alone, monitoring, choosing, confirming or revising and making appropriate links. This is an assessment, and the teacher analyses the record daily for the kinds of processing initiated by the reader.

3.   Letter identification

The teacher expands the range of known letters, using manipulation of magnetic letters in 'compare and contrast' tasks, aiming for speeded perception and discrimination of letters one from the other. This is the time when teachers aim for fast recognition of letters in isolation, knowing that the reader will use this during text reading to pick up visual information in upcoming new text. There can be no rapid sensory association of letter forms with possible sounds without working through the visual perception of letters.

The brief time given to speeded single-letter activities expands, as competence increases, to taking known words apart into component letters and reassembling them, and to taking them apart to construct new (similar) words. The perceptual and cognitive challenges are to attend to detail in print, to have maximum opportunities to construct or act on the task, to attend to order (that is, sequences of letters), and, increasingly, to phonemes, patterns, clusters, syllables and words, for the speeding up of processing. The teacher prompts and his or her actions and demonstrations are speeded, fractionally faster than the child's.

4.   Composing orally and then writing a self-composed message

The child learns to compose something orally to be written and then to compile it letter by letter and word by word. The child segments his or her speech, finding individual words and breaking them into phonemes. Then the child writes (re-constructs) the word. Within this task the teacher insists upon the learner hearing and recording the sounds in some words in the message, helps the learner to use what he or she knows to get to new words, and expects high frequency words to be put down quickly. The teacher writes into the story what is beyond the competency of the child at this point in the lesson series. The child may do a slow tedious analysis as he or she writes a new word, and rehearses the production of that word several times, increasing the production speed.

This is an opportunity to do a slow phonemic analysis, to find ways of spelling the sounds heard (with a helpful teacher sometimes acting as scribe), to revisit words partly known, to use what the child knows to get to new words, to practise spelling with and without a copy, to reread the message so far and to start the cycle again. The teacher teaches whatever he or she judges will take the child's processing to a higher level, and otherwise shares the task to end up with a readable text, part of which the teacher may have written. As the task gets easier the recorded messages get more complex and generally longer. As the sentences get more complex and challenge the child's competencies there may still be a need for teachers to 'write in' a word or two.

Words are rich in information. To be known any letter, cluster or word must eventually be known in every respect — its phonological, visual and spelling features, and its place in reading or writing text.

At the end of the lesson there are two further important steps: the teacher introduces a new book, carefully selected to suit the child's level of processing and to present new challenges, tempting the child to lift his or her processing to another level. Teacher and child will interact over the challenges as the child reads this new book. (See Table 3A, pp. 226–227.)

General comments

The tasks of the daily lesson (Clay 1993) provide an opportunity to examine some cognitive issues which are inherent in the theoretical framework I have just described. What is taught within each slot in the lesson framework is determined by:

a) a particular child's strengths and competencies, and

b) the level of text (read or written) currently supporting and challenging the child.

A specific teaching emphasis occurs when it is required, and not in a particular sequence at a particular time for all children. The psychological orientation or theoretical rationale of each activity in the lesson framework remains more or less the same throughout the lesson series. The rationales for including the activities relate to cognitive issues.

Moving up through a gradient of text and task difficulty, children read and write (they may read four or five little stories and write one or more sentences in each lesson), every day, with zero tolerance of interruption to the daily lessons. This provides opportunities:

- to orient to, talk over, read and understand a new story every day (strengthening oral language and comprehension)

- to revisit known vocabulary in novel contexts, increasing familiarity (developing direct access to a reading vocabulary)

- to reconstruct recent successful experience and to orchestrate complex interacting processes on partially known material (developing text processing)

- if necessary, to develop a component skill in isolation but, *without delay*, to use it in text settings and settle the new knowledge into the interactive network of text-reading skills which are already controlled

- to use writing as a resource for reading and vice versa (a kind of double chance for 'bootstrapping' to occur)

- to segment words in speech, in print and in writing, and relate one to another (for example articulating phonemes, writing phonemes and reading phonemes, establishing a rapid link from visual form to sound in reading, and from sound to visual form in writing)

- to integrate information from different sources — to read, anticipate, monitor and self-correct, guided by information in print, by language and by meaningfulness, while constructing messages word by word.

Using the table of lesson components for professional development

Table 3A is a new representation of the RR lesson framework (Clay 1993). The components of the lesson are listed in the first column, the lesson requirements are listed in column 2, and the final column contains comments on things that teachers might write into their daily lesson record. That is a standard feature of every RR lesson. In column 3 I have used the heading 'Issues' to record some of the issues about cognitive gains that might be raised for discussion.

Discussing 'Why do you do this?' with teachers

I have found it useful when working with trained RR professionals to leave column 3, labelled 'Issues', blank, a place for them to record their thinking. (The worksheets I, II, III and IV in Table 3B at the end of this chapter, pages 239–242, suggest a useful format.) The worksheet task can be varied to suit the level of the completed professional training of those working on the exercise, and to take in the flurry of topical issues which are up for debate at any one time in the current literature. For teachers I have used a simple question: Why is each of these activities included in the lesson framework? Teachers have reasons for what they do, and 'why' questions are a good place to begin. One study which praised RR teachers quite dramatically ignored the 'why' questions. Their teaching was reported in this way.

> Teachers trained in Reading Recovery seem to know from moment to moment what text to focus on, when and how to prompt, when to tell, when to coach, and when to allow readers to direct their own reading. Learning to teach within the student's zone of proximal development enables the teacher to determine with some confidence what text will be challenging enough and when each scaffolding behaviour is appropriate. (Wong, Groth and O'Flahaven 1994)

At first RR teachers regard that as a great statement but then they complain that the writers provide no reasons why teachers focus, prompt, tell, coach, or let the child work independently. The researchers had not detected any theoretical framework like literacy processing (or some alternative), that pulled the conceptualisation of the teaching together. The statement gave teachers no credit for knowing when and why to make the next move. At a practical level thousands of teachers across the world deliver lessons according to the framework in Table 3A every school day in RR while at the same time ensuring that the actual content of the lesson meets the fine-grained learning needs of a particular individual at a particular time. Teachers must come to articulate their reasons for doing what they do so well.

Discussing 'processing' with tutors/teacher leaders

Those professionals who train RR teachers are called tutors or teacher leaders. They need to be able to lead teachers into discussions of the 'why' questions but their personal challenge is to become more articulate about what they understand by the term 'literacy processing', the theory of reading and writing with which they work. Their discussions should be about the kinds of processing which might be developed in each of the components of the lesson. The discussions will relate to the psychological processes described in current models of reading and writing acquisition. They may deal with text meaning and comprehension; with direct and rapid access to known vocabulary prompted both by visual recognition and phonological learning; with problem-solving new texts using knowledge of any kind interactively (visual, phonological, word, syntactic, language, book knowledge and world knowledge); and with monitoring whether a 'good fit' of all information has been achieved, and if not, then operating error detecting and correcting strategies. For them to understand why current practices are recommended, and to decide whether variants threaten or might potentially increase the effectiveness of a learner's learning, such topics must be part of professional discussions.

Discussions among trainers

Trainers in training for RR will be exploring literacy learning theories and evaluating research critiques of literacy teaching and early interventions, and they could use the empty column of the worksheets to test out theories, or criticisms, or advocacies, or new ideas in a variety of ways. Column 3 allows for discussions of perceptual/cognitive theories and learning opportunities associated with each component. (What in-the-head processes could be tentatively inferred by the teacher? and what checks for evidence can the teacher make to see whether his or her inference is supported or negated?) Two examples of issues trainers might explore may help to illustrate this.

Example 1. What would be the progressive changes through which low-achieving children might be expected to move?

Most theorists use a model of the possible progressions in beginning reading which they derive either from the averaged scores from some representative sample, or for selected groups of readers. The outcome descriptions are mainly controlled by the theory behind the tests used, or by an adopted curriculum, or studies of children with reading problems. An inescapable conclusion of all that theory and research has disclosed is that the progressions which researchers are able to 'discover' are mainly *the outcomes of the input programme of instruction that has been delivered to the research population in their schools prior to the time the researchers began their model-building research.*

RR did not escape this problem: however, *it was guided initially by descriptive research of competent readers and writers who had been taught in a first programme in which text processing was the focus of instruction.* Component skills were taught in order to facilitate text processing (Clay 1982). I monitored changes in processing behaviours in the individual learners in a classroom programme in five schools using a representative sample. I took records of reading and writing behaviours over very short periods of time (weekly intervals) in all their variety, and divided the children after one year of instruction into high, high average, low average, and low progress groups. From the averaged test outcomes for each quartile group it was concluded that children were significantly different in their literacy learning, and that how they dealt with the errors as they read text (a processing variable) varied from child to child (Clay 1982).

When the mounting control of learners allows them to assemble the necessary information to solve a focal difficulty (Singer 1994), this contributes to the beginning of a positive cycle of slow improvement. Signs that this is occurring are that:

- the rate of acquisition accelerates

- work on novel (new) texts generates more surprisingly 'good' responses than 'problem' responses

- work on familiar texts is faster and more flexible

- the need for teacher support, guidance, input or questioning is diminished, and the reader does more of the problem-solving on material selected to be appropriate for him or her

- children's progress allows teachers to lift the challenge steadily to new levels of text complexity

- the reader begins to work independently with success on an appropriately chosen, new literacy task.

These shifts are clearly observable if the teacher can choose from available reading material so that a learner can read new material on the same level of difficulty (new book, same level) or at a higher level of difficulty (new book, higher challenge). In either case the teacher governs the challenge of the new book by his or her introduction to the new material for he or she can scaffold the task minimally or extensively or anywhere in-between. What began as 'a cycle of interacting skill deficits'

(Stanovich 1986) gradually changes to a cycle of interacting competencies for most children, and teachers, noticing the shifts, enter them into their records.

Some of the changes that occur over an average series of early intervention lessons in RR are that:

- letter identification and concepts about print come to require little attention as they are both closed sets of information which can be mastered, and attention shifts to speed of response

- the learner gains an independent control over hearing sounds in words needed for writing and other ways to get to new words and the teacher calls overtly for this new knowledge to also be used in reading

- the child who at first reads text by attending to different sources of information separately, and in sequence, comes to use meaning, syntax, visual and sound information as if having orchestrated the processing of information from several different sources rapidly, if not simultaneously

- sentences being read, word after word, are monitored for the constructed meaning that is emerging, errors are detected, action is initiated, self-corrections can be heard, until the processing becomes much faster and self-corrections are no longer heard.

Children adopt a pace for reading which can support the selection of responses allowing for monitoring of correctness and problem-solving of errors to occur. A slow initial pace increases as the system becomes more effective in all these activities (see Singer, Table 2, p. 113).

So, trainers in training have to achieve some theoretical perspectives on what opportunities the lesson components provide for learning what has to be learned. The third column in Table 3A very briefly nominates *some* of the cognitive learning opportunities associated with this activity (the in-the-head processes tentatively inferred by the teacher who checks for evidence of whether his or her inference is supported or negated). These brief references provide starting points for theoretical explorations.

Example 2.   Theorists differ. Compare two theoretical explanations for the learning of RR children.

To clarify what is meant by 'literacy processing theory' compare the way Adams (1990) described what RR children do with the description from a literacy processing theory viewpoint used in Table 3A. The characteristics of RR teaching are recognisable in Adams' account (pp. 419–420), and hers is one of the better 'translations' of RR thinking in the general literature. So where do the differences lie? They lie in the language used but the language stems from the theoretical conceptualisation.

Adams wrote:

Rereading of a familiar book has been shown to be a superlative way of refining and reinforcing word recognition and comprehension skills, [and] bolstering self-confidence and accomplishment.

Clay replies:

Rereading several familiar texts increases the volume of reading, and the opportunities for compiling and orchestrating of successful processing; meaning, structure and print guide successful anticipation, self-correction and decision-making during 'print to message to print to message decision-making', word after word (Table 3A).

Adams wrote:

[The teacher records] mis-readings, stumbles, impasses, appeals for help, repetitions, pauses and directional difficulties [and] can learn much about how the child prioritises and exploits the information and strategies available when reading.

Clay replies:

The teacher records, on the second reading without interacting, problem-solving alone, monitoring, choosing, confirming or revising, making appropriate links and self-correcting (Table 3A).

Adams wrote:

Secure learning of letter identities is supported through key words, exercises with magnetic letters, verbal description, directed attention to similarities and differences, finger tracing and printing. The importance of phonological awareness and linguistic awareness is also explicitly recognized. The child is asked to clap out syllables, point to each separate word while reading, focus on letter recognition, spelling patterns, spelling-sound relationships, and words.

Clay replies:

Letter identification is linked to forming letters in readable ways, to quick response of sounds for letters, to fast recognition of upcoming new text, and to using letter-to-sound consistencies. The teacher prompts for attention to letter detail when letters are embedded in print — in words, syllables, clusters or chunks.

The contrast between the words used to describe these three sets of observations is predominantly between an item and skills-based theory and a literacy processing theory; the explanation of what is occurring is different because of the theory-in-use in the heads of each author. *Obviously literacy professionals across countries operate effectively using a skills-based, surface behaviour approach; my argument is that a theory of literacy processing is, to date, more helpful for teachers of young children having severe difficulty learning to read and write.*

A preventive approach ...

Learners need to be able to use the opportunities they get, in school (where they get help and guidance from teachers) and out of school, to assemble for themselves a read/write action system. An early intervention teacher, who is focused upon preventing subsequent literacy learning difficulties, will need to do more than teach a child to decode a book or spell correctly. Supportive interactions in one-to-one instruction could aim only to foster such limited behaviour but I would argue that merely increasing sounds and words known (that is, the contents of some knowledge stores) would not count as preventive. The early intervention teacher who strives to prevent later learning difficulties must help pupils to build towards a self-extending literacy learning system which allows the child to learn from his or her own efforts (which must go far beyond sounding out the letters of the word). There must be scope for independent responding and independent learning in every lesson from the beginning, working up towards a self-extending system in the long term. At discontinuing from RR we must look for signs that the child is initiating and generating new responses, going it alone beyond what previous lessons have provided.

The most spectacular signals which help the teacher to scaffold new challenges for the constructive learner appear when the learner goes beyond prior competence independently. *This constructive 'going beyond the known' is not an outcome of the final weeks of the lesson series; it has to be fostered as independent processing from the beginning of a lesson series. It is the insurance taken out to ensure that the programme will be preventive and not merely a temporary catch-up on items known or skills mastered.*

This is an important aspect of one-to-one intensive teaching of children who begin with few literacy behaviours. Early intervention teachers who give daily instruction can monitor the shifts made by children who are tentatively trying to become constructive in solving literacy tasks. The incipient moves are rarely fully fledged, accurate responses; it is the knowledgeable, observing and well-trained teacher who recognises the potential in the child's formative attempt. 'Actively constructive from the start' means from the first invitation such as, 'Where do we start reading?' or the request to put the full stop (period) at the end of the day's written message which the teacher had to scribe for the reluctant beginner. Table 3A provides an overview of the kinds of cognitive issues that could be hypothesised to be important.

RR must continue to derive deeper insights from research but research designs must be carefully crafted and cautiously interpreted to be logically consistent with RR's developmental and preventive view of early intervention. Requiring preventive outcomes from early interventions has serious consequences for the research questions posed and the research designs used. These are discussed in Chapter 7. There are also problems raised if treatments are varied according to client need. An interesting question of research logic arises when someone asks which child characteristics are related to the outcomes of a RR treatment. It is typical in educational research to explore the differential outcomes of characteristics of children like gender, home background factors, language factors, prior experience and knowledge on entry to the programme. Relationships would frequently be expressed as correlations. But what happens if the treatments were planned to diminish the effects of any such differences? Adjusting the treatments on a daily basis to the differences between children, while expecting them all to reach a common goal, must diminish the usual correlational relationships.

RR has a common goal for children: average band performance within the child's own classroom. It is the intent of the programme to produce common outcomes for children who do differ in a multitude of different ways. That is the logic of the treatment, to produce a working level of literacy skills despite predictions which might be made if the treatment were not available. This point is developed further in Chapter 7.

There are three levels of professionals in RR and the trainers are the theoreticians and the lead researchers. Other researchers who want to mine practices from RR for use in the classroom should consult trainers as RR theorists, rather than teachers, during the design of their projects. They should not be surprised if they find that many trainers agree with Clay, and do not recommend trying to drag the advantages which naturally accrue from a one-to-one teaching opportunity into small- or large-group teaching situations of the classroom. It is necessary to start over and work out how the literacy behaviours, which change over time in RR, can be developed in group situations. For it is not what the teachers do that induces the necessary changes but rather it is how they understand the developmental changes they are trying to bring about that leads to their selection of what to attend to and to their prompting behaviours (see quote on page 231).

RR teachers make use of a theory which enables them to reshape the foundational learning of the child who is confused about early literacy learning, and to do this in a short period of time. Individually designed and individually delivered instruction by a well-trained teacher is the price we have to pay to allow the flexibility of the adjustments described above to occur: the clinical reality is that they do not work in every case given the time limit placed on the treatments, and the vagaries of delivery systems by education authorities.

... requires a developmental perspective

In contrast to a 'critical variable' approach to literacy difficulties, RR theory is based on a complex theory which includes both reading and writing and hypothesises that simple initial behaviours of various kinds (visual, motor, auditory and verbal) become interrelated. The changes which can be observed as a result of learning are integrative, and different working systems combine rather than act alone. Some early behaviours disappear, and 'the reading act' must be described differently on different tasks and at different periods of acquisition. Thousands of replications of these kinds of changes have been demonstrated by low-achieving children, more than 50 children every school day completing the intervention successfully (called discontinuing) in New

Zealand, and more than 500 each school day in the United States. This is replicated in many different education systems (New Zealand; Victoria, Canberra, New South Wales, and Queensland in Australia; and hundreds of different education systems in the various states of the United States; most provinces in Canada; 34 Local Educational Authorities of the United Kingdom; and the island territories of Jersey and Bermuda).

What earlier outcomes make for specified later outcomes in literacy learning? Two forms of that question have been used by policy planners in the last decade:

1. What would have to change to have all children readers and writers with average for age competencies by age nine or ten years?

2. For the many RR children who have a satisfactory immediate result from their series of lessons, can we describe in detail what type and variety of later outcomes are likely to follow?

If the questions of educators and politicians are to be answered then research must be designed from a developmental perspective and follow through from early outcomes to some later end-point. Researchers must consider seriously that a developmental perspective is crucial if we want answers to questions like that. Otherwise we can only continue down an old unsatisfactory path, hypothesising from small clusters of variables in cross-sectional research designs and only considering what Karoly (1993) called fragments of achievement. Moderate group predictions do not protect us from large prediction errors for individuals, or for outlier subgroups, and so they do not allow planners to make sound policy for individuals in outlier groups. (See discussions about collecting data on individuals in the next chapter.)

Case and Okamoto (1995) and Karmiloff-Smith (1995) have respectively taken a developmental view of mathematics achievement and oral language shifts over time in cognitive activities. In literacy learning the research of Vellutino et al. (1996) graphed five differential paths of progress towards the early outcomes but the study had not been designed to lead to differential, practical treatment options for those groups. Although educators often ask developmental questions there are not many examples of research designs which provide answers.

Accepting for the sake of argument that satisfactory results occur in this intervention partly as a result of these daily activities and their rationales, this must lead researchers to consider seriously that a developmental perspective is crucial if we are to explain what makes for efficiency in subsequent literacy learning. Without a developmental perspective which flows through from early acquisition to advanced mature processing, many intervention initiatives have probably had crippling effects on low achievers and maintained their low status relative to their peers.

Table 3B Distinguishing prevention from mere early intervention

Worksheet I

Activity	Lesson requirements	Issues	Lesson records
Rereading several familiar texts	Books read before, still allowing some processing challenges.		Word recognition. Use of meaning. Phrasing. Enjoying the story. Attention to print detail. Speeded recognition.
Yesterday's new book and Running Record	Second reading. Behaviour record for analysis. No teaching until task has been completed.		Independent reconstruction of a near-novel experience. Successful problem-solving. Teach on both successful reading and errors.

Worksheet II

Activity	Lesson requirements	Issues	Lesson records
Letter identification	Manipulate magnetic letters. Known range extended in 'compare and contrast' tasks. Speeded perception.		Speeded recognition of any form or feature in isolation, among many, and embedded in words.
Shift to include making and breaking, taking words apart in isolation	Take known words apart and construct new from old. Avoid word families or prescriptive sequences. Maximise *the child's* construction opportunities. Prompt and assist.		Learners notice/use previously taught cluster components during reading and writing. Learning to use these and commenting.

Worksheet III

Activity	Lesson requirements	Issues	Lesson records
Composing and writing own sentence/story	Child composing a story. Shared production, child or teacher or both. Change over time, lift amount, complexity and increase independence. Hearing and recording the sounds in words. High-frequency words written quickly. Known words written quickly. Read and reread the composition as necessary.		Produce print versions of words and messages one can speak. Able to get to new words. Phonological analysis, by letters and by clusters. Look for how this knowledge is used while reading and writing texts. Speeded recognition and production. Self-correcting while writing — noticing, rereading, composing again, referring back. Examples of initiating word-solving.
Cut-up story	Reconstruction of teacher's copy of the child's story cut up.		Monitoring and correcting behaviour, verbal and in movements, and comments on these.

Worksheet IV

Activity	Lesson requirements	Issues	Lesson records
Introduce carefully selected new book	Text not read. Teacher and child discuss sense, plot, vocabulary. Use and emphasise new language terms and language structures.		Participation with the teacher orienting to a new text. Record child's comments and questions.
First reading of carefully selected new book	Not interrupted by too much teaching. Read with the help of the introduction, some prompting to support reading of continuous text. Analysis at sub-word level usually after successful word- or text-solving. A teaching opportunity may occur because some new difficulties arise		Independent on novel text, reads easily, and mainly correct. Problem-solves the hard bits, pauses, tries and tests. Sounds good.

References

Askew, B.J., I.C. Fountas, C.A. Lyons, G.S. Pinnell and M.C. Schmitt. 1998. *Reading Recovery Review: Understandings, Outcomes, and Implications.* Columbus, OH: Reading Recovery Council of North America.

Bradley, L. and P. Bryant. 1983. Categorizing sounds and learning to read — A causal connection. *Nature* 301: 419–421.

Case, R. and Y. Okamoto. 1995. *The Role of Central Conceptual Structures in the Development of Children's Thought. Monographs of the Society for Research in Child Development,* No. 246, 60: 5–6.

Clay, M.M. 1979. *Reading: The Patterning of Complex Behaviour.* Auckland: Heinemann.

———. 1982. *Observing Young Readers: Selected Papers.* Portsmouth, NH: Heinemann.

———. 1985. Reading Recovery: Systemic adaptation to an educational innovation. *New Zealand Journal of Educational Studies* 22, 1: 35–58.

———. 1993. *Reading Recovery: A Guidebook for Teachers in Training.* Auckland: Heinemann.

———. 1997. International perspectives on the Reading Recovery program. In J. Flood, S.B. Heath and D. Lapp, eds, 1997, *Handbook of Research on Teaching Literacy Through the Communicative and Visual Arts.* Macmillan Reference Series on Educational Research.

Clay, M.M. and B. Tuck. 1993. The Reading Recovery sub-groups study, 1991. In M.M. Clay, *Reading Recovery: Guidelines for Teachers in Training,* pp. 86–95. Auckland: Heinemann.

Gittleman, R. 1985. Controlled trials of remedial approaches to reading disability. *Journal of Child Psychology and Psychiatry* 26: 843–846.

Gittleman, R. and I. Feingold. 1983. Children with reading disorders I: Efficacy of reading remediation. *Journal of Child Psychology and Psychiatry* 24: 167–192.

Johnston, P.H. and R.L. Allington. 1991. Remediation. In R. Barr, M.L. Kamil, P. Mosenthal and P.D. Pearson, eds, *Handbook of Reading Research,* Vol. II, pp. 984–1012. White Plains, NY: Longman.

Karmiloff-Smith, A. 1992. *Beyond Modularity: A Developmental Perspective on Cognitive Science.* Cambridge, MA: MIT Press.

Karoly, P. 1993. Mechanisms of self-regulation: A system view. *Annual Review of Psychology* 44: 23–52.

Kerslake, J. 1998. Annual monitoring of Reading Recovery: The data for 1997. *The Research Bulletin* 9, October: 43–47. Wellington: Ministry of Education.

Masson, M.E.J. 1987. Remembering reading operations with and without awareness. In B.K. Britton and S.M. Glynn, eds, *Executive Control Processes in Reading,* pp. 253–277. Hillsdale, NJ: Lawrence Erlbaum.

O'Leary, S. 1997. *Five Kids: Stories of Children Learning to Read.* Bothell, WA: The Wright Group/ McGraw-Hill.

Phillips, G. and P. Smith. 1997. *A Third Chance to Learn: The Development and Evaluation of Specialised Interventions for Young Children Experiencing the Greatest Difficulty in Learning to Read.* Wellington: New Zealand Council for Educational Research.

Pinnell, G.S. 1996. Reading Recovery: A Review of Research. *Educational Report #23.* Columbus, OH: Martha King Language and Literacy Center, OSU. Also in J. Flood, S.B. Heath and D. Lapp, eds, 1997, *Handbook of Research on Teaching Literacy Through the Communicative and Visual Arts.* Macmillan Reference Series on Educational Research.

Rumelhart, D.E. 1994. Toward an interactive model of reading. In R.B. Ruddell, M.R. Ruddell and H. Singer, eds, *Theoretical Models and Processes of Reading* (Fourth Edition), pp. 864–894. Newark, DE: International Reading Association.

Singer, H. 1994. The substrata-factor theory of reading. In R.B. Ruddell, M.R. Ruddell and H. Singer, eds, *Theoretical Models and Processes of Reading* (Fourth Edition), pp. 895–927. Newark, DE: International Reading Association.

Stanovich, K.E. 1980. Toward an interactive-compensatory model of individual differences in the development of reading fluency. *Reading Research Quarterly* 16: 32–71.

———. 1986. Matthew effects in reading: Some consequences of individual differences in the acquisition of literacy. *Reading Research Quarterly* 21, 4: 360–406.

Vellutino, F.R., D.M. Scanlon, E.R. Sipay, S.G. Small, R. Chen, A. Pratt and M.B. Denckla. 1996. Cognitive profiles of difficult-to-remediate and readily remediated poor readers: Early intervention as a vehicle for distinguishing between cognitive and experiential deficits as basic causes of specific reading disability. *Journal of Educational Psychology*, APA, 88, 4: 601–638.

Wong, S., L. Groth and J. O'Flahaven. 1994. *Characterizing teacher-student interaction in Reading Recovery lessons.* Reading Research Report No. 17, National Reading Research Center, Universities of Georgia and Maryland.

7 Planning research for early literacy interventions

7 Planning research for early literacy interventions

Eliot Eisner of Stanford University addressed the future of educational research when he wrote this:

> ... the major aim of the common enterprise in which we are engaged ... has to do with the improvement of educational practice so that the lives of those who teach and learn are themselves enhanced ... we do research to understand. We try to understand in order to make our schools better places for both the children and the adults who share their lives ... In the end, our work lives its ultimate life in the lives that it enables others to lead. Although we are making headway toward that end, there will continue to be difficulties and uncertainties, frustrations and obstacles. (Eisner 1993, p. 10)

Those comments could have been specially crafted for those who work internationally in the general field of early literacy interventions. Reading Recovery (RR) professionals recognise their relevance.

As far as possible this chapter takes a global perspective and explores the potential of research to contribute to RR's future in any country, despite the fact that many of the recent research reviews which have examined RR's research credentials have been conducted or published in the United States (Shanahan and Barr 1995; Askew et al. 1998; Jones and Smith-Burke 1999; Pinnell 2000). New ideas must be tested and contested, especially those which claim to improve the performance of low achievers. However, if we are to demonstrate how they can make a contribution to teaching practice we must also fund the opportunity for those new ideas to be trialled for an extended period in appropriate conditions. Such opportunities were provided for RR by the Department of Education in New Zealand, and the National Diffusion Network in the United States. If the guillotine of cost effectiveness falls too early as new developments struggle for resources, this deprives us of new solutions to old educational problems. It is clear from RR's history that research evaluating an early intervention must report on four aspects: the learning of the children; the training and practices of the teachers; the quality of the implementation in the system; and the longitudinal progress of the children in subsequent years.

Twenty-two years of working with RR in several different countries has produced many arguments about how it should be researched and improved. While the discussion in this chapter relates specifically to the RR experience, what we have learned has implications for the wider field of early literacy intervention.

Reading Recovery's concept of early intervention

Prevention is a central concept of RR, not a catchphrase

RR is designed to reduce the incidence of literacy learning problems among individual young children and it is supplemental to the classroom programme. It can be described as clinical because it delivers different programmes to different children according to their strengths and learning needs. It became an intervention adopted by an education system when administrators in New Zealand supported it through three years of development (Clay 1979) and four years of researched trials (Clay 1985b). Guided by a model of prevention (Caplan 1964; Pianta 1990), it seeks to treat a critical group after they have been exposed to literacy learning opportunities and before the onset of serious difficulties. This is commonly called secondary prevention.

One criterion of RR's success is the number of ex-RR children who can continue literacy learning with success back in their own classrooms after the intervention. That depends, obviously, on whether the quality of instruction in classrooms can sustain the progress of ex-RR children; sometimes it can and sometimes it cannot. Intervening variables will seriously affect long-term outcomes: these include children's life circumstances, the quality of subsequent school instruction, and cumulative variables like enough opportunities to read and write to sustain subsequent success. Critics and cost-conscious administrators want RR to show significantly different effects four or more years after the intervention, a demand rarely made of any educational programme. It cannot be predicted by the developmental theories which spawned the intervention. Progress would probably be sustained under optimum circumstances but immunisation against all future conditions of learning is an absurd expectation not sustainable by learning theory or by developmental theory. (See O'Leary 1997 for five illustrative cases.)

RR had to be designed to work in schools of different size, using different curricula emphases, in communities with different populations, and with different levels of achievement in different schools (for example, under the decile categorisation of New Zealand schools). So relative criteria were adopted. The lowest achievers in any school will be at risk because by definition there are great distances between them and the main thrust of instruction in that school. RR must take children from any classroom programme and return them to effective functioning in that classroom programme. Such flexibility is surprising, but essential and not usually acknowledged.

Reducing the predictive correlations

One question asked by many people is about the characteristics of these low achievers: do personal, home or community characteristics of subgroups of children predict outcomes, and in particular, the children who will be referred for longer-term help? A RR programme delivered impeccably should lower predictive correlations from any initial characteristic to any criteria for outcomes. The treatment, delivered individually and designed to suit the individual's strengths and pace of learning, is designed to iron out differences *and avoid the negative effects of any prior variables.* There are as many examples of how this is done as one can think of but the following provide illustrations.

- Time in the programme is varied from twelve to twenty weeks.

- Amount of conversation is varied to meet oral language needs.

- Absence is reduced to an absolute minimum by several manoeuvres.

- It is recommended that missed lessons are made up (temporarily two a day).

- If people at home cannot be persuaded to have the child read to them and assemble his or her cut-up story, someone at school will take on the role.

- Activities within lesson components and the time spent on them vary with individual need.

- Pace of lesson is managed by the teacher to adjust to the learner.

- Particular books are chosen for a child, considering gender, interests, cultural experiences as well as progress to date.

- Time on hearing sounds in words, on letter work, on phonemic awareness, on word work and the cut-up story is increased or decreased according to learner needs.

- Progression up a gradient of difficulty in books differs: some children move through levels rapidly while others read different books on one level for several lessons, and this is varied at different times in a lesson series.

- Close additional attention is paid to having weak areas of individual responding linked in association with strong responses.

- In the last month the child's way of working is adjusted to take account of the idiosyncratic demands of the class teacher.

It is the aim of the treatment to deliberately interfere with and minimise any factors which might reduce learning and it is the logic of the treatment to diminish predictive correlations. Sometimes the clusters of negative factors are more complicated than teacher ingenuity can deal with and then case guidance from the professional who trained that teacher is available. Individually designed and individually delivered instruction by a well-trained teacher allows for such adjustments to be made: the clinical reality is that they do not work in every case.

Such deliberate manipulation of the treatment to minimise any effects resulting from child characteristics must surely diminish predictive correlations. It is the intent of the programme to produce common outcomes from children who differ in a multitude of ways. That is the logic of the treatment, to produce a working level of literacy skills despite predictions which might be made were the treatment not available. When treatments are varied according to client need and are planned to diminish the effects of existing differences between the clients, then predictions made from differences among clients on entry to the programme should be lowered by the treatment. The RR treatment aims to produce a common outcome despite initial differences. Research designs must take into account the effects of treatment on predictive correlations.

Four endorsements

Four endorsements from very different sources, all independent of RR professionals, speak to the conceptual basis of RR, and offer some challenges.

1.   From literacy research

In the *Reading Research Quarterly* Shanahan and Neuman (1997) reviewed studies that they believed:

- addressed important issues and/or genuine questions (strongly driven by theory)

- were rhetorically powerful and simply executed

- speculated boldly on broad issues of learning, teaching and instruction.

They wrote:

> No study has so successfully influenced remedial reading instruction as [the] Reading Recovery program ... In a series of studies conducted over a 5-year period, Clay examined the effects of her innovative one-on-one tutorial program to intervene early in reading failure. Up to then, remediation was usually delayed until students were in the fourth grade, as it was assumed that they might catch up on their own. Clay intervened, often successfully, after only one year of instruction. Unlike traditional remedial programs, Clay emphasized instruction in the context of real reading, observation as a key assessment technique, high-quality teacher education as a fundamental part of the intervention, and

individualized instruction that would raise student achievement to the average level [sic] of class performance. (p. 207)

2. From the special education field

Vellutino, Scanlon, Sipay, Small, Chen, Pratt and Denckla (1996) reported an extensive study of early intervention for 'Reading Disability' funded by the National Institute of Child Health and Human Development in the United States. In a large-scale study of kindergarten children from middle class suburbs 1400 were followed into Grade 1, and those showing reading impairment were given daily individual tutoring. The intervention programme placed most of the children *within or above the average range* after one or two semesters of remedial instruction *and a group of hard-to-teach children were identified*. The approach, the tests, the research logic, the tutoring, and the conclusions are not derived from RR sources, but the study was motivated by a paper I wrote on 'Learning to be learning disabled' (Clay 1987). That paper argued:

> ... that most children who have difficulty learning to read are encumbered by experiential and/or instructional deficits, rather than basic deficits in cognitive abilities underlying reading ability. [Clay] pointed out that interpretation of results from reading disability research is generally compromised by the failure to evaluate and control for the child's educational history, and underscored the need for longitudinal studies that included an intervention component to correct for this design problem ... Following Clay's lead we designed and conducted such a study. (Vellutino and Scanlon 1999, p. 8)

3. From school inspectors

Two inspectors of primary schools (Frater and Staniland 1994) reported to the British government on whether a programme like RR could be implemented in a whole education system. After an inspection visit to RR in New Zealand they concluded that:

> ... the low and generally stable figures for the proportions of pupils referred on for longer term help prompt further thought. Most prominently, perhaps, they suggest that the scheme may have told us something fundamental about the remediable nature of much of the incidence of early reading difficulty encountered not only in New Zealand but in similarly long-established education systems in other advanced industrial societies. (p. 12)

The mean percentage of children who could not meet the stringent discontinuing criteria of average band performance in both reading and writing *was below 1 per cent of the birth cohort.* They added:

> ... the New Zealand system is well on the way to identifying the next frontier, the third wave children, that small core who do not appear able to accelerate at the rates of the majority of pupils for whom the scheme is the appropriate measure. As yet, the third wave is not favoured with similar nationally coherent and systematic provision. (p. 23)

That is fair comment, for the next step is taking far too long, according to national figures published annually by the Ministry of Education. Recent research on a third wave of assistance for these children in New Zealand (Phillips and Smith 1997a, 1997b) points to a development area which deserves serious and urgent attention.

4. *From* Redesigning Education

The fourth endorsement also comes with a challenge. In *Redesigning Education* Wilson and Daviss (1994) were searching for effective ways for education to redesign itself, perpetually. They described RR as a prototype of an effective design process for change in education, but they insist that a prototype is not an ideal or mature model of an effective redesign process. RR must be progressively redesigned to incorporate insights from cognitive research and teachers' growing experience, and independent evaluations must be compared in effectiveness to a range of other innovations pursuing similar objectives. Progressive redesign of RR has occurred and must continue. Since the Wilson and Daviss publication an evaluative process for assessing the quality of site, state and country implementations of RR has been developed. Three-day implementation meetings have been undertaken in several states in the United States, and their reports published. Two 'Academies for Administrators' have been held in the United States, both extending the range of feedback from 'user' comments on RR. A renewed interest in research on the cognitive aspects of children's learning in RR is emerging. RR should change:

- when replicated research establishes the advantage of a change,

- or when the political, economic and policy environments change in characteristics,

- or when educational goals and standards shift,

- or when teacher innovations engage academic and research attention and are rigorously trialled and evaluated.

The redesign process must be responsive to several different sources of challenge to change.

The four reviews saw that literacy problems were responding to the treatment and recommended that changes in the RR programme must be directed to the success of more children.

The current status of monitoring research

When RR was adopted by an education system and money was spent on training and teaching, the immediate questions became 'Who is entering RR?' and 'What changes are occurring in children's performance?'

RR is delivered to diverse children in diverse settings, and has a large database. The progress of thousands of students (436,249 students over a twelve-year period in North America [Askew et al. 1998], 11,000 a year in New Zealand [Kerslake 1998], over 3000 a year in the United Kingdom [Hobsbaum 1997], 9000 in Canada in 1998–99 [Canadian Institute of Reading Recovery 2000], and increasing numbers in Australia) is recorded daily by every teacher and a summary is sent to a national or regional data-collecting centre. Documentation in different countries provides the basis for decisions about changes to the implementation of the programme in that country. That the intervention strategy has been replicable across settings and countries by many teachers and under many different educational policies is in itself an outcome to be valued, and allows information to be shared internationally. An early intervention programme profits from recent, relevant data providing annual confirmation that it is working towards its goals, and available to inform new educators and new critics.

1. At the level of the school

In the first year of trials in New Zealand schools administrators were able to 'read' progress in the daily lesson records of individual children. They could see the trajectories of change in the records kept by teachers; they could see change from slow to fast learners in the weekly graphs of progress in reading and writing. They could check the outcomes with their personal knowledge of average-for-age in local schools. The progress was detailed for individuals and pre- and post-test results were kept. Schools are encouraged to make the intervention work effectively for them by documenting their own results.

2. At the district, region, or state level

Districts develop a plan for RR and the district's monitoring of each yearly operation should inform its planning. Success of RR in a district is dependent on well-managed school level programmes, and solving problems at the school level will strengthen the district programme. Effective management at district level must consider issues like funding, the requirements of sound teacher training, geography, teacher mobility, population characteristics, attitudes, misinformation, priorities, regular monitoring, and the continuing education of RR teachers and those who train them.

3. At the national level

RR is unusual in that there is careful, detailed and consistent monitoring in each country. Annual monitoring by the Research Division of the New Zealand Ministry of Education began in 1984. Teachers' records on each child are independently checked by tutors/ teacher leaders before being sent for collation and analysis of national trends. The system knows precisely what is happening, year by year, in every location where the system operates, and private schools who opt into RR comply with the same rules.

Monitoring in the United Kingdom is done by the Institute of Education at the University of London; national results are published and local education authorities receive individual reports.

National data collection for the United States is a huge operation, carried out by the National Data Evaluation Center (NDEC) at the Ohio State University in Columbus, Ohio. NDEC collects descriptive and standard pre- and post-test assessment data annually on every RR student in schools, including Department of Defence schools located in several countries, with high standards of data integrity and timely reporting. Data, entered by RR teachers on specially designed scan forms and sent to NDEC for processing, undergo a rigorous quality control edit including a manual review of each data sheet, and this is followed by a multi-stage computer diagnostic procedure designed to detect and correct for erroneous data. Additional corrections are made after edit reports are sent to each site.

During the summer NDEC provides each site with a group of computer-generated tables and figures to support the preparation of evaluation reports required of each RR site. Each year numerous special data sets and reports are requested and provided to sites. These analyses are timed to allow sites to adjust their goals and practices for the following school year.

These data from a total population of children in certified RR sites, and not merely a sample of the children served, allow NDEC to conduct studies of long-term programme impact and validation of the assessment procedures. In addition NDEC encourages and supports the efforts of university training sites and individual RR sites to engage in further independent research.

Reviews of research on early interventions

Attempts to reduce difficulties in literacy learning can be grouped under the following three headings.

Traditional treatments

Examples would be programmes associated with special funding sources like Title 1 and Learning Disability programmes in the United States, and dyslexia programmes in the United Kingdom. Despite careful selection of children and organised training programmes for teachers, two persistent criticisms of such programmes has been their high rates of identification of children in the middle primary or elementary school who did not have access to a good early intervention programme, and their low rates of success with treatments.

Changes to classroom programmes

Plans are made to teach first instruction in classrooms differently in the belief that this will reduce or eliminate the need for special help. Most curriculum revisions for beginning literacy programmes claim that fewer literacy difficulties will follow implementation of the new curriculum.

Early interventions

A shift has occurred in the past ten to twenty years a) to reduce the incidence of literacy problems among the lowest-achieving children in their first year(s) at school, and b) to provide supplementary individual help for children to catch up to classmates by the end of the first year of formal schooling.

The research challenge for RR has been to show what is possible under the last option. To what extent can initial low achievement be overcome? Appropriately, people have asked what happens to ex-RR children in subsequent school learning. People also ask whether the delivery system can be adapted for different education settings.

Speigel 1995

Several reviewers have tried to extract the important features common to very different early intervention projects. Speigel (1995) recommended that traditional remedial programmes which often have a positive but marginal impact could be more successful if they adopted some instructional principles gleaned from RR. She called for teachers to:

- start early
- use connected text
- spend more time on reading
- provide many opportunities to learn
- have tasks matched to instructional level
- teach strategies and how to apply them to new tasks
- include writing
- teach phonemic awareness
- use direct instruction
- teach individuals
- select the best teachers
- plan for accelerated progress.

Pikulski 1994

Pikulski (1994) reviewed five early intervention programmes for first grade students: Success for All (Wasik and Slavin 1993); the Winston Salem Project (Hall et al. 1993); the Boulder Project (Hiebert et al. 1992); the Early Intervention in Reading (Taylor et al. 1992); and Reading Recovery (Pinnell 1989; Pinnell, Fried and Estice 1990).

For a successful early intervention programme he recommended attention to a different list of important features:

- the students' total programmes should add up to co-ordinated instruction

- quality instruction for increased time

- individual tutoring for some children and small groups for others

- starting in first grade with support beyond the classroom

- using easy texts which lead to success

- reading the same text several times

- attending to words and letters, phonemic awareness and phonics

- writing

- assessment to monitor progress

- communication with homes

- preparing accomplished teachers.

These two lists imply many plausible hypotheses of improvements which should be treated with caution. In 1967, and again in 1985, I published research in classrooms where teachers were meeting all those criteria, and still the high progress readers pulled away from their slower classmates at a fast rate. That classroom research suggested that something more was required. Long lists of important principles, factors or practices are useless unless they are *woven into a theory of how children learn, how teachers can teach, and how a sound delivery system can be mounted. Each teacher has to change how particular children learn.*

One-to-one tutoring deserves an important place in discussions of reform in preventive, compensatory, remedial and special education strategies (Walmsley and Allington 1995, Pikulski 1994, Wasik and Slavin 1993); it is, potentially, an effective means of responding to student reading failure. I agree with these authors that if we know how to ensure that students will learn to read in the early grades, we have an ethical and perhaps legal responsibility to see that they do so. None of these reviewers has specified what it is about the one-to-one teaching that produces success for children at risk. What has much to do with success in early interventions is a well-trained special teacher, given the opportunity to design a programme to suit each child and taking each child by a somewhat different path to the desired outcome of satisfactory work in a classroom, documenting the progress made daily.

The most useful reviews to lead us forward will be extensive, recent, evaluative and balanced. It is helpful to know something about the professional orientation of the reviewer and to track down some of the individual research reports because important variables can become invisible in a condensed account. Reviews may be 'insider' evaluations by professionals interested in the development and explanation of the work they are engaged in, or they may be completed by researchers making independent evaluations of the intervention. From many available I have selected three for comment.

Pinnell 1996

Pinnell (1996, 1997) published a comprehensive review of over 50 studies of RR research from North America which is a rich source of information for new research and collates criticisms and answers criticisms. Pinnell suggested that ideas for further research are lurking in the surprising things that RR is able to do. She wrote:

> The studies were undertaken in different contexts and for a variety of purposes. All studies found RR to be very powerful in the initial intervention, and long-term results are positive in most studies, although there is some variation by context. The program's unique features — intensive teaching, professional development, and a network of professional support — are highlighted in the research on teacher learning and illustrate why a program for children has captured so much attention in the research community.

Pinnell drew these three conclusions from her review of studies in the United States.

- RR offers powerful learning opportunities for children and teachers. *More research is needed on the nature of this learning and factors related to it.* [My italics.]

- Children who do not reach the discontinuing criteria make progress in RR but need further special instruction in subsequent years. More research is needed that examines children for whom RR was not a sufficient intervention programme. (Torgesen 2000)

- The implementation plan for RR offers a self-renewing system that continues to improve over time. Rather than concentrating on first-year implementations, *more research is needed on the long-term implementation of RR* as projects mature over several years.

Shanahan and Barr 1995

The International Reading Association awarded the Albert J. Harris Award in 1997 to Shanahan and Barr (1995) for a comprehensive, critical review of RR's research and effectiveness. They reported positively that RR leads to learning, that students make greater than expected gains in reading, that the effects are comparable to those accomplished by the most effective educational interventions, and that RR merits continued support. They report negatively that it is less effective and more costly than has been claimed, and that it does not lead to systemic changes in classroom instruction. The authors make several recommendations for monitoring the programme more effectively and for encouraging innovations that might lower costs while maintaining effectiveness. These are hypotheses and their worth has yet to be tested, and RR professionals would want to see replicated results at several different sites before new findings could lead to changing the programme. We do not gamble with children's treatments by discarding tested effectiveness for an untested possibility. In summary of their extensive critique the authors write:

> It has proven to be a robust program both in terms of its consequences and its replicability across sites. Further, it has become a significant force in shaping the way we view early literacy development. (1995, p. 992)

They add that it would be appropriate to continue to expend public funds on RR, and public policies should permit education agencies to adopt RR or other proven approaches, and should encourage local experimentation and innovation to identify even better approaches.

Reading Recovery Review 1998

A further source of 'insider' debates about RR is *Literacy, Teaching and Learning,* a refereed journal published by the Reading Recovery Council of North America (RRCNA). This journal has two editorial thrusts: it reports important research pertaining to the programme — about children's learning, about training professionals, and about implementing the programme, but it also reports important research and reviews of new developments that RR professionals should become aware of. A collection of research papers from that journal was published (Swartz and Klein 1997).

In a bid to reduce insider/outsider bias a team of RR trainers prepared for publication by RRCNA two tabular summaries of a) five published reviews of research on the effectiveness of RR under the headings 'Source, Purpose, Scope of Review, Conclusions and Comments' and b) fourteen research studies on aspects of the intervention under the headings 'Source, Purpose, Sample, Measures, Basic Findings/ Conclusions and Comments'. The final manuscript which provided an explanatory text about RR was then submitted to a panel of (named) independent reviewers for critical appraisal and revised in the light of their comments. It provides a valuable reference to RR research at the turn of the century (Askew, Fountas, Lyons, Pinnell and Schmitt 1998).

Administrators' questions

Early administrative support

I began to work with an early intervention designed to address a problem faced by education systems in advanced industrial countries. My background was in classroom teaching, special education and academic developmental psychology. I had taught about how children and young people develop for most of my academic career to educators, educational psychologists, and people in schools and communities who worked with children in their homes and schools.

An administrator hoping to initiate RR in an Australian state came to New Zealand on an official visit. He was shown children learning, how teachers were trained, the involvement of the university in academic training, and the books and materials used. He visited schools and talked with principals, and then he asked, in a tone which conveyed puzzlement and complaint, where was the guiding hand of an administrator? We had been underestimating the importance of administrators. We began to acknowledge the great contribution of two chief inspectors of primary schools in Auckland, Terry Walbran and Ash Newth, and of the Director-General of Education, Bill Renwick, and his adviser, Ken Foster, and other significant administrators who understood the logic of the early intervention strategy in its earliest days in New Zealand.

In the United States an early emphasis of the administrators' needs came from the Deputy Superintendent in Ohio, Bob Bowers, and from Glen Robinson, the Director of the Educational Research Service (ERS) in Arlington, Virginia (a national clearing-house for school research and information, compiling, analysing and sharing information that is essential to effective decision-making). It is an independent, not-for-profit corporation serving the research and information needs of school systems in the United States, their administrative staffs, school boards, and the public. Robinson commissioned a monograph entitled *Reading Recovery: Early Intervention for At-Risk First Graders* written by Pinnell, DeFord and Lyons (1988). The publication was timely as an early 'good reference' for the programme.

It had become apparent that administrators were asking new questions mostly to do with implementation factors.

RR was designed to be a system intervention

In the United Kingdom the initial support came from educational psychologists and school inspectors in Surrey. Against a backdrop of conservative political reform in British education with strong advocacy for 'phonics instruction' as a panacea for all literacy evils, a fledgling RR programme was just beginning to train its first teachers and tutors. After three years two school inspectors visited New Zealand and provided a good reference on the most novel aspect of RR, the fact that it was designed to be adopted, implemented and evaluated by and for an education system; in 21 years the training has not been available without the backing of an education system. These school inspectors were directed to study RR 'in its original setting and to report on it in the context of the local initial reading instruction where it is offered as "something extra" for those children who are making a slow start to reading, at the end of their first year of schooling'. Their report (Frater and Staniland 1994) was critically evaluative (see pages 245–246). The final sentence reads:

> The essential conditions for the success of RR, as a system [intervention], lie in the coherence, the resourcing, and the reach of the support and quality assurance which are put in place for its implementation.

How to question research reports

Administrators seek research reports on interventions to identify promising models of service and service delivery at the level of the education system. Because RR is designed to be adopted by an education system, future RR researchers would do well to add the particular viewpoint of administrators to the research-planning agenda.

The first group of questions addresses the quality of the implementation which is being studied. The most elegant of research designs only provides acceptable test results of RR's effectiveness for administrators if the researchers:

a) provide evidence that the programme which was delivered conformed with the accepted guidelines approved for their education system,

b) used experienced teachers, and

c) worked in an education system which had a minimum of three years' experience of making the programme work.

Otherwise the report may merely document the growing pains of starting something new rather than provide a valid test of the programme's effectiveness. The report needs to address the integrity of the instruction and also to explain how the programme is managed in the school and district. Administrators should ask, 'Does the research report give me firm assurance that the treatment was implemented as designed?' The first cluster asks questions about:

1. The sample of children studied.

2. The integrity of the implementation.

3. The quality of the instruction.

4. How many schools were studied, and how varied they were?

1.   The sample of children

What group of children did the research study? If the research does not use similar children of similar ages in similar communities with similar prior experiences, in comparison with those the administrators are concerned about, the research may have little bearing on the decisions being made. The characteristics of the sample used are important to consider.

2.   The integrity of implementation

Was the research about an established implementation of RR or a beginning one? Authorities suggest that it may take three to five years to bed down a new programme in a new school setting.

3. The quality of the instruction

Were the teachers trained and experienced, with easy access to tutors or teacher leaders? Were they inexperienced, or without guidance during their apprenticeship? Many studies (Sylva and Hurry 1995; Center et al. 1995) proceed as if one has only to consider the children's learning, without weighing up the teacher experience, or the school's experience of mounting the programme. Administrators will fully understand how the two latter factors influence the learning. The fact that teachers need a year-long training course points to the need to evaluate the programme when it is delivered by experienced RR teachers, not by teachers receiving their training or in their first years after training.

4. What type and number of schools participated?

It has been argued that knowing how many schools an intervention works with at some level of effectiveness may be more important to the administrator than the gain score differences (Pogrow 1998). The logistics of servicing the programme are extremely important.

A second group of questions relates to how the findings were reported, and include the following:

5. What outcomes for individuals were reported?

6. Was the teaching a variant of the standard?

7. Is this a critical evaluation? Is a viable alternative offered?

5. What outcomes for individuals were reported?

Are findings about groups of children in an intervention enough? While clinical psychologists and medical practitioners know that eliminating problems at the individual level has good effects when these are reported at the systems level for groups, most educational administrators act as though delivery of education services to individuals is too detailed for their consideration, and if the system level results look good they choose to assume that individuals will be well-served. This is not true in early intervention. Change should always be reported at the level of individuals. Administrators should look for research that reports *the outcomes for individuals as well as group results.*

Do average (mean) score differences tell administrators what they need to know? Is it also important to know how many and what kind of individuals were successful? In intervention research we want to know for which individuals the treatment was satisfactory. Some research designs have powerful analyses which separate out which of two groups gained significantly higher scores than some alternative group; for example, control group studies usually of two or three groups, treated and untreated (see pp. 266–267). That design cannot tell us whether a RR programme reaches its goals of average band performance for individuals; a significantly higher group score for the RR group would tell us nothing about their relationship to the normally-achieving children, but only whether the treated group was better than an untreated group.

Two quite different questions need to be asked. Faced with a number of individuals who are each at risk of making a slow start in literacy learning we need to distinguish two groups:

- individuals who can be predicted to make progress in a classroom programme

- and individuals who have made considerable progress but who will need continuing support for a much longer period.

It is legitimate to complete mean score analyses in addition to reporting the progress of individuals, but it is unsatisfactory to have *only mean scores* because this is a clinical programme in which individuals get treatments designed to suit individual needs (see pp. 266 and 274). One obvious external factor which points to that is 'time in the programme'. This varies from child to child and is a signal to the administrator that the treatments are different (O'Leary 1997). Many research designs preclude reporting on individuals, and for intervention studies the progress of individuals must be available.

6.   *Was the teaching a variant of the standard?*
This could be difficult for the reader of a research report to judge. Sometimes researchers change the RR programme, adjusting it to suit the theoretical needs of their research design. Standardising the time in treatment when it was designed to vary is one such change. So a study which defined the length of the RR programme as fifteen weeks and eliminated the period during which the very-hardest-to-teach children make their biggest shifts did not give RR a fair trial (Center et al. 1995). Others have used RR as a vehicle for delivering a different lesson component (in, say, phonological awareness) so trained the teachers differently (Hatcher 1994; Iversen 1991). This makes the interpretation of results difficult; was it the RR framework, or the variant, which produced the success or failure? It has been possible to design research which rigorously tested standard RR against several alternative variants (Pinnell et al. 1994).

7.   *Is this a critical evaluation? Is a viable alternative offered?*
If the authors are presenting an alternative treatment, how strong are their data about a) what happened to individual children, b) how well the teachers delivered the programme, and c) the range of schools that could make it work?

The final group of questions is directed to future research in RR:

8. Is any long-term follow-up reported?

9. Is reliability of measures reported?

10. What were the positive outcomes for the system?

8.   Is any long-term follow-up reported?

What does the administrator expect the longitudinal outcomes to be? RR supplements the child's classroom programme and good outcomes are dependent upon good classroom teaching in the year of RR placement *and in subsequent grades/classes.*

A high energy, well-resourced RR programme should place all but 1–2 per cent of children in their second year at school within the average band in both reading and writing, which means within easy reach of a good classroom programme. One to two per cent will have made literacy gains but are not predicted to hold their own without further help for a longer period of time. Administrators would like more than this for their investment of money and effort but better results have not been demonstrated. They expect RR to immunise children against poor teaching in the next grades, against several changes of teachers, against social upheavals in children's personal lives in and out of school, and all of life's ups and downs like health and family problems. No programme can do this. The call for long-term outcomes for a short-term investment has been made by administrators, but is not predicted by the developmental theory of RR.

Some researchers find that other low-achieving children receiving class teaching do catch up to ex-RR children, and they regard this as suggesting that this could happen for all RR children. In the real world the classroom instruction provided subsequent to RR is critical for children's subsequent progress and if other slow learners caught up with the ex-RR children that showed that class teachers were doing their job well (Clay 1979, 1993b). It must be a positive outcome if untreated children can be brought to this achievement by classroom teachers. Schools in New Zealand were urged to work towards this.

To conduct research extending more than three years beyond RR seemed to me unrealistic because as a developmental psychologist, I could anticipate the statistical effects of the increasing number of intervening variables. Sustaining what was learned and building on to it for a three-year-period was success in my terms (Clay 1993b, 1997b). However, Rowe's research (1997, p. 264–265) encourages a more optimistic view.

Other questions from administrators might be these. Could what happened have been due to some other concurrent event or process? Were there enough subjects to show whether a difference existed? What were the different outcomes of the treatment for different groups? Was enough treatment delivered or did it stop too soon? I close this section with two recommendations to researchers which may increase the effective use of their results by administrators.

9.   Is reliability of measures reported?

Recently research analysts (Eyberg 1995; Goldstein 1998; Rowe 1997) have called for the reliability of the measures to be reported for the sample of children used in the research and not merely the ones in the test manual, or in a pilot study.

10.   What were the positive outcomes for the system?

Henggeler (1994) recommended a list of outcomes (derived for children's mental health services) which could easily be applied to some education services like RR and the questions would look like this. Does the intervention lead:

- to reduction in the use of restrictive services (like retention, special education, remedial education)?

- to increase in accountability for detailing progress during the programme and outcome at the individual level?

- to increase in delivery of cost-effective services?

- to increase in flexible services?

- to movement towards comprehensive services, which are well-integrated one with another?

- to movement towards individualised services?

- to empowering providers such as individual schools?

Educational research is not usually designed with such questions in mind but hopefully decision-makers may be able to read comments on such positive outcomes in future studies.

Administrators need to be critical of a research report's recommendations. They should isolate the particular problem for which they need an answer, formulate some simple questions about it, and make a critical appraisal of whether the research provides answers to their questions. It would be appropriate to ask a RR professional at the tutor/teacher leader or trainer level some questions relating to the integrity of an implementation in a research report. Researchers' questions are of critical and ultimate importance, but administrators need to know how to 'read' the researchers' reports and how to determine which are the critical features of the research for their own administrative decisions.

Long-term outcomes: research about 'change over time'

Rowe 1997

Rowe (1997) reported that Australian administrators might expect a strong long-term effect from RR. Research from the University of Melbourne on educational policy and school effectiveness reported a longitudinal study of 5000 children, plotting the progress of readers as they moved through two or three grades and showing increases in the means and the spread of scores. (The cross-sectional sequential type of research design that was used has strong support for studying this type of problem — see Baltes, Reese and Nesselroade 1977.) Within the 5000 children randomly sampled from many schools there were 147 ex-RR children from the earliest days of the programme in Victoria, Australia. How had they progressed in relation to the total group? The distribution of these children across the range of achievement in the school had not been foreseen but was totally predictable. *Children who would have been the lowest achievers clustered around 0–10 percentile as six-year-olds were at nine, ten and eleven years of age spread across the achievement range in the same way as the main research sample, and the lower limits of their distribution tended to be higher than those of their non-RR peers.* The general message was that the schools had done as much for the treated RR group as they had done for the other children who were originally more competent — they had spread them through the same range of achievement. That is as good as it gets; I think that is the best result we could expect from an early intervention without subsequent interventions. It was fortunate that Rowe captured this in his analysis for several reasons, but one reason is that we now know what kind of outcome it would be sensible to predict in future studies.

The graphical representation in Rowe's research data by box and whisker plots is a useful descriptive tool enabling a reader to see at a glance the mean, the standard deviation and the range of the group scores.

Longitudinal results from some states in the United States

The *Reading Recovery Review* (1998) reports Ohio Fourth Grade Proficiency test results for two years from 1991 to 1993; Massachusetts Grades 2 and 3 studies across three years; a four-year follow-up in the New York regional site; and two sets of longitudinal studies using the Texas Assessment of Academic Skills. There have been important changes in research designs over this decade with an acceptance now that the appropriate comparison group for evaluating outcomes of the RR intervention is a randomly sampled group from the cohort of school entrants from which the RR children will subsequently be drawn.

The cluster of studies also throws up what I consider to be a very important finding, illustrated by the Massachusetts report:

> This study supported the notion that somewhat tentative literacy performance immediately after the intervention seems to become stronger in subsequent years. (Askew et al. 1998, p. 31)

As many factors would be predicted to contribute to a washout of the effect of a short period of help in early intervention, such results imply that something about the intervention is making a contribution. Whether it is the extra help delivered early or individually designed daily lessons or teachers with a coherent theory of what literacy processing systems must be constructed or all of these or none of these is not yet known.

This strengthening of literacy performance in contrast to a washout effect agrees with Rowe's findings from another continent.

What questions does a control-group study answer?

Control-group experiments set up two competing hypotheses about the population from which the experimental and control group are selected, preferably by random allocation to the two groups. One hypothesis says that the mean scores of tests for these two samples at the end of the treatment are more or less equal and there is no effect from the treatment. The alternative hypothesis says that the means of the populations are significantly different (meaning that a real effect probably did arise as a result of the treatment). An appropriate statistical analysis is made and a table of critical values confirms whether the result is significant or not. A recent review by Dracup (1995) claimed that this process based on probability is imperfect.

The control-group design is not well-suited to measuring longitudinal effects. One difficulty is that over time as all children move through their schools, the spread of achievement scores widens and significant differences are more difficult to demonstrate with older groups. This is a statistical phenomenon discussed by Wasik and Slavin (1993).

The control-group design also masks complexity. An advocate for this research would claim that the 'methods used' must be specified in detail. In my view it avoids the necessity of specifying the detail of the instruction given: the important interactions of teacher and pupil, the details of what is changing over time day by day, week by week, and how the interactions differ from child to child. No control-group study can specify the variations in individual lessons designed by teachers to suit the different processing profiles of different children.

A quantitative analysis of multivariate factors gives a standard answer that 'A' produces higher scores than 'B' or vice versa, or there is no difference. It may help administrators to choose between two possibilities but it will not help administrators to decide for whom and for how long and with what results for individuals, the programme could work. It is a powerful instrument that develops big problems when it tries to inform an intervention which is trying to deliver different treatments adjusted to individual differences. In two studies which have been highly critical in the history of RR research (Iversen 1991 and Center et al. 1995), the research reports require the reader to have faith in the treatment labels and concise descriptions attributed by the authors to their treatments. A close reading of Iversen's original thesis convinces me that no group received an authentic RR treatment and that there were two experimental treatments being delivered. There was no independent check on this. The Center et al. team took many liberties with the RR treatment, the most obvious being to limit the calculations to fifteen weeks of tuition. The Ohio State University study (Pinnell et al. 1994, see below) added an analysis of the lessons delivered in the RR treatment group as a way of overcoming this problem.

If researchers want to run a traditional control-group design and randomly allocate children to treatment and non-treatment groups, they must overcome a tough ethical problem about whether the RR programme can be withheld from a randomly selected group named as a control group.

Finally there is a very serious problem with the control-group study. Assume that random allocation of low achievers to experimental and control groups could be achieved *that would never produce an answer to a question that RR needs to answer which is, 'Do the RR children perform within the average band of their classroom programme?'* If we only ever compare them with low achievers we are not likely to get an answer to that question. *It is not enough to achieve significant improvement over their starting scores;* the aim is to be reasonably confident of subsequent progress through day-to-day participation in their classroom instruction. This is the difference between the 'discontinued' children and the 'referred' children when they leave RR. The exit or post-test scores are of some interest but it is whether new cognitive processes have been put in place that provides a basis for predicting subsequent progress.

Naturally administrators find the logic of the control-group design apparently suited to their needs: on the surface it tells them on the average which of two programmes gives significantly higher scores, reducing the complexity to simplicity. Academic researchers tell administrators that this is the best design; district research departments believe this. But administrators are short-changed on the information they get.

Shanahan (1987) reviewed Clay's 1985 edition of *The Early Detection of Reading Difficulties* and concluded that the New Zealand RR research was designed in such a way that it was impossible to know whether or not the programme worked. Presumably he sought a control-group design, and would have been satisfied with a significant difference between means (rather than with the fate of individuals). The only comparison group available was with children who did not receive the programme, so all RR children were compared with all the rest of the children in the same schools and age group. The low-end subgroup at the beginning was compared with the entire age cohort of untreated children at the end. The treated group fell mainly within the average band. *The evidence was published as individual scores for every child across the test battery.* The changes in reading levels made by these individuals convinced administrators that these children had surely moved. The New Zealand Director-General of Education and his advisers found the evidence of the movement of individual children from minimal achievements at entry to performance within the average band of their class at exit readable in the changes of texts they could read. They saw the amount of change worth having on the ground in real schools.

Traditional reasoning is inverted when thinking about RR. A group of children is shown to be significantly different prior to treatment from the rest of the bunch. What the school needs to achieve is that following RR instruction the lower-scoring group is found *to be not significantly different* from a group selected randomly at the beginning of the treatment from among the whole population. They can then be taught within the average group in their classroom.

Sylva and Hurry 1995

The Department for Education in Britain requested and funded a control-group research design which was more sensitive to the characteristics of the treatments. The authors were required by the funding body to compare RR, based on a theory of how children learn, with another programme derived from theory of how to teach the phonemic characteristics of English, a theory of teaching rather than a theory of learning. Such a programme was created for the research project. Favourable results for RR were reported from the classical control group study with short-term follow-up, conducted by an independent research unit.

The Ohio State University report 1994

A carefully designed and informative research study was conducted by an Ohio State University team (Pinnell, Lyons, DeFord, Bryk and Seltzer 1994). *They fully understood the intricacies of the early intervention challenges and designed a control-group study which overcame many of the problems.* It compared each of four different instructional models for helping high-risk first-graders with each of four control groups receiving an existing intervention programme (Title 1). From their results they judged RR to be the best choice of the five instructional alternatives tested (Pinnell et al. 1994; or Pinnell 1996). The study included an analysis of time and content for each of the five instructional treatments delivered, an excellent practice rarely undertaken.

Researchers must choose research designs which are appropriate for the questions to be answered. Different research designs are associated with different kinds of knowledge and different kinds of questions, and they produce different kinds of evidence. Comparative control-group designs are legitimate if they address the questions raised. Two examples of the appropriate use of this type of research design with RR have been discussed, but the best 'trace' of long-term effects which exists (Rowe 1997, see above) could not have been produced using a simple control-group comparison design.

Other approaches to 'change over time'

Literacy achievements are acquired cumulatively over time and RR records are able to capture data on changes in individuals over the course of their twelve to twenty weeks of lessons. Further research may need to involve the study of how learning changes over short, medium and long periods of time.

Systematic observation

Shanahan and Neuman (1997) saw observation as a key *assessment* technique. I would argue:

- that scientists observe as a discovery or fact-finding technique establishing what exists

- that teachers dare not overlook observation as a basic phase of teaching

- and that assessment then becomes a third and later use of observation.

Bakeman and Gottman (1986) defined systematic observation as 'a particular approach to quantifying behaviour concerned with naturally-occurring behaviour observed in naturalistic contexts' (p. 4). Records of behaviour collected by observers are the measuring instruments of observational research; they specify which behaviour is to be selected from the passing stream and recorded for subsequent study. The hallmarks of systematic observation are:

- the use of predefined behaviour codes

- by observers of demonstrated reliability

- and demonstrations (results) which can be replicated.

The methodological issues which arise when data are collected by direct observation are thoroughly reviewed by Hops, Davis and Longoria (1995) and include a section on my next topic, sequential analysis.

Systematic sequential observation

If systematic observation is used to record *sequential behaviours* we can explore a series of events or a series of interactions as they occur in real time. For example, all teaching can be viewed as a series of interactions. Test scores have commonly been a way of reporting the outcome of teaching but when we study the process of teaching we have to observe and record child-teacher-child-teacher... interactions in episodes (Watson 1999). Test scores do not lead directly to teaching but coded observations, supported by a theory of what changes to expect, can be used to guide teaching (Clay 1985a). If a researcher asked, 'Does this antecedent event increase the probability of a consequent event?' or 'Does this behavioural chain herald an integration shift when two behaviours seem to merge?' then systematic sequential analysis might lead to interesting results (Hops et al. 1995).

A second example may be familiar to many readers. In the first years of literacy instruction the Running Record is the systematic observation tool devised to code sequentially the events that occur as a child reads continuous text. The sequential events are recorded for later analysis. The record is not of teaching interactions because the teacher refrains from interacting during the taking of a Running Record. The reading is done independently of the teacher.

Researchers must observe, and they need to do it well, with imagination, with boldness, with dedication and in valid and reliable ways (Bakeman and Gottman 1986, p. 200). Controlled observations taken sequentially make us *aware of patterns in the record*. Discovering patterns can give rise to theories. These authors make the following three statements:

- Only a small percentage of research in education involves systematic observation.

- Very little of that uses sequential observation.

- Three possibilities for observing sequential observation in education are learner behaviour, or teaching moves, or both in interaction.

So systematic observations which are analysed for sequential patterns usually yield new insights in areas previously restricted to quantitative analysis of tests scores or probes at several isolated points of time. A sequential analysis of patterns in reading behaviours could lead to what I call a literacy processing theory, a theory of assembling perceptual and cognitive working systems needed to complete increasingly complex tasks (see Chapter 3).

Take, for example, self-correction while reading aloud (see Chapter 5). A quantitative study might only consider accuracy and error, and tally the initial error. A sequential study of reading aloud yields records of error, puzzlement, repeated efforts to correct the error, and self-correction. Such an approach gives rise to new questions with theoretical consequences like, 'What made the reader initiate self-correction?' Quantitative studies produce a large body of evidence which may push aside the rare evidence from systematic observation of events in sequence, even when that latter evidence may be very important for teaching and learning. Attention to how patterns of behaviour change over time in individuals could result in a different acquisition theory (see Chapter 2).

Some attempts to take systematic sequential observations of children and teachers in writing interactions (Girling-Butcher, Phillips and Clay 1991; Boocock, McNaughton and Parr 1998) reported many difficulties in coding and recording behaviours, and how they change, in reliable ways. One study of RR writing interactions provided new insights and possibilities for research (Hobsbaum, Peters and Sylva 1996).

Scientists demand data that be replicable, amenable to scientific analysis and faithful to the phenomena studied. They need to answer the questions that need answering: too often in RR's experience the research was not designed to answer the questions for which administrators needed answers. Observations are useless if carried out in a slipshod way exercising little control over what is being studied. They also need to study and report patterns of change over time.

Replication of research studies

Replication (to make a replica) is an important concept in the history and theory of science. It is how science verifies research results. If a scientist reports findings that other scientists cannot verify when they try to repeat a study then the original findings will be questioned. If other scientists use the same definitions, procedures, and design and arrive at the same results, then the findings in the first study are supported by the subsequent studies.

The call for replication is made by scientists to *force the difference between fact and fiction*. If observations can be repeated by several observers in different settings the risk of the single observer having influenced the result in some way is reduced. RR results have been *repeated* across teachers, children, sites, countries and languages. The change patterns across a series of lessons appear similar, despite individual differences in the lessons given. Different teachers get similar results from delivering different lessons. RR lesson series across the world bring children to criterion levels at the rate of something like 150,000 or more per year. The results have been repeated many times.

However, there are some problems with this kind of evidence. On the one hand people holding similar opinions will tend to make identical observations which support their view. Training to take observations sets up a social group (an in-group) and by definition cannot be objective. That is why people challenge RR's claims that replication supports RR's effects. That is why having administrators assess the change with different criteria (like progress on the school's curriculum) is helpful. That is why independent (outsider) research using a conceptual base that is related (such as Vellutino et al. 1996) but not seen as 'insider research' is very important to RR.

On the other hand research evaluations that are independent of the treatment research raise a different problem. People who are not RR professionals often do not understand the intervention nor the underlying theory well enough, may not use appropriate criteria for judging it, and are at risk of not replicating the treatment. Independence can include ignorance, in that basic qualities or adjustments of the treatment can be overlooked.

Replication is useful because it provides evidence of accountability once a programme is established and can be made open to the scrutiny of the administrators, but it is difficult to achieve true replication in the social sciences and in education, because something almost always gets varied, such as the instruments used, the treatment procedures, the time line, and/or modifications to fit local circumstances, limited budgets, or the requirements of the selected statistical analysis. Researchers want to improve on what earlier researchers did so they 'repeat the study' but do not replicate it.

Repeated demonstrations are a strength and should be highly valued by administrators, but the critical research reviewer will demand more than that. Researchers must search for safeguards against unchecked subjectivity. They are obliged to support and test interpretations in each research project by carrying out more than one type of analysis, seeking additional sources of confirmation, looking for and discussing counter instances, considering alternative explanations and checking with respondents.

Simultaneous replication

When different schools use the same standardised test at the same time in the school year they are actually engaging in simultaneous replication. Researchers at different sites study the same problem in the same way at the same time, using the same definitions, procedures and instruments and they collect data according to the same time line. In other words the same study is reported tens or hundreds of times. RR already operates like this, and it would be easy to design and record simultaneous replication studies across multiple sites. My original studies were designed to meet the same research directives as simultaneous replication; they were designed to replicate the same effect across individual cases (Frymier, Barber, Gansneder and Robertson 1989).

Simultaneous replication is particularly suited to school districts. The technique is most effective for organisations that have sub-units which are separated geographically, that have a central headquarters with communication and dissemination capabilities, that have a consensus on organisational purposes, and that have a commitment to research as one way to attain those purposes.

Historical replication

The need for historical replication arises in RR because it has lasted for many years. Assuming that the societies and school systems in which it exists are changing dynamically over time, and the rationales and theories which provide RR's explanations for its success are also dynamically responding to new information, it is necessary to have replication studies. Research funding should support quality proposals for replication studies if, after ten years or so, a legitimate question is 'Do the same results and explanations still hold true?' given that times and settings have changed. Sometimes the answer will be yes, they still hold true; at other times a search for explanations of the directions of change will be indicated.

Individual replications or repeated measures

Individual RR records change over the period of twelve to twenty weeks of lessons. From hundreds of replications of that change sequence we can predict some changes which are likely to occur for individuals and therefore for groups. Most research designs average out individual variability, and cannot report or predict a result at the individual level; or not without considerable risk of being wrong. This is unacceptable in a treatment or prevention programme, and when the effect occurs for each individual we can be more confident of the treatment effects reported for a group.

Replication across different education systems

In the United Kingdom, the United States, Canada and Australia, data have been collected for local education authorities, in ways in which it would be possible to compare implementations across comparable units on scope and quality of implementation of early intervention. This has not typically been done. The preferred comparison is for an educational system to compare itself with some national figures.

Single-subject research designs

The single-subject experiment uses the subject as his or her own control. (Other names for this type of research are intra-subject designs and within-subject designs.) This kind of research appeared in the literature of applied behaviour analysis about 1970, but it is not often described in educational research textbooks. Researchers repeatedly observe the performance of individuals at close intervals during learning (which would sound familiar to RR professionals). They record how performance changes in the days following the introduction of the experimental treatment and in particular, how this compares with the same subject's performance in the days prior to the treatment. This is how the learner is used as his or her own control (instead of using a control group). This is a research model which can record the particular effects of particular teaching procedures on the learning of individual children. Strict rules of research logic governing this type of research must be respected. The performance of small groups could be reported in such research but each individual child is traceable. It is no coincidence that Running Record graphs of individual progress over time look somewhat like those used in single-subject research designs.

These designs (Church 1997) are useful for studying how treatment or instruction influences skill development in individuals and to identify the factors upon which human behaviour change depends. To make repeated observations frequently is to create very detailed pictures of change in performances. This is a useful approach for studying many aspects of learning:

- the appearance of new behaviours

- the acquisition of a sequence of steps in a particular order

- learning new stimulus-response correspondences

- some concept or rule learning

- new knowledge responses

- changes in response frequency.

Different kinds of behaviour change include improvements in accuracy, improvements in fluency, and improvements in maintenance of the responses. This research design was used by Phillips and Smith (1997b) to study improvements in a 'Third Wave' literacy intervention with children who did not discontinue from RR after a full 20 weeks of lessons.

Necessary features of single-subject research include standardising the recording procedures and measuring the effects of treatments. The experiment can apply to a few subjects of a defined population. This kind of experiment tends to generate results of a kind that RR could use to trial slight modifications of parts of a programme. Instead of asking questions about the whole treatment would it be possible to ask questions about the effects of specific instructional variables, the kind of experiment in which the experimenter changes just one aspect of teaching? This kind of experimental analysis might advance our understanding of the effects of particular teaching variables on learning. If only one instructional variable changes as we move from one experimental treatment to the next, any changes in rate of learning which were observed might be directly attributed to the variable which has changed.

The research design is far from perfect for studying change in RR, however. An important assumption in RR's theory is that what has caused children to have difficulty will vary from child to child. At any one time their repertoires of competencies will be grossly different child from child. If every child is taken from where he or she is to somewhere else then their starting points and most rapid route to success must be different and lessons must be designed to suit the processing strengths and weaknesses of particular children. A single-subject research design allows the researcher to determine whether the adjustments made by the teacher achieved a change in that child's literacy behaviours. However, none of a particular teacher's students will read the same books, and the items learned will vary from child to child just as much as the words he or she writes daily will vary with the topic he or she has chosen to write about and his or her control of language. That being the case it is not a research design which can easily lead to aggregating the findings across subjects.

Another problem for researchers of RR instruction is that none of the lesson activities is directed to a particular facet of reading and writing. To omit the writing activity is to reduce learning to compose text, hearing and recording sounds in words, taking words to fluency in writing, building a writing vocabulary linked to a reading vocabulary, practice with breaking speech into words, and words into letters, and practice in combining letters into words and words into phrases and sentences.

To omit familiar reading is to reduce the amount of reading done, reduce word and letter revision, deprive the child of fluent reading opportunities, and the easy use of syntactic and semantic sources of information, limit the sense of control and well-being, omit practice for the book to be taken home, and miss out on authentic reading that gets a reading process going well.

Letter identification is practised in every lesson slot and when the teacher introduces a new challenge in letter learning there will be interactive effects with this learning across the lesson in all activities. The good teacher links whatever the child is working on from one section to what arises as a challenge in any other part of the lesson. These things make it difficult to 'investigate' the instructional activities of a RR lesson.

Single-subject research designs were most often used by behaviourists, which is perhaps why readers from the field of literacy learning may know little about them *but they are just as useful when using a cognitive theory of learning (Greer 1983) as long as researchers keep in mind where behavioural data ends and inference begins.*

The challenges of longitudinal intervention research

When an intervention is delivered we are interested in more than mere description of changes to learning, or behaviour or health; we want to understand those changes, to explain them, and to choose between different treatments. To be able to do these things longitudinal research will be necessary extending across a period of years in addition to short-term effectiveness trials.

The advantages and disadvantages of longitudinal research must be weighed carefully. Advantages listed by Black and Holden (1995) include:

- the possibility of capturing the heterogeneity of the outcomes

- the study of changes in individuals

- the precision of timing and measurement of experiences

- how chains of changes can be related one to another (in causal chain analysis)

- and improvement in the chances that critical variables will not be missed.

On the other hand these authors list the problems to be overcome during the designing of research as:

- small numbers of subjects are used

- evaluators from within the intervention are used because outside evaluators do not understand the essential components of the intervention

- funding is required for a long period

- subjects leave the project (called sample attrition)

- measures become outdated

- state-of-the-art theories change between the beginning and end of the longitudinal project

- major societal events change the contexts under study

- theory is needed to predict the outcomes but the study is usually undertaken in order to formulate that very theory.

A longitudinal intervention in education is highly likely to produce different outcome effects for different groups of children, it will certainly lose many children from the sample due to family mobility, and it will be hard-pressed to monitor some of the reasons for change occurring (such as when the child affects his or her own condition and lifts himself or herself out of the risk categories).

It has been argued by Bryant and Bradley (1985) that an approach which avoids most of the research design traps involves three types of research. It must: 1) describe what occurs in controlled studies (experimental or non-experimental); 2) use a longitudinal study to place your exciting find in a developmental perspective stretching before and after; and 3) develop a training intervention which produces or prevents certain behaviours. Garmezy (1988) argued that longitudinal research in intervention studies is vital to understanding developmental processes and adaptation, but they could be implemented in the final phases of a research programme after earlier studies have pointed to their worth. That is consistent with the Bryant and Bradley plan.

Black and Holden (1995), following Feinstein (1977), described three categories of longitudinal intervention research focused on questions of efficacy, effectiveness and efficiency. I quote the questions each category raises because I think these distinctions are important for RR.

- Efficacy trials are conducted to determine if the intervention works under optimal or ideal conditions.

- Effectiveness trials assess whether an intervention works in the field and can be integrated into existing systems.

- Efficiency refers to an analysis of the costs and benefits needed to move from research to policy, and widespread implementation.

There is a need to know not only whether an intervention is useful but for whom it works, and at what cost. To move forward we also need to know, if possible, why it works. Ramey and Ramey (1998) summarise early intervention research evidence over four decades and outline six principles about efficacy. They conclude that intensive, high-quality, ecologically pervasive interventions can and do work.

When planning for a follow-through design which plans to map the progress of an intervention group and a non-intervention group, random assignment of subjects to both groups at the beginning should be the goal. To escape ethical constraints this must be done before you know you have a successful intervention. That may introduce some organisational constraints and extra work. However, in the case of low-achieving groups the research design also needs to report where the research groups stand in relation to the rest of the population. Which members of the treated group can reach average band performance, for example? Or is the outcome to be described as improvement of the quality of life?

Two other checks should be included in the research designs of interventions. There should be a research report on treatment integrity (whether the treatment was delivered as designed), and it is important to provide evidence of who were trained to deliver the intervention, who trained them, how they were trained, and how experienced and successful they were as teachers. (See p. 261.)

There is a basic theoretical question which rocks the foundations of longitudinal interventions. Their strength lies in being able to predict children's development but some developmental theorists say that outcomes for individuals are unpredictable because of the complexity of the 'causes' of success or difficulties. The folly of extending longitudinal intervention research for too long arises from the difficulties of dealing with the effects of all the intervening factors that influence children's learning. This led me to limit my own follow-up studies to three years.

It is clearly appropriate to plot the progress of individuals from some beginning point to some end-point across a span of time. Applied behaviour analysis has been used to do this over short periods of time and is particularly suitable for the study of individuals (Phillips and Smith 1997b). However, change theorists like Fullan (1999) suggest that change tends to be better explained by chaos theory than by predictable causes.

Research issues for RR interventions

Three aspects of RR are constantly under revision: the teaching practices, the training of teachers, and the implementations in education systems. These are codified in several editions of texts, changes to educational policies, changes to the guidelines of existing programmes, and changes to training courses.

Variants in the lesson interactions (the teaching practices)

To be effective RR must be responsive to the discourse of new research and theory and not be locked into the theory of the late 1970s when it was developed (Pearson 1994). Uncertainty in theory and practice must continue to be probed and practices changed in the direction of better results for a wider variety of children. Has the intervention varied (Clay 1997b)? Here are three examples which illustrate where change has occurred, or where current enquiry is focused.

(a)   Recent research on phonemic awareness called for little change in actual procedures. In 1976–77 we observed that some children had extreme difficulty with 'hearing sounds in words' in isolation and in text reading. Effective teaching to deal with this was built into the programme in 1977, prior to the research and theoretical formulations of the 1980s about phonemic awareness. New evidence confirmed existing practice; what changed was the research read by RR professionals during the training of trainers, tutors or teacher leaders, and teachers, that is, course-work at three levels. RR children performed as well on phonemic awareness tests in comparison with a special treatment group studied by Iversen (1991) and Iversen and Tunmer (1993). Children are trained to hear and record the sequence of sounds in words in their writing and teachers prompt them to use this knowledge as they *read* new words. The new phonemic awareness research led to an increased emphasis on the reciprocity of reading and writing (see Wasik and Slavin 1993).

(b)   RR trainers have sought better theoretical articulation of what children have to learn about looking at print. We search for a stronger theoretical basis for how children weave visual perception learning (the identity of letter forms in letter sequences) into their early construction of inner control over literacy. Research on eye movements (Rayner and Pollatsek 1989) and research on the sequence and timing of visual and phonological information and how they enter into fast, competent processing of print in mature readers captures my interest (Barnea and Breznitz 1998). Usually a reader attends to and identifies visual information which then triggers access to phonemic information. We search for findings about the role of increased speed of visual perception of the symbols of the code during the earliest stages of acquisition.

(c)   Research about onsets, rimes and analogy clarified how children can develop effective procedures for working at the sub-word level with parts of words in English, creating units or patterns to be recognised rapidly. Using phonologically regular and orthographically regular onsets and rimes allows for word-solving that is faster than letter by letter. Teachers learned to support children when reading words that are not regular in either sound or spelling with some variant of 'It looks/sounds like X [using the word the child had selected] but it's Y.' That prompt has proved helpful with low achievers. It seems to alert children to the problem that, in English, sounds can appear as different spellings, and the same spellings can have different sounds. The implication is 'be ready to be flexible', and 'if it is not your first choice try an alternative'. A prescribed teaching sequence or undue stress upon regularity and word families does not foster the flexibility required to read English. Onset and rime breaks have been found to be appropriate in English but not in some other languages (Goswami 1999). This body of research allowed for changes to the teaching manual for better teaching in the 'making and breaking' segment of the lesson in the 1985 edition of RR teaching procedures.

RR professionals work with a dynamically changing theory (witnessed by the discussions aired in this book) and a multivariate and interactive view of change (rather than a single causal theory). This forces an openness to new knowledge. If 'RR helps children to integrate a wide range of skills involved in reading and writing'

(Sylva and Hurry 1995) then there are a myriad of unknowns hidden in the words 'to integrate' that need to be explored in future research.

What is particularly challenging for theory construction about literacy learning is that during the time of reading and writing acquisition, each one of the multivariate processes is in a state of early development and though primitive and immature, the processes are being continually transformed by use, and being modified by changes in each of the others. Errors occur in all of the processes.

New editions of the teachers' texts covering theory (Clay 1991), assessments (Clay 1993a), and teaching procedures (Clay 1993b) are essential if a programme is evaluating itself and responding to shifts in available knowledge from observations and from research. RR trainers monitor these needs.

Variants developed outside the intervention

What happens when variants are added to the teaching practices? If good results are reported with the inclusion of a variant procedure it is not acceptable merely to claim that the variant produced the good outcome, for it is plausible to suppose that the broad-band intervention may have sustained the progress despite the variant. Hatcher (1994), for example, introduced a systematic, detailed and prescriptive phonological training into his recommended programme and, unless we are shown otherwise, a protagonist might hypothesise that the wrap-around RR programme carried the variant to its success. Care must be taken with research designs where lesson components are added or withdrawn or varied so that it is clear whether gains or losses or equivalence are demonstrated.

Speakers of a language other than English

Hiebert (1994) reported that children learning English as a second language are, or should be, excluded from RR. *This has never been the practice wherever RR operates.* In RR children's individual lessons are monitored and changed daily, according to idiosyncratic needs. The 'English for Speakers of Other Languages' (ESOL) group perform well in RR where they are given 30 minutes every day with a teacher who increases their time for talking and personalises their instruction, while teaching them to read and write. Research from California (Neal and Kelly 1999; Gentile, 1997), from New York (Ashdown and Simic 2000), from New Zealand (Smith 1994) and from the United Kingdom (Hobsbaum 1997) reports that ESOL children in RR reach the same levels as English-speaking children and do not take longer to do this. Hobsbaum's concluded that:

> We need to be aware that younger and less fluent bilingual children, in effect, those who are struggling at the early stages of learning English, have difficulties with the programme. We shall be addressing the problem of how to find ways to match the early texts we offer them to their style and level of English. At present it may be premature to use lack of fluency with English as a reason for excluding young bilingual learners from the programme. (p. 146)

It is not widely understood that RR has no problems with the selection of ESOL children as suitable for the intervention. They must be next in literacy achievement rank among the lowest achieving group in their school. However, entry to RR may be delayed a few months *if a child is unable to understand what he or she is being asked to do when given the tasks of the Observation Survey. As long as the child knows enough language to be able to engage with the tasks it can be predicted that his or her literacy achievement will be helped by RR's approach in spite of low or zero entry scores.*

Some educators question the ability of ESOL children to continue to gain after RR is no longer available to them. This is not a literacy learning question; it is a question of whether the school is providing them with the opportunities to advance in their control of English.

The neglect of writing

Progress in RR is measured for both reading and writing and children are expected to survive back in the classroom in both curriculum areas. A large body of research shows that readers and writers have to develop phonemic awareness and build the use of the sound system of their spoken dialect into their developing network of strategies for the two similar but different processing systems of reading and writing. These two activities can have reciprocal effects on each other. Teachers can retard the progress of children in reading when they skip writing or give it minimal attention, assuming that they should give priority to reading and attend to writing as a later learning task. Teachers have to actively teach for a transfer of reading knowledge to writing or vice versa; the learner, like most adults, does not automatically connect the two. In early intervention teaching these links must be established. (See Chapter 1.)

Scaffolding in RR and in classrooms

Scaffolding (or teacher support for) new learning in RR was studied in the research reported by Hobsbaum, Peters and Sylva (1996) and opens an exciting vista for the study of writing. However, the authors concluded:

> Although the scaffolding process has been shown here [in RR] to underpin the teaching of writing in a reading intervention, we are less confident that it is useful in the ordinary classroom teaching.

Can we accept that? It is possible that the benefit of scaffolding and support may still be possible and beneficial in a classroom but that the practice would have to look different, and perhaps be delivered more intensively at a crucial time, and not for everyone all of the time. RR children need to have the beginning phases of literacy learning scaffolded on a daily basis but with such help can become average readers and writers.

Changes beyond discontinuing from RR

I would expect RR to continue to derive deeper insights from the theories and methodologies of developmental psychology in the future.

Many opportunities are opening up for researchers who understand RR to pose questions and carry out research among the age group in the next year or two after completion of a RR programme. What does the transition look like? (Researchers would probably be advised to first find out what RR professionals think supports the transition out of RR for their graduates.) What does the classroom learning of the next year after RR look like for all children, and what does the subsequent learning of discontinued children look like? What does the self-extending system (Clay 1991) look like and how do the self-extending systems of discontinued RR children change after their RR lessons have ended? How does this change compare with the progress made by other children in the same age group who did not have RR? Further insights into literacy processing at higher levels than the RR age group could lead to new understandings and changes in practices during RR lessons. It is not difficult to find evidence in existing research for this conclusion: RR children who have been successful in RR make variable progress in the subsequent school year in classrooms and then annually show more and more consistent progress as they move up through their school programmes. The tentativeness of the early success and the consistency of the later progress are trends to be carefully documented and explained.

References

Ashdown, J. and O. Simic. 2000. Is early literacy intervention effective for English language learners? Evidence from Reading Recovery. *Literacy Teaching and Learning: An International Journal of Early Reading and Writing* 5, 1: 27–42.

Askew B.J., I.C. Fountas, C.A. Lyons, G.S. Pinnell and M.C. Schmitt. 1998. *Reading Recovery Review: Understandings, Outcomes, and Implications.* Columbus, OH: Reading Recovery Council of North America.

Bakeman, R. and J.M. Gottman. 1986. *Observing Interaction: An Introduction to Sequential Analysis.* Cambridge: Cambridge University Press.

Baltes, P.B., H.W. Reese and J.R. Nesselroade. 1977. *Life-span Developmental Psychology: Introduction to Research Methods.* Monterey, CA: Brooks/Cole.

Barnea, A. and Z. Breznitz. 1998. Phonological and orthographic processing of Hebrew words: Electro-physiological aspects. *The Journal of Genetic Psychology* 159, 4: 492–504.

Black, M.M. and E.W. Holden. 1995. Longitudinal intervention research in children's health and development. *Journal of Clinical Child Psychology* 24, 2: 163–172.

Boocock, C., S. McNaughton and J.M. Parr. 1998. The early development of a self-extending system in writing. *Literacy, Teaching and Learning* 3, 2: 41–58.

Bryant, P. and L. Bradley. 1985. *Children's Reading Problems.* Oxford: Blackwell.

Canadian Institute of Reading Recovery, Toronto, Canada, personal communication 2000.

Caplan, G. 1964. *Principles of Preventive Psychiatry.* London: Tavistock Publications.

Center, Y., K. Wheldall, L. Freeman, L. Outhred and M. McNaught. 1995. An evaluation of Reading Recovery. *Reading Research Quarterly* 30: 240–263.

Church, J. 1997. *Within-Subject Experimental Analysis.* State of the Art Monograph, No. 5. New Zealand Association for Research in Education.

Clay, M.M. 1979. *Reading: The Patterning of Complex Behaviour* (Second Edition). Auckland: Heinemann.

———. 1985a. Engaging with the school system: A study of interactions in new entrant classrooms. *New Zealand Journal of Educational Studies* 20, 1: 20–30.

———. 1985b. *The Early Detection of Reading Difficulties* (Third Edition). Auckland: Heinemann.

———. 1987. Learning to be learning disabled. *New Zealand Journal of Educational Studies* 22, 2: 155–173.

———. 1991. *Becoming Literate: The Construction of Inner Control.* Auckland: Heinemann.

———. 1993a. *An Observation Survey of Early Literacy Achievement.* Auckland: Heinemann (First Edition 1972; Second Edition 1979; Third Edition 1985; title change 1993).

———. 1993b. *Reading Recovery: A Guidebook for Teachers in Training.* Auckland: Heinemann.

———. 1997a. The development of literacy difficulties. In D. Corson, 1997, *Encyclopaedia of Language and Education, Volume 2: Literacy.* Dordrecht, Netherlands: Kluwer Academic Publishers.

———. 1997b. International perspectives on the Reading Recovery program. In J. Flood, S.B. Heath and D. Lapp, eds, *Handbook of Research on Teaching Literacy Through the Communicative and Visual Arts.* Macmillan Reference Series on Educational Research.

Clay, M.M. and B. Watson. 1993. The three-year follow-up in 1981. In M. Clay, *Reading Recovery: A Guidebook for Teachers in Training.* Auckland: Heinemann.

Dracup, C. 1995. Hypothesis testing — what it really is. *The Psychologist* (UK), August: 359–362.

Eisner, E. 1993. Forms of understanding and the future of educational research. *Educational Researcher,* October, 1993: 5–11.

Eyberg, S.M. 1995. Jigsaws: Introduction to the special issue on methodological issues in clinical child psychology research. *Journal of Clinical Child Psychology* 24, 2: 122–124.

Feinstein, A.R. 1977. *Clinical Biostatistics.* St Louis: Mosby.

Frater, G. and B. Staniland. 1994. Reading Recovery in New Zealand: A Report from the Office of Her Majesty's Chief Inspector of Schools. *Literacy, Teaching, and Learning* 1, 1: 143–162. Also available from the Office for Standards in Education, Her Majesty's Stationery Office, London.

Frymier, J., L. Barber, B. Gansneder and N. Robertson. 1989. Simultaneous replication: A technique for large-scale research. *Phi Delta Kappa,* November 1989: 228–231.

Fullan, M. 1999. *Change Forces: The Sequel.* Philadelphia, PA: Falmer Press.

Garmezy, N. 1988. Longitudinal strategies, causal reasoning and risk research: A commentary. In M. Rutter, ed., *Studies of Psychosocial Risk: the Power of Longitudinal Data*, pp. 29–44. Cambridge, England: Cambridge University Press.

Gentile, L.M. 1997. Oral language: Assessment and development in Reading Recovery in the United States. In S.L. Swartz and A.F. Klein, eds, *Research in Reading Recovery.* Portsmouth, NH: Heinemann.

Girling-Butcher, W., G. Phillips and M.M. Clay. 1991. Fostering independent learning. *The Reading Teacher* 44, 9: 694–697.

Goldstein, H. 1979. *The Design and Analysis of Longitudinal Studies.* New York: Academic Press.

———. 1998. *Models for Reality: New Approaches to the Understanding of Educational Processes.* London Institute of Education, University of London.

Goswami, U. 1999. Spelling it out …. Book review of *Learning to Spell: Research, Theory and Practice Across Languages,* C.A. Perfetti, L. Rieben and M. Fayot, eds, in *The Psychologist* 12, 7: 360–361.

Greer, R.D. 1983. Contingencies of the science and technology of teaching and pre-behavioristic research practices in education. *Educational Researcher* 12: 3–9.

Hall, D.P., C. Prevatte and P.M. Cunningham. 1993. Elementary Ability Grouping and Failure in the Primary Grades. Unpublished manuscript quoted by Pikulski (1994).

Hatcher, P.J. 1994. *Sound Linkage: An Integrated Programme for Over-coming Reading Difficulties.* London: Whurr Publishing.

Henggeler, S.W. 1994. A consensus: Conclusions of the APA Task Force Report on innovative models of mental health services for children, adolescents and their families. *Journal of Clinical Child Psychology* 23 (Suppl.), 2: 2–6.

Hiebert, E.H. 1994. Reading Recovery in the United States: What difference does it make to an age cohort? *Educational Researcher* 23: 15–25.

Hiebert, E.H., J.M. Colt, S.L. Catto and E.C. Guy. 1992. Reading and writing of first-grade students in a restructured Chapter 1 program. *American Education Research Journal* 29: 545–572.

Hobsbaum, A. 1997. Reading Recovery in England. In S.L. Swartz and A.F. Klein, eds, *Research in Reading Recovery.* Portsmouth, NH: Heinemann.

Hobsbaum, A., S. Peters, and K. Sylva. 1996. Scaffolding in Reading Recovery. *Oxford Review of Education* 22, 1: 17–35.

Hops, H., B. Davis and N. Longoria. 1995. Methodological issues in direct observation. *Journal of Clinical Child Psychology* 24, 2: 193–203.

Iversen, S.J. 1991. Phonological Processing Skills and the Reading Recovery Programme. Master of Arts dissertation, Massey University Library, Palmerston North, New Zealand.

Iversen, S. and W. Tunmer. 1993. Phonological processing skills and the Reading Recovery program. *Journal of Educational Psychology* 85, 1: 112–126.

Jones, N.K. and M.T. Smith-Burke. 1999. Forging an interactive relationship among research, theory and practice: Clay's research design and methodology. In J.S. Gaffney and B.J. Askew, eds, *Stirring the Waters: The Influence of Marie Clay*. Portsmouth, NH: Heinemann.

Kerslake, J. 1998. Annual monitoring of Reading Recovery: The data for 1997. *The Research Bulletin* 9, October: 43–47. Wellington: Ministry of Education.

Neal, J. and P.R. Kelly. 1999. The success of Reading Recovery for English language learners and Descubriendo la Lectura for bilingual students in California. *Literacy Teaching and Learning: An International Journal of Early Reading and Writing* 4, 2: 81–108.

Nesselroade, J.R. and P.B. Baltes. 1979. *Longitudinal Research in the Study of Behavior and Development*. New York: Academic Press.

———. 1984. Sequential strategies and the role of cohort effects in behavioral development: Adolescent personality (1970–72) as a sample case. In S.A. Mednick, M. Harway and K.M. Finello, eds, *Handbook of Longitudinal Research*. New York: Praeger.

O'Leary, S. 1997. *Five Kids: Stories of Children Learning to Read*. Bothell, WA: The Wright Group/McGraw-Hill.

Pearson, D.P. 1994. Notes on Reading Recovery Opportunities and Obligations. Speech to deans of colleges of education with Reading Recovery training programmes. Personal communication.

Phillips, G. and P. Smith. 1997a. *Closing the Gaps: Literacy for the Hardest-to-teach*. Wellington: New Zealand Council for Educational Research. (An abridged version.)

———. 1997b. *A Third Chance to Learn: The Development and Evaluation of Specialised Interventions for Young Children Experiencing the Greatest Difficulty in Learning to Read*. Wellington: New Zealand Council for Educational Research.

Pianta, R.C. 1990. Widening debate in educational reform: Prevention as a viable alternative. *Exceptional Children* 56: 306–313.

Pikulski, J.J. 1994. Preventing reading failure: A review of five effective programs. *The Reading Teacher* 48, 1, September: 30–39.

Pinnell, G.S. 1989. Reading Recovery: Helping at-risk children learn to read. *The Elementary School Journal*, 90, 2: 159–181.

———. 1996. Reading Recovery: A Review of Research. *Educational Report #23*. Columbus, OH: Martha King Language and Literacy Center, OSU. Also in J. Flood, S.B. Heath and D. Lapp, eds, 1997. *Handbook of Research on Teaching Literacy Through the Communicative and Visual Arts*. Macmillan Reference Series on Educational Research.

———. 2000. *Reading Recovery: An Analysis of a Research-based Reading Intervention*. Columbus, OH: Reading Recovery Council of North America.

Pinnell, G.S., D.E. DeFord and C.L. Lyons. 1988. *Reading Recovery: Early Intervention for At-Risk First Graders*. Arlington, VA: Educational Research Service.

Pinnell, G.S., M.D. Fried and R.M. Estice. 1990. Reading Recovery: Learning how to make a difference. *The Reading Teacher* 43: 282–295.

———. 1991. Reading Recovery: Learning how to make a difference. In D. DeFord, C.A. Lyons and G.S. Pinnell, eds, *Bridges to Literacy: Learning from Reading Recovery*. Portsmouth, NH: Heinemann.

Pinnell, G.S., C.A. Lyons, D.E. DeFord, A.S. Bryk and M. Seltzer. 1994. Comparing instructional models for literacy education of high-risk first-graders. *Reading Research Quarterly* 29, 1: 9–39.

Pogrow, S. 1998. What is an exemplary program, and why should anyone care? *Educational Researcher*, 27, 7: 22–29.

Ramey, C.L. and S.L. Ramey. 1998. Early intervention and early experience. *American Psychologist* 53, 2: 109–120.

Rayner, K. and A. Pollatsek. 1989. *The Psychology of Reading.* Englewood Cliffs: Prentice Hall.

Rowe, K.J. 1997. Factors affecting students' progress in reading: Key findings from a longitudinal study. In S.L. Swartz and A.F. Klein, eds, *Research in Reading Recovery*, pp. 53–101. Portsmouth, NH: Heinemann.

Shanahan, T. 1987. Review of *The Early Detection of Reading Difficulties* (Third Edition) by Marie Clay. *Journal of Reading Behavior* 19: 117–119.

Shanahan, T and R. Barr. 1995. Reading Recovery: An independent evaluation of the effects of an early instructional intervention for at-risk learners. *Reading Research Quarterly* 30, 4: 958–996.

Shanahan, T. and S. Neuman. 1997. Conversations: Literacy research that makes a difference. *Reading Research Quarterly* 33, 2: 202– 210.

Slavin, R.E., N. Madden, N. Karweit, L. Dolan, and B. Wasik. 1991. Research directions: Success for All; Ending reading failure from the beginning. *Language Arts,* 68: 404–409.

Smith, P. 1994. Reading Recovery and children with English as a second language. *New Zealand Journal of Educational Studies* 29, 2: 141–159.

Speigel, D. 1995. A comparison of traditional remedial programs and Reading Recovery: Guidelines for success for all programs. *The Reading Teacher* 49, 2: 86–96.

Swartz, S.L. and A.F. Klein. 1997. *Research in Reading Recovery.* Portsmouth, NH: Heinemann.

Sylva, K. and J. Hurry. 1995. *Early intervention in children with reading difficulties.* School Curriculum and Assessment Authority Discussion Paper No. 2, London.

Taylor, B.M., B.J. Frye, R. Short and B. Shearer. 1992. Classroom teachers prevent reading failure among low-achieving first grade students. *The Reading Teacher* 45: 592–597.

Torgesen, J.K. 2000. Individual differences in response to early interventions in reading: The lingering problem of treatment resisters. *Learning Disability Research and Practice* 15, 1: 55–64.

Vellutino, F.R. and D.M. Scanlon. 1999. Focus, Funding, Phonics — What's the point: A reply to Pressley and Allington, *Issues in Education*, e-journal, p. 8.

Vellutino, F.R., D.M. Scanlon, E.R. Sipay, S.G. Small, R. Chen, A. Pratt and M.B. Denckla. 1996. Cognitive profiles of difficult-to-remediate and readily remediated poor readers: Early intervention as a vehicle for distinguishing between cognitive and experiential deficits as basic causes of specific reading disability. *Journal of Educational Psychology*, APA, 88, 4: 601–638.

Walmsley, S.A. and R.L. Allington. 1995. Redefining and reforming instructional support programs for at-risk students. In R.L. Allington and S.A. Walmsley, eds, *No Quick Fix: Rethinking Literacy Programs in America's Elementary Schools.* Newark, DE: International Reading Association.

Wasik, B.A. and R.E. Slavin. 1993. Preventing early reading failure with one-to-one tutoring: A review of five programs. *Reading Research Quarterly* 28, 1: 179–200.

Watson, B. 1999. Creating independent learners. In J.S. Gaffney and B.J. Askew, eds, *Stirring the Waters*, pp. 47–74. Portsmouth, NH: Heinemann.

Wilson K.G. and B. Daviss. 1994. *Redesigning Education.* New York: Henry Holt.

8   Change over time
in children's literacy development

8   Change over time in children's literacy development

Some biographical history

Students chide me that they cannot find my biographical details: what follows is an account of some historical settings and research origins from the latter years of my career when Reading Recovery (RR) was developed. I entered upon an exploration of early literacy learning because of my work in normal and clinical developmental psychology, following my first training as a teacher. I began to explore literacy processing. That involved a search for how children become readers and writers, using a methodology common in developmental psychology, the meticulous recording of surface behaviours and how these change over time. The search for understanding the changes led me to the psychological processing that produces those behaviours and more recently to the writing of Holmes (1960) and Singer (1994) (see Chapter 3). In this book 'Acts of literacy processing: an unusual lens' tells some of that history and exploration. In my view literacy processing theory has immediate potential for going beyond RR:

- to shorten the effort and time given to some special education students in the literacy area, and

- to contribute to resolving some of the polarities which bedevil literacy discussions.

I have never believed that new applications for classroom learning would come from direct transfer of teaching tricks from RR and have tried to discourage others from expecting this to occur. It may be, however, that some understandings derived from the experience of RR may provide a basis for conceptualising or investigating other problems.

The academic discipline of developmental psychology, known popularly as child development, had become established as a sub-discipline of psychology by the time I came upon it in the 1950s at the University of Minnesota, in one of five research units initiated to study normal and clinical aspects of child development. Developmental psychology is a study of change over time in growing organisms, attempting to describe or explain or optimise development (Baltes, Reese and Nesselroade 1977; Baltes and Schaie 1973). Describing is a legitimate first step for when one asks, 'What occurs?'

So that is where I began my research in literacy learning. A few correlations produced a shock. Where children were at the end of their first year of instruction was where they were ranked in relation to peers one and two years after that. This led to the idea of early delivery of a second chance to learn and what I have called 'spoiling the predictions or expectations'. My original study in 1963–66 followed 100 five-year-old children from their fifth to their sixth birthdays with weekly observations and I watched the multi-factored way in which they constructed complex literacy processing systems for both reading and writing.

Half of my university career in teaching and research was spent in developmental psychology with projects ranging from infancy through childhood and adolescence. I spent evenings and weekends with parent education groups (like Play Centre and Parents Centre), I taught the Psychology of Adolescence for twenty years, and completed a national research project on children who were *Round-About Twelve*. Children's language development held a special interest for me, and led to my first research monograph, an analysis of syntactic awareness in children published by the Society for Research in Child Development (1971). That led to the publication of two language assessments in the *Record of Oral Language and Biks and Gutches* (Clay, Gill, Glynn, McNaughton and Salmon 1983). I prepared an extensive literature survey of the development of quadruplets and children of higher multiple births (1974, 1989) and a study of children of parents who separate (Clay and Robinson 1978).

I taught graduate students who were training to be educational psychologists for thirty years, working as a clinician and a supervisor of probationer clinicians until 1990. In a small country developmental and educational psychologists were given a broad brief. We battled for professional status in the New Zealand Psychological Society, and worked for change in the provisions for the mentally retarded, for the emotionally disturbed, for children with cerebral palsy, sight and hearing problems, and we supported the strong growth of counsellor training in our country. I participated in the early efforts to create services for victims of child abuse and rape, and to respond to children's needs arising from traffic accident traumas and community disasters. My efforts were diverse but with a common focus — providing messages and tools which helped teachers and the community to think about change as children develop into young citizens.

Alongside a strong emphasis on what occurred in normal developmental psychology ran the clinical aspects of my work with educational psychologists as we explored the limitations of testing and diagnosis, and difficulties of the controlled study of treatments, and how to think theoretically about leading children from the brink of trouble back to a more secure developmental track, that is, *to the recovery of a more normal trajectory*. It was after I began teaching a course called 'Changing Deviant Development', in about 1972, and exploring innovative ideas in the literature, that something became obvious to me. If we were to change deviant patterns of development then detailed accounts of how optimum development came about were critical. Descriptions of optimum development provide both the step-wise goals of change to aim for and the indicators of desired outcomes. (This is only one of my heresies.) Theories of deviance rarely specify how and when it might be possible to build bridges for a return to a normal trajectory of progress. I watched the Illinois Test of Psycholinguistic Abilities and the Frostig Tests of Visual Perception rise and fall from favour and the critique of intelligence testing shake its very foundations. I was asked to write an article on learning disabilities for a book about special education, and the editors allowed me to write a critique rather than a review (Clay 1972). At this time the new concept of learning disability was rapidly gaining favour and even people I had taught were writing newspaper articles about how naughty brains twisted the stimuli around back to front so the child could not deal with it. There was a kind of 'What's this?' reaction to my article from my colleagues. Within four years I had begun something more positive than a critique, and the research and development phase of RR was under way, but ten years later the urge to clarify dyslexia and learning disability took control again, and I presented a paper to the NZ Psychological Society on 'Learning to be learning disabled' (1987). More recently a major research report gave empirical substance to my hypotheses (Vellutino et al. 1996).

My interest in preventive interventions took shape in the 1970s as I explored with my students the theories in lifespan developmental psychology. The aim was to describe change during development, to find ways to explain it, and to find ways of modifying change for optimum outcomes. It might even be possible to develop effective programmes which prevented dysfunctional developments by optimising functional developments. While not distinct from conventional child development research, lifespan developmental psychology was more articulate about the conceptualisation of change. In lifespan developmental psychology attention was paid to the past as a prologue to the present, and the present as a prologue to the future. And to know how to guide treatments as a series of changes towards optimal development, individual change must be conceptualised in terms of both the individual in context and, over time, the context of a changing society.

I described changes in early literacy development at weekly intervals in my first longitudinal research study throughout a school year in a random sample of children in their first year at school. This provided the map or trajectory of normal literacy acquisition in one society (New Zealand) at one time (the 1960s). An optimising intervention could be provided at some point where a failure could be predicted with minimum error, and would lead to changing the interactions of individuals with their environments and social contexts. The lifespan paradigm has a focus:

- on change rather than stability

- on interactions or opportunities to learn

- on the conjoint analysis of individual and environment systems

- on models that intertwine genotypic and phenotypic analysis
- and on research designs which seek to explain the dynamic interplay between ontogenetic and historical events.

The lifespan view of development draws attention to how dramatically development can be modified across the lifespan (Baltes, Reese and Nesselroade 1977).

The theoretical origins of RR and the subsequent development of an optimum intervention lies in lifespan developmental psychology of the 1970s. Some of the capacity of this intervention to adapt to different educational systems lies in the tenet of its original theoretical base that dynamic change in environments or social contexts must be taken into account in any treatment or optimisation paradigm.

The other aspect of lifespan developmental psychology theory that pervades the RR programme is adherence to the relativity of all judgements — whether made by theorist, researcher, teacher or learner. This leads to the conclusion that when the interactions between individual and society are complex and changing it is the tentative decisions operating in a flexible system that provide the suitable base from which to get change. And literacy learning is an encyclopaedic series of changes.

Why is this explanation important? I think it provides a sense of the depth and breadth of the theoretical thinking behind RR which is more than a package of teaching tricks, a collection of bright ideas, or some fashionable procedures to be changed when the next innovation comes along. RR draws strengths from many disciplines — education, educational psychology, instructional psychology, psychological assessment, research in classrooms, and what is known about atypical developmental psychology, clinical child psychology, and genetics. I have approached literacy learning from a developmental viewpoint: that has been my personal unusual lens.

In the 1970s I could think of no way to design a research study which would convince the various groups of professionals that the concept of learning disability was overgeneralised (and I certainly would not have been able to obtain research resources to begin that challenge). I adopted the pragmatic strategy of demonstrating on a large scale that with effective intervention the world could be different. Rowe (1997) gave that pragmatism a respectability with a well-designed longitudinal research project which established that if education systems were given low achievers-turned-into-average band achievers they would, over time, distribute them across the whole range of achievement. In other words, the range of variables affecting the progress of all children was now operating 'normally' for what was once an outlier group. I had not been developmentally astute enough to predict that, but immediately saw that this was precisely what one should have predicted. Vellutino and his research team (1996) provided research evidence of differences within the literacy difficulties area at an early age which require expertise and services of different kinds. The quality of that research project gave empirical support to my position on the need for early intervention. From my 1987 paper on 'Learning to be learning disabled' the team was interested in the argument that failure to control for the child's educational history is a major impediment to differential diagnosis of reading disability because the adverse effects of inadequate pre-reading experience, inadequate instruction, or both can often mask or even mimic the adverse effects of constitutionally based deficits.

Studies that have sought to evaluate basic process deficit explanations of reading disability are confounded by this problem. The authors drew attention to intervention studies that have shown that most impaired readers can acquire at-level reading skills if they receive early and labour-intensive intervention to correct the reading deficiencies (Clay 1985; Iversen and Tunmer 1993; Pinnell et al. 1994; Wasik and Slavin 1993), and reported that:

> [Our results], like those obtained in the previous intervention studies, are consistent with Clay's (1987) contention that most impaired readers, who might be classified as learning disabled, are probably not learning disabled in the stereotypic sense in which this term is used. (p. 608)

> ... it should be apparent, both from this study and from other intervention studies that have appeared in the literature ... *that to render a diagnosis of specific reading disability in the absence of early and labour-intensive remedial reading that has been tailored to the child's individual needs is, at best, a hazardous and dubious enterprise, given all the stereotypes attached to that diagnosis.* (p. 632) (Vellutino et al. 1996, pp. 601–638. The italics are mine.)

This suggests that the majority of children who might be diagnosed as 'reading disabled' are impaired by experiential and instructional deficits rather than basic cognitive deficits. The study of change over time in developmental psychology had a great deal to do with the logic of my initial arguments.

As new research questions arise there will be rich resources of professional talent both within and beyond RR for exploring them. I think we could aim for above 99 per cent success with literacy instruction in education systems with a bit more exploration, critical thinking, quality training for teachers, quality early intervention, and astute implementation policies. It is becoming evident that in all education systems some children do not learn well among other children in their first classroom groups but respond to individual help. Both RR in practice operating across the world, and Vellutino's team in particular, have found children who are extremely hard to teach, even one to one. Therein lies a challenge for future developments. While maintaining ongoing programmes there should be altogether separate efforts to discover, by carefully designed research, further 'different paths to common outcomes' for those who find literacy learning difficult. But the exploration of those horizons should not call for the demolition of what works at this time.

Before we divert resources from what is currently working well, new solutions must be tested and proved to be just as useful in the field. Those who develop new solutions must go beyond discovery under controlled research conditions. *Their first challenge is to show that teachers can be trained to deliver the appropriate interactions which produce the necessary results. Their second challenge is to implement a new treatment in the field in critical mass to produce an effect.* In a curious way those two challenges have been revealed during the twenty years that RR has been making its contribution to the resolution of many learning difficulties, under the critical eyes of administrators and researchers.

I argued that we should try to take a large proportion of the learning disability population away by providing opportunities for a second chance to learn, and RR continues to work on that. Despite the thoroughness and winning logic of the Vellutino study, I dislike the new argument that appears at the end of their article and is echoed in the learning disability literature. It claims that if we could identify the children with phonological deficits when children are aged about five years of age and treat the deficit then and there, we might be able to deal with the learning disability. I retain a different view, historical in its origin, and never fashionable because of its complexity. I think different children fail to learn to read for different reasons, and many fail because of a cluster of problems. Until we try to teach them to read and write, to learn a double-coded code, we cannot identify who will be successful.

RR works well in many settings at this time and it is tentative and flexible enough to push the boundaries of our understanding and refine our teaching and decision-making much further. Several authors have used this memorable parable to highlight the need for early intervention programmes (Slavin et al. 1991; Pikulski 1994):

> The authors write of a mythical town where 30 per cent of the children were falling ill from contaminated drinking water; many died. The town spent millions for the medical care of these victims. A town engineer proposed building a water treatment plant that could virtually eliminate the illnesses. The town council rejected the proposal as being too expensive, because funds would not be available to treat current victims and because 70 per cent of the children never fell ill.

It is sad but true that thinking about educational provisions for children with literacy difficulties often follows a similar line.

New theoretical images from developmental psychology

The chapters in this book contain provocative hypotheses intended to invite exploration in well-designed research. Collectively they argue for using a complex theory of literacy learning with children who need extra help for many different reasons early in their schooling. My questions have been about the perceptual and cognitive changes that exist irrespective of teaching or materials, changes that teachers respond to as they teach day by day. Those changes occur rapidly over a short period of time. My focus is narrowly on young, low-achieving children. I conclude that we need better theory, more research and programmes that bring about life-saving changes for the young children getting left behind. I selected five largely neglected areas for discussion because of their challenge to early intervention professionals — writing, working on the information in print (processing), reading continuous text, explaining self-correction, and becoming self-initiating and constructive. Observant, flexible and tentative teachers take children along different paths because of their current strengths and weaknesses but bring them to common outcomes with the independence to take themselves further.

Emerging theory in developmental psychology today contributes new images of how complex the changes in children's development may be. Two geographical metaphors alert us to this. The first is a powerful metaphor of an ontogenetic landscape (see Figure 4). We know how landforms are shaped and changed under the long-term influences of climate, and how young rivers cut into plateaus and create hills and valleys and plains. An 'ontogenetic landscape for locomotion' is a metaphor used to describe learning to crawl and walk (Muchisky, Gershkoff-Stowe, Cole and Thelen 1996); it represents the development of the infant as a landscape in which behaviours appear, change rapidly at times, and progressively develop many stable features. (It must be stated that the stable features of the individual's development are not necessarily standard features of a group's development.) *New learning at any one time must depend on the nature of the landscape formed by the past experiences of the learner up until this moment in time.*

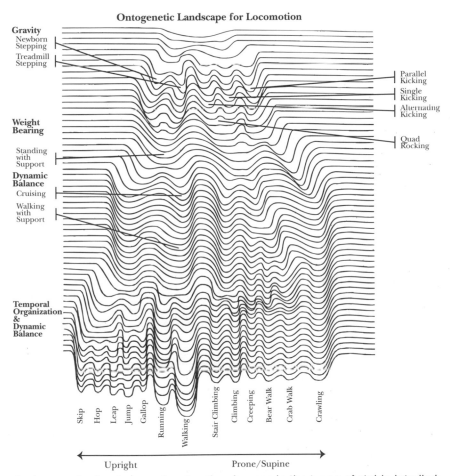

Figure 4 Locomotor landscape showing the changes in the types of stable interlimb co-ordinations over the first years of life. The increasing number of stable configurations denotes a growing repertoire of locomotor behaviours. Reprinted with permission.

For children who enter school these 'landscapes' are different from child to child depending upon what their developmental histories have been. Formal instruction makes a deliberate attempt to shape the existing landscape, and whenever school instruction begins it is directed to many different 'landscapes' already in existence. The authors explained that time runs from the top of the model to the bottom and *each horizontal line represents the probability that certain actions will occur, given a supporting context*. As time passes the landscape develops multiple stable behavioural attributes (Thelen 1995, p. 78); they may be hard but not impossible to change.

A second image representing how complex developmental change is comes from extensive research (Thelen and Ulrich 1991; Thelen 1995; Thelen and Smith 1994) conducted with the motor behaviour of very young children as they reached, kicked, crawled and walked. Separate performances are developed by the infant for kicking to shake a mobile, and for standing up, but gradually, as a wider range of experience is gained, common aspects of each solution overlap and *a superordinate category of movement may emerge*. The separate skills might be pictured in what Thelen calls a very crude model as four separate clouds (reaching, kicking, crawling, walking). (See Figure 5.)

> At first the clouds are separate and accessed by constrained situations ... Knowing how to kick a mobile does not help with knowing how to adjust forces to stand up. However, as infants gain a wide range of experience, these clouds enlarge ... [and] the solution spaces intersect where the common features of each solution overlap ... an action in one context is influenced by a history of actions in a wider variety of contexts. (Thelen 1995, p. 97)

> It is as if there were a superordinate category of abstract force that emerged from these specific experiences. (Thelen and Smith 1994, p. 326)

The power to go beyond prior performance lies in bringing the processes of interacting groups of neurons together. A change in the merging of different processes heralds the appearance of new behaviours.

Thelen and Smith used these metaphors to describe changes in motor behaviours like learning to walk, a type of learning that is very different from the coded activities of literacy. Eminent reviewers of their books, however, described their theory as 'an exciting, powerful way of thinking that will serve as a new foundation for helping to remake the study of developing behaviour' (Fischer, jacket review of Thelen and Smith 1994) and 'a strong view that change and development have to be the result of the interactions of multiple factors, not single causes, either environmental or genetic' (E. Gibson and Sage, jacket review of Thelen and Smith 1994).

Care must be taken not to transfer the images from what these authors call 'dynamical systems theory' uncritically and in a cavalier manner to early literacy learning. We can hypothesise that integrated processing in early literacy learning takes over from some originally isolated and independent control systems. As such changes become mapped in well-designed research we may glimpse how perceptual/cognitive

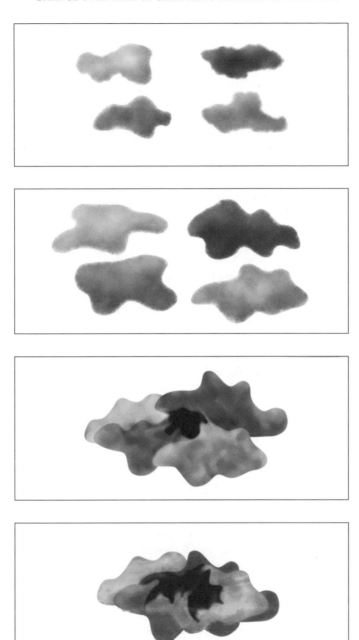

Figure 5 Clouds have a non-structured, process-like character. Thelen (1995) used them to represent the changes which occur in reaching, kicking, stepping, crawling and walking in infancy. Superordinate controls (black areas) emerge from a wide range of different experiences. Note that access to the subordinate controls remains available. Reprinted with permission.

activity in literacy learning becomes developmentally constructed, and perhaps eventually get some rough neurological mapping of major integrations. Kay's early school reading behaviour (see Chapter 2) seems to exemplify the overlapping of some very diverse competencies, and Thelen and Smith provide one metaphor of how we might begin to understand integrative change in complex systems.

For me there is a particular attraction in Thelen's theory because her research analysis overcomes some problems in literacy research which I have struggled with. If I interpret her report correctly, some infants would use a stepping motion on a walking treadmill at one month and others not until five or six months. To take a group mean from such subjects would lead to the variability being treated as noise rather than as information about what is stable at what age in which children. Thelen holds that clearer identification of transitions will open up windows which allow us to explore processes and identify what allows a system to move into new forms of process. Thelen proposes that:

> Continuous changes in one or a few organic or environmental components are sufficient to cause wide-ranging reorganisation. Developing systems are nonlinear and may respond with large effects to small changes. (Thelen and Ulrich 1991, p. 97)

As I try to remember my experience with infants stepping, standing when held, standing alone, and walking, I am intrigued to think through how Thelen's studies of transitions might help us understand what has yet to be studied and explained in literacy learning — how do separate ways of functioning in early learning make it through transitions to integrated and co-ordinated functioning during the first year or two of reading instruction? How fascinating it would be to begin the study of emergent literacy again with tools shaped by such concepts.

Clark (1996) invites us to loosen up our thinking about children's decision-making and to consider how complex it is for any of us to fit one piece into a jigsaw puzzle:

> One (unlikely) way to tackle such a puzzle would be to look very hard at a piece and try to determine by reason alone whether it will fit in a certain location. Our actual practice, however, exploits a mixed strategy in which we make a rough mental determination and then physically try out the piece to see if it will fit. We do not, in general, represent the detailed shape of a piece well enough to know for certain if it is going to fit in advance of such a physical manipulation. … Completing a jigsaw puzzle thus involves an intricate and iterated dance in which 'pure thought' leads to actions which in turn change or simplify the problems confronting 'pure thought.'

Clark called this the simplest example of what is known as an action loop. (In Chapter 3, pp. 102 and 122, the discussion of cycles of parsing provides another example.)

While Clark's whole theoretical approach to the brain and psychology is refreshingly different some of his ideas fit quite easily into a RR professional's day-to-day attempts to explain observed literacy behaviours. He refers to some development occurring without blueprints (p. 39), to soft assembly of patterns of behaviour which can then change rapidly (p. 42), to self-organisation by learners, and to how learners use the environment to scaffold their own learning (p. 44). His notion of scaffolding is broader than Vygotsky's version of expert support, since it can encompass all kinds of external aid, non-social as well as social. Clark discusses how we use our environment to support what we are trying to do (and my aging brain understands that I need to do more of this deliberately). I hear a similar discussion among RR people about how well the children's texts are supporting the reader's primitive processing systems.

Consider Clark's notion of *soft assembly* (1996, p. 42). Clark gives us an everyday image of what he calls 'soft-assembly in learning' using human walking as an example. It is soft-assembled in that it naturally compensates for quite major changes in walking conditions. Quoting Thelen and Smith (1994) he asks us to think how icy sidewalks, blisters, and high-heeled shoes all 'recruit' different patterns of gait and muscle control while we keep to the main goal of locomotion. Hard-assembled solutions controlled by a centralised system (the brain, or central nervous system) are contrasted with the fluid adaptation to context and task which is 'soft-assembled'. How could this work? Clark asks us to imagine several systems each controlling its own workload, one sending out a 'request for bids' to other systems which respond giving estimates of the time they would require to complete the job, and the best bidder takes over. The solution gets the job done and is soft-assembled. No single system is crucial; posting and bidding occurs among whatever systems are currently active. It seems to me that his bidding system is very close to Rumelhart's bidding from different knowledge sources and perhaps this is a primitive text-processing example:

Text: Ben   went   to   look   on   the   television.
Child: /   /   /   /   /   /   T-
                                                      TV. No.
                                                      TV station. No.
                                                      It's television.

When Thelen and Smith found individual differences in infant reaching it turned out, in each individual case, to be soft-assembled from somewhat different components in different children. They concluded that large degrees of individual variability are a powerful clue to the nature of the underlying processes of soft assembly (p. 44). Different individuals produce the same outcome by different assemblies of systems. Although we look for milestones in infant development, think how much variability we allow for when babies will cut their first teeth, crawl, walk, or put their first two words together. It is fine to be months later than someone else.

Such images provide glimpses of possible directions and futures in describing change over time in early literacy learning but offer us no immediate leads or theories or models. They inform us that psychologists are grappling with change over time in complex behaviours and suggest that we should be looking for fresh conceptualisations about the complexities of literacy processing. To me, working with a preventive early intervention, I think this conclusion deserves pre-eminence. Complex theory leads rather naturally to an increased respect for, and theoretical interest in, what might be termed the historical idiosyncrasies of individual development, wrote Clark (p. 42). There is a delicate balance between individual variation and developmentally robust achievements.

What enables RR to work in educational settings internationally?

RR is unusual in this way: it is designed to be adopted by education systems and an individual cannot buy it, get the training, watch the video, or apply it in a classroom. It is a programme of effort to be added to the ongoing offerings of an education system and it works like an insurance against having more than a tiny group of children in the upper grades with literacy problems. Long-term planning by an education system can result in that long-term view.

The RR intervention has been delivered by well-trained and dedicated professionals in each of its many different settings. The integrity of the programme has been maintained with vigilance. An independent study of ten promising programmes commended the staff development model in these terms:

> The intensity and the methods utilized by RR in training and the insistence on high level RR performance provided an almost singularly attractive model for future staff development efforts, regardless of the program type. As schools systematize and create opportunities for serious staff development, the thoroughness of the RR model seems to be well worth emulating. (Herman and Stringfield 1997, p. 86)

Through local initiatives RR has spread throughout New Zealand, to several Australian states, to remote and urban areas of Canada, to most states of the United States, to Northern Ireland, Wales and England and to island territories like Jersey and Bermuda. It has responded to the needs of children and the administrative values of many different education systems. This early intervention is like a standard boat tossed into several turbulent rivers and struggling to master the rapids and stay afloat in each of them.

Central tenets of RR have been tentativeness, flexibility and problem-solving. These qualities have surfaced in the ways in which the teaching addresses individual patterns of strengths and weaknesses in children, and in how the teachers are training to design lesson series for individual children, and again in the solutions people have found for implementing RR. Somehow RR professionals have learned how to hold fast to principles, practices and rationales while at the same time allowing for variability in the educational practices and beliefs, and change over time in society.

The important answers to RR's international success probably cluster in five areas, in each of which the need for tentativeness and flexibility is great. The five areas are guidelines for programme delivery, the training of teachers, the lesson components, the complex theory of literacy learning, and theories about children's development.

1. Guidelines for programme delivery
The programme guidelines guard against shifts towards ineffective practices. Shifts can occur so easily for many reasons, and monitoring research has indicated many ways in which changes can limit the programme's potential for success. Adaptations may arise because it makes someone's life easier to do standard things in a standard way, and adopt less demanding objectives.

When operated with tentativeness and flexibility RR's guidelines guard against prejudicing any child's chances of learning. Research and experience support the conclusions that the programme guidelines lead to the best outcomes for the most children. Let me give one example. There are recommendations about how many children a RR teacher might teach individually each day. A minimum of four is suggested in the training year, and wherever this is possible in subsequent years. Many people cannot understand why an experienced teacher should not work with as few as two children each day. Well, RR teachers are decision-makers; they design individual programmes to suit individual children. When they meet only two children each day over the period of a year they are not challenged to make enough varied decisions and their teaching tends to drift away from the innovative. Enter an exceptionally challenging child and the teacher is not ready for the task ahead.

RR has been able to work in systems that are large and small, church and secular, public and private, in State Education Departments and in private universities, small and remote, or large and urban. It prepares children for very different classroom programmes, to achieve much the same level of outcomes, and it does this in English and Spanish. Education systems differ and at any one time they are changing in different ways depending on their social and educational histories. RR has to acknowledge and work with those differences. Problem-solving the programme into different education settings is one essential feature of this early intervention.

2. The long period of training prepares teachers to be decision-makers
Neither a practical apprenticeship nor an explicit text alone was considered sufficient for training RR professionals. It was assumed that teachers could understand a new approach in a short course but would they change their daily practice in appropriate ways? An apprenticeship might create some inspired teaching but would teachers be able to put what they did and why they did it into words to share with others? What were needed were new understandings, new practices, different decisions for different children, and a means of sharing new insights and unsolved problems with colleagues. The professional networks of expertise would be very important in RR. From the trainers who train the tutors/

teacher leaders, to the tutors/teacher leaders who train the teachers, to the teachers who make decisions by the minute in their individual lessons with children, every one has to understand the child, the possibilities and the potential of the programme to reach its goals for individual children.

RR training is thorough wherever it occurs, a year-long training in which teachers must change their practices in a supervised apprenticeship, as well as their understanding. They must learn to articulate rationales for children's observed behaviours and for the teaching that must follow, and they must continue to learn from children, and from colleagues.

3. Lesson components support perceptual/cognitive processing

In spite of limitations in individual profiles teachers find ways around the children's problems, in most cases. RR lessons must be relatively short (30 minutes), streamlined, brisk, varied, with scope for established skill and knowledge to be consolidated, responses produced at speed with not too much attention, but time to work on new challenges which lift competency to higher levels. We tend to give tasks in a RR lesson simple labels (the economy of words) but a couple of examples may illustrate their complexity:

Rereading several familiar texts achieves a number of things: it increases the amount of reading done, it results in much successful processing so that children 'orchestrate' the complex set of things they already do well, it allows for independent problem-solving, recognition is speeded, phrasing is possible, there is attention to print detail, and the stories are enjoyed. Teachers may be working on several of these goals in one lesson.

Writing a sentence or 'story' requires the child to take the first steps towards composing. The production is shared between teacher and child; there is a gradual lift over time in the amount, quality and independence of the child's writing. The child comes to know how texts are compiled from letters and words, that writing involves segmentation of speech, is related to the sounds of speech, can be read, and that there are different ways to construct new words.

These are simple tasks which call for complex learning. A great deal of learning is being achieved in the 30-minute lesson, and much of it is clearly learning how to do 'literacy things' which should be useful for more independent work in classrooms. The teacher attends to many aspects of literacy learning. The results should provide an insurance of success whatever the demands of the classroom programme.

4. The utility of a complex theory of literacy learning

In contrast to a simple theory of learning, such as one which rates the learning of phonemic awareness or some other single variable as the first significant thing to learn about literacy, RR's complex theory of literacy learning supports the view that there are many parts of literacy processing which can be difficult for children. Different children have different strengths and weaknesses, and there may be many causes of difficulty varying from child to child. One child may have a single difficulty or a cluster of several difficulties. The challenges for the teacher come in making teaching decisions which adapt to each child's idiosyncratic patterns of competencies. Using a complex theory, RR hopes to be able to serve both children with one type of problem and children with several different problems. Some children find bringing one competency into a working relationship with another competency is nearly impossible, making this integrating of complex behaviours of literacy activities an important part of what RR teachers attend to.

RR theories face the issue of multiple causes head on: the need for help arises for multiple reasons (causes) across children in the treatment group, but the individual learner is challenged by multiple causes within his or her own individual functioning. While that position is realistic, it is also theoretically frustrating for many people.

5. A theory about constructive individuals independently pushing the boundaries of their own knowledge, rather than groups led through each step by a teacher

This applies to the low achievers as much as to the proficient ones. Independence is encouraged in simple ways to allow children to solve problems. RR theory assumes that the goal of early literacy learning is to have children who can in time read silently and compose and write relatively independently and who teach themselves more by engaging in these activities. The constructive child is the one who makes something of the instruction and becomes a fluent processor of printed messages.

How do these five things explain RR's success in a variety of settings? If we assume that we need constructive children in classrooms who can independently solve many literacy learning problems for themselves, then by the end of a series of lessons a successful RR child should be able to use the activities of the classroom to push his or her own knowledge even further. The well-trained teacher will be tentative and flexible in his or her interactions with a range of children each of whom present somewhat different problems. The cognitive processing and the wide range of competencies developed in the children should prepare them for performance in almost all classroom programmes. But here comes another qualification: there must be minor adjustments to tune in a particular child to the particular demands of his or her classroom teacher in the last few weeks of the RR programme.

At the level of the education system the intake, teaching and discontinuing procedures are easy to manage, the progress of every child is monitored, and quality control measures operate whatever the administrative structure. The ex-lowest achievers must ideally be able to learn within the classroom programme without special programming, but with an attentive teacher.

There has to be a reason why we have high rates of success across each of the countries we work in. That consistency, despite vast differences in educational practices, policies and provisions, implies that a) the teaching procedures must be appropriate for children's learning needs and b) there must be scope for a large range of individual differences to be addressed. In general RR gets close to what is needed in an early intervention.

Readers' questions

Reviewers of my manuscript gave me food for thought. It is only fair to say I asked them to be critical and pass over the things that they found helpful. Perhaps my readers have some of the same questions in their heads so here are a few of my reactions to reviewers' questions.

1. Is it the author's intention to leave some things open, not answered?

All the assumptions about early interventions should be open to examination and any one assumption may be challenged by new evidence. We live and breathe by asking questions. Satisfactory but inefficient procedures will be discarded, and replaced by better formulations. Current procedures will serve children well enough until new evidence provides teachers with a better understanding and/or a more effective way of acting. And with the passage of time the questions we need to ask will also change.

2. The subsystems discussed under assembling working systems should have been discussed in detail.

Any theory of complex learning must work with an incomplete description of processing. First, there are many things we do not know. Second, today's way of conceptualising what goes on in the brain will become inadequate as theory, research and practice 'on the ground' combine to show that this is necessary. Third, theoretical concepts sometimes get in the way of progress. For example, a claim that three cue systems are the explanation of processing, or that there is a hierarchy of knowledge sources are two descriptions used in RR which are proving too narrow to characterise the brain's many complex networks of activity. By changing the discourse to 'assembling working systems' I hope to escape from those problems and give myself scope to pay more attention in the future to the news reaching us from neurologists and neuro-psychologists. RR professionals need to:

- think more tentatively and flexibly about processing

- think about changes in early primitive systems moving to become more complex systems

- think about larger systems like input, mediation and output

- think about several language systems (sounds, structures and meanings) which interact with one another

- think more about visual and motor systems in early reading

and to observe how gradually two, three, four or more of these systems are pulled together and applied, as if instantaneously, to the task of reading or writing.

3.   Are we looking at acts of literacy processing and constructing processes to get away from strategies?

I certainly am. We need something less ambiguous than strategies which is used in three different ways in literacy education. Assembling working systems may help us to think about, articulate and discuss what the children seem to be doing and how they are changing, and hopefully bring us to more researchable questions.

4. a) *Reading: the Patterning of Complex Behaviour* was well-founded in Russian developmental psychology with researchers like Luria, Zaporozhets, Zinchenko, Sokolov, Leontiv, Elkonin and Vygotsky. *Change Over Time in Children's Literacy Development* avoids mention of neurology and yet the links seem obvious. Why is this? Paediatric neurology today has much to offer.

   b) This made me want to replay a series of television tapes called *TV on the Brain*. Why have you not made links with this new knowledge?

I think the new formulations in *Change Over Time in Children's Literacy Development* are positioned to link well with the new knowledge emerging from neuropsychology.
      Under a 20-year test RR has demonstrated itself as a safety net which works very well but could do better. We have tested an explanation of how to undercut the literacy difficulties problem. We have explored changes over time deeply and thoroughly at the clinical level of the individual child. That no child is excluded for any reason is a tough test of that theory. But despite the daily attention to sequential change we do not have an articulate description of what processing changes occur. However, processing changes have to be elaborated for competent children before we can establish their existence because the literacy field would consider our low-achieving cases to be outliers or exceptional rather than the rule. We need to sharpen our theorising about what it is that changes over time to prepare ourselves to debate with the neuropsychologists. We are probably not ready to evaluate the value to our children of the advice they give us.

5.   Are you worried that the changes from primitive to more complex processing will be seen as stages? Could it be more fluid? Can we avoid levels, and states?

Yes, I debated whether to include Table 1 (see Chapter 2). My judgement is that early intervention professionals need some vague hypothetical progressions in processing in order to take their thinking and teaching to higher levels. The labels on the table are vague. I tried age and discarded it; that differs in different countries (opportunities to learn are different). I tried time at school but that does not work (it rather depends on how old you were and how much you knew when you started). So I come back to my old description of the teacher's task. The teacher has to find out what the child knows, thinks and is able to do, and take the child from there to somewhere else. There are many paths to common outcomes of sound literacy processing.

There is nothing stage-like in what we observe as RR children make progress, and Table 1 means what it says, repeatedly — any of the following in any order or combination and any of these achievements might combine at any time to bring about a significant shift. It could be helpful for early intervention teachers to have some idea, however vague, of the progressions or sequences that could occur.

If anything the table is a confession of what we do not know. We do not know anything about the gross order in which things occur. We cannot claim any precise sequence to be preferable and would not want to. We have no idea what things become integrated and what that means. Early interventions have to take children by the fastest route from where they are to discontinuing. The entries are descriptions of process — how to do something, not what to know. The things listed are not items, or performance criteria which educational programmes usually look for to mark progress: they are what teachers can observe children doing. To use the table as a list of things to teach would waste teaching time.

Research questions for the future might ask, 'What has to become integrated or used together to bring about a shift from one description to another?' I suspect that RR teachers will notice when an integration has taken place and be able to talk about how separate things were before the shift and what is different now. That has always been true for directional behaviour, or when information is cross-checked, or when errors show that visual, structural and meaning information were all used in an error substitution.

Draft readers did not like Chapter 2 yet I retained it. It may not be interesting or forward looking, but it is the critical data set, the historical case from which my alternative view was formulated. Several things in Chapter 2 are of current relevance for the delivery of RR:

- It uncovers areas where early intervention has little knowledge, for example in the processing of writing, and at the higher levels of reading.

- Except for Ng's study there is almost nothing on integration, and Ng's shifts in proficient children's management weighting of attention are interesting.

- The link of early motor behaviour is very interesting and virtually ignored (despite my study of identical quadruplets).

- Reference to Table 1 could provide guidance for teachers experiencing difficulties at the lowest levels, at the highest levels, and with difficult decisions over discontinuing.

Hopefully in the next ten years some of the hypotheses in the progressions table will be discarded and some will be written up as fully as the self-correction chapter in this book. I am only opening up the discussion.

The view is preventive, developmental and provocative

Theoretical views compete with one another in the search for better explanations. Let me set my current view of learning to read over against a view expressed by two prestigious authors, Athey and Singer (1987 and yes, the same Harry Singer), reviewing an important publication called 'Becoming a Nation of Readers' (Anderson, Hiebert, Scott and Wilkinson 1985) in the *Harvard Educational Review*.

> The development of general reading ability consists of two overlapping phases: learning how to read (reading acquisition) and learning how to gain information (ability to learn from texts). Learning to read takes place normally in the primary grades and involves two major tasks: acquiring the concept of reading, its purpose and uses; and learning the code. Learning the code involves (1) word identification processes, (2) use of language and cognitive resources in response to text characteristics, and (3) integration of (1) and (2) ... Children begin to achieve this integration by the end of first grade and many tend to complete the acquisition process by the end of the third grade when they achieve automaticity of decoding and word identification skills. By contrast, the second phase of reading (learning from text) is open-ended and infinite. During this phase, there must be continuous development of background information, vocabulary, knowledge structures, and familiarity with writing patterns including such features as rhetorical structures, cohesive ties, and signalling terms ...

Despite the careful wording of this explanation, the division of the task into learning to read and reading to learn has made life harder for our lowest achievers. They rarely got past the first phase. A different metaphor, that of organismic growth, would leave us free to hypothesise that the changing organisation of literacy learning can be viewed as creating the primitive forms of necessary working systems from the time when literacy awareness begins. As is the case with oral language development, linkages and reciprocity and the production of simple responses that work lead the organism to learn how to use the environment out there with its people, print and symbols, to build processing systems that work and because they work expand and extend in speed, range, effectiveness and complexity.

Teaching practices that flow from the two-stage theory of literacy learning create learning barriers for confused young learners. A second chance programme which aims to build effective processing in all its surface and strategic complexity in both reading and writing, and to do this at accelerated rates, has been successful with low achievers. In fact longitudinal data suggests that their literacy learning becomes stronger as they proceed through school. My change over time view of children's literacy learning is inconsistent with a two-stage theory of literacy teaching discussed in the quote above.

Some cautions

All research data, experimental or descriptive, is contaminated by the education programme the children have passed through, because the programme constrains the opportunities to learn. We are unable to watch an unfolding process free from a contaminating effect of prior experiences steeped in instructional bias. (For example my research findings reflect the New Zealand teaching programme; Biemiller's, Ehri's, and Juel's reflect instructional emphases in different parts of North America; Ferreiro and Teberosky's accounts reflect Argentinian cultural practice interpreted through a Piagetian explanatory theory.) Research can report only what children have been taught or had the opportunity to learn for themselves — different things are emphasised in different societies and in different programmes.

The view I have described is derived from detailed records of active learners changing over a brief stretch of historical time. When the researcher works with short intervals of learning time, stage theories become untenable, and individual differences loom large. This is a function of the data collection. However, this view produces information which teachers can use to improve their teaching day by day.

Many of my observations have come from watching the progress of individuals rather than from averages calculated from heterogeneous individuals of the same or different age groups. In terms of early learning, averages are unable to inform the teacher who is dealing with children who are of similar age *but at different levels of building a literacy processing system*. Whether teaching in classrooms might be driven by a complex theory to foster these such changes over time would be a topic for another paper. For now I find it essential for a successful early intervention programme. I think that Holdaway's (1979) description of a goal for literacy teachers could also be the goal for early intervention teachers:

> *There is no better system to control the complexities and intricacies of each person's learning than that person's own system operating with genuine motivation and self-determination within reach of humane and informed help.* (p. 170)

References

Athey I. and H. Singer. 1987. Developing the nation's reading potential for a technological era. *Harvard Educational Review* 57, 1: 84–93.

Baltes, P.B., H.W. Reese and J.R. Nesselroade. 1977. *Life-span Developmental Psychology: Introduction to Research Methods*. Monterey, CA: Brooks/Cole.

Baltes, P.B. and K.W. Schaie, eds. 1973. *Lifespan Developmental Psychology: Personality and Socialization*, Epilogue, pp. 365–395. New York: Academic Press.

Clark, A. 1996. *Being There: Putting Brain, Body, and the World Together Again*. Cambridge, MA: MIT Press.

Clay, M.M. 1971. *Sentence Repetition: Elicited Imitation of a Controlled Set of Syntactic Structures by Four Language Groups. Monograph of the Society for Research in Child Development*, 36, No. 143.

———. 1972. Learning disorders. In S.J. Havill and D.R. Mitchell, eds, *Issues in New Zealand Special Education*. Auckland: Hodder and Stoughton.

———. 1974. The spatial characteristics of the open book. *Visible Language* 8, 3: 275–282.

———. 1985. *The Early Detection of Reading Difficulties* (Third Edition). Auckland: Heinemann.

———. 1987. Learning to be learning disabled. *New Zealand Journal of Educational Studies* 22, 2: 155–173.

———. 1989. *Quadruplets and Higher Multiple Births*. Oxford: Blackwell Scientific Publications.

Clay, M.M., M. Gill, T. Glynn, T. McNaughton and K. Salmon. 1983. *Record of Oral Language and Biks and Gutches*. Auckland: Heinemann.

Clay, M.M. and V.M.J. Robinson. 1978. *Children of Parents Who Separate*. Wellington: New Zealand Council of Educational Research.

Herman and Stringfield, 1997. *Ten Promising Programs For Educating All Children: Evidence and Impact*. Arlington, VA: Educational Research Service.

Holdaway, D. 1979. *The Foundations of Literacy*. Sydney: Ashton Scholastic.

Holmes, J.A. 1953. *The Substrata-factor Theory of Reading*. Berkeley, CA: California Book.

———. 1960. The substrata-factor theory of reading: Some experimental evidence. In the *Proceedings of the Fifth Annual Conference of the International Reading Association New Frontiers in Reading*, and reprinted in H. Singer and R.B. Ruddell, eds, 1970, *Theoretical Models and Processes of Reading* (First Edition), pp. 187–197. Newark, DE: International Reading Association.

Iversen, S. and W. Tunmer. 1993. Phonological processing skills and the Reading Recovery program. *Journal of Educational Psychology* 85, 1: 112–126.

Muchisky, M., L. Gershkoff-Stowe, E. Cole and E. Thelen 1996. The epigenetic landscape revisited. A dynamic interpretation. In C. Rovee-Collier and L. Lipsitt, eds, *Advances in Infancy Research* 10: 121–159.

Pikulski, J.J. 1994. Preventing reading failure: A review of five effective programs. *The Reading Teacher*, 48, 1, September: 30–39.

Pinnell, G.S. 1996. Reading Recovery: A Review of Research. *Educational Report #23*. Columbus, OH: Martha King Language and Literacy Center, OSU. Also in J. Flood, S.B. Heath and D. Lapp, eds, 1997, *Handbook of Research on Teaching Literacy Through the Communicative and Visual Arts*. Macmillan Reference Series on Educational Research.

Pinnell, G.S., C.A. Lyons, D.E. DeFord, A.S. Bryk and M. Seltzer. 1994. Comparing instructional models for literacy education of high-risk first-graders. *Reading Research Quarterly* 29, 1: 9–39.

Rowe, K.J. 1997. Factors affecting students' progress in reading: Key findings from a longitudinal study. In S.L. Swartz and A.F. Klein, eds, *Research in Reading Recovery*, pp. 53–101. Portsmouth, NH: Heinemann.

Singer, H. 1994. The substrata-factor theory of reading. In R.B. Ruddell, M.R. Ruddell and H. Singer, eds, *Theoretical Models and Processes of Reading* (Fourth Edition), pp. 895–927. Newark, DE: International Reading Association.

Slavin, R.E., N. Madden, N. Karweit, L. Dolan and B. Wasik. 1991. Research directions: Success for All; Ending reading failure from the beginning. *Language Arts* 68: 404–409.

Thelen, E. 1995. Time scale dynamics and the development of an embodied cognition. In R. Port and T. van Gelder, eds, *Mind in Motion*. Cambridge: MIT Press.

Thelen, E. and L. Smith. 1994. *A Dynamic Systems Approach to the Development of Cognition and Action*. Cambridge, MA: MIT Press. Fischer's and Gibson's review comments are on the jacket of this book.

Thelen, E. and B.D. Ulrich. 1991. *Hidden Skills. Monographs of the Society for Research in Child Development*, Serial No. 223, 56, 1.

Vellutino, F.R., D.M. Scanlon, E.R. Sipay, S.G. Small, R. Chen, A. Pratt and M.B. Denckla. 1996. Cognitive profiles of difficult-to-remediate and readily remediated poor readers: Early intervention as a vehicle for distinguishing between cognitive and experiential deficits as basic causes of specific reading disability. *Journal of Educational Psychology*, APA, 88, 4: 601–638.

Wasik, B.A. and R.E. Slavin. 1993. Preventing early reading failure with one-to-one tutoring: A review of five programs. *Reading Research Quarterly* 28, 1: 179–200.

Complete references

Anderson, R.C. 1985. The role of reader's schema in comprehension, learning and memory. In H. Singer and R.B. Ruddell, eds, *Theoretical Models and Processes of Reading* (Third Edition). Newark, DE: International Reading Association.

Anderson, R.C. and P.D. Pearson. 1984. A schema-theoretic view of basic processes in reading comprehension. In P.D. Pearson, ed., *Handbook of Reading Research*. New York: Longman.

Ashdown, J. and O. Simic. 2000. Is early literacy intervention effective for English language learners? Evidence from Reading Recovery. *Literacy Teaching and Learning: An International Journal of Early Reading and Writing* 5, 1: 27–42.

Askew, B.J. 1993. The effect of multiple readings on the behaviors of children and teachers in an early intervention program. *Reading and Writing Quarterly: Overcoming Learning Difficulties* 9: 307–315.

Askew, B.J., I.C. Fountas, C.A. Lyons, G.S. Pinnell and M.C. Schmitt. 1998. *Reading Recovery Review: Understandings, Outcomes, and Implications*. Columbus, OH: Reading Recovery Council of North America.

Askew, B.J. and D. Frasier. 1999. Early writing: An exploration of literacy opportunities. *Literacy, Teaching and Learning* 4, 1: 43–66.

Athey I. and H. Singer. 1987. Developing the nation's reading potential for a technological era. *Harvard Educational Review* 57, 1: 84–93.

Bakeman, R. and J.M. Gottman. 1986. *Observing Interaction: An Introduction to Sequential Analysis*. Cambridge: Cambridge University Press.

Baltes, P.B., H.W. Reese and J.R. Nesselroade. 1977. *Life-span Developmental Psychology: Introduction to Research Methods*. Monterey, CA: Brooks/Cole.

Baltes, P.B. and K.W. Schaie, eds. 1973. *Lifespan Developmental Psychology: Personality and Socialization*, Epilogue, pp. 365–395. New York: Academic Press.

Barnea, A. and Z. Breznitz. 1998. Phonological and orthographic processing of Hebrew words: Electro-physiological aspects. *The Journal of Genetic Psychology* 159, 4: 492–504.

Biemiller, A. 1970. The development of the use of graphic and contextual information as children learn to read. *Reading Research Quarterly* 6: 75–96.

Bissex, G. 1980. *GNYS AT WRK: A Child Learns To Write and Read*. Cambridge, MA: Harvard University Press.

Black, M.M. and E.W. Holden. 1995. Longitudinal intervention research in children's health and development. *Journal of Clinical Child Psychology* 24, 2: 163–172.

Boocock, C. 1991. Observing Children Write in the First Four Years of School. Master of Arts thesis, University of Auckland Library.

Boocock, C., S. McNaughton and J.M. Parr. 1998a. The early development of a self-extending system in writing. *Literacy, Teaching and Learning* 3, 2: 41–58.

———. 1998b. The early development of a self-extending system in writing. *Literacy Teaching and Learning* 3, 2: 41–59.

Booth, D. 1999. Personal communication, University of Toronto.

Bradley, L. and P. Bryant. 1983. Categorizing sounds and learning to read — A causal connection. *Nature* 301: 419–421.

Britton, B.K. and S.M. Glynn, eds. 1967. *Executive Control Processes in Reading*. Hillsdale, NJ: Lawrence Erlbaum.

Britton, B.K. and S.M. Glynn. 1987. *Executive Control Processes in Reading*. Hillsdale, NJ: Lawrence Erlbaum.

Brown, A.L., A.S. Palincsar and B.B. Armbruster. 1994. Instructing comprehension-fostering activities in interactive learning situations. In R.B. Ruddell, M.R. Ruddell and H. Singer, eds, *Theoretical Models and Processes of Reading* (Fourth Edition), pp. 757–787. Newark, DE: International Reading Association.

Brown, J., K.S. Goodman and A.M. Marek. 1996. *Studies in Miscue Analysis*. Newark, DE: International Reading Association.

Brown, R. 1976. *A First Language: The Early Stages*. Harmondsworth, England: Penguin Education.

Bruner, J. 1957. On perceptual readiness. *Psychological Review* 64: 123–152.

———. 1971. *Going Beyond the Information Given: Studies in the Psychology of Knowing*. New York: W.W. Norton.

———. 1974. Organization of early skilled action. In M.P.M. Richard, ed., *The Integration of the Child into the Social World*, pp. 167–184. London: Cambridge University Press.

Bryant, P. and L. Bradley. 1985. *Children's Reading Problems*. Oxford: Blackwell.

Campbell, R.L. 1993. Commentary. In A. Demetriou, A. Efklides and M. Platsidou, *The Architecture and Dynamics of Developing Mind*. *Monographs of the Society for Research in Child Development*, No. 234, 58: 5–5.

Canadian Institute of Reading Recovery, Toronto, Canada. 2000. Personal communication.

Caplan, G. 1964. *Principles of Preventive Psychiatry*. London: Tavistock Publications.

Case, R. and Y. Okamoto. 1995. *The Role of Central Conceptual Structures in the Development of Children's Thought*. *Monographs of the Society for Research in Child Development*, No. 246, 60: 5–6.

Cazden, C.B. 1974. Play with language and meta-linguistic awareness: One dimension of language experience. *Organization Mondiale Pour l'Education Prescolaire* 6: 12–24.

Center, Y., K. Wheldall, L. Freeman, L. Outhred and M. McNaught. 1995. An evaluation of Reading Recovery. *Reading Research Quarterly* 30: 240–263.

Chall, J.S. 1983. *Stages of Reading Development*. New York: McGraw-Hill.

Chapman, J. 1981. *The Reader and the Text*. London: Heinemann.

Chomsky, C. 1971. Write first; Read later. *Childhood Education* 1971, 47: 396–399.

———. 1972. Stages in language development and reading exposure. *Harvard Educational Review* 42: 1–33.

———. 1975a. How sister got into the grog. *Early Years*: 36–39.

———. 1975b. Invented spelling in the open classroom. *Word* (Special Issue entitled *Child Language Today*) 27: 499–518.

———. 1979. Approaching reading through invented spelling. In L.B. Resnick and P.A. Weaver, eds, *Theory and Practice of Early Reading*, Vol. 2, pp. 43–64. Hillsdale, NJ: Lawrence Erlbaum.

Chomsky, N. 1957. *Syntactic Structures*. The Hague: Mouton.

Church, J. 1997. *Within-Subject Experimental Analysis*. State of the Art Monograph, No. 5. New Zealand Association for Research in Education.

Clark, A. 1996. *Being There: Putting Brain, Body, and World Together Again*. Cambridge, MA: MIT Press.

Clark, M.M. 1992. Sensitive observation and the development of literacy. *Educational Psychology* 12, 3–4: 216–223.

Clay, M.M. 1966. Emergent Reading Behaviour. Doctoral dissertation, University of Auckland Library.

———. 1967. The reading behaviour of five-year-old children: A research report. *New Zealand Journal of Educational Studies* 2, 1: 11–31.

———. 1968. A syntactic analysis of reading errors. *Visible Language* 8, 3: 275–282.

———. 1969. Reading errors and self-correction behaviour. *British Journal of Educational Psychology* 39: 47–56.

———. 1970. An increasing effect of disorientation on the discrimination of print: a developmental study. *Journal of Experimental Child Psychology* 9: 297–306.

———. 1971. *Sentence Repetition: Elicited Imitation of a Controlled Set of Syntactic Structures by Four Language Groups. Monograph of the Society for Research in Child Development,* 36, No. 143.

———. 1972. Learning disorders. In S.J. Havill and D.R. Mitchell, eds, *Issues in New Zealand Special Education.* Auckland: Hodder and Stoughton.

———. 1974a. The spatial characteristics of the open book. *British Journal of Educational Psychology* 39, 1: 47–56.

———. 1974b. The spatial characteristics of the open book. *Visible Language* 8, 3: 275–282.

———. 1975. *What Did I Write?* Auckland: Heinemann.

———. 1979. *Reading: The Patterning of Complex Behaviour.* Auckland: Heinemann.

———. 1979a. *Reading: The Patterning of Complex Behaviour* (Second Edition). Auckland: Heinemann.

———. 1979b. *The Early Detection of Reading Difficulties: A Diagnostic Survey with Recovery Procedures* (Second Edition). Auckland: Heinemann.

———. 1982. *Observing Young Readers: Selected Papers.* Portsmouth, NH: Heinemann.

———. 1985a. Engaging with the school system: A study of interactions in new entrant classrooms. *New Zealand Journal of Educational Studies* 20, 1: 20–38.

———. 1985b. Reading Recovery: Systemic adaptation to an educational innovation. *New Zealand Journal of Educational Studies* 22, 1: 35–58.

———. 1985c. *The Early Detection of Reading Difficulties* (Third Edition). Auckland: Heinemann.

———. 1987a. Learning to be learning disabled. *New Zealand Journal of Educational Studies* 22, 2: 155–173.

———. 1987b. *Writing Begins At Home.* Auckland: Heinemann.

———. 1989. *Quadruplets and Higher Multiple Births.* Oxford: Blackwell Scientific Publications.

———. 1991. *Becoming Literate: The Construction of Inner Control.* Auckland: Heinemann.

———. 1993a. *An Observation Survey of Early Literacy Achievement.* Auckland: Heinemann (First Edition 1972; Second Edition 1979; Third Edition 1985; title change 1993).

———. 1993b. *Reading Recovery: A Guidebook for Teachers in Training.* Auckland: Heinemann.

———. 1997a. The development of literacy difficulties. In D. Corson, 1997, *Encyclopaedia of Language and Education, Volume 2: Literacy.* Dordrecht, Netherlands: Kluwer Academic Publishers.

———. 1997b. International perspectives on the Reading Recovery program. In J. Flood, S.B. Heath and D. Lapp, eds, 1997, *Handbook of Research on Teaching Literacy Through the Communicative and Visual Arts.* Macmillan Reference Series on Educational Research.

———. 1998. *By Different Paths to Common Outcomes.* York, ME: Stenhouse Publishers.

———. 2000a. *Running Records for Classroom Teachers.* Auckland: Heinemann.

———. 2000b. *Concepts About Print For Teachers of Young Children.* Auckland: Heinemann.

Clay, M.M. and C. Cazden. 1990. A Vygotskyan interpretation of Reading Recovery. In L. Moll, ed., *Vygotsky and Education.* Cambridge, UK: Cambridge University Press.

Clay, M.M., M. Gill, T. Glynn, T. McNaughton and K. Salmon. 1983. *Record of Oral Language and Biks and Gutches.* Auckland: Heinemann.

Clay, M.M. and R.H. Imlach. 1971. Juncture, pitch and stress as reading behaviour variables. *Journal of Verbal Behaviour and Verbal Learning* 10: 133–139.

Clay, M.M. and V.M.J. Robinson. 1978. *Children of Parents Who Separate.* Wellington: New Zealand Council of Educational Research.

Clay, M.M. and B. Tuck. 1993. The Reading Recovery sub-groups study, 1991. In M.M. Clay, *Reading Recovery: Guidelines for Teachers in Training*, pp. 86–95. Auckland: Heinemann.

Clay, M.M. and B. Watson. 1993. The three-year follow-up in 1981. In M. Clay, *Reading Recovery: A Guidebook for Teachers in Training.* Auckland: Heinemann.

Clay, M.M. and B. Williams. 1973. The reading behaviour of Standard One children. *Education (New Zealand)* 2: 13–17.

Daniels, J.C. and H. Diack. 1954, 1958. *The Royal Road Readers.* London: Chatto and Windus.

Department of Education. 1963. The *Ready to Read* series. Wellington: School Publications (now Learning Media).

DeStephano, J. 1978. *Language, the Learner and the School.* New York: John Wiley and Sons.

Dewey, G. 1970. *English Spelling: Roadblock to Reading.* New York: Teachers College Press, Columbia University.

Donald, D. 1981. The role of illustrations in children's oral reading accuracy, strategies and comprehension at different developmental and progress levels: A psycholinguistic guessing game. Unpublished doctoral dissertation, University of Cape Town Library.

Downing, J. and C.K. Leong. 1982. *Psychology of Reading.* New York: Macmillan.

Dracup, C. 1995. Hypothesis testing — what it really is. *The Psychologist* (UK), August: 359–362.

Durrell, D. 1958. First grade reading success study. *Journal of Education* 140, February.

Dyson, A.H. 1994. Viewpoints: The word and the world — reconceptualizing written language development or do rainbows mean a lot to little girls? In R.B. Ruddell, M.R. Ruddell and H. Singer, eds, 1994, *Theoretical Models and Processes of Reading.* Newark, DE: International Reading Association.

———. 1997. *Writing Superheroes: Contemporary Childhood, Popular Culture, and Classroom Literacy.* New York: Teachers College Press.

Ehri, L.C. 1991. Development of the ability to read words. In R. Barr, M.L. Kamil, P. Mosenthal, and P.D. Pearson, eds, *Handbook of Reading Research*, Vol. II, pp. 383–417. White Plains, NY: Longman.

Eisner, E. 1993. Forms of understanding and the future of educational research. *Educational Researcher,* October, 1993: 5–11.

Elkonin, D.B. 1971. Development of speech. In A.V. Zaporozhets and D.B. Elkonin, eds, *The Psychology of Preschool Children.* Cambridge, MA: MIT Press.

———. 1973. USSR. In J. Downing, ed., *Comparative Reading*, pp. 551–580. New York: Macmillan.

Elley, W.B. 1989. Vocabulary acquisition from listening to stories. *Reading Research Quarterly* 24, 2: 174–187.

Evans, M.A. 1985. Self-initiated repairs: A reflection of communicative monitoring in young children. *Developmental Psychology* 21, 2: 365–371.

Eyberg, S.M. 1995. Jigsaws: Introduction to the special issue on methodological issues in clinical child psychology research. *Journal of Clinical Child Psychology* 24, 2: 122–124.

Feinstein, A.R. 1977. *Clinical Biostatistics.* St Louis: Mosby.

Ferreiro, E. and A. Teberosky. 1982. *Literacy Before Schooling.* Portsmouth, NH: Heinemann.

Frater, G. and B. Staniland. 1994. Reading Recovery in New Zealand: A Report from the Office of Her Majesty's Chief Inspector of Schools. *Literacy, Teaching, and Learning* 1, 1: 143–162. Also available from the Office for Standards in Education, Her Majesty's Stationery Office, London.

Frith, U. 1980. *Cognitive processes in spelling.* London: Academic Press.

Frompkin, V.A. 1971. The non-anomalous nature of anomalous utterances. *Language* 47, 1: 27–52.

———, ed. 1973. *Speech Errors as Linguistic Evidence.* The Hague: Mouton.

———, ed. 1980. *Errors in Linguistic Performance: Slips of the Tongue, Ear, Pen, and Hand.* New York: Academic Press.

Frymier, J., L. Barber, B. Gansneder and N. Robertson. 1989. Simultaneous replication: A technique for large-scale research. *Phi Delta Kappa,* November 1989: 228–231.

Fullan, M. 1999. *Change Forces: The Sequel.* Philadelphia, PA: Falmer Press.

Garmezy, N. 1988. Longitudinal strategies, causal reasoning and risk research: A commentary. In M. Rutter, ed., *Studies of Psychosocial Risk: the Power of Longitudinal Data,* pp. 29–44. Cambridge, England: Cambridge University Press.

Gentile, L.M. 1997. Oral language: Assessment and development in Reading Recovery in the United States. In S.L. Swartz and A.F. Klein, eds, *Research in Reading Recovery.* Portsmouth, NH: Heinemann.

Gibson, C.M. and I.A. Richards. 1957. *First Steps in Reading English: A Book for Beginning Readers of All Ages.* New York: Pocket Books.

Gibson, E.J. 1969. *Principles of Perceptual Learning and Development.* New York: Appleton, Century, Crofts.

Gibson, E.J. and H. Levin. 1975. *The Psychology of Reading.* Cambridge, MA: MIT Press.

———. 1991. *An Odyssey in Learning and Perception.* Cambridge, MA: MIT Press.

Girling-Butcher, W., G. Phillips and M.M. Clay. 1991. Fostering independent learning. *The Reading Teacher* 44, 9: 694–697.

Gittleman, R. 1985. Controlled trials of remedial approaches to reading disability. *Journal of Child Psychology and Psychiatry* 26: 843–846.

Gittleman, R. and I. Feingold. 1983. Children with reading disorders I: Efficacy of reading remediation. *Journal of Child Psychology and Psychiatry* 24: 167–192.

Glynn, T., S. McNaughton and A. Wotherspoon. 1975. Modification of reading, writing and attending behaviour in a special class for retarded children. Unpublished research paper, Department of Education, University of Auckland.

Goldstein, H. 1979. *The Design and Analysis of Longitudinal Studies.* New York: Academic Press.

———. 1998. *Models for Reality: New Approaches to the Understanding of Educational Processes.* London Institute of Education, University of London.

Goldstone, R.L. 1998. Perceptual learning. *Annual Review of Psychology* 49: 585–612.

Goodman, K.S. 1994. Reading, writing, and written texts: A transactional-sociopsycholinguistic view. In R.B. Ruddell, M.R. Ruddell and H. Singer, eds, *Theoretical Models and Processes of Reading* (Fourth Edition), pp. 1057–1093. Newark, DE: International Reading Association.

Goodman, K.S. and Y.M. Goodman. 1979. Learning to read is natural. In L.B. Resnick and P.A. Weaver, eds, *Theory and Practice in Early Reading*, Vol. 1, pp. 137–154. Hillsdale, NJ: Lawrence Erlbaum.

Goodman, Y., ed. 1990. *How Children Construct Literacy: Piagetian Perspectives.* Newark, DE: International Reading Association.

Goodman, Y.M. and C. Burke. 1972. *The Reading Miscue Inventory.* New York: Macmillan.

Goodman, Y.M. and K.S. Goodman. 1994. To err is human: Learning about language processes by analysing miscues. In R.B. Ruddell, M.R. Ruddell and H. Singer, eds, *Theoretical Models and Processes of Reading*, pp. 104–123. Newark, DE: International Reading Association.

Goswami, U. 1998. The role of analogies in the development of word recognition. In J.L. Metsala and L.C. Ehri, eds, *Word Recognition in Beginning Literacy*, pp. 41–63. Mahwah, NJ: Lawrence Erlbaum.

———. 1999. Spelling it out …. Book review of *Learning to Spell: Research, Theory and Practice Across Languages*, C.A. Perfetti, L. Rieben and M. Fayot, eds, in *The Psychologist* 12, 7: 360–361.

Gough, P.B. 1985. One second of reading. In H. Singer and R.B. Ruddell, eds, *Theoretical Models and Processes of Reading* (Third Edition), pp. 661–689. Newark, DE: International Reading Association.

Greer, R.D. 1983. Contingencies of the science and technology of teaching and pre-behavioristic research practices in education. *Educational Researcher* 12: 3–9.

Guthrie, J.T. 1973. Reading comprehension and syntactic responses in good and poor readers. *Journal of Educational Psychology* 65: 294–299.

Haber, R.N. 1978. Visual perception. *Annual Review of Psychology* 29: 31–59.

Hall, D.P., C. Prevatte and P.M. Cunningham. 1993. Elementary Ability Grouping and Failure in the Primary Grades. Unpublished manuscript quoted by Pikulski (1994).

Harris, T.L. and R.E. Hodges. 1995. *The Literacy Dictionary: The Vocabulary of Reading and Writing.* Newark, DE: International Reading Association.

Hart, B. and T.R. Risley. 1999. *The Social World of Children Learning to Talk.* Baltimore: Paul Brookes Publishing.

Hatcher, P.J. 1994. *Sound Linkage: An Integrated Programme for Over-coming Reading Difficulties.* London: Whurr Publishing.

Hebb, D.O. 1949. *The Organization of Behaviour*, pp. 101–102. New York: Wiley.

Henggeler, S.W. 1994. A consensus: Conclusions of the APA Task Force Report on innovative models of mental health services for children, adolescents and their families. *Journal of Clinical Child Psychology* 23 (Suppl.), 2: 2–6.

Herman and Stringfield, 1997. *Ten Promising Programs For Educating All Children: Evidence and Impact.* Arlington, VA: Educational Research Service.

Hickman, M.E. 1985. The implications of discourse skills in Vygotsky's developmental theory. In J.V. Wertsch, ed., *Culture, Communication and Cognition: Vygotskian perspectives.* Cambridge: Cambridge University Press.

Hiebert, E.H. 1994. Reading Recovery in the United States: What difference does it make to an age cohort? *Educational Researcher* 23: 15–25.

Hiebert, E.H., J.M. Colt, S.L. Catto and E.C. Guy. 1992. Reading and writing of first-grade students in a restructured Chapter 1 program. *American Education Research Journal* 29: 545–572.

Hobsbaum, A. 1997. Reading Recovery in England. In S.L. Swartz and A.F. Klein, eds, *Research in Reading Recovery.* Portsmouth, NH: Heinemann.

Hobsbaum, A., S. Peters, and K. Sylva. 1996. Scaffolding in Reading Recovery. *Oxford Review of Education* 22, 1: 17–35.

Holdaway, D. 1979. *The Foundations of Literacy*. Sydney: Ashton Scholastic.

Holmes, J.A. 1953. *The Substrata-factor Theory of Reading*. Berkeley, CA: California Book.

———. 1960. The substrata-factor theory of reading: Some experimental evidence. In the *Proceedings of the Fifth Annual Conference of the International Reading Association New Frontiers in Reading*, and reprinted in H. Singer and R.B. Ruddell, eds, 1970, *Theoretical Models and Processes of Reading* (First Edition), pp. 187–197. Newark, DE: International Reading Association.

Holmes, J. and H. Singer. 1961. The substrata-factor theory: Substrata-factor differences underlying reading ability in known groups. US Office of Education, Final Report No. 538, SAE 8176.

———. 1964. Theoretical models and trends toward more basic research in reading. *Review of Educational Research* 34, April: 127–155.

Hops, H., B. Davis and N. Longoria. 1995. Methodological issues in direct observation. *Journal of Clinical Child Psychology* 24, 2: 193–203.

Howard, I.P. and W.B. Templeton. 1966. *Human Spatial Orientation*. London: Wiley.

Hurry, J. 1996. What is so special about Reading Recovery? *The Curriculum Journal* 7, 1: 93–108.

Iversen, S. and W. Tunmer. 1993. Phonological processing skills and the Reading Recovery program. *Journal of Educational Psychology* 85, 1: 112–126.

Iversen, S.J. 1991. Phonological Processing Skills and the Reading Recovery Programme. Master of Arts dissertation, Massey University Library, Palmerston North, New Zealand.

Johnston, P.H. 1997. *Knowing Literacy: Constructive Literacy Assessment*. York, ME: Stenhouse Publishers.

———. 2000. *Running Records: A Self-tutoring Guide*. York, ME: Stenhouse Publishers.

Johnston, P.H. and R.L. Allington. 1991. Remediation. In R. Barr, M.L. Kamil, P. Mosenthal and P.D. Pearson, eds, *Handbook of Reading Research*, Vol. II, pp. 984–1012. White Plains, NY: Longman.

Jones, N.K. and M.T. Smith-Burke. 1999. Forging an interactive relationship among research, theory and practice: Clay's research design and methodology. In J.S. Gaffney and B.J. Askew, eds, *Stirring the Waters: The Influence of Marie Clay*. Portsmouth, NH: Heinemann.

Juel, C. 1980. Longitudinal research on learning to read and write with at-risk students. In M.J. Dreyer and W.H. Slater, eds, *Elementary School Literacy: Critical Issues*. Norwood, MA: Christopher-Gordon.

———. 1988. Learning to read and write: a longitudinal study of 54 children from first through fourth grades. *Journal of Educational Psychology* 4: 437–447.

———. 1991. Beginning Reading. In R. Barr, M.L. Kamil, P.B. Mosenthal and D. Pearson, eds, *Handbook of Reading Research*, Vol. 2, pp. 759–788. London: Longman.

Karmiloff-Smith, A. 1979. *A Functional Approach to Child Language*. Cambridge: Cambridge University Press.

———. 1992. *Beyond Modularity: A Developmental Perspective on Cognitive Science*. Cambridge, MA: MIT Press.

Karoly, P. 1993. Mechanisms of self-regulation: A system view. *Annual Review of Psychology* 44: 23–52.

Kerslake, J. 1998. Annual monitoring of Reading Recovery: The data for 1997. *The Research Bulletin* 9, October: 43–47. Wellington: Ministry of Education.

Kress, G. 2000. *Early Spelling: Between Convention and Creativity.* London: Routledge.

Learning Media. 1985. *Reading in the Junior Classes.* Wellington: Ministry of Education.

Levy, Y. 1999. Early metalinguistic competence: Speech monitoring and repair behavior. *Developmental Psychology* 35, 3: 822–834.

Lynn, R. 1966. *Attention, Arousal and the Orientation Reaction.* London: Pergamon.

MacKinnon, A.R. 1959. *How Do Children Learn to Read?* Toronto: Copp Clark Publishing.

Marshall, J.C. and J. Morton. 1978. On the mechanics of EMMA. In A. Sinclair, R.J. Javella and W. Klein, eds, *The Child's Conception of Language,* pp. 225–239. Berlin: Springer-Verlag.

Masson, M.E.J. 1987. Remembering reading operations with and without awareness. In B.K. Britton and S.M. Glynn, eds, *Executive Control Processes in Reading,* pp. 253–277. Hillsdale, NJ: Lawrence Erlbaum.

McKoon, G. and R. Ratcliff. 1998. Memory-based language processing: Psycholinguistic research in the 1990s. *Annual Review of Psychology* 1998, 49: 25–42.

McNaughton, S. 1974. Behaviour Modification and Reading in a Special Class. Unpublished Master of Arts thesis, University of Auckland Library.

———. 1978. Instructor Attention to Oral Reading Errors: A Functional Analysis. Unpublished doctoral dissertation, University of Auckland.

———. 1981. Becoming an independent reader: Problem-solving during oral reading. *New Zealand Journal of Educational Studies* 16: 172–185.

———. 1985. Beyond teaching: The development of independence in learning to read. Conference address, 11th Annual Australian Reading Association, Brisbane.

———. 1987. *Being Skilled: The Socialization of Learning to Read.* London: Methuen.

———. 1988. A history of errors in the analysis of oral reading behaviour. *International Journal of Experimental Educational Psychology* 8, 1 and 2: 21–30.

———. 1995. *Patterns of Emergent Literacy: Processes of Development and Transition.* Auckland: Oxford University Press.

McNaughton, S. and T. Glynn. 1981. Delayed versus immediate attention to reading errors: effects on accuracy and self-correction. *Educational Psychology* 1: 57–65.

McNaughton, S., T. Glynn and V. Robinson. 1981. *Parents as Remedial Reading Tutors: Issues for Home and School.* Wellington: New Zealand Council for Educational Research. Reprinted 1987 as *Pause, Prompt and Praise: Effective Tutoring for Remedial Reading.* Birmingham: Positive Products.

McQueen, P.J. 1975. Motor Responses Associated with Beginning Reading. Master of Arts thesis, University of Auckland Library.

Meek, M. 1988. *How Texts Teach What Readers Learn.* South Woodchester, Stroud: The Thimble Press.

Miller. G.A. 1981. *Language and Speech.* San Francisco: S.F. and W.H. Freeman.

Morais, J. 1995. Do orthographic and phonological peculiarities of alphabetically written languages influence the course of literacy acquisition? *Reading and Writing: An Interdisciplinary Journal* 7: 1–7.

Muchisky, M., L. Gershkoff-Stowe, E. Cole and E. Thelen 1996. The epigenetic landscape revisited: A dynamic interpretation. In C. Rovee-Collier and L. Lipsitt, eds, *Advances in Infancy Research* 10: 121–159.

Nalder, S. 1984. Emergent Reading: A Development Year Project. Report distributed by the Reading Advisory Service, Ministry of Education. Author address, 10B Nea Place, Glenfield, Auckland, New Zealand.

Neal, J. and P.R. Kelly. 1999. The success of Reading Recovery for English language learners and Descubriendo la Lectura for bilingual students in California. *Literacy Teaching and Learning: An International Journal of Early Reading and Writing* 4, 2: 81–108.

Neale, M. 1958. *The Neale Analysis of Reading Ability.* London: Macmillan.

Nesselroade, J.R. and P.B. Baltes. 1979. *Longitudinal Research in the Study of Behavior and Development.* New York: Academic Press.

———. 1984. Sequential strategies and the role of cohort effects in behavioral development: Adolescent personality (1970–72) as a sample case. In S.A. Mednick, M. Harway and K.M. Finello, eds, *Handbook of Longitudinal Research.* New York: Praeger.

Ng, S.M. 1979. Error and Self-correction in Reading and Oral Language. Doctoral dissertation, University of Auckland Library.

Nicholson, T. 1984. Experts and novices. *Reading Research Quarterly* 19, 4: 436–450.

O'Leary, S. 1997. *Five Kids: Stories of Children Learning to Read.* Bothell, WA: The Wright Group/ McGraw-Hill.

Paley, V.G. 1981. *Wally's Stories.* Cambridge, MA: Harvard University Press.

Pearson, P.D. 1990. Foreword. In T. Shanahan, ed., *Reading and Writing Together: New Perspectives for the Classroom.* Norwood, MA: Christopher-Gordon.

———. 1994. Notes on Reading Recovery Opportunities and Obligations. Speech to deans of colleges of education with Reading Recovery training programmes. Personal communication.

Penton, J. and D. Holdaway, 1973. *The Early Reading In-Service Course.* Report to the Director-General of Education. Wellington: Department of Education.

Perfetti, C.A., L. Rieben and M. Fayol, eds. 1997. *Learning to Spell: Research, Theory and Practice Across Languages.* Hillsdale, NJ: Lawrence Erlbaum.

Phillips, G. and P. Smith. 1997a. *Closing the Gaps: Literacy for the Hardest-to-teach.* Wellington: New Zealand Council for Educational Research. (An abridged version.)

———. 1997b. *A Third Chance to Learn: The Development and Evaluation of Specialised Interventions for Young Children Experiencing the Greatest Difficulty in Learning to Read.* Wellington: New Zealand Council for Educational Research.

Pianta, R.C. 1990. Widening debate in educational reform: Prevention as a viable alternative. *Exceptional Children* 56: 306–313.

Pikulski, J.J. 1994. Preventing reading failure: A review of five effective programs. *The Reading Teacher* 48, 1, September: 30–39.

Pinker, S. 1994. *The Language Instinct: How the Mind Creates Language.* New York: William Morrow.

Pinnell, G.S. 1989. Reading Recovery: Helping at-risk children learn to read. *The Elementary School Journal,* 90, 2: 159–181.

———. 1996. Reading Recovery: A Review of Research. *Educational Report #23.* Columbus, OH: Martha King Language and Literacy Center, OSU. Also in J. Flood, S.B. Heath and D. Lapp, eds, 1997. *Handbook of Research on Teaching Literacy Through the Communicative and Visual Arts.* Macmillan Reference Series on Educational Research.

———. 2000. *Reading Recovery: An Analysis of a Research-based Reading Intervention.* Columbus, OH: Reading Recovery Council of North America.

Pinnell, G.S., D.E. DeFord and C.L. Lyons. 1988. *Reading Recovery: Early Intervention for At-Risk First Graders.* Arlington, VA: Educational Research Service.

Pinnell, G.S., M.D. Fried and R.M. Estice. 1990. Reading Recovery: Learning how to make a difference. *The Reading Teacher* 43: 282–295.

———. 1991. Reading Recovery: Learning how to make a difference. In D. DeFord, C.A. Lyons and G.S. Pinnell, eds, *Bridges to Literacy: Learning from Reading Recovery.* Portsmouth, NH: Heinemann.

Pinnell, G.S., C.A. Lyons, D.E. DeFord, A.S. Bryk and M. Seltzer. 1994. Comparing instructional models for literacy education of high-risk first-graders. *Reading Research Quarterly* 29, 1: 9–39.

Pogrow, S. 1998. What is an exemplary program, and why should anyone care? *Educational Researcher*, 27, 7: 22–29.

Ramey, C.L. and S.L. Ramey. 1998. Early intervention and early experience. *American Psychologist* 53, 2: 109–120.

Randell, B. 1999. Shaping the PM story books. *The Running Record*, RRCNA 11, 2: 1–12.

Rayner, K. and A. Pollatsek. 1989. *The Psychology of Reading.* Englewood Cliffs: Prentice Hall.

Rayner, K., G.E. Raney and A. Pollatsek. 1995. Eye movements and discourse processing. In R.F. Lorch and E.J. O'Brien, eds, *Sources of Coherence in Reading.* Hillsdale, NJ: Lawrence Erlbaum.

Read, C. 1975. *Children's Categorization of Speech Sounds in English.* Urbana, Illinois: National Council of Teachers of English.

———. 1986. *Children's Creative Spelling.* London: Routledge, Kegan Paul.

Recht, D.R. 1976. The self-correction process in reading. *The Reading Teacher*, April: 633 ff.

Robinson, S.E. 1973. Predicting Early Reading Progress. Master of Arts thesis, University of Auckland Library.

Rogoff, B. 1990. *Apprenticeship in Thinking — Cognitive Development in Social Context.* New York: Oxford University Press.

Rosenblatt, L. 1994. The transactional theory of reading and writing. In R.B. Ruddell, M.R. Ruddell and H. Singer, eds, 1994, *Theoretical Models and Processes of Reading* (Fourth Edition), pp. 1057–1093. Newark, DE: International Reading Association.

Rowe, K.J. 1997. Factors affecting students' progress in reading: Key findings from a longitudinal study. In S.L. Swartz and A.F. Klein, eds, *Research in Reading Recovery*, pp. 53–101. Portsmouth, NH: Heinemann.

Ruddell, R.B., M.R. Ruddell and H. Singer, eds. 1994. *Theoretical Models and Processes of Reading* (Fourth Edition). Newark, DE: International Reading Association.

Rumelhart, D.E. 1994. Toward an interactive model of reading. In R.B. Ruddell, M.R. Ruddell and H. Singer, eds, 1994, *Theoretical Models and Processes of Reading* (Fourth Edition), pp. 864–894. Newark, DE: International Reading Association.

Schwartz, R.M. 1997. Self-monitoring in beginning reading. *The Reading Teacher* 51, 1: 40–48.

Shanahan, T. 1987. Review of *The Early Detection of Reading Difficulties* (Third Edition) by Marie Clay. *Journal of Reading Behavior* 19: 117–119.

———, ed. 1990. *Reading and Writing Together: New Perspectives for the Classroom.* Norwood, MA: Christopher-Gordon.

Shanahan, T and R. Barr. 1995. Reading Recovery: An independent evaluation of the effects of an early instructional intervention for at-risk learners. *Reading Research Quarterly* 30, 4: 958–996.

Shanahan, T. and S. Neuman. 1997. Conversations: Literacy research that makes a difference. *Reading Research Quarterly* 33, 2: 202– 210.

Share, D.J. 1990. Self-correction rates in oral reading: Indices of efficient reading or artefact of text difficulty? Research Note, c/o the author, Haifa University, Haifa, Israel.

Singer, H. 1994. The substrata-factor theory of reading. In R.B. Ruddell, M.R. Ruddell and H. Singer, eds, *Theoretical Models and Processes of Reading* (Fourth Edition), pp. 895–927. Newark, DE: International Reading Association.

Singer, H. and R.B. Ruddell, eds. 1970. *Theoretical Models and Processes of Reading* (First Edition). Newark, DE: International Reading Association.

Singh, N.N., A.S.W. Winton and J. Singh. 1984. Effects of delayed versus immediate attention to oral reading errors on the reading proficiency of mentally retarded children. *Applied Research in Mental Retardation* 6: 295–305.

Slane, J. 1979. An individual audiovisual in-service course for teachers: The Early Reading In-service Course. *Programmed Learning and Educational Technology* 16, 1: 38–45.

Slavin, R.E., N. Madden, N. Karweit, L. Dolan and B. Wasik. 1991. Research directions: Success for All; Ending reading failure from the beginning. *Language Arts* 68: 404–409.

Smith, F. 1971. *Understanding Reading* (First Edition). New York: Holt, Rinehart and Winston.

———. 1978. *Understanding Reading* (Second Edition). New York: Holt, Rinehart and Winston.

Smith, J.W.A. and W.B. Elley. 1997. *How Children Learn to Write*. Auckland: Addison Wesley Longman.

Smith, P. 1994. Reading Recovery and children with English as a second language. *New Zealand Journal of Educational Studies* 29, 2: 141–159.

Solley, C.M. and G. Murphy. 1960. *Development of the Perceptual World*. New York: Basic Books.

Spalding, R.B. and W.T. Spalding. 1962. *The Writing Road to Reading*. New York: William Morrow.

Spear-Swerling, L. and R.J. Sternberg. 1996. *Off-Track: When Poor Readers Become "Learning Disabled"*. Boulder, Colorado: Westview Press.

Speigel, D. 1995. A comparison of traditional remedial programs and Reading Recovery: Guidelines for success for all programs. *The Reading Teacher* 49, 2: 86–96.

Spiro, R.J., R.L. Coulson, P.J. Feltovich and D.K. Anderson. 1994. Cognitive flexibility theory: Advanced knowledge acquisition in ill-structured domains. In R.B. Ruddell, M.R. Ruddell and H. Singer, eds, *Theoretical Models and Processes of Reading* (Fourth Edition), pp. 602–615 and 895–927. Newark, DE: International Reading Association.

Spiro, R.J., W.L. Vispoel, J.G. Schmitz, A. Samarapungavan and A.E. Boerger. 1987. Knowledge acquisition for application: Cognitive flexibility and transfer in complex content domains. In B.K. Britton and S.M. Glynn, eds, *Executive Control Processes in Reading*. Hillsdale, NJ: Lawrence Erlbaum.

Stanovich, K.E. 1980. Toward an interactive-compensatory model of individual differences in the development of reading fluency. *Reading Research Quarterly* 16: 32–71.

———. 1986. Matthew effects in reading: Some consequences of individual differences in the acquisition of literacy. *Reading Research Quarterly* 21, 4: 360–406.

Swartz, S.L. and A.F. Klein. 1997. *Research in Reading Recovery*. Portsmouth, NH: Heinemann.

Sylva, K. and J. Hurry. 1995. *Early intervention in children with reading difficulties*. School Curriculum and Assessment Authority Discussion Paper No. 2, London.

Taylor, B.M., B.J. Frye, R. Short and B. Shearer. 1992. Classroom teachers prevent reading failure among low-achieving first grade students. *The Reading Teacher* 45: 592–597.

Thelen, E. 1995. Time scale dynamics and the development of an embodied cognition. In R. Port and T. van Gelder, eds, *Mind in Motion.* Cambridge: MIT Press.

Thelen, E. and L. Smith. 1994. *A Dynamic Systems Approach to the Development of Cognition and Action.* Cambridge, MA: MIT Press. Fischer's and Gibson's review comments are on the jacket of this book.

Thelen, E. and B.D. Ulrich. 1991. *Hidden Skills. Monographs of the Society for Research in Child Development,* Serial No. 223, 56, 1.

Thompson, G. 1981. Individual differences attributed to self-correction in reading. *British Journal of Educational Psychology* 51: 228–229.

Thorndike, R.L. 1973. *Reading Comprehension Education in Fifteen Countries.* Uppsala: Almqvist and Wiksell.

Torgesen, J.K. 2000. Individual differences in response to early interventions in reading: The lingering problem of treatment resisters. *Learning Disability Research and Practice* 15, 1: 55–64.

Treiman, R. 1993. *Beginning to Spell: A Study of First Grade Children.* New York: Oxford University Press.

Vellutino, F.R. and D.M. Scanlon. 1999. Focus, Funding, Phonics — What's the point: A reply to Pressley and Allington, *Issues in Education,* e-journal, p. 8.

Vellutino, F.R., D.M. Scanlon, E.R. Sipay, S.G. Small, R. Chen, A. Pratt and M.B. Denckla. 1996. Cognitive profiles of difficult-to-remediate and readily remediated poor readers: Early intervention as a vehicle for distinguishing between cognitive and experiential deficits as basic causes of specific reading disability. *Journal of Educational Psychology,* APA, 88, 4: 601–638.

Vernon, M.D. 1957. *Backwardness in Reading: a Study of its Nature and Origin.* Cambridge: Cambridge University Press.

Vygotsky, L.S. 1962. *Thought and Language.* Cambridge, MA: MIT Press.

Wagner, R.K. and R.J. Sternberg. 1987. Executive control in reading comprehension. In B.K. Britton and S.M. Glynn, eds, *Executive Control Processes in Reading.* Hillsdale, NJ: Lawrence Erlbaum.

Walmsley, S.A. and R.L. Allington. 1995. Redefining and reforming instructional support programs for at-risk students. In R.L. Allington and S.A. Walmsley, eds, *No Quick Fix: Rethinking Literacy Programs in America's Elementary Schools.* Newark, DE: International Reading Association.

Wasik, B.A. and R.E. Slavin. 1993. Preventing early reading failure with one-to-one tutoring: A review of five programs. *Reading Research Quarterly* 28, 1: 179–200.

Watson, B. 1980. An Observation Study of Teaching Beginning Reading to New Entrant Children. Master of Arts thesis, University of Auckland Library.

———. 1999. Creating independent learners. In J.S. Gaffney and B.J. Askew, eds, *Stirring the Waters,* pp. 47–74. Portsmouth, NH: Heinemann.

Watson, S. and M.M. Clay. 1975. Oral reading strategies of third form students. *New Zealand Journal of Educational Studies* 1, May: 43–51.

Weber, R. 1970. A linguistic analysis of first grade reading errors. *Reading Research Quarterly* 5: 427–451.

Weinberger, J., P. Hannon and C. Nutbrown. 1990. *Ways of Working With Parents to Promote Early Literacy Development.* Sheffield: University of Sheffield Educational Research Centre.

Wheldall, K. and T. Glynn. 1988. Contingencies in contexts: A behavioural interactionist perspective in education. *International Journal of Educational Psychology* 8, 1 and 2: 5–20.

White, D.N. 1984. *Books Before Five*. Portsmouth, NH: Heinemann.

Williams, B. 1968. The Oral Reading Behaviour of Standard One Children. Master of Arts thesis, University of Auckland Library.

Williams, J. 1995. Phonemic Awareness. In T. Harris and R.E. Hodges, *The Literacy Dictionary: The Vocabulary of Reading and Writing*, pp. 185–186. Newark, DE: International Reading Association.

Wilson K.G. and B. Daviss. 1994. *Redesigning Education*. New York: Henry Holt.

Wimmer, H. and U. Goswami. 1994. The influence of orthographic consistency on reading development: word recognition in English and German children. *Cognition* 51: 91–103.

Wong, P. and S.S. McNaughton. 1980. The effects of prior provision of content on the oral reading proficiency of a low progress reader. *New Zealand Journal of Educational Studies* 15, 2: 159–175.

Wong, S., L. Groth and J. O'Flahaven. 1994. *Characterizing teacher-student interaction in Reading Recovery lessons*. Reading Research Report No. 17, National Reading Research Center, Universities of Georgia and Maryland.

Wood, D. 1978. Problem-solving: the nature and development of strategies. In A. Underwood, ed., *Strategies of Information Processing*. London: Academic Press.

———. 1988. *How Children Think and Learn* (First Edition). Oxford: Blackwell.

———. 1998. *How Children Think and Learn* (Second Edition). Oxford: Blackwell.

Wood, D., J.S. Bruner and G. Ross. 1976. The role of tutoring in problem-solving. *Journal of Child Psychology and Child Psychiatry* 17, 2: 89–100.

Wotherspoon, T. 1974. Modification of Writing Behaviour in a Special Class. Master of Arts thesis, University of Auckland Library.

Yopp, H.K, and H. Singer. 1994. Toward an interactive reading instruction model: Explanation of activation of linguistic awareness and meta-linguistic ability in learning to read. In R.B. Ruddell, M.R. Ruddell and H. Singer, eds, *Theoretical Models and Processes of Reading* (Fourth Edition), pp. 381–390. Newark, DE: International Reading Association.

Index

activities
  in a lesson   226–231
  visual, complex   165
  visual, simple   165
  writing   26
acts   *See also* Running Records
  of processing   39–88, 83 (Note 3), 84–85, 95–107, 225
  record of   43–46
administrator(s)
  how to question reports   260–264
    implementation integrity   260
    long-term follow-up   262
    outcomes for individuals   261
    outcomes for the system   263
    quality of instruction   261
    reliability of measures   263
    research samples   260
    schools, type and number   261
    standard or nonstandard teaching   262
    viable alternative   262
  support   251–252, 258
assembling
  a complex system   114
  behaviour signals   199
  complex processing   96, 199
  messages   29
  sentences   28, 30, 30–31
  stories   116
  working systems   89–142, 219
assumptions about reading texts   91–93
attending   158
  superficial   163
  to features   20–21
  to information   29
  to letters   20, 29, 146–148, 160–161, 175
  to old symbols   162
  to print   19–20
  to several knowledge sources   120
  to sounds   26, 32, 175
  to visual input   156–163
  to words   175
  weighting of   69–70, 159
attention
  directing it inwards   119, 151
  directing it outwards   19–20, 118, 151
  fading   174
  minimal   29
  shaping   174
  sharpening   174
  shifting   29, 69
  switching   118
  weighting   159
behaviour(s)
  surface   111–115
books   *See also* text(s)
  familiar   228
  yesterday's new book   228
case studies   74–75, 115–123
change
  beyond discontinuing   280
  complexity, and the cloud image   293
  continuous   296
  in self-corrections   202
  in visual learning   148–149
  in word knowledge   123
  ontogenetic landscape   293

open to change   80–81, 297
over time   41–43, 57–58, 77, 123, 202, 287–305
  in literacy development   287–293
  in Reading Recovery teaching   76, 221–222
  research   264–267
  Rowe   264–265
  successive integrations   131–132
choosing   *See also* decision-making   125–126
  among difficult choices   174
  between alternatives   120–121, 126, 184, 201–202
chunks
  of print   170
Clay   287
code(s)   169
  how to look at a code   145
  messages   169
  new   160–161
  old   162
  printed
  symbols   168, 169
  units of a code   159, 166, 170
  visual   116, 146, 172
composing
  messages   229
  orally   229
  quickly, on the cut-up story   28–29
  sentences   98
  stories   27–28
comprehension   106–107
constructing
  networks   80, 198, 224
  sentences   34, 98
  words   21–23, 33
  words from clusters   21–23
  words from phonemes   21–23
constructive
  becoming   5, 219, 224, 226–227
  beyond the known   236
  children   215, 223, 301
  from first lessons   236
  lessons in being   5, 224, 226
  readers   102, 105
  writers   15–17
correlations
  lowering   249–250
cut-up stories   30
decision-making   50, 149, 157
  in controlled sequences   168
dedication   6
definitions
  acts   41
  literacy   41
  perceptual learning   148
  processing   41–42
  reading   1, 102, 112
  recovery of normal trajectory   289
  self-correction   184
  unusual lens   42
  visual perception   154, 175
developmental
  lags   217
  psychology   6, 288–289, 290–292, 305
    lifespan   289–290
    new images   292–298
    view   219, 238
differentiation   159
discrimination

Index of illustrative examples